Secret Intelligence
and Public Policy

Secret Intelligence and Public Policy

A DILEMMA OF DEMOCRACY

Pat M. Holt

A Division of Congressional Quarterly Inc.
Washington, D.C.

Library of Congress Cataloging-in-Publication Data

Holt, Pat M.
    Secret intelligence and public policy : a dilemma of democracy /
Pat M. Holt.
        p. cm.
    Includes bibliographical references and index.
    ISBN 0-87187-683-3
    1. Intelligence service--United States.   2. Democracy--United
States.   I. Title.
JK468.I6H64   1994
327.1273--dc20   94-32202
                                                                      CIP

Contents

Preface

The purpose of this book is threefold:

1) To provide a general introduction to the intelligence community (what it is, what it does, how it fits in the government).

2) To illuminate the tradeoffs involved in making decisions about intelligence operations (the risks versus the anticipated gains).

3) To examine the yet unsolved problem of how an open society, such as the United States, can exercise political control over activities that are necessarily secret.

The book is designed primarily for advanced undergraduate and graduate students of international affairs or political science. But any student contemplating a career in foreign affairs, whether in government, journalism, or international business, is going to have to deal with the intelligence community in one way or another and may even have to make some of the murky choices that the book discusses. The book also should be of interest to the general public. All citizens need to think more deeply about the book's central problem—who watches the watchdogs?

Despite a voluminous literature—and to some degree because of it—much of the intelligence community is surrounded by mythology. The leading protagonist in the myths, either as hero or villain, is the Central Intelligence Agency, followed in second place at some distance by the Federal Bureau of Investigation. Of course, the CIA is not responsible for everything bad (or good, depending on one's point of view) that happens in the world. The CIA is both criticized and praised for its actions, or attempts at action; it has accomplished some things so well that they remain publicly unknown and others so poorly that the national embarrassment lingers. But in almost every case, the CIA was doing what it had been told (or thought it had been told) to do by a higher authority.

Some of the principal concerns of this book are who the higher authority ought to be (the president? National Security Council? Congress? others?), how that authority reaches its decisions, and how the lines of communication from authority to operational officer can be unclogged. The Department of Defense pays great attention to what it calls "command and control" of the nation's military forces. Similar attention has not been given—in some respects, deliberately so—to command and control of intelligence. Can, or should, this be changed?

There is no classified information in this book; no secrets are revealed or scandals exposed. The author was a member of the professional staff of the Senate Foreign Relations Committee for twenty-seven years. During seventeen of those years, he was the committee's principal point of contact with the intelligence community and was in charge of the committee's activities relating to intelligence. He learned a great many secrets and failed to learn others despite diligent efforts to penetrate the obfuscation that is a bureaucrat's natural defense. Some of the secrets he learned (and some he failed to learn) have since been revealed by somebody else. They are freely discussed; the others remain secret.

The most valuable thing the author learned is not secret but only obscure. It has to do with the problems the intelligence community faces in trying to do its job and the problems the rest of the government faces in trying to deal with the community. It was in the course of pondering these mysteries that the idea of this book gradually developed.

The scheme of the book is in four parts. Part I establishes the theoretical framework for the problem of political control of secret activities in an open society. It also traces the origins and growth of the intelligence community.

Part II describes the community, what it is, and what it does. The role of each agency that is a part of the community is explained, and separate chapters discuss the four functions of intelligence: collection, analysis, counterintelligence, and covert action.

Part III considers the mechanisms of public control—the media, the presidency, and Congress—in both theoretical and practical terms. The media are included because they are central to the basic dilemma that is at the heart of the book: secrecy and democracy are fundamentally incompatible; yet it is necessary that they coexist, however uneasily.

Part IV looks to the future. The growth of the intelligence community was largely a phenomenon of the cold war, but in the post-cold war world, those who make foreign policy continue to need the community's product. What have we learned that will help us avoid the mistakes of the past?

In the course of preparing this book, I interviewed scores of present and past intelligence officers, diplomats, journalists, and members of Congress and their staffs—all on a background, not-for-attribution, basis. Some of those I interviewed would be embarrassed even to be included in a listing, so I have decided that it is best not to acknowledge any publicly. They know who they are; let them know also that I am enormously grateful.

Four people who contributed a great deal to the manuscript can be named. Brenda Carter of CQ Press was unfailingly helpful. Loch K. Johnson of the University of Georgia and John Macartney of American University read the manuscript and made many constructive suggestions. This is a better book as a result. The book was also improved by the deft editing of Barbara de Boinville. Any errors that remain are mine.

Pat M. Holt
Bethesda, Md.

PART I

The Problem and How It Grew

The nation's founders were preoccupied with balance—between the union and the states, among the three branches of the federal government, between the government and the people. The American government is built on the premise that balance is the best protection against abuse by any element of the whole. But the founders also recognized that the ultimate protection had to lie in the people themselves who could, at stated intervals, turn out one president or one Congress and get a new one.

This ultimate protection is effective only if the people are well informed about what their government is doing. And there's the rub when the government engages in secret activities. Chapter 1 sketches the framework of this problem. Chapter 2 describes its origin and traces its growth.

The essence of the problem is that secrecy and democracy are incompatible; yet some intelligence activities are necessarily secret. The intelligence community gives the president the means, if he wishes, to carry out in secret programs that would involve him in contentious political debate if he attempted to carry them out in public.

The origin of espionage is lost in the mists of history, but its existence is documented in the Old Testament. The public control of secret activities became a problem only with the development of free societies, something that occurred much later.

From his embassy in Paris during the American revolution, Benjamin Franklin spied on the British and was spied on by them. He was also the beneficiary of a French covert action to extend military assistance to the rebellious colonies. Generally, however, intelligence did not become a matter of serious concern for the United States until after World War II.

The Central Intelligence Agency was created in 1947 to coordinate intelligence activities, but other agencies were added over the next fifteen years. The growth of this community and the evolution of public attitudes toward it were heavily influenced by the cold war.

CHAPTER 1

Secrets in an Open Society

Quis custodiet ipsos custodes! (Who will watch the watchdogs!)
—Juvenal

"If men were angels," the authors of the *Federalist* wrote, "no government would be necessary. If angels were to govern men, neither external nor internal controls on government would be necessary. In framing a government which is to be administered by men over men, the great difficulty lies in this: you must first enable the government to control the governed; and in the next place oblige it to control itself." [1]

The framers attempted to solve this "great difficulty" through building the system of checks and balances and the separation of powers into the Constitution. The goal was to construct a government in which no single part could predominate. The president was made dependent on Congress for authority and especially for money. Congress needed the president's signature on a bill before it could become law, or else Congress had to pass the bill by a two-thirds majority.

This relationship was intended to make it difficult for the government to act; it was intended to slow things down. Delay, the framers thought, would help reason prevail. The Supreme Court has put it this way: "Convenience and efficiency are not the primary objectives—or the hallmarks—of democratic government." [2] But presidents, not being angels, get impatient. They stretch their constitutional powers. When they have an intelligence community at their beck and call, they have an instrument by which they can do this in secret. Unless Congress is vigilant, presidents can defeat the Constitution's checks and balances.

The separation of powers is an internal control on government. The more important control is external. It is what the *Federalist* calls "a dependence on the people." [3] The ability of the people to change the government is the ultimate safeguard against the abuse of governmental power and the ultimate corrective if power is abused. Oliver North referred to this safeguard when questioned about his key role in the Reagan administration's illegal sale of arms to Iran and secret diversion of the funds to Nicaraguan rebels (the Contras):

> . . . the President is the highest official in the land answerable to the American people and ultimately, under the Constitution, answerable to the people

through a variety of means, re-election—they can vote him out of office. They chose not to do so." [4]

Of course, if the people do not know what the government is doing, they cannot exercise this power intelligently and responsibly. Secrecy is the enemy of democracy. This is the contradiction posed by the growth of the intelligence community in the United States since World War II.

THE ROLE OF INTELLIGENCE

The problems caused by secrecy in the making of foreign policy become clearer if we look briefly at what the intelligence community does. There are four principal intelligence functions: collection, analysis, counterintelligence, and covert action. Chapters 4, 5, 6, and 7 discuss them in more detail.

COLLECTION

Collection is gathering information from whatever source. It may be as humdrum as reading a newspaper, as glamorous as bugging a foreign minister's office (or bribing his secretary), as sophisticated as taking pictures from space. Collection generally creates a foreign policy problem only when a hazardous technique goes astray. The loss of the U-2 reconnaissance aircraft over the Soviet Union in 1960 is perhaps the outstanding example.

ANALYSIS

Analysis is making sense out of what is collected. It is the intelligence product that goes to the policy maker. The interaction between analyst and policy maker is beset with uncertainties. Is the analyst under pressure (or does the analyst think he or she is under pressure) to tell the policy maker what the latter wants to hear? Is the policy maker willing to listen to something he or she does not want to hear? Does the analyst have an axe to grind? Bad analysis, or bad interaction between analyst and policy maker, can lead to bad policy.

Inappropriate dissemination also can lead to bad policy. For security reasons, intelligence is compartmented: the more sensitive the intelligence, the more restricted its distribution. Sometimes collectors don't tell analysts everything. For that matter, sometimes presidents and secretaries of state do not give the Central Intelligence Agency (CIA) important information they have received in private conversations with foreign leaders. [5]

However complete or incomplete the intelligence that goes into the analytic product, the question remains of how widely that product should be disseminated within the policy-making or operational community. If dissemination is too slow or too restricted, the intelligence may be overtaken by events, sometimes with disastrous results, as in the case of Pearl Harbor. On December 7, 1941, the United States had advance warning of a Japanese attack in the Pacific, though not the specific target. The warning was relayed too late and to the wrong people.

In recent years Congress has shown a growing tendency to make policy dependent on certain presidential findings, which in turn are dependent on intelligence analysis. An example is a law that directs that foreign aid be cut off to any country building nuclear weapons. The president's determination as to whether a country is doing that, and therefore whether it may continue to receive foreign aid, depends on what the president is told by the analysts in the intelligence community. The president may very much want to continue aid to that country for what he regards as higher reasons of state. In these circumstances the intelligence community is under pressure to make the president's decision easier, and the president is under pressure to distort the community's analysis if he thinks it necessary. There are similar examples in laws making foreign aid or trade concessions dependent on a country's human rights performance.

Sooner or later, every president faces the temptation to exaggerate intelligence reports in order to support a predetermined result. For example, the president might be tempted to depict a situation abroad as more urgent than is suggested by intelligence. The fact that the intelligence is secret makes it easier for the president to succumb to this temptation and more difficult for the public to come to informed judgments about policy. Repeated statements which are at odds with publicly known facts damage the credibility not only of an administration but of the intelligence community generally.

COUNTERINTELLIGENCE

Counterintelligence is protecting secrets from outsiders who are trying to learn them. It is keeping foreign intelligence services from doing to you what you are trying to do to them. The main policy problem arising from counterintelligence is that its techniques (wiretapping, covert surveillance) are generally intrusive and violate the constitutional rights of American citizens when used in the United States.

COVERT ACTION

Covert action is an effort to influence a foreign government or group without the hand of the United States being evident. It may be secretly publishing a newspaper or magazine to promote a particular point of view. It may be secretly bribing journalists to slant news stories or editorials. It may be subsidizing a group or organizing a riot. It may be using mercenary troops as guerrillas or in civil wars. It may be giving monetary or other help to foreign political parties. It may be any number of other things.

In all cases elaborate precautions are taken so that covert action cannot be traced to the United States. As is well known, these precautions have not always been successful. Some of the United States' greatest embarrassments have resulted from disclosure of the U.S. role in a covert action. The Iran-Contra scandal is one prominent example. Another is the total defeat of CIA-trained Cuban exiles who invaded their homeland at the Bay of Pigs in 1961. Some of the most bitter controversies about U.S. foreign policy have arisen from such covert actions.

DO WE NEED INTELLIGENCE?

With the end of the cold war, does the United States still need a foreign intelligence program? Sen. Daniel Patrick Moynihan, D-N.Y., has proposed that the Central Intelligence Agency be abolished and residual intelligence activities be transferred to the State Department.[6] Moynihan served as ambassador to India and to the United Nations before coming to the Senate. He also served for a time as a member of the Senate Intelligence Committee. This experience has given him more than an ordinary acquaintance with intelligence, and he has a record on other issues of prescient, original thinking, and therefore his views deserve to be taken seriously. But abolishing the CIA begs the question of whether the U.S. government needs to continue to deal in international secrets.

Half of the resources of the intelligence community were devoted to the Soviet Union before that entity's dissolution.[7] There remain things in the constituent parts of the former Soviet Union that the United States still needs to know—the state of nuclear weapons and their delivery systems, if nothing else—but the new circumstances argue powerfully for a substantial reallocation of resources and probably for a contraction of resources as well. This does not, however, get the United States out of the business of international secrets.

Although no single country looms as threateningly as the Soviet Union once did, the United States needs to know more about other countries and movements—China, the increasingly vociferous Islamic world, and assorted terrorist groups, to pick three priorities. Some may find a kind of quixotic appeal in Senator Moynihan's proposal, but a bureaucracy as massive as that of the intelligence community, or even of the smaller CIA, is not easily disbanded. As a practical matter, intelligence will continue to be with us. The challenge is to deal with it, not to escape it.

Secrets have always been a part of all governments, democratic or not. Nor do all secrets have to do with foreign intelligence. Some things are secret by act of Congress, and Congress has put some of them beyond even its own reach. Examples are income tax returns, information furnished to census takers, and certain proprietary information that businesses are required to report to the Commerce Department. Some of this data shielded from public view is used to support decisions about public policy, just as intelligence is used to support decisions about foreign policy. The Treasury Department uses the data it extracts from tax returns to analyze tax rates and to write new tax legislation. Congress uses demographic data from the census when writing legislation about education, health, and housing. In these and other instances Congress and the public are dependent on, and are disposed to accept, the analyses of the executive branch. But they are not totally dependent. The General Accounting Office is a congressional agency, and occasionally it goes behind the material the executive branch presents to Congress and reviews the raw data and the analytical methodology.

There is another safeguard. These subjects have to do with domestic policy. If the executive branch tries to manipulate or distort analyses based on secret data relating to domestic matters, some of the affected groups may object. More Americans are likely to know the truth about domestic matters than about foreign policy, simply because they are affected by them and can see what is going on. In matters of foreign policy with which intelligence is concerned, manipulations or distortions based on secrecy are less likely to be noticed publicly until it is too late for corrective action.

Some legitimately argue that more intelligence is secret than needs to be, but much intelligence is necessarily secret. It cannot be shared with the public. As a consequence, the public has to take certain things on faith. That is antithetical to democracy. It helps if secret intelligence is shared with Congress, acting as the trustee of the public. But that still leaves the public having to take Congress on faith. Discussions of this subject come back to the frequently stated principle that, without honesty and trustworthiness, the American system of government cannot work. And there is no fail-safe way to guarantee that the men and women who run the government will be honest and trustworthy. This problem has been at the heart of much of the debate about intelligence.

SECRECY AND INTERNATIONAL AGREEMENTS

From its earliest days the U.S. government has been marked by clashes between the president and Congress over what information the president should furnish Congress and what information he can legitimately withhold. An early attempt to resolve this conflict, at least with regard to the treaty-making process, was made by John Jay, whose undercover negotiations with the British led to the 1783 Treaty of Paris recognizing American independence:

> It seldom happens in the negotiation of treaties, of whatever nature, but that perfect *secrecy* and immediate *despatch* are sometimes requisite. There are cases where the most useful intelligence may be obtained, if the persons possessing it can be relieved from apprehensions of discovery. These apprehensions will operate on those persons whether they are actuated by mercenary or friendly motives; and there doubtless are many of both descriptions, who would rely on the secrecy of the President, but who would not confide in that of the Senate, and still less in that of a large popular Assembly. The [constitutional] convention have [sic] done well, therefore, in so disposing of the power of making treaties, that although the President must, in forming them, act by the advice and consent of the Senate, yet he will be able to manage the business of intelligence in such a manner as prudence may suggest. [Italics in original.][8]

This is as good a statement as any of the importance of protecting intelligence sources. The risk of disclosure of a secret increases with the number of people who know it. Sources get nervous and uncooperative if they think what they report is going to be widely repeated. A knowledgeable person may be able to identify the source of certain information even if the source is not explicitly revealed. In Jay's construction, a source might feel secure telling the president, but not the Senate, let alone the more numerous House. In modern terms the source would be willing to talk to the CIA but only on condition that the agency not pass the report on to Congress.

In this framework the interest of the Senate and the public is protected by the process: the president can use secret intelligence, known only to him, to negotiate a treaty, but then the treaty that results must be made known to, and can be debated by, the Senate and the public. However, the treaty's public provisions might have been shaped by secret intelligence known only to the president. If this is the case, then neither the Senate nor the public can make an informed appraisal of the treaty. They will know what is before them, but they will not know what *might* have been before them.

President Woodrow Wilson was disillusioned by the revelation of secret agreements among the European allies during World War I. Wilson proclaimed "open covenants openly arrived at" to be one of the objectives of the peace settlement, but he only got more disappointment. Few, if any, international agreements have ever been negotiated totally in public; it was considered a great step forward when secret annexes came into disfavor.

There are solid diplomatic reasons not to negotiate in public: for one, publicity makes compromise more difficult. Congress has never had all the information about secret diplomacy. Most of the time this has not made much difference, but it occasionally becomes an issue.

Panama Canal Treaties

One of the crowning achievements of Jimmy Carter's presidency (1977-1981) was a pair of treaties that returned total control of the Panama Canal to Panama in the year 2000, abolished the U.S.-controlled Canal Zone, and relinquished U.S. military bases. The treaties, which were signed in 1977, had been thirteen years in negotiation, and they removed an even older contentious issue in U.S.-Panamanian relations. The treaties were approved by the Senate in 1978 by votes of 68-32, one more than the required two-thirds.

During Senate consideration, a story was broadcast, originally by CBS News, that the United States had planted microphones in the Panamanian embassy in Washington. According to the story, the Panamanians discovered the bugs and then blackmailed the United States into making concessions during the negotiations. The Senate Intelligence Committee investigated this story and concluded that it was without substance. But the embassy had, in fact, been bugged by someone. The Panamanian ambassador showed the bugs, still in place, to an American visitor, who pronounced them obsolete. (In the murky world of intelligence, one should allow for the possibility that the Panamanians put the bugs there themselves so that they could show them off. But the Panamanians had no rational motive for doing this. They wanted the treaties ratified, and the bugs merely confused the issue. There is also the possibility that the CIA had done it after all and had conned the Senate Intelligence Committee into believing its denial.)

Sen. Howard H. Baker, Jr., R-Tenn., then the Senate minority leader, demanded that the administration supply the complete negotiating record. He was joined in this request by Sen. Claiborne Pell, D-R.I., then a member and later the chairman of the Foreign Relations Committee. This enormously upset the Carter administration, which foresaw leaks from Congress causing renegotiation of the entire treaties. In the end the administration persuaded the senators to accept summaries and a few excerpts.[9]

This was one of the first demonstrations of the utility of the Senate Intelligence Committee. It investigated the embassy bugging story, and its credibility was such that the Senate accepted its conclusion that there was no bugging.

The administration was not always so fortunate in persuading the Senate to back away from its demands for a treaty's negotiating record.

THE ANTIBALLISTIC MISSILE TREATY

This treaty with the Soviet Union was a major arms control accomplishment of the Nixon administration (1969-1974). It limited development of antiballistic missile defenses of the superpowers. More than a decade later it came into conflict with the Reagan administration's Strategic Defense Initiative (SDI), which was designed precisely to do what the ABM treaty forbade. The conflict first arose with respect to testing during the research and development phase of SDI.

The ABM treaty prohibited most kinds of testing, or so it was thought when the treaty was before the Senate in 1972. In 1985, when the constraints of the ABM treaty were felt to be threatening the development of SDI, the Reagan administration announced a reinterpretation of the treaty to loosen the constraints. This provoked a wave of protests in the Senate, none stronger than those voiced by Sen. Sam Nunn, D-Ga., chairman of the Armed Services Committee. Nunn demanded, and got from the Reagan administration, the ABM negotiating record. He found the record to be lacking in support for the Reagan reinterpretation. Other senators read the record and thought it supported Reagan.

Nunn and other senators had another, more fundamental objection. They believed a reinterpretation of what a treaty meant required joint action by the president and the Senate, just as ratification of a treaty required joint action.

So far as the ABM treaty was concerned, the issue became moot with the end of the cold war. In July 1993 the Clinton administration formally announced its agreement with the narrow interpretation of the ABM treaty on which Nunn had insisted.[10] The controversy, however, had established an important precedent when the Reagan administration sent the negotiating record to the Senate. This was more than Carter had been willing to do with the Panama Canal treaties. The Reagan administration had lifted a little the curtain of secrecy surrounding negotiations and a little of the protection, of which Jay wrote, from "apprehensions of discovery." At the same time the larger constitutional issue of how the United States might reinterpret a treaty remained unresolved. One could say the Senate had won a battle but not the war.

INTELLIGENCE IN A DEMOCRATIC GOVERNMENT

The instruments of a democratic government must be responsive to the will of the people; otherwise, the government is not democratic. The United States has well-developed mechanisms for ensuring this responsiveness with respect to most government agencies and programs. If, for example, the National Park Service does a poor job of managing the national parks, visitors to those parks notice. They complain to Congress or write letters to newspapers. Reporters investigate. Congress holds hearings. Action is taken. If the intelligence community does a poor job of collecting and analyzing intelligence, the public does not know it, but the public will have to pay if this leads to bad foreign policy. The intelligence community also gives the president the means, if he is inclined to use them, to do in secret things that most Americans would disapprove of if they knew about them.

Yet much of what the intelligence community does necessarily has to be done in secret. The great question is how to reconcile that with public accountability.

There are four levels at which control or accountability can be enforced. First is the president, who is the head of the executive branch and is the official most directly responsible. Second is the Congress, which is responsible for general oversight of executive branch agencies and most importantly for the appropriation of money. Then there is the media. In many respects it is like a fourth branch of the government with extra-official watchdog responsibilities. And finally there is the public, which always has the last word but which is critically dependent on the others for information.

It is in the public's name that any governmental activity, covert or overt, is undertaken in the first place. That is the source of the term "public interest." Consider again the example of the National Park Service. If the parks are poorly managed and maintained, those members of the public who use the parks will organize themselves into an interest group that will maintain a lobby in Washington and eventually bring about reform of the National Park Service. That cannot happen with respect to the intelligence community. For intelligence, control and accountability have to be enforced at other levels than the public.

It was only at the end of World War II that the United States seriously got into intelligence in a big way. When the Central Intelligence Agency was created in 1947, it was put under the control of the National Security Council; for practical purposes, that meant the president. He is the only member of the NSC who matters when the time comes to make a decision.

During the Truman and Eisenhower administrations (1945-1961), the intelligence community operated mainly on the basis of personal, informal relationships between the president and whoever happened to be director of central intelligence (DCI). This worked reasonably well. But by 1960 changes began to occur. The community grew considerably larger and more institutionalized—that is to say, more bureaucratic. It also began to make mistakes—some fortuitous, some the fault of the CIA, some the fault of the president. The U-2 spy plane was shot down in 1960 and wrecked a Khrushchev-Eisenhower summit. The Bay of Pigs invasion of Cuba failed in 1961. Other mishaps and disclosures followed.

By the mid-1970s Congress, which had been a largely somnolent watchdog, roused itself, investigated, and established permanent committees in both the House and Senate to oversee the intelligence community. Many observers thought this solved the problem. It still appears that the mechanism for a solution is in place, but the mechanism is not automatic. Congress has to make it work. The failure of the mechanism to prevent the Iran-Contra scandal in the 1980s raised anew the question of whether it is adequate.

As Congress has learned more, the task appears more complicated. Oversight of intelligence is more than preventing scandals à la Iran-Contra, though that is elementary. Intelligence generates many problems of public policy. Some have to do with foreign affairs. Some have to do with the way the government works. There is a fine line between policy oversight and micromanagement, or unwarranted interference with day-to-day administration.

The media is thrust into this process by the theory of the First Amendment's guarantee of freedom of the press. This theory is that the public interest is served when the media have free rein to keep the government honest. The intelligence community presents a particular challenge in that it is not open, as the other departments of the government are open, to prying reporters. The intelligence community is hard for a journalist to cover. It has to be this way because the community cannot function in public. And so we come back to the basic dilemma.

The intelligence community presents another challenge to the media, this one a reflection of the symbiotic nature of the relations between the media and the government. The media and the intelligence community each has something the other one wants. Each can help the other. They can exchange information, and sometimes they have gone beyond exchanging information.

The role of the media is discussed in detail in Chapter 8, with examples of when the media has been a watchdog, when it has been a lapdog, and when it has been a (sometimes unwitting) messenger boy. Chapter 9 discusses the record of the president and the National Security Council as overseers, and Chapter 10 the record of Congress.

MAKING AND IMPLEMENTING FOREIGN POLICY

It is important to keep firmly in mind the distinction between making and implementing foreign policy. Making policy is deciding what to do. Implementing is doing it.

With the important exception of covert action, intelligence is used in making policy. Collection provides the raw data. Counterintelligence protects collection's sources and methods from penetration by hostile services. Analysis organizes the data in a usable form. It then becomes one of the factors to be taken into account by the policy makers.

And who are the foreign policy makers? The most important, by far, is the president. Others include the relevant officials of the executive branch—always the national security adviser, the secretary of state and his or her principal subordinates; in addition, depending on the subject matter, the secretary of defense and officials from the Defense Department and the Joint Chiefs of Staff, or perhaps the secretary of the treasury, or commerce, or agriculture. Note that the director of central intelligence and other officials of the intelligence community are not included. William Casey, the DCI under President Ronald Reagan from 1981 to 1986, was a conspicuous exception. Casey had managed Reagan's 1980 presidential campaign, and some people say he really wanted to be secretary of state in the Reagan administration. Instead, he was made DCI and given cabinet rank, a policy-making position that no other DCI has had. He was absorbed in policy, insisted on participating in policy, and Reagan apparently welcomed it. Other DCIs and other presidents have generally taken the view that participating in making policy, or even in giving policy advice, would interfere with objective intelligence assessment. The DCI's role was described by

Richard Helms, who held the job under Presidents Lyndon Johnson and Richard Nixon, as helping "to keep the game honest." [11]

Each of the principals named in the preceding paragraph is the head of a large and generally disorderly bureaucracy that is an important part of the policy-making process. The bureaucracy writes the option papers that usually set the framework for the discussion. It asks (sometimes) the tough "what if?" questions. It briefs the principals for interagency meetings. It may even set the agendas for those meetings. And it is the source of the internecine conflicts that are the bane of every White House official trying to manage the executive branch.

Foreign policy is not the exclusive preserve of the executive branch, though most of it originates there. Congress is an important participant. The Senate has its special constitutional responsibilities with respect to treaties and nominations. Most foreign policy requires money for its implementation, and a good deal of it requires legislative authority. Both of these requirements involve the House as well as the Senate. Finally, Congress is a bridge between the executive branch and the people. It is a sounding board for public opinion and a forum for debate.

The proper role of Congress in making foreign policy has been controversial from the beginning. Congressional involvement has varied over time depending on several factors—among others, the relative importance of foreign policy in American life, whether a policy was controversial or had general public support, and the strength and skills of the president as a political leader. Informal ties are forged between elements of the executive bureaucracy and congressional staff or committees in order to further or impede a particular proposal. Regardless of such ties, the executive branch has often resisted what it regards as congressional interference with its foreign policy prerogatives. But it is a misguided president who ignores Congress's political clout.

Besides Congress, the public is an important participant in making foreign policy. There are, in fact, several publics, some more important in this respect than others. There is, first, the media—newspapers, magazines, radio, and television. The media are crucial because they are one of the principal means by which the government and the public communicate with each other. Second, there is the foreign policy community—academia, think tanks, organizations of various kinds with international interests. Third and finally, there is the public at large. The American people's attention waxes and wanes as they feel their varied interests threatened or advanced by particular policies. These interests may be ethnic, reflecting Americans' emotional ties to the lands of their ancestors. The interests may be economic, reflecting the desire of some Americans to sell their products abroad and the fear of other Americans of foreign competition. There may be any of a number of other interests.

The public participates in making policy indirectly but no less powerfully. Most interest groups maintain lobbies in Washington to see to it that their views are heard in the proper quarters. The power of the Jewish American lobby to support Israel is legendary. Greek Americans successfully raised a storm of protest against aid to Turkey when Turkey invaded Cyprus in 1974. Cuban Americans are vigilant to protest any warming trend toward Cuban Prime Minister Fidel Castro.

Out of this vast and usually disorganized array of interests—presidential, bureaucratic, congressional, academic, economic, ethnic—a policy eventually emerges. Secret intelligence is usually a crucial input into this policy, but only the president, the bureaucracy, and selected members of Congress (and congressional staff) know what the intelligence is. Others may know parts of it, based on leaks of selected material to selected recipients. But most people have to take on faith that an important underpinning of the policy is what the president and a few other policy makers say it is.

Sometimes this does not matter. One could make up one's mind about the North American Free Trade Agreement (NAFTA) without access to secret intelligence. There are enough facts about it in the public domain to come to a reasonable conclusion about its merits. Problems arise when there are not enough facts in the public domain, and access to secret intelligence is crucial to making a reasoned judgment.

LONG-TERM AND SHORT-TERM POLICY

There is a distinction to be made between the long term and the short term in policy making. The making of long-term policy almost always involves all the individuals and groups mentioned above, and it usually develops over a period of months or even years. It is concerned with reaching a consensus on a definition of basic national interests and with building an enduring framework within which short-term policies can fit. The making of short-term policy usually involves only the president, his closest advisers, and possibly a few selected members of Congress. It is usually made in days or even hours as a response to an unexpected situation.

The decision that the Iraqi invasion of Kuwait in the summer of 1990 should not go unchallenged by the United States was part of a long-term policy. It reflected a consensus about collective security in the face of aggression as well as about the strategic importance and the resources of the area. There was debate aplenty about the tactics and timing of the U.S. response, but the basic policy was generally accepted. Nor did one need access to secret intelligence to form an opinion about the policy.

One did need access to secret intelligence to evaluate the decision to make the retaliatory cruise missile strike against Iraqi intelligence headquarters in June 1993. The crucial factor in this short-term U.S. policy was whether Iraq was, or was not, responsible for an alleged assassination attempt against former president George Bush in Kuwait in April 1993. After the strike the Clinton administration described the evidence of Iraqi complicity as conclusive, based on what it said was a meticulous investigation by the Federal Bureau of Investigation (FBI). But in reporting the evidence to the U.N. Security Council, U.S. ambassador Madeleine K. Albright was specific only with respect to the bombs that the Iraqis intended to use (they were like bombs Iraqis had used elsewhere). She said suspects had made incriminating statements, but she did not say what those statements were. She referred to other "classified intelligence sources" without saying what they were or what they revealed.[12] Thus, the public was asked to take the administration's statements on faith. If a member of the public chose not to do that, there was no way to argue about it.

More careful investigation of the FBI report raised some doubts. One anonymous senior White House official was quoted as calling one of the report's most persuasive points "overstated and . . . essentially incorrect." Other White House aides, also anonymous, said the president was moved to order the retaliation by his expectation that the report would be leaked.[13]

In the short term there is sometimes a fine line between making policy and implementing it. Most Americans would probably agree with the general proposition that the United States should not tolerate the attempted assassination of former presidents. The question then becomes one of what to do about such an attempt when it occurs. First, we must be sure that an attempt was in fact made, and we must be sure of who made it. Then a range of options present themselves as possible responses. If we decide on a military response, do we use cruise missiles or manned aircraft? Do we hit Iraqi intelligence headquarters (as in fact we did) or other targets? Or do we opt for tighter economic sanctions? The choice among these and other possible options is the point at which policy making becomes policy implementation. Perforce this choice must be left to the president. It will be affected by secret intelligence, but those are secrets the public does not need to know. What the public does need to know is that the president is responding to a real attack and that the response is directed against the real perpetrators.

The Use of Secrets in Making Policy

The proper use of intelligence in policy making is to inform or enlighten the process. The more the policy maker knows about the problem he or she is dealing with, the more likely it is that an intelligent and workable policy will result. Intelligence helps the policy maker avoid mistakes. It serves as an antidote to preconception, prejudice, and ideological rigidity. In Helms's phrase, it helps to "keep the game honest."

But it is a rare policy maker who has the self-discipline to hew to such a rigorous use of intelligence. Policy makers are frequently tempted to look to intelligence for support of what they want to do rather than for clues as to what they ought to do. Policy makers who succumb to this temptation reveal only that portion of the intelligence, warped or distorted though it may be, that supports their position, and they suppress the remainder of the intelligence that presents a more rounded picture. In doing this they render a disservice to the public interest, but unless somebody is looking over their shoulder, no one will ever know.

The argument is, "We have intelligence to show that [a given situation exists]. I wish I could tell you what it is, but it is from a very sensitive source that I must protect." Dean Rusk was secretary of state in the Johnson administration, which used this argument many times. Rusk later described it as "the worst argument in politics that I know of . . . a phony argument from the very beginning.[14] In justifying the Johnson administration's intervention in the Dominican Republic in 1965, the State Department told the Senate Foreign Relations Committee, "If you knew what we know, you would agree with what we did." The committee challenged the department to tell what it knew; when the department did so, it was dumbfounded that the committee in fact did not agree. The department's secret files did not support the administration's public position.

The Reagan administration consistently exaggerated intelligence reports from Central America in a way that supported its controversial policies there. The congressional intelligence committees knew the truth but felt constrained from making it public because of security considerations.

The Johnson administration misrepresented the U.S.-North Vietnamese naval encounter in the Tonkin Gulf in August 1964. It concealed its own provocative actions in the gulf and perhaps exaggerated the attacks that were alleged to have been made by North Vietnamese PT boats against American destroyers. The truth came out later in bits and pieces but too late to affect either the congressional or public debate at a meaningful stage. In the meantime, Congress, which did not yet know the truth, passed the Gulf of Tonkin Resolution delegating massive authority to the president to act as he saw fit in Southeast Asia. The Johnson administration later heavily relied on this resolution as authority for its controversial policy in Vietnam.

Intelligence is not always abused. The United States has negotiated and ratified a number of arms control treaties. All of them have been crucially dependent on verification and on the capability of American intelligence to detect violations. The techniques for verifying compliance involve some very sophisticated and secret methods. In the case of the early arms control treaties, the executive branch in effect asked the Senate to trust it, to take on faith its assurances that verification was technically feasible. When the Senate approved the treaties, it not only expressed its own trust in the executive branch; it also in effect asked the public to agree that the trust was warranted. To a large degree, this had to be taken on faith. But not entirely. The nongovernmental scientific community did not have access to secret data, but it could at least explain physics.

By the time of the later treaties, the Senate Intelligence Committee had been established. This introduced a check on the executive. The committee had access, it said, to all the technical details of the sensitive methods of verification.

But the rest of the Senate and the public at large still had to trust the Intelligence Committee. Strictly speaking, the rest of the Senate was not dependent on the committee. Any senator had the right to read any of the data and reports received by the committee, but few took advantage of this, and fewer still were capable of understanding the technical reports without devoting substantial time to study and briefing. As a practical matter, not all the members of the Intelligence Committee devoted the time and effort necessary to familiarize themselves with these problems and processes. The watchdogs acting on behalf of the Senate were in fact the committee staff and a handful of members. This is also true, however, of other committees dealing with less sensitive programs. Congressional committees generally perform their oversight functions with a handful of members and staff.

Even so, establishment of the intelligence committees in the House as well as in the Senate was a significant step toward the principle of public accountability of the intelligence community. Most members of the committees feel this responsibility and take it seriously. Sen. David L. Boren, D-Okla., who was chairman of the Senate committee from 1987 to 1993, talked frequently of the committee's "first responsibility . . . to the American people" and of how its members were "acting as trustees for the people." [15] Others have spoken in a similar vein.

There is no evidence that the executive branch or the Senate Intelligence Committee has misled either the Senate or the public about the American verification capability. This raises an interesting question: Can the public interest be protected without the public knowing it? These matters are discussed in more detail in Chapter 5 on analysis.

THE USE OF INTELLIGENCE IN IMPLEMENTING POLICY

Although a great many people are involved, directly or indirectly, in making policy, its implementation is the exclusive prerogative of the executive branch. This means that the president is at the center of both making and implementing policy. This dual role tends to blur the distinction between the two functions, especially in the mind of the president, with particular consequences in the use of covert action.

To implement policy the president has many tools: traditional diplomacy, bilateral diplomacy with respect to a specific country, and multilateral diplomacy carried out through the United Nations or one of the regional organizations of which the United States is a member. There are the various informational, educational, and cultural programs of the U.S. Information Agency. There is economic and trade policy. With respect to many countries, there is economic assistance or the multilateral programs of the international financial institutions such as the World Bank, the International Monetary Fund, and regional development banks. (These multilateral economic programs are not, strictly speaking, instruments of the U.S. government, but the United States can powerfully influence them when it wants to.) There is a wide range of military tools, ranging from friendly (military assistance and training) to hostile (blockades, warfare). And then there is covert action.

Of all the functions of intelligence, covert action is the only one with the exclusive purpose of implementing foreign policy and of doing it secretly without the knowledge either of the American people or the people of the foreign country concerned. This raises two problems relevant to the democratic control of secret activities. One concerns ends (the purpose of the covert action); the other concerns means (the form the covert action takes).

Some covert actions are unexceptional on both counts. During one period, the CIA secretly subsidized Americans' attendance at meetings of international students. It was considered in the national interest that the United States be represented, and the CIA was the most readily available source of money. From time to time the CIA has secretly subsidized the living expenses of impecunious delegations to international conferences. It was considered in the national interest that the conferences succeed. (In at least one case, the conference failed, but that was not for lack of trying.) These things could just as well have been done by the State Department, but due to a quirk in the congressional appropriations process, the CIA always has more money for miscellaneous expenditures than does State.

In these examples nothing was done that was inappropriate. There was a happy harmony of ends and means. Covert action was used to support an established policy with widespread, if not universal, public support, but public acknowledgment of U.S. government financing would have detracted from the policy's effectiveness.

Other covert actions have ends that are congruent with openly established, well-known policy, but the means are questionable. In the Italian elections of 1948, the United States publicly showed its desperation to prevent a victory by the Communist Party. Italian Americans were openly urged to write to their relatives to vote against the Communists. On a parallel but covert track, the CIA poured money and other assistance into the campaign of the Christian Democratic Party, which won the election. Some people who agreed with the desired outcome nonetheless felt that direct, covert intervention in a foreign election was inappropriate.

The same questions are raised, even more acutely, when we move from electing governments to overthrowing them. One could argue that the Bay of Pigs operation against Castro was a covert action in support of an openly established policy. But the anti-Castro policy in question was by no means universally accepted, and even some who did accept it were not prepared to support an action to overthrow the Cuban regime. Even less were they prepared to accept assassination of Castro, which was attempted more than once during the Kennedy administration.

Finally, some covert actions have ends *and* means that are unacceptable to most Americans. These actions may be attractive to a president because they enable him to do something that he could not otherwise do without becoming embroiled in major political controversies.

Nicaragua during Reagan's presidency (1981-1989) provides a classic example. The Reagan administration had a firm ideological commitment that the national interest of the United States required the failure of the Nicaraguan government then in power. Most Americans held no particular brief for that government, but there was vigorous controversy over the proposition that the national security of the United States depended on its overthrow. Thus was born the most contentious foreign policy issue since the Vietnam War, and out of this came not only the Iran-Contra scandal, but a host of other inappropriate covert actions (see Chapter 7).

The Reagan administration tried to use covert action to do secretly what it knew it could not do publicly. This is inappropriate for a government in a democratic country. Worse, the Reagan administration tried to use covert action to do secretly what it had been expressly forbidden by law to do at all. This is subversive in a democratic country.

This subversion was not uncovered by the vigilance of either Congress or the press, the two institutions that are supposed to act as a free society's watchdogs. The affair began to unravel by sheer chance: an American survived a plane crash in Nicaragua and then talked to his captors. It can be argued that the affair was so vast that it would have come to light sooner or later anyway. However, that is a tenuous safeguard. One would want a more reliable restraint on a government that does not, as the *Federalist* put it, consist of angels.

CONCLUSION

Many things must be done secretly or not at all. These things include some methods of collecting intelligence and, by definition, all covert action. The government is therefore constantly faced with a tradeoff between secrecy and not doing something. Despite the popular image of dawdling bureaucrats, the impulse is to do something.

This was reinforced during the cold war when there was an even greater than normal atmosphere of urgency. This encouraged a tendency to cut corners. In an *ex post facto* investigation the General Accounting Office found that the Defense Department persuaded Congress to authorize several weapons systems by deliberately overstating the capability of Soviet defenses and the vulnerability of U.S. defenses.[16] This tendency permeated the foreign policy agencies of government and acquired a momentum that produced a pervasive climate of deceit.

The first U.S. spy is generally held to have been Nathan Hale, a young graduate of Yale University who was caught and hanged by the British during the Revolutionary War. His statue stands today outside the Yale Club in New York and the CIA headquarters in Langley, Virginia. Hale referred to espionage as a "peculiar service," and he justified it by saying that "every kind of service necessary for the public good becomes honorable by being necessary."[17] No doubt unwittingly, Hale cut to the heart of the problem of public policy in intelligence. Who determines what is the public good? Who determines what kind of service is necessary for it, especially when the service in question is secret? What seems necessary to one person may seem only desirable or even immaterial to another. What one person sees as the public good, another may see as a public abomination.

In essence, Hale said that the end justifies the means. This is one of the oldest problems in ethics, but it has also been the rationalization of many intelligence operations. Taken by itself, the statement is meaningless. The "means" here is action necessary to achieve an objective. If the objective itself is worthless, then there is no reason to take any action. If the objective is national survival, then strong action is justified. But even in these extreme cases, one has to ask if the action in question is the only way, or the best way, to ensure survival. An infinite number of less clear cases crowd across the broad spectrum between the extremes.

The American political system is designed so that when people disagree about such things, as they certainly will, there is public debate and discussion and eventually elections to settle the matter. But this cannot happen if the public does not know what its government is doing. If the public does know, then most intelligence operations, being dependent on secrecy, cannot be undertaken in any event. This is the catch-22 of intelligence and policy.

Is there a valid distinction between peacetime and wartime? Most people think there is. The argument over whether the end justifies the means is muted in wartime when usual peacetime considerations are submerged in the overriding drive for military success. But this is not absolute; witness the arguments over the use of nuclear weapons, poison gas, or germ warfare. The public tends to be more tolerant of government in wartime, to accept more secrecy, and to ask fewer questions. Objections, if any, are generally withheld until the war is over. But even the distinction between war and peace is blurred. World War II was the last American war that was declared by Congress as the Constitution requires and that directly and immediately affected our national life. The Korean and Vietnam wars were fought on the other side of the world while life in the United States went on more or less as usual. Vietnam eventually became so controversial it disrupted our national life, but that merely underlines the point that it did not reflect a consensus.

One possible way out is for those in control of intelligence (mainly the president) to apply an informal rule of thumb: If the people knew about this, would they support it? This has to be a seat-of-the-pants judgment, but presidents have pretty good political instincts; otherwise they would not have become president in the first place. (Sometimes these instincts are dulled by long occupation of the White House, but that is a separate problem.) It can be argued that President Harry Truman's instincts would have told him the people would have supported aid to the Christian Democrats against the Communists in the Italian elections of 1948. President Johnson could have been reasonably sure that the people would have supported aid to the Christian Democrats against the Socialists in the Chilean elections of 1964. But President Richard Nixon had reason to doubt the people would have supported his secret campaign to destabilize the regime of Chilean president Salvador Allende from 1970 to 1973, and President Reagan certainly knew that the people would have opposed arms deals with Iran and aid to the Nicaraguan Contras, especially since Congress had voted four times against aid to the Contras. One can argue further that it was precisely because they knew the public would oppose their policies that Nixon and Reagan tried to keep the implementation of those policies secret. And that is subversive of the American political process.

An even more informal and personal rule of thumb can usually be relied on to produce the same result. And it is perhaps easier to apply. In a previous incarnation as a staff member of the Senate Foreign Relations Committee, this writer devoted an inordinate amount of time to an effort to draft legislative guidelines for intelligence operations. He finally decided it could not be done and summarized his work with only this guidance, which is inappropriate for a statute but apropos here. If a proposed action gives you the kind of feeling you got when you were a little boy and were thinking about doing something you did not want your mother to know about, you had better not involve the U.S. government in it now that you are grown up.

NOTES

1. *The Federalist*, no. 51. Attributed to either Alexander Hamilton or James Madison.
2. *Immigration and Naturalization Service* v. *Chadha et al.*, 462 U.S. 919 (1983).
3. *The Federalist*, no. 51.
4. Senate Select Committee on Secret Military Assistance to Iran and the Nicaraguan Opposition, and House Select Committee to Investigate Covert Arms Transactions

with Iran, *Iran-Contra Investigation*, Joint Hearings, 100th Cong., 1st sess., 1987, vol. 100-7, pt. II, 37. Hereafter cited as Iran-Contra Hearings.

5. See, for example, Dean Rusk, Oral History (Rusk Y), Dean Rusk interviewed by Loch Johnson and Richard Rusk, Richard B. Russell Memorial Library, University of Georgia, Athens, Ga., January 18, 1985, 19. "A president and secretary of state usually know things, which are not passed on to the intelligence community to be taken into account when they make their estimates. For example, in my own very private talks with Andrei Gromyko [longtime Soviet foreign minister], there were times when we would talk about certain things over in the corner somewhere and I would not write a memorandum on it and circulate it all through the government. But I would take those talks into account when I was making my own judgment as to the product of the intelligence community on those same issues."

6. See S. 236, 102d Cong., *To repeal certain Cold War legislation and for other purposes.* The bill was referred to the Intelligence Committee, which took no action on it.

7. Robert N. Gates, "CIA and the Collapse of the Soviet Union: Hit or Miss?" Speech to Foreign Policy Association, New York, May 20, 1992. Text from CIA Public Affairs Office.

8. *The Federalist,* no. 64.

9. William J. Jorden, *Panama Odyssey* (Austin: University of Texas Press, 1984), 467-468, 470-471.

10. Letter, Thomas Graham, Jr., acting director, Arms Control and Disarmament Agency, to Sen. Claiborne Pell, chairman, Senate Foreign Relations Committee, July 13, 1993. Text in committee press release, July 14, 1993.

11. Richard Helms oral history interview, Lyndon Baines Johnson Library, Austin, April 4, 1969, 7.

12. R. Jeffrey Smith and Ann Devroy, "Clinton Says U.S. Action 'Crippled' Iraqi Intelligence," *Washington Post*, June 29, 1993.

13. Seymour M. Hersh, "A Reporter at Large: A Case Not Closed," *New Yorker*, Nov. 1, 1993, 80.

14. Dean Rusk Oral History *(Rusk AA)*, Richard B. Russell Memorial Library, University of Georgia, Athens, Ga., 12.

15. Senate Select Committee on Intelligence, *Nomination of Robert M. Gates*, Hearings, 102d Cong., 1st sess., 1991, 5.

16. Tim Weiner, "Military Accused of Lies Over Arms," *New York Times*, June 28, 1993.

17. Quoted in Charles W. Brown, *Nathan Hale: The Martyr Spy* (New York: J.B. Ogilvie, 1899), 61.

CHAPTER 2

Origins and Evolution of American Intelligence

I think it was a mistake. And if I had known what was going to happen, I never would have done it.

—Harry S. Truman

Espionage has been aptly called the world's second oldest profession,[1] and there are many examples of its joint practice with the oldest. The Old Testament tells the story of the two spies whom Joshua sent to Jericho. They went into "the house of a harlot whose name was Rahab." She hid them from the king of Jericho and even sent the king's men (possibly the first counterintelligence agents) on a wild goose chase to look for them outside the city. In return Rahab received protection for herself and her family. When the Israelites sacked the city, Rahab and family were spared, and she lived happily in Israel ever after.[2]

In another biblical example Moses, acting under divine direction, sent men "to spy out the land of Canaan." He directed them to

> see what the land is, and whether the people who dwell in it are strong or weak, whether they are few or many, and whether the land that they dwell in is good or bad, and whether the cities that they dwell in are camps or strongholds, and whether the land is rich or poor, and whether there is wood in it or not. Be of good courage and bring some of the fruit of the land.

This would be a good checklist for a modern intelligence report. Moses's agents spent forty days on their mission. They returned with grapes, pomegranates, and figs. They agreed that the land "flows with milk and honey. . . . Yet the people are strong, and the cities are fortified and very large." But their analysis of this intelligence differed. A few wanted to go anyway "and occupy it; for we are well able to overcome it." But others said, "We are not able to go up against the people; for they are stronger than we. The land . . . is a land that devours its inhabitants; and all the people that we saw in it are men of great stature." Some millennia later President John F. Kennedy sent Gen. Maxwell Taylor and Walt Rostow, then the president's deputy national security adviser, to report on Vietnam. Their conclusions were so different he asked if they had gone to the same country. Moses might have felt the same way. God was displeased and sent the faint of heart to wander in the wilderness for forty years—one year for every day of their espionage mission.[3]

Governments have always tried to learn other governments' secrets and to conceal their own in order to protect themselves or to gain an advantage in commerce, in negotiations, or in war. As international relations have become more complex, the importance of intelligence to policy makers has increased. Technology has provided better tools of the trade, but the fundamentals are basically unchanged. Intelligence is valuable in dealing with friendly nations, even allies, as well as hostile nations and putative enemies. Nor is the practice of gathering intelligence limited to governments. Businesses try to find out what their competitors are planning. Advance knowledge is deemed so unfairly advantageous in trading securities and commodities that such insider trading has been made illegal in the United States.

Writing in the fifth century B.C., the Chinese sage Sun Tzu identified foreknowledge as "the reason the enlightened prince and the wise general conquer the enemy whenever they move." [4] Sun Tzu also described five categories of secret agents: agents in place, double agents, deception agents, expendable agents, and penetration agents. This typology is still generally valid.

Intelligence received a boost in Europe in the fifteenth century with the rise of city states that began to carry on diplomatic relations with each other through the establishment of embassies. These embassies provided splendid cover for secret activities. They also provided diplomatic immunity for the spies unfortunate enough to be caught. They still do. The principal state secretary of Elizabeth I, Sir Francis Walsingham, developed a considerable intelligence network in Europe using graduates of Oxford and Cambridge, universities that continue to be a rich source for recruitment by the British intelligence agencies.

FROM THE REVOLUTION TO WORLD WAR I

About the time the British were hanging the American spy Nathan Hale, Benjamin Franklin was making his way to Paris, where he set up shop as the first American diplomat. He had a twofold mission: to get military and economic assistance from France, and to establish and run a network of agents in London following developments in the British government. He was successful on both counts.

The French had their own reasons to cause trouble for the British, but they did not want to be aboveboard about it. The aid that they readily supplied (a total of about $8.3 million—a great deal of money in the eighteenth century) was secret. Military supplies were funneled through a fictitious trading organization called Rodrigue Hortalez and Company. This was the creation of Caron de Beaumarchais, who was also the author of the play *The Marriage of Figaro* on which Mozart's better known opera of the same name is based. Today the company would be called a proprietary, many of which have been created by the CIA. Thus was the United States involved in covert action even before it was independent.[5]

Franklin not only spied on the British; he was also the target of British espionage. A member of his staff, it was disclosed later, was being paid by the

British to deliver data that he had stolen from Franklin. He also delivered British data to Franklin. It is not known yet, and probably never will be, which side he was really working for or whether he was milking both.

As what became the War of 1812 with Great Britain approached, President James Madison undertook a covert action in the Spanish territory of Florida. In 1811 Madison sent George Mathews to Florida to preempt British intrigues there and turn them to America's advantage. Mathews's instructions were to accept Florida for the United States if he could persuade the Spanish, who were having their own troubles, to let go of it. Otherwise, he was to take it anyway and set up a provisional government. Spain refused to cede Florida (there was no reason to think it would), so Mathews incited an insurrection by the English-speaking inhabitants, who declared their independence March 27, 1812. The next day Mathews's forces moved in.

Spain protested, and Madison ordered Mathews to suspend the operation. Secretary of State James Monroe, who had not known about it before, said that Mathews had "misunderstood" his instructions. The United States had to wait until 1819 to get Florida.

This early example has many of the elements of covert action today, especially that which utilizes military or paramilitary forces: secret incitement of foreigners to stage what will appear to be a spontaneous uprising, immediate American help for them, national embarrassment when the operation becomes public, and a president who does not tell his secretary of state everything.

Such examples were rare in the nineteenth century when in truth the United States did not have an intelligence service. Such intelligence as it did have was largely an opportunistic, hit-or-miss wartime endeavor limited to tactical military intelligence, the kind Nathan Hale was trying to learn. Even the Civil War did not occasion much spying, despite the fact that the circumstances were made for espionage. The two sides shared a common language and culture, making it easy for spies to blend into the general population. Post-World War II Germany had the same characteristics, and it was a hotbed of spies.

During the U.S. Civil War, the South made a greater intelligence effort than the North, though without many concrete results. The Confederate Secret Service conducted covert actions to supply arms and encouragement to southern sympathizers in the North, especially in Maryland. It also tried guerrilla warfare (including a raid from Canada on St. Albans, Vermont), and it attempted some sabotage. The assassination of Abraham Lincoln, some say, was a Confederate covert action. In one version the original intention was to kidnap Lincoln and hold him hostage.[6] It is well established that the attempted assassination of Secretary of State William Seward was part of the same plot (whatever the plot's origins) in which the president was killed.

The navy got a permanent intelligence unit in 1882, mainly because of an interest in learning about foreign ship construction methods. The army got an intelligence unit in 1885. These are the attaché services that establish relations with their foreign counterparts with the avowed purpose of collecting military and naval intelligence.

The most significant beginnings of U.S. intelligence activities came with cryptanalysis—code breaking—in World War I. The State Department, army, and navy all independently began efforts to read other countries' codes and ciphers and to make their own more secure.[7] The pioneers were Herbert O. Yardley, who started work in the State Department as a $900 a year code clerk in 1912, and William Friedman who (with his wife Elizebeth) worked in the Army Signal Corps. Both efforts started in World War I but came to fruition in the 1930s.

THE INTERWAR PERIOD

Yardley presided over a secret effort jointly funded by the State and War departments and operated in a presumably residential house in Manhattan. It was called the Black Chamber. Over a twelve-year period Yardley's group managed to decode or decipher more than 45,000 telegrams from nineteen countries: among others, Argentina, Brazil, Chile, China, Costa Rica, Cuba, France, Germany, Japan, Liberia, Mexico, Nicaragua, Panama, Peru, the Soviet Union, Spain, and the United Kingdom. Nothing was sacred; they even took a crack at the Vatican's codes.[8]

When Herbert Hoover became president in 1929, he made Henry L. Stimson secretary of state. After a few months Yardley sent Stimson the texts of an important series of intercepted and decoded messages. Apparently, Yardley did this more to impress Stimson with the value of the Black Chamber than to convey intelligence to the secretary of state, but the move was fatally counterproductive. Stimson was aghast that such activity would be going on in peacetime and ordered it stopped. Years later, in Stimson's memoir-biography written jointly with McGeorge Bundy, the action was explained:

> This act he [Stimson] never regretted. In later years he was to permit and indeed encourage similar labors in another Department [that is, War], but in later years the situation was different. In 1929 the world was striving with good will for lasting peace, and in this effort all the nations were parties. Stimson, as Secretary of State, was dealing as a gentleman with the gentlemen sent as ambassadors and ministers from friendly nations, and as he later said, "Gentlemen do not read each other's mail."[9]

The U.S. government closed the Black Chamber on October 31, 1929. Yardley and the other employees were each given three months severance pay. It was supposed to last until they found other jobs, but with the onset of the depression, it did not. Broke and embittered, Yardley wrote a book, *The American Black Chamber*, which revealed the Chamber's secrets and became a publishing sensation. He soon wrote another book-length manuscript, which he titled *Japanese Diplomatic Secrets, 1921-22*. The book was rejected by the publisher, the respected house of Bobbs-Merrill, which was worried that the government might try to ban further publication of *The American Black Chamber*. Bobbs-Merrill did not wish any more trouble at that time. It went further and secretly notified the Justice Department of the existence of the manuscript. A grand jury was convened in New York under the direction of a young assistant U.S. attorney named Thomas E. Dewey. It subpoenaed the manuscript and simply kept it. Dewey sent the manuscript to the Justice Department, where it remained under lock and key until it was declassified in 1979 at the request of James Bamford, who was writing a book about U.S. code breaking.[10]

Yardley's writings inspired Congress in 1933 to enact a law providing criminal penalties for disclosing cryptologic data obtained "by virtue of . . . employment by the United States." It is still in effect as 18 U.S.C. 952.

By 1944 Assistant U.S. Attorney Dewey had become governor of New York and was the Republican presidential candidate against Franklin Roosevelt, then running for a fourth term. Information came to the attention of Gen. George C. Marshall, army chief of staff, that Dewey was planning to charge in the campaign that code breaking had given Roosevelt advance knowledge of the Japanese attack on Pearl Harbor and that the president had failed to warn American commanders in Hawaii. Marshall wrote a long letter, which was hand delivered to Dewey, outlining the disastrous consequences of publicizing the code-breaking success. Not the least of these was that it would interfere with the continued receipt of German cryptanalytic intelligence from the British. Dewey's first reaction was that he had known about the broken Japanese codes for years, and he refused to believe the Japanese were still using them. He was persuaded to hold his tongue by Marshall's argument that disclosure would also affect the war in Europe. Marshall's approach to Dewey, incidentally, was made without Roosevelt's knowledge.[11]

While Yardley was creating a stir with his revelations, the War Department had another cryptologic genius at work in the person of William Friedman, who was picked up by the Army Signal Corps in 1921. During the 1920s and 1930s, Friedman directed a small group, importantly including his wife Elizebeth, and by the beginning of World War II they had made up most of the ground the State Department had lost with the closing of the Black Chamber. The navy during this time also mounted a major effort against Japanese naval codes. By the time of Pearl Harbor, this effort involved 700 people and was achieving major successes.

Thus, the United States entered World War II in December 1941 with considerable code-breaking ability in place. The problem was that the United States did not know what to do with it. The government was so impressed with the need for secrecy—as it should have been—that intelligence derived from cryptanalysis was withheld from people, especially those in the navy in Hawaii, who should have had it. (There was probably some bureaucratic jealousy involved in this tightfistedness as well.)

In addition, the government misinterpreted the intelligence it had: it expected a Japanese attack, but in the Philippines or Southeast Asia, not Hawaii. So strong was this mindset that when Secretary of the Navy Frank Knox was told of the attack on Pearl Harbor, he is said to have exclaimed, "My God! This can't be true; this must mean the Philippines." The final relevant message intercepted from the Japanese reached Washington in the early hours of December 7, 1941. It indicated the time of the attack as 1:00 p.m. Washington time but did not say where. Even this message was not forwarded to the Pacific in timely fashion because of organizational, bureaucratic, human, and even technical communications shortcomings.[12] This sad story provided one of the strong arguments for the establishment of the *Central* Intelligence Agency after the war. The creators of the CIA sought to centralize intelligence activities so that never again would the government suffer the results of too many intelligence agencies working at cross-purposes.

THE BEGINNINGS OF COUNTERINTELLIGENCE

The 1930s brought a rising concern over German espionage. This resulted from a series of coincidences, each building on the last. Taken together they provide a remarkable demonstration of the loose, happy-go-lucky state of American counterintelligence at that time.

The story begins in the spring of 1935 with pillow talk between an employee of Maj. Truman Smith, the American army attaché in Berlin, and a woman employed by the Abwehr, the German High Command's intelligence service. She told her lover that the Abwehr was operating in New York and that it was using German merchant ships to carry information back and forth. Maj. Smith's report of this information came to the attention of Major Joe N. Dalton, an army intelligence officer at Governor's Island in New York. Dalton asked customs officials to pay particular attention to German ships.

Some months later, in September, a customs agent had his suspicions aroused by a heated conversation between one of the stewards of the liner *Europa* and an unknown man. A search of the man yielded negatives of films and a packet of letters in German. The agent arrested the man, who turned out to be a German citizen named William Lonkowski. The films were of plans for a new experimental plane under development for the navy in Buffalo.

When Lonkowski was questioned the next day, he said he was a piano tuner and correspondent for an aviation magazine. With the concurrence of the army, the customs agents pretended to accept this story and released Lonkowski, asking only that he return in three days for a further interview. The army's hope was that Lonkowski would lead them to others. The hope was not misplaced. Lonkowski beat a path to the office of Dr. Ignatz Theodor Griebl, a medical reserve officer in the U.S. Army who was prominent in the American Nazi movement. Dr. Griebl drove Lonkowski to Canada. From there Lonkowski returned to Germany, where his surveillance was handed over to the attaché, Major Smith. Lonkowski later had a prominent career in German air intelligence.

At this point Major Dalton of Governor's Island took his problem to the FBI—not officially but informally to an FBI agent in New York who happened to be a friend. Even for a doctor's office, there were a great many visitors to Dr. Griebl's establishment. Again informally, Major Dalton went to another friend, this one the postal inspector in charge of overseas mail in New York. Arrangements were made to receive the names and addresses of the people to whom Dr. Griebl and his visitors were sending letters and packages. Most of them were in Germany, and Major Smith reported that they were cover names.

By this time it was 1937, and an informal collection of Americans from a variety of agencies had been chasing Nazi spies for more than two years without notable result. Then the mail cover began to show repeated mailings to a Mrs. Jessie Wallace Jordan in Dundee, Scotland. Dalton asked the army attaché in London to determine if the British might be interested in the contents of Mrs. Jordan's mail. The attaché had lunch with the head of the British Secret Service at their London club. The British would indeed be very interested. And since at that time the British were less queasy than the Americans about opening other people's mail, they proceeded to find out. What they found out was that Mrs. Jordan was not only a spy herself, reporting British defense information to Germany, but she was also a relay agent for Dr. Griebl's net as well as other Nazi activities in the United States.

At this point Major Dalton and his friend in the FBI brought the matter to the attention of higher authority. Far from reproving his agent for acting out of channels, the director of the FBI, J. Edgar Hoover, was happy to bask in the reflected glory of smashing a spy ring. The first arrests were made in February 1938; eighteen people were indicted. Of these, only four were within the jurisdiction of the United States. Those four were convicted in December 1938.[13]

A political row ensued over the weak state of American defenses, intelligence, and counterintelligence services. In June 1938 President Roosevelt pronounced himself in favor of increased army and navy appropriations, as the *New York Times* story put it, "for running down foreign spies in the United States." Roosevelt added that he "wanted it clearly understood he would not sanction espionage by American agents abroad."[14] Despite this presidential stricture, the increased appropriations were used in part for more attachés abroad and for more counterintelligence activity by both the military and the FBI in Latin America.

Roosevelt returned to the subject in October 1938 in another press conference when he noted a considerable increase in foreign spy activity throughout the country. He said that the government was reexamining the status of unnaturalized foreigners employed by defense contractors, and he indicated that he would propose to the next session of Congress that federal counterespionage activities be intensified and coordinated to protect the nation's military and naval defense plans. The president also drew a clear distinction between foreign government propaganda activities in the United States and the efforts of undercover foreign agents.[15]

WORLD WAR II

World War II started in Europe in September 1939. Within days British prime minister Neville Chamberlain appointed Winston Churchill first lord of the admiralty. Shortly thereafter Churchill and President Roosevelt began a secret collaboration which bypassed both Chamberlain, Churchill's nominal superior, and U.S. ambassador Joseph P. Kennedy, Roosevelt's nominal representative in London (and father of the future U.S. president). The go-between was a remarkable British agent named William Stephenson (code named Intrepid).

Stephenson arrived in the United States in the early spring of 1940 with the twin objectives of enlisting U.S. cooperation in British intelligence and in work on the atomic bomb. U.S. participation in the secret intelligence project was initially channeled through the FBI and was limited to Director Hoover. But even Hoover could not keep up with everything. Stephenson shortly began looking for an American whom he could recommend to Roosevelt as the president's personal agent for liaison with the British. This person had to be someone who would have the total trust of both Roosevelt and Churchill. Stephenson turned to William J. Donovan, whom he had come to know between the wars and who proved to be acceptable to the president and to Churchill, by then the prime minister.[16]

Donovan was fifty-seven years old in 1940. He had had a distinguished military career in World War I, winning the Medal of Honor, among other decorations. He practiced law in New York City and dabbled in New York state Republican politics, incurring Franklin Roosevelt's dislike (which Donovan reciprocated). He was well acquainted in Europe, and John Lord O'Brian, a prominent New York lawyer, convinced Roosevelt that Donovan could be useful to him for "special assignments." Roosevelt sent Donovan on a number of secret missions, including several to Great Britain where he bypassed Ambassador Kennedy, who was out of sympathy with the president's pro-British policy.

The Stephenson-Donovan-Hoover triangle was inherently unstable. Donovan had no staff, and Hoover, who had a staff, was constrained by secrecy. Hoover had acquired a dislike of Donovan almost twenty years before when Donovan had served briefly in the Justice Department. In the summer of 1941, Roosevelt brought Donovan to public view and gave him the title Coordinator of Information with some vague instructions to gather information and to dispense it worldwide. The first function was secret intelligence; the second was public propaganda.

The attempt to carry out both overt and covert activities in the same organization did not last long, and the Office of the Coordinator of Information was split into two parts. The Office of War Information coordinated the government's wartime public information activities. It is the bureaucratic ancestor of the U.S. Information Agency. The Office of Strategic Services (OSS), with Donovan in charge, conducted covert intelligence activities, and the Central Intelligence Agency is its lineal descendant.

The OSS was born and lived in a world of bureaucratic jealousies and turf wars. The army and navy continued their intelligence collection, the most important aspect of which, by far, was signals intelligence. The FBI kept the OSS out of Latin America, and neither Gen. Douglas MacArthur nor Adm. Chester Nimitz would allow it to operate in the Pacific. (The CIA and MacArthur were still sniping at each other during the Korean War.) Thus, in World War II the OSS perforce was largely limited to Europe. Its principal activities were in covert action or unconventional warfare and in research and analysis. Veterans of the OSS provided the core of the CIA when that agency was created in 1947.

INTELLIGENCE COMES OF AGE

The ink was scarcely dry on the Japanese surrender document in September 1945 when President Truman abolished the OSS. Clandestine intelligence collection was given to the War Department and the army; research and analysis went to the State Department. Covert action was dropped because the president saw no need for it.

This arrangement was satisfactory to almost nobody. Although some upper level officials of the State Department (principally Undersecretary Dean Acheson) wanted the department to develop a strong, centralized, civilian-controlled intelligence collection capability, the department's geographic and functional bureaus rebelled. They feared that centralization, even in the State Department, would threaten their own activities. Spruille Braden, then the assistant secretary for Latin America, protested: "... [T]here is not one single item or function . . . which is not being fully and competently performed by the Office of American Republic Affairs." [17] (There are some people in the State Department who still feel that they do it best. Indeed, both State and CIA are supposed to report on conditions and developments abroad, a duplication of mission that remains the source of bureaucratic conflict.) The State Department's internal disarray was not the only problem. The War and Navy departments (the air force did not yet exist independently) resisted the idea of transferring any of their civilian personnel to State and quarrelled between themselves over the division of military intelligence functions.

Meanwhile, the intelligence reaching the president's desk was a mishmash of uncoordinated, unevaluated reports. In January 1946 an exasperated Truman established a Central Intelligence Group to coordinate intelligence under a National Intelligence Authority, which consisted of the secretaries of state, war, and the navy. Truman designated Rear Adm. Sidney W. Souers, then the deputy chief of naval intelligence, to be the director of the Central Intelligence Group (CIG). Souers was a reserve officer from Missouri and a good friend of the president in civilian life. Dependent on other agencies for funds and personnel, the CIG had no real authority to coordinate intelligence, but at least Admiral Souers regulated the flow of intelligence reports to the president and briefed the president every morning. This gave Truman the impression the system was working better, and from his point of view it was.

An intelligence historian of this period has written that the CIG "originated as a personal instrument of President Truman" and has called it Truman's "personal information service." [18] Although the intelligence community has expanded enormously since then, its sole purpose (except for covert action) continues to be to provide information to a select clientele. Its most important client by far is the president. Thus, to a considerable extent, the intelligence community remains the president's personal information service.

Some presidents have tried to make the intelligence community their personal instrument of foreign policy as well, free of the constraints of the State and Defense departments. At the same time, the growth of the intelligence community and of U.S. involvement in the world has broadened the community's clientele. Intelligence has become more important to many people, both civilian and military, involved in the operational aspects of foreign policy. This has made problems of dissemination more acute, but the problems have existed for a long time.

The Central Intelligence Group continued until Congress passed the National Security Act of 1947. The principal purpose of this landmark legislation was to unify the armed forces. To this end it created the National Military Establishment (later converted into the Department of Defense), the Joint Chiefs of Staff, and a separate air force. It also, almost incidentally, created the Central Intelligence Agency.

This was the first time American intelligence activity was given any kind of statutory authority. And there was an urgent need for it from a practical, if not a constitutional, viewpoint. In the process of tidying up the government after the war, Congress had inserted in the Independent Offices Appropriation Act of 1945 a provision that forbade making funds available to any agency in existence for more than a year without a specific appropriation by Congress.

The National Security Act of 1947 solved this problem, after a fashion. Except for some housekeeping items (such as contributions to its retirement fund), the CIA has never received a specific appropriation by Congress; rather, its appropriations are disguised and buried elsewhere, mainly in the Defense Department appropriation bill.

Despite the agency's fiscal crisis, Truman thought so little of the CIA's creation at the time that he described it as simply the renaming of the Central Intelligence Group.[19] Twenty years after leaving office, Truman had a different view: "I think it was a mistake. And if I'd known what was going to happen, I never would have done it." The former president's further explanation of his change of view is worth quoting at some length, because it deals directly with the fundamental policy problem that is the heart of this book:

> Now, as nearly as I can make out, those fellows in the CIA don't just report on wars and the like, they go out and make their own, and there's nobody to keep track of what they're up to. They spend billions of dollars on stirring up trouble so they'll *have* something to report on. They've become . . . it's become a government all of its own and all secret. They don't have to account to anybody.
>
> That's a very dangerous thing in a democratic society, and it's got to be put a stop to. The people have got a right to know what those birds are up to. And if I was back in the White House, people would know. You see, the way a free government works, there's got to be a housecleaning every now and again, and I don't care what branch of the government is involved. *Somebody* has to keep an eye on things.
>
> And when you can't do any housecleaning because everything that goes on is a damn *secret*, why, then we're on our way to something the Founding Fathers didn't have in mind. Secrecy and a free, democratic government don't mix. . . . [Emphasis in original.][20]

It should be pointed out that it was under Truman that the CIA embarked on covert action, beginning with the Italian election of 1948. (Even then the director and the general counsel were dubious of their authority.) This is discussed further below.

Truman was not alone in his belief that the CIA had grown beyond what had been intended. Clark Clifford was White House counsel during the Truman administration and one of the principal drafters of the National Security Act. Speaking in 1978, Clifford said that "the Central Intelligence Agency was to be mainly a depository of information." He also said: "I seriously doubt that the legislative branch contemplated [covert] activities in passing the legislation, and it is my belief that President Truman did not have them in mind at the time he signed the bill."[21]

Writing in 1991, Clifford had a different recollection. "We understood," he said, that the CIA's functions "would include covert activities." But, he added, "we expected them to be limited in scope and purpose." He continued:

> But over the years, covert activities became so numerous and widespread that, in effect, they became a self-sustaining part of American foreign operations. The CIA became a government within a government, which could evade oversight of its activities by drawing the cloak of secrecy around itself.[22]

However the CIA may have outgrown the expectations of its creators, it failed to live up to them in one respect: It did not perform the centralizing role envisioned for it. From the beginning the army and the navy retained their intelligence organizations, and the new air force acquired one. They were reluctant to share what they learned with the CIA, especially when sensitive signals intelligence was involved. The State Department had its Bureau of Intelligence and Research—not the focal point of the government's intelligence efforts, as Acheson had wanted, but enough to keep the department's hand in. The FBI also stayed stubbornly in the field.

There was more to come. In 1952 President Truman established the National Security Agency (NSA) as part of the Defense Department. He did this through a simple directive addressed to the secretaries of state and defense. The agency's purpose was, and is, to break the codes of other countries and to make the codes used by the United States. It also deals in signals intelligence generally—intercepted communications whether encoded or not and intelligence derived from electronic emissions (see Chapter 3). Even the existence of NSA was scarcely acknowledged for years.

The Defense Intelligence Agency (DIA) was created in 1961 by Secretary of Defense Robert S. McNamara. The purpose was to coordinate the military intelligence organizations and to further the centralization of the Defense Department, one of the unfulfilled purposes of the National Security Act. In this respect, at least, DIA was spectacularly unsuccessful. It had minimal impact on the military services and simply added a new layer of bureaucracy to the intelligence community. Thereby, it increased, rather than decreased, the problem of centralization of the intelligence community as well as of the Defense Department.

All three of these agencies—CIA, NSA, and DIA—were created rather offhandedly—almost, as has been said of Britain's acquisition of its empire, in a fit of absentmindedness. The CIA's original statutory authority consisted of less than three pages of a much longer law to which the CIA was incidental. Congress was not involved at all in the origins of either the National Security Agency or the Defense Intelligence Agency. The former sprang from a simple presidential directive without even the dignity of an executive order. The latter sprang from action by a cabinet officer without even White House approval.

Mention should also be made of the National Reconnaissance Office. It was established in the air force in 1960 to manage satellite reconnaissance programs, which were then just becoming significant.

Except for the CIA, the major intelligence agencies in terms of money spent and people employed are in the Department of Defense. The figures are secret, but it is commonly thought that the agencies in Defense account for approximately 80 to 85 percent or more of the U.S. intelligence budget.[23] The proportion varies from year to year, the principal determinants being the amount of expensive technology and the costliness of covert actions. No wonder that the director of central intelligence (DCI), who is supposed to coordinate all intelligence operations, sometimes feels lonely and outnumbered.

The DCI's life was worse in the beginning. The creation of the CIA was welcomed by virtually no one outside the White House. Army and navy intelligence, joined by the new air force intelligence, brawled among themselves but made common cause against the new kid on the block. The military agencies resisted sharing intelligence with the CIA and resisted personnel assignments to the new agency. So, to a degree, did the State Department; but one account has it that between 1946 and 1949, first the Central Intelligence Group and later the CIA received almost all their current information from State.[24]

Admiral Souers had agreed to become the first director of the Central Intelligence Group in January 1946 with the understanding that he would stay only six months. He was succeeded in June by Lt. Gen. Hoyt S. Vandenberg, the forty-seven-year-old star of the army air corps (later chief of staff of the air force) and the nephew of Sen. Arthur H. Vandenberg, R-Mich., chairman of the Foreign Relations Committee in 1947-1948. General Vandenberg, as much as anybody, was responsible for the provisions of the National Security Act creating the CIA. He also obtained J. Edgar Hoover's agreement to get the FBI out of Latin America, which turned out to be a time-consuming process.

THE KOREAN WAR

Vandenberg was followed as DCI by Rear Adm. Roscoe H. Hillenkoetter, who had spent most of his thirty-year naval career at sea. Hillenkoetter lacked the rank, the prestige, and the bureaucratic skills to perform a coordinating function. Under his direction the CIA developed some capacity as an intelligence producer, but it failed to foresee either the North Korean attack on South Korea in June 1950 or the Chinese intervention in the war on the side of North Korea later that year.

In this failure the CIA had plenty of company. G-2, the military intelligence component of General MacArthur's command in Tokyo, also missed the call, though it had an abundance of what in retrospect looked like warning signals: creation of a North Korean tank brigade, evacuation of farm families living within two miles of the border between North and South Korea, and banning of civilian traffic on rail lines between the North Korean capital of Pyongyang and the border. The State Department also missed the signs of an imminent invasion. Dean Rusk, then the assistant secretary for the Far East, said to the House Foreign Affairs Committee on June 20, 1950 (five days before the North Korean attack), "We see no present intention that the people across the border have any intention of fighting a major war for that purpose [seizing the South]."[25] The CIA at least had the excuse that it had virtually no intelligence collection capability in the Far East. Its entire Tokyo station consisted of three people working out of a hotel. MacArthur, still carrying on his vendetta against the OSS, denied the CIA office space in his headquarters.

Later in 1950 and with less reason, the CIA, MacArthur's G-2, and the State Department misread signs of the impending Chinese intervention in the war. All agreed the Chinese had the capability to intervene; none discerned a Chinese intention to intervene. In retrospect, the Chinese seemed to be trying to send warnings that they did, in fact, intend to do exactly that if American troops crossed the South-North border of the thirty-eighth parallel and entered North Korea. South Korean troops did not matter, the Chinese said; it was the Americans who worried them. The chosen messenger for these warnings was the Indian ambassador in Beijing. The Chinese calculated that his reports to his foreign office in New Delhi would get to Washington in one way or another. In this the Chinese were correct, but what they did not foresee was that although the reports would lead some State Department officials to urge caution, they would be ignored by the higher officials who were managing the war.[26]

Nonetheless, Washington approached the problem of China with great caution. MacArthur was directed not to bomb targets within five miles of the Chinese border and not to send U.S. troops to the border. The United States was concerned about the Soviet Union as well as about China. Washington took it for granted that the Soviet Union was behind the North Korean invasion of South Korea and feared that a strong provocation of China might bring the Soviets into the war, an event that would surely have meant a nuclear confrontation between the superpowers.

Fear of a wider war was at the bottom of Washington's differences with MacArthur, differences that led President Truman to relieve the general of his command in April 1951. This firing of an American icon set off a tremendous political furor that was eventually defused by extensive joint hearings before the Senate Armed Services and Foreign Relations committees. During these hearings, the matter of Soviet-Chinese relations was aired in detail, as were the differing views held about them by MacArthur and the Truman administration.

Two points involving intelligence are worthy of note. MacArthur's fate was sealed, so far as Truman was concerned, by intercepted communications from Spanish and Portuguese diplomats in Tokyo reporting conversations with MacArthur. The diplomats said the general had talked of his intention to use the Korean War as a means to dispose of what he called the Chinese Communist question once and for all. The Soviet Union, MacArthur continued, would either keep out of the war or face destruction itself. The United States picked up this intelligence in the course of monitoring Spanish and Portuguese diplomatic traffic.[27] It was really intelligence about the United States, not foreign governments. U.S. intelligence agencies are not supposed to gather intelligence about the United States, but in this case the information gave the president evidence of what was, at best, insubordination on the part of a key military commander.

The second point has to do with Washington's prevailing mindset about the role of the Soviet Union in the Korean conflict and the likelihood of Soviet intervention on behalf of the Chinese. When a government's mind is firmly made up, it is very difficult to change it. That phenomenon was noted earlier in connection with where the Japanese were likely to attack in December 1941. It occurred again in the 1970s with respect to the shah of Iran (see Chapter 5). In the case of Korea, unlike Iran, there was not much countervailing intelligence anyway; there were only the differing views of MacArthur, and these were largely discounted by the Joint Chiefs of Staff and the White House.

Soviet Foreign Ministry archives, newly opened after the end of the cold war, reveal a Soviet government much more conservative and cautious than had previously been thought. Premier Josef Stalin reluctantly approved the North Korean invasion of the South only after repeated appeals from North Korean leader Kim Il Sung. Stalin did not anticipate the U.S. reaction and was alarmed by it. He sent limited military forces to Korea to aid China but took pains to keep them secret. He was, in short, as fearful of direct conflict with the

United States as the United States was of conflict with the Soviet Union.[28] Failure to understand this was perhaps the most monumental intelligence shortcoming of all, but given the difficulty of penetrating the Soviet government at that time, it is easily excusable. It was a failure not only of intelligence but also of political judgment. In this respect, it must be assessed in light of the period's heavy pressures for political orthodoxy.

In October 1950, the month before the Chinese intervention in Korea, Hillenkoetter was replaced as DCI by Army general Walter Bedell Smith. Smith had been Eisenhower's chief of staff in the European theater during World War II and thereafter had served as Truman's ambassador to the Soviet Union. He was tough, hard-driving, blunt, and he had the rank to make what he said stick. He had been selected for West Point from the army's enlisted ranks. He had held every rank in the army from private to four-star general and once said that some of his most valuable and awe-inspiring characteristics were acquired while serving as a first sergeant.

Even Smith could not bring total order out of the disparate intelligence community, but he significantly reduced the bureaucratic brawling and went a measurable distance toward asserting the dominance of the CIA. He got control of covert action by summarily ending an argument over interagency relationships, and he established within the CIA the Office of National Estimates, which remained the focal point of analysis for twenty years.

Evolution of Collection and Analysis

Members of the intelligence community have never lived in total harmony with each other, but the discord was greater in the early years. It arose principally over collection. Everywhere except in the CIA, there was a feeling that the CIA should confine itself to coordination of the intelligence product and leave collection to the other agencies, principally the military services. There was a contradiction involved in this argument because the other agencies were markedly reluctant to share what they collected with the CIA, which in their view was supposed to coordinate and assemble it. But coordinating did not, in their view, include telling them what to do or dividing the work among them.

The opposition of other agencies notwithstanding, the CIA simply began to collect and thereby got a foot in the bureaucratic door. It forced the door wider because its early directors had more influence in the White House and in Congress than did the military intelligence chiefs and also because it did a better job at clandestine collection. A White House directive gave it authority to collect foreign intelligence from businesses and individuals in the United States; the other agencies were frozen out.

Analysis remained a problem on two counts. The agencies continued to withhold intelligence from policy makers, usually pleading that the information was too sensitive. Equally serious was the problem of coordination. The analytic product was supposed to be a coordinated statement by the community (though it was signed by the DCI), and this proved to be an exceedingly time-consuming process. The resulting estimate frequently reflected the lowest common denominator of agreement. There were dissents even to this, some of them based on bureaucratic bias. Although still problematic, the coordination process works better now than it did then.

EVOLUTION OF COVERT ACTION

In late 1947 the National Security Council directed the CIA to conduct covert psychological operations against the Soviet Union and its satellites in reprisal for what the council saw as similar operations by the Soviets against the United States. Admiral Hillenkoetter, then the DCI, did not welcome the assignment. He thought the agency had enough to do establishing its role in collection, analysis, and coordination. Hillenkoetter also felt that the OSS had had a bad experience in combining clandestine propaganda and intelligence. Furthermore, his legal counsel was telling him he did not have authority for this initiative without going back to Congress. Given the expansive powers that the NSC and the CIA have since then claimed for covert operations, Hillenkoetter's view has a quaintly old-fashioned ring to it.[29]

Hillenkoetter got perhaps unexpected support from the National Military Establishment (the bureaucratic predecessor of the Defense Department), where Secretary James V. Forrestal and the service secretaries and chiefs thought the responsibility ought to be in the State Department. Secretary of State George Marshall strongly objected, arguing that, if exposed, clandestine propaganda would damage the department's reputation for honesty. Undersecretary of State Robert Lovett did not even want to know very much about the project, arguing that the less the department knew of the details, the better its strategic position would be. But George Kennan, then head of the State Department's Policy Planning Staff, objected that putting responsibility in the CIA might lead to action independent of national policy considerations. One of these considerations during the Berlin blockade in 1948 was, as Kennan put it, not "to hurt Russian feelings."[30]

The upshot of all this was the creation of a Special Procedures Group, which later became the Office of Special Projects, and still later had a variety of other names. By the summer of 1948, the mandate had expanded from clandestine propaganda to other covert measures, and the United States was in the business of covert action. The interagency committee, under whatever name, was responsible for control, and the CIA was responsible for operations. Hillenkoetter thought that the State Department and the National Military Establishment, soon to become the Defense Department, had worked together to put the activity in the CIA because neither wanted the other to have it.

THE COLD WAR

Historians will argue for a long time about precisely when, where, and how the cold war began and ended. As good markers as any are the division of Europe between East and West in 1946 and the ending of that division with the breach of the Berlin Wall in 1989. In that span of forty-three years, almost everything the United States did in foreign affairs—and a good deal of what it did in domestic affairs—was related to the cold war. By and large, this was seen as a period of pervasive conflict between the United States and the Soviet Union. No shots were fired in anger between the contending superpowers, but their animosity was no less deadly for that fact. No facet of the American government during this period can be understood outside the context of the cold war, and the American intelligence community least of all.

The anxiety level of the cold war was intensified because the United States and the Soviet Union were the only two countries capable of destroying each other, and much of the rest of the world, with nuclear weapons. That is what made them superpowers. Throughout the cold war other countries had nuclear weapons, but only the United States and the Soviet Union had them in super-abundance and with delivery systems capable of putting them on targets thousands of miles away.

Added to the nuclear threat was an ideological component that gave the cold war an almost religious fervor. For some, it became a crusade—a western counterpart of an Islamic *jihad* or holy war. The cold war was political, economic, psychological. It was worldwide in scope. The superpowers did not fight each other with military weapons, but they supplied plenty of weapons to proxies who could fight among themselves while the respective superpowers encouraged them.

The intelligence services of the superpowers went at each other hammer and tongs in the back alleys, as well as the diplomatic salons, of the world. The United States was trying to ensure that other governments were on its side; the Soviets were trying to ensure that other governments were on their side. Few holds were barred. In many countries each side spent a good deal of time spying, not on the local government, but on each other.

This sub rosa aspect of the cold war was fought on a world stage where, in Asia, Africa, and Latin America, the dominant political force was nationalism. Each superpower tried to turn third world nationalism to its advantage. Each supported, opposed, overthrew, or installed third world governments—or tried to. Each accused the other of doing so—frequently, but not always, with reason.

In the United States the cold war was not conducive to calm discussion or reasoned argument about public control of secret activities. Nevertheless, little by little, over time, it began to take place. The intelligence community was different at the end of the cold war than at the beginning. It was different again in the cold war's aftermath. So were the government's mechanisms for ensuring its responsiveness to the public will. But the basic challenge of how to solve this problem endured.

NOTES

1. Phillip Knightley, *The Second Oldest Profession: Spies and Spying in the Twentieth Century* (London: A. Deutsch, 1986).
2. Joshua 2:1-21, 6:17, 6:25.
3. The story of spying on Canaan is told in Numbers, chapters 13 and 14.
4. Sun Tzu, *Ping-fa (The Art of War)*. Quoted in Allen Dulles, *The Craft of Intelligence* (New York: New American Library, 1963), 11.

5. Samuel Flagg Bemis, *A Diplomatic History of the United States* (New York: Henry Holt, 1942), 15-31; and Loch K. Johnson, *America's Secret Power: The CIA in a Democratic Society* (New York: Oxford University Press, 1989), 12-13.

6. William A. Tidwell, "Target: Abe Lincoln," *Washington Post*, Oct. 16, 1988. For a more extensive treatment, see William A. Tidwell, with James O. Hall and David Winfred Gaddy, *Come Retribution: The Confederate Secret Service and the Assassination of Lincoln* (Jackson: University Press of Mississippi, 1988).

7. A code is a group of symbols (usually numbers) used to represent a word, a number, or a phrase. Thus, the code value 1234 might mean "aircraft" or "tank" or "convoy sighted." In a cipher, each letter of the text is replaced by another letter. The replacement follows an orderly procedure, which is known to the sender and receiver of the message, and without which the message is gibberish. Thus, "aircraft" might be "zxptp zmq." Ciphers are usually sent in groups of five letters, regardless of the length of the words that they are disguising. Codes can be enciphered for transmittal. Thus, the code group 1234 might be enciphered as 6051. To read an enciphered coded message (encicode, in the technical term), one needs first the cipher key and second the code book. For our purposes in this book, the differences between codes and ciphers do not matter; we are interested in the fact that somebody is trying to communicate privately, and somebody else is trying to find out what is being communicated. For those who wish to explore further the fascinating field of cryptanalysis, the best work is David Kahn, *The Codebreakers: The Story of Secret Writing* (New York: Macmillan, 1967).

8. Kahn, 359.

9. Henry L. Stimson and McGeorge Bundy, *On Active Service in Peace and War* (New York: Harper, 1947), 188.

10. James Bamford, *The Puzzle Palace: A Report on America's Most Secret Agency* (Boston: Houghton Mifflin, 1982), 16-25. See also Kahn, *Codebreakers*, 360-369.

11. Ronald Lewin, *The American Magic: Codes, Ciphers and the Defeat of Japan* (New York: Farrar, Straus and Giroux, 1982), 5-14.

12. The standard work on the Japanese attack on Pearl Harbor is Roberta Wohlstetter, *Pearl Harbor: Warning and Decision* (Palo Alto: Stanford University Press, 1962). The most detailed account is the thirty-nine volumes of hearings by the congressional Joint Committee on the Investigation of the Pearl Harbor Attack, *Pearl Harbor Attack*, 79th Cong., 1st and 2d sess., 1946. An excellent short account is in Kahn, *Codebreakers*, 1-67. A more extensive treatment with abundant anecdotes (including the Knox quote, p. 314) is Edwin T. Layton with Roger Pineau and John Costello, *"And I Was There": Pearl Harbor and Midway—Breaking the Secrets* (New York: William Morrow, 1985). Layton was Pacific Fleet intelligence officer at the time of Pearl Harbor.

13. This story is told in considerably more detail in William R. Corson, *The Armies of Ignorance: The Rise of the American Intelligence Empire* (New York: Dial Press, 1977), 79-91. See also Ladislas Farago, *The Game of the Foxes: The Untold Story of German Espionage in the United States and Great Britain during World War II* (New York: McKay, 1971).

14. "President Urges Fund to Fight Spies," *New York Times*, June 25, 1938. Under the then prevailing rules of presidential press conferences, the president could be quoted only in indirect discourse. The direct quotations are those of the *Times* reporter.

15. Felix Belair, Jr., "Roosevelt Plans Nationwide Drive on Foreign Spies," *New York Times*, Oct. 8, 1938.

16. For a gripping account of Stephenson's operations in the United States, see William Stevenson, *A Man Called Intrepid: The Secret War* (New York: Ballantine Books, 1976). For Donovan's role, including the OSS experience, see Richard Dunlop, *Dono-*

van: America's Master Spy (New York: Rand McNally, 1982); and Anthony Cave Brown, *The Last Hero: Wild Bill Donovan* (New York: Times Books, 1982). For the Hoover-Donovan relationship see Curt Gentry, *J. Edgar Hoover: The Man and the Secrets* (New York: W. W. Norton, 1991).

17. Quoted in Dean Acheson, *Present at the Creation: My Years in the State Department* (New York: W. W. Norton, 1969), 160.

18. Arthur B. Dowling, *The Central Intelligence Agency: An Instrument of Government, to 1950* (University Park: Pennsylvania State University Press, 1990), 180.

19. Harry S. Truman, *Years of Trial and Hope*, vol. 2 of *Memoirs* (New York: Doubleday, 1956), 58.

20. Merle Miller, *Plain Speaking: An Oral Biography of Harry S. Truman* (New York: G. P. Putnam's Sons, 1973), 391-392.

21. Senate Select Committee on Intelligence, *National Intelligence Reorganization and Reform Act of 1978*, Hearings. 95th Cong., 2d sess., 1978, 8, 10.

22. Clark Clifford with Richard Holbrooke, *Counsel to the President: A Memoir* (New York: Random House, 1991), 170.

23. The 80 percent estimate is cited in House Armed Services Committee, *Intelligence Authorization Act for Fiscal Year 1989*, H. Rept. 100-591, pt. 2, dissenting views. Eighty-five percent or more is cited in *Congressional Record*, 101st Cong., 2d sess., Aug. 3, 1990, S12300 (daily ed.), remarks of Sen. William S. Cohen. At the time, Cohen was ranking Republican on the Intelligence Committee.

24. Anne Karalakas, *History of CIA*, in Senate Select Committee to Study Governmental Operations with Respect to Intelligence Activities (Church Committee), Final Report, Book IV, 15. This is S. Rept. 94-755, 94th Cong., 2d sess., 1976.

25. Joseph C. Goulden, *Korea: The Untold Story of the War* (New York: Times Books, 1982), 37-41.

26. Ibid., 274-285.

27. Ibid., 477. Goulden erroneously attributes the intercepts to the National Security Agency, which was not created until 1952. Earlier that work was done by the Army Security Agency.

28. See the following publications of the Cold War International History Project, Woodrow Wilson International Center for Scholars, Washington, D.C.: Jian Chen, *The Sino-Soviet Alliance and China's Entry into the Korean War*, Working Paper 1, June 1992; Kathryn Weathersby, "New Findings on the Korean War," *Cold War International History Project Bulletin* (Fall 1993); and Kathryn Weathersby, *Soviet Aims in Korea and the Origins of the Korean War, 1945-1950: New Evidence from Russian Archives*, Working Paper 8, November 1993.

29. Dowling, *The Central Intelligence Agency*, 245-281.

30. Ibid., 263.

PART II

The Community:
What It Is and What It Does

This part of the book describes what the intelligence community is all about. Chapter 3 sets forth the community's organization and what each of its member agencies does.

Chapters 4 through 7 deal with the four functions of intelligence—collection, analysis, counterintelligence, and covert action—and with the problems they raise. These problems are of two kinds. There are, first, what might be called technical or operational problems. How do you do something? How do you collect? How do you protect yourself against penetration? And many other issues. There are, second, more fundamental questions of public policy. Is a given task worth doing? Who decides? And many more.

The intelligence process begins with collection. By volume, far the largest part of intelligence comes from open, public sources. Some of the most valuable intelligence comes from old-fashioned spies or from new-fangled reconnaissance satellites or listening techniques.

Collection provides a flood of intelligence that pours into Washington every day. Making sense out of this deluge is the task of analysis. The other big problem of analysis is ensuring objectivity. Objectivity may be threatened by bias (sometimes subconscious) on the part of the analyst. It may be threatened by pressure from policy makers who are looking more for support than for enlightenment. Or the policy maker may have such a fixed mindset that he or she ignores the message the intelligence analyst is trying to send.

Counterintelligence is the effort to keep foreign intelligence services from doing to us what we are trying to do to them. It is conducted in the United States as a law enforcement activity by the Federal Bureau of Investigation. It is conducted abroad by the Central Intelligence Agency. Much counterintelligence work consists of spying on people who are suspected of spying on us. A continuing problem is how to ensure that the government can protect its secrets while also protecting the civil liberties of its citizens. A further problem is how to determine whether foreign defectors are really defecting (in which case they can be very helpful) or whether they are sent to spy on us from within (in which case they can be very damaging).

Finally, the many forms and uses of covert action are described in Chapter 7. Covert action is an effort by the U.S. government to influence a foreign situation through means that cannot be traced to the United States. The purpose of a given covert action, as well as the means to achieve it, may be unexceptional (for example, paying an impecunious delegation's travel expenses when publicity would be embarrassing to all concerned). Or both the purpose and the means may be highly controversial as well as illegal; the Iran-Contra affair is an example. Between these two extremes of the spectrum are many gradations.

CHAPTER 3

The Intelligence Community: Who Does What

"The question is," said Humpty Dumpty, "which is to be master—that's all."

—Lewis Carroll

The intelligence activities of the U.S. government are carried on by a variety of agencies that collectively are called the intelligence community. The work of the community is divided into two major parts: the National Foreign Intelligence Program (NFIP) and Tactical Intelligence and Related Activities (TIARA). In general, TIARA is military intelligence—what a commander needs to know to manage a battle or a campaign. NFIP is everything else. The line between them is not always clear. One way to distinguish them is to think of NFIP as the kind of intelligence foreign policy makers need and to think of TIARA as the kind of intelligence military combat commanders need. There are obvious overlaps. For example, the strength and composition of foreign military forces are of interest to foreign policy makers and to military commanders. But NFIP deals more with overall totals (How many tanks?), while TIARA is concerned with details (Where are the tanks? How much gasoline do they have available? What are the road conditions?).

In the Intelligence Authorization Act for Fiscal Year 1993, Congress provided some definitions that are legally controlling if not substantively enlightening:

> The term "National Foreign Intelligence Program" refers to all programs, projects, and activities of the intelligence community, as well as any other programs of the intelligence community designated jointly by the Director of Central Intelligence and the head of a United States department or agency or by the President. Such term does not include programs, projects, or activities of the military departments to acquire intelligence solely for the planning and conduct of tactical military operations by United States Armed Forces.[1]

The distinction between NFIP and TIARA is somewhat artificial and occasionally the source of confusion. A common analogy is that it is easy enough to tell the difference between day and night but not so easy around dawn and twilight. The NFIP/TIARA dichotomy, such as it is, is rooted in committee

jurisdictions in Congress and in bureaucratic divisions of labor in the executive branch. In the Senate the Intelligence Committee has jurisdiction over
NFIP; the Armed Services Committee has jurisdiction over TIARA. In the
House the Intelligence Committee has jurisdiction over both, but the Armed
Services Committee has concurrent jurisdiction over TIARA. In fact, most
intelligence agencies collect both types of intelligence, and most intelligence
officers would regard it as a waste of time to try to categorize each piece of
intelligence as one or the other. They know what is relevant to their concerns
and what is not.

There are broad areas of overlap. These are most evident in connection
with ongoing military operations, of which the Vietnam and Persian Gulf wars
are conspicuous examples, but they are seen also in other respects. During most
of the 1980s, the CIA coordinated a program in which hundreds of millions of
dollars were spent to buy, deviously and secretly, Soviet weapons from certain
countries in Eastern Europe. Some weapons were given to anticommunist guerrillas to use against Soviet troops in Afghanistan; others were studied by U.S.
armed forces to learn more about what they might some day be up against.[2]

As the Clinton administration grappled with the problems of proliferation
of weapons of mass destruction, it found that the intelligence community had
focused on foreign acquisition efforts to the neglect of questions of control and
operation. What might trigger the use of such weapons by a given country?
What was the doctrine, if any, for using them? A joint effort was mounted by
the CIA, Defense Intelligence Agency, and other elements of the Defense Department to address these questions, which clearly lay on both sides of whatever line there is between NFIP and TIARA. Notwithstanding, Congress and
the Office of Management and Budget insist the line is there, even if it cannot
always be seen. So long as this is recognized, arguments over where to draw the
line become rather sterile.

The size of the intelligence community, in its totality and in its components, is secret. A guess, confirmed as close by some who know, put the fiscal
year 1994 budget for the intelligence community at $28 billion, of which $16
billion was for NFIP and $12 billion for TIARA. Over the years the total has
varied because of several factors: bureaucratic upward creep, the expansion and
contraction of covert action, and the cost of new technology. The budget's high
point came during the Reagan administration (1981-1989) at something more
than $30 billion.

One of the enduring points of contention in the intelligence community is
the control of this budget. Presidents Gerald Ford, Jimmy Carter, and Ronald
Reagan all issued executive orders lodging control in the DCI, and the DCI annually prepares a consolidated intelligence budget. (One former director of the
Office of Management and Budget says that the DCI deceived him about what
was in the budget. If the president's own budget officer can't find out, one wonders how Congress can. Congress thinks it has changed enough budget procedures so that it can and does.)

Most intelligence funds are hidden in the Defense Department appropriations bill, and most of them are spent by agencies of the Defense Department,
and therefore the DCI's control is less than total. In the Intelligence Authorization Act of 1993, Congress attempted to strengthen the DCI by giving him legal

authority over the NFIP budget, including reprogramming and transfers of funds.

ORGANIZATION

One should keep firmly in mind the distinction between the director of central intelligence and the director of the Central Intelligence Agency. These two functions are combined in the same individual, but conceptually they are quite different.

The director of central intelligence (DCI) is the head of the intelligence community. He is the official whom President Truman wanted to *centralize* intelligence. The director of the Central Intelligence Agency is the operating head of the CIA, which is one (and not the largest) member of the intelligence community.

From time to time voices are raised in Congress and elsewhere to suggest that these roles should be filled by two people instead of competing for the attention of a single person. It is also sometimes suggested that the DCI should devote his full time to managing the community, leaving the operation of the CIA to his deputy (DDCI). Such suggestions arise not only because of the overwhelming workload produced by combining the roles, but also because the community is plainly neither centralized nor coordinated. Its members exist in a state somewhere between uneasy tension and unseemly bureaucratic squabble.

The workload is a very real constraint, both on the DCI and his deputy. When Stansfield Turner was DCI, he gave President Carter two thirty-minute briefings a week and spent ten to twelve hours preparing for each.[3] That is half a normal work week. Granted, he worked more than a normal week; but one still wonders how other things got done. Even so, the more important constraint is in the structure of the intelligence community. The DCI is supposed to run it, but the secretary of defense controls most of the money and people.

The DCI and the deputy DCI are appointed by the president, subject to Senate confirmation, and serve at the pleasure of the president. At least one of them must be a civilian. The Intelligence Authorization Act for Fiscal Year 1993 expresses the sense of Congress that

> it is desirable that either the Director or the Deputy Director be a commissioned officer of the Armed Forces or that either such appointee otherwise have, by training or experience, an appreciation of military intelligence activities and requirements.[4]

To help the DCI manage the community, there is a group called the Community Management Staff. Before the tenure of Robert Gates as DCI (1991-1993), it was called the Intelligence Community Staff. This group led a murky existence, less because what it did was secret than because it did not do very much. It was most active and most influential during the Nixon and Ford administrations (Nixon, 1969-1974; Ford, 1974-1977). Some career intelligence professionals give George Bush, who was Ford's DCI in 1976, particular credit for strengthening the Intelligence Community Staff's power over the budget. The staff also fixes collection priorities. As discussed further in Chapter 4, these priorities are useful in preventing wasted effort, but in fact agencies collect what is available to be collected. A priority may be interception of Chinese diplomatic messages, but if they cannot be decoded, the collecting agency is going to report whatever it can decode.

When William H. Webster became DCI in 1987, he inherited the legacy not only of the Iran-Contra scandal but also of the reign as DCI of William Casey, who had been much more interested in policy than in administration. Webster set about strengthening the hand of the DCI. During his incumbency (1987-1991) and that of his successor, Robert M. Gates (1991-1993), several centers were created specifically to serve the DCI. There was the Counterintelligence Center in the CIA's Directorate of Operations; one of its interesting assignments was considering what foreign satellites could learn about the United States and how U.S. satellites could be deceived. There was the Counterterrorism Center, also in the Directorate of Operations. The Counternarcotics Center was put in the Directorate of Intelligence, and the Nonproliferation Center was put in the Office of the DCI's Special Assistant for Arms Control. Later there was added a Covert Action Task Force.[5]

When Gates became DCI in the fall of 1991, he instituted a review of the organization and role of the CIA in particular and of the intelligence community in general in the post-cold war world. One of the results that came about as a result of that review was a refurbishing of the Intelligence Community Staff, complete with a name change, to emphasize its function as the instrument through which the DCI manages the community. Many of the functions of the old staff were distributed to elements of the intelligence community. What remained was put under a new official, the executive director for intelligence community affairs, who was to exercise the DCI's day-to-day responsibilities for managing the community.

In the Intelligence Authorization Act for Fiscal Year 1993, Congress strengthened the DCI's position. The DCI was given authority to establish requirements and priorities for intelligence collection. He already had this authority under sundry executive orders, but it is more impressive to put it in a law. And the 1993 law added more: The secretary of defense is directed to consult with the DCI before appointing the heads of the National Security Agency, the National Reconnaissance Office, and the Defense Intelligence Agency. The law also created a central imagery authority in the Defense Department, the head of which is to be appointed by the secretary of defense on the recommendation of the DCI. Finally, the law gave the DCI, subject to the president's discretion, the right to attend and participate in meetings of the National Security Council. Taken together, these items are a significant upgrading of the status and authority of the DCI.

LAWS AND EXECUTIVE ORDERS

The most comprehensive authoritative statement of the organization, composition, and duties of the intelligence community is Executive Order 12333, signed by President Reagan December 4, 1981. The Intelligence Authorization Act for Fiscal Year 1993 also formally lists the members of the community.

It was not until 1976—almost thirty years after the CIA was created—that a president seriously looked at the community as a whole. Gerald Ford was driven to do it then only by the wave of revelations that followed the Watergate scandal in 1972, the overthrow of Chilean president Salvador Allende in 1973, and the sundry investigations of the mid-1970s.

President Ford issued Executive Order 11905 on February 18, 1976. Generally, it tightened the control of the community by the National Security Council (and, therefore, by the president), made a start at spelling out the functions of the components of the community, and set forth certain restrictions (for example, no assassinations). Most of the restrictions were aimed at abuses that were then in the news: no unlawful surveillance or searches of American citizens; no opening of mail "except in accordance with applicable statutes and regulations"; no infiltration of U.S. organizations or attempts to influence them; and no drug experimentation on unwitting subjects. This was the first time there had been any restrictions.

President Carter issued his own executive order governing intelligence operations (12036, January 24, 1978). This coincided with the beginning of hearings by the Senate Intelligence Committee in what proved to be a fruitless attempt to write a comprehensive legislative charter for the community. The Carter executive order created an NSC Policy Review Committee for general oversight and an NSC Special Coordination Committee to deal with covert action ("special activities" in the words of the order) and sensitive collection operations. It also created a National Intelligence Tasking Center to set targets and priorities for collection. In most other respects, Carter's executive order followed the Ford order. It tightened Ford's restrictions on intelligence activities somewhat, and it added an important new one: Intelligence agency participation in contracts with private institutions had to be known to appropriate officials of the institution concerned. In other words, if a college professor is doing research for the CIA, the college has to know it.

Finally, the Carter order directed the DCI to keep the congressional intelligence committees "fully and currently informed" and to provide any information or document requested by the committees. This was a signal advance in White House cooperation with Congress, but it did not long survive the Carter presidency.

The Reagan executive order (12333, December 4, 1981), still in force in mid-1994, begins with a statement of the goals of U.S. intelligence activities. Three of these go beyond the usual statements of helping policy makers reach more informed judgments. One says that "maximum emphasis should be given to fostering analytical competition" (Sec. 1.1(a)). This means that intelligence estimates should reflect input from different points of view. Such competition is an important tool of analysis and is discussed further in Chapter 5. Reagan's order also calls for "a balanced approach between technical collection efforts and other means" (Sec. 1.1(b)). This goes to a continuing controversy over the relative merits of human sources compared with communications intercepts and satellite photography. Third, the order calls for "special emphasis" on counterintelligence (Sec. 1.1(c)).

The Reagan order reopened some of the loopholes the Carter order had closed in restrictions on intelligence activities. The attorney general was given somewhat broader authority to approve wiretaps, and penetration of domestic organizations was authorized if the head of the agency deemed it essential. And the Carter mandate to cooperate with Congress disappeared.

MEMBERS OF THE INTELLIGENCE COMMUNITY

The Reagan order also listed the agencies comprising the intelligence community and set forth their duties. The intelligence community includes, in addition to the CIA, agencies in the Defense, Justice, State, Treasury, and Energy departments.

CENTRAL INTELLIGENCE AGENCY

The CIA is the preeminent member of the intelligence community. It is an important collector. It takes the lead in analysis; any analytic product involving more than one agency goes through the CIA. It is the designated instrument for covert action. The CIA conducts counterintelligence abroad but yields to the FBI on counterintelligence in the United States. The Reagan executive order gives the CIA responsibility for intelligence on the foreign aspects of narcotics production and trafficking, but the Drug Enforcement Administration has since become much more important in this respect.

The 1993 Intelligence Authorization Act strengthened the CIA's analytic leadership by establishing the National Intelligence Council in the office of the DCI. The council is composed of senior analysts from the intelligence community and substantive experts from outside the community. The primary function of the council is to produce national intelligence estimates, these to include alternative views of elements of the community "whenever the Council considers appropriate." In other words, the council is in control. And the DCI is in control of the council: He appoints its members, they report to him, and they serve at his pleasure.

Most of the CIA's work is humdrum searching of open source material. The CIA is also the cloak-and-dagger agency. It has carefully cultivated an image of mysterious omnipotence (something that in turn has led it to be charged with a good many things it has not done). It has more Ph.D.s than many medium-sized universities (in almost every scholarly field from anthropology to zoology), but it won't say how many. It has physicians who diagnose the ailments of foreign leaders on the basis of fragmentary reports of symptoms. It has psychiatrists who make long distance assessments of the mental health of foreign leaders and prepare personality profiles. It has technicians who can cram a message into a dot that looks like a period at the end of an innocuous sentence. It has historians, linguists, economists. It has technicians who can alter your appearance or your voice and who can forge a passport (or almost anything else).

To do all these things, and more, the CIA has a secret number of people spending a secret amount of money. In fact, the size of the agency, especially so far as the budget is concerned, is subject to considerable annual variation, depending mainly on the number and extent of the covert action programs in which it is engaged. The NFIP budget increased rapidly, by as much as 17 percent a year, in the 1980s. A good deal of this increase went to the CIA because the agency was involved in three major covert actions (Nicaragua, Angola, Afghanistan) and a number of minor ones. In 1986 the CIA budget was estimated at $2.8 billion;[6] in 1994 it was reported at $3 billion.[7] The number of people is usually put at about 15,000, but a recent well-informed writer says 22,000 is the true number, not including 4,000 contract and part-time employees.[8]

DEPARTMENT OF DEFENSE

The big money, perhaps as much as 85 percent of the total intelligence budget, is in the Department of Defense. There are highly technical operations tucked away as appendages in some assistant secretary's office. We shall concern ourselves here only with those that have a significant impact on public policy.

DEFENSE INTELLIGENCE AGENCY.   The DIA coordinates Defense Department collection requirements and manages the defense attaché system. It represents Defense on the National Foreign Intelligence Board (NFIB), thus displacing the army, navy, and air force and providing one voice instead of three. But the uniformed services still send observers to NFIB meetings. The DIA also prepares its own analyses. For several years prior to the breakup of the Soviet Union, the DIA published an annual unclassified report, *Soviet Military Power.*

The director of the DIA is also the intelligence deputy of the Joint Chiefs of Staff (JCS) and as such is the JCS principal intelligence officer.

The DIA was supposed to unify the intelligence services of the uniformed armed forces, but instead it has only added another layer of bureaucracy. In retrospect, one wonders why anybody thought it would do more, given the uniformed services' jealousy of their historical prerogatives. Now, in addition to army, navy, and air force attachés in American embassies, there is a defense attaché who is senior to the others. The defense attaché represents the Defense Intelligence Agency but is an officer of the army, navy, air force, or marines.

Most countries have military attachés in their embassies in other countries. The role of the attachés is to serve as a liaison with the armed forces of the country to which they are accredited and at the same time to gather intelligence about those forces. Some of the intelligence is collected clandestinely, but the mission is perfectly open, as is a good part of the collection.

The first U.S. naval attachés were sent abroad in the 1880s to learn about shipbuilding. The army was not far behind with its attachés. The Marine Corps has its own intelligence unit for tactical, battlefield purposes, but there are no marine attachés. Marine Corps officers sometimes serve as naval attachés. The air force naturally insisted on its own attaché service, and its own intelligence, when it was created in 1947.

Each service has an attaché, and usually several assistant attachés, in large countries. In small countries all services are not always represented (the navy rarely sends an attaché to a land-locked country, for example). In very small countries the defense attaché may be the only one.

The DIA is thought to be the smallest of the major intelligence agencies. In 1978 it was estimated to have approximately 5,000 employees and a budget of

$200 million to $250 million.[9] For fiscal year 1995 its budget was estimated to be $500 million.[10]

ARMY, NAVY, AIR FORCE, MARINES.   The job of the intelligence components of the uniformed services is to supply the intelligence that commanders need in operational situations. Intelligence officers serve at all levels of command—in the army, from a company to the chief of staff. The chief of army intelligence is a lieutenant general who is also deputy chief of staff, but the more than 25,000 army intelligence personnel worldwide work not for the deputy chief of staff but for army field commanders.[11]

The Reagan executive order tasks the intelligence agencies in the armed forces with collecting "information on the foreign aspects of narcotics production and trafficking." This puts yet another group of counternarcotic intelligence agents in the field along with the CIA and DEA. The DEA is not named in the Reagan order as part of the intelligence community, but its intelligence functions are included in congressional authorizing legislation.

Uniformed intelligence agencies are also responsible for a good deal of peacetime tactical intelligence. What is the depth of harbors? What is the capacity of airfields? At one time they made a major effort to collect data on Central American power grids and water systems so that an expeditionary force would know the location of switches and valves.

NATIONAL SECURITY AGENCY.   The National Security Agency (NSA) is the U.S. government's cryptologic service. It makes the codes, ciphers, and equipment used by American agencies, and it tries to break those used by foreign countries. It has a huge headquarters building at Fort Meade, Maryland, just off the Baltimore-Washington Parkway. It has listening posts scattered around the world.

NSA works through subsidiary organizations in each of the three uniformed services: the Army Intelligence and Security Command, the Naval Security Group Command, and the Air Force Electronic Security Command. Altogether these NSA organizations involve thousands of uniformed personnel at overseas bases, in addition to thousands of civilians at headquarters. The cost is thought to be about $4 billion in 1994.[12] In terms of people, NSA is the biggest component of the intelligence community.

NSA's raw material comes from the interception of electronic emissions. In the jargon of the trade, these provide signals intelligence (SIGINT). They may be messages, either in voice or code, transmitted by radio, in which case they are communications intelligence (COMINT). Or they may be the signals that active radars emit, in which case they are electronic intelligence (ELINT). There is other even more esoteric signals intelligence, such as the telemetry sent by a missile during a test flight (TELINT), from which it is possible to learn the missile's characteristics. The Reagan executive order makes NSA the only agency authorized to engage in signals intelligence unless the secretary of defense orders otherwise.

NSA is one of the agencies where NFIP and TIARA come together. When NSA intercepts and decodes foreign diplomatic traffic, it is producing political or national foreign intelligence. Most of the tactical intelligence in NSA is produced by its uniformed subsidiaries (who may also produce NFIP).

There is a tactical intelligence need for SIGINT. In a battlefield situation the army needs to know, for example, where the enemy's tanks are and what they are doing, and to know it, if possible, in real time. ("Real time" is military jargon for simultaneous, or right now. When you carry on a conversation, you hear the other party in real time. To know something in real time is to know it as it is happening; this military phrase has nothing to do with distinguishing from unreal time.) The air force needs the same kind of intelligence about the enemy's planes; the navy, about his ships. The air force and navy also need to know the frequencies and technical specifications of potentially hostile radars. It was the navy's involvement in efforts to learn these things that led to the Gulf of Tonkin incident during the Vietnam war and to the seizure of the *Pueblo* off the coast of North Korea a few years later.

NATIONAL RECONNAISSANCE OFFICE.   Although President Dwight D. Eisenhower established the National Reconnaissance Office (NRO) in 1960, the government would not even admit it existed until 1992. Reagan's executive order discreetly refers to it as "offices for the collection of specialized intelligence through reconnaissance programs."

For fiscal 1994 the office had a budget estimated at more than $7 billion.[13] But NRO does not have many people. It needs a great deal of money because it builds, or contracts for the building of, extremely expensive satellites.

NRO suffered a costly failure in August 1993. Shortly after liftoff from Vandenberg Air Force Base in California, a Titan IV rocket blew up while carrying three satellites that it was supposed to put into orbit. The total cost of the rocket and its payload was about $1 billion, and the program was put on hold until investigators could determine what went wrong.

NRO's budget had already become a matter of dispute in the congressional intelligence committees, where some members were skeptical of how many satellites the United States needed in the aftermath of the cold war. But then an offsetting problem arose, one not much talked about because of the political sensitivity of its subject matter. Because of the costliness of reconnaissance satellites, there has developed a kind of intelligence industrial complex. Defense contractors who build the satellites, and the communities where the contractors' plants are located, have a special interest in building more. Besides the parochial (or pork barrel) politics involved in keeping these plants in business, is there a national interest involved in keeping together a hard core of skilled people with the requisite know-how? And if there is such a national interest, can it be served by building fewer satellites over longer time spans—say one every three years instead of three every year?

The satellites not only take remarkably clear pictures from hundreds of miles up, they also collect a variety of signals intelligence. The government's adamant refusal to admit the existence of NRO, long after it was widely talked about in the press and other public forums, is a classic example of bureaucratic inertia in continuing to do something after the reason for having done it in the first place no longer exists. The original reason for the secrecy was extreme Soviet sensitivity about aerial or space reconnaissance at any altitude. In

May 1960, with the crash of the U-2 and its aftermath, the United States lost its capability to overfly the Soviet Union and take aerial photographs (see Chapter 4). NRO was established in August 1960 to run a high priority program to develop reconnaissance satellites to replace the U-2. Given the fragile state of U.S.-Soviet relations at that time, it was prudent to do this in deepest secrecy.

Later during the 1960s and continuing in the 1970s, as the United States and the Soviet Union got into serious arms control negotiations, each superpower saw the advantage of using reconnaissance satellites to verify compliance by the other with arms limitation agreements. Each was still inhibited from saying so, however, and the magic phrase "national technical means" was invented so that the parties could talk to each other about reconnaissance satellites without using those words. With the end of the Soviet Union, even that ruse was no longer necessary. Yet years after the reason for secrecy had passed, the government clung to it until, surprisingly, the Defense Department announced the NRO's existence in a press release in September 1992.

The Reagan executive order provides that the NRO (not called that, to be sure) should carry out "consolidated reconnaissance programs for specialized intelligence." [14]

CENTRAL IMAGERY AUTHORITY.   The Central Imagery Authority in the Defense Department coordinates the processing and exploitation of the imagery obtained by the NRO's satellites. The satellites no longer simply take pictures; they produce images, or more precisely, streams of computer code that are converted into images. The 1993 Intelligence Authorization Act states that the head of the new imagery authority is to be appointed by the secretary of defense upon the recommendation of the DCI.

STATE DEPARTMENT

The State Department's link to the intelligence community is its Bureau of Intelligence and Research, headed by an assistant secretary. The bureau prepares analyses and reports based on open sources, on the classified reporting of embassies abroad, and on intelligence disseminated by other agencies in the community. It prepares a special daily briefing for the secretary of state in addition to that which the secretary receives from the CIA as a member of the National Security Council. The bureau represents the department on the National Foreign Intelligence Board, but the undersecretary for political affairs speaks for State on the Policy Coordination Group with respect to covert action.

The bureau does no intelligence collection; that is performed by embassy personnel overseas. The Reagan executive order says State's collection shall be overt. It is, in the sense that everybody knows that diplomats are sent abroad, among other purposes, to collect information. But much of the information is sensitive and classified. So, indeed, is some of the collection, the executive order notwithstanding. When an ambassador calls on a foreign minister in the minister's office, the two may talk alone or with only a few aides present. The fact that the meeting took place is publicly known (overt), but what transpired at the meeting is not known. Nor is it unusual for ambassadors and foreign ministers or other officials to meet privately after office hours in somebody's home. In these cases even the meeting itself may not be publicly known.

The State Department has another role in the intelligence community, this one related to its primacy in the government in matters of foreign policy. Both the law and executive orders give ambassadors (who report to the secretary of state) authority over American government personnel abroad, including intelligence officers. If the secretary of state objects to a particular intelligence activity, only the president can override him. Secretaries of state have objected and have made it stick.

JUSTICE DEPARTMENT

The Federal Bureau of Investigation and the Drug Enforcement Administration both perform intelligence functions. The Justice Department also has important responsibilities in implementing the Foreign Intelligence Surveillance Act of 1978 and the Classified Information Procedures Act of 1980. These laws, which are discussed further in Chapters 6 and 10, deal with the relationship between the intelligence community and the judicial process.

FEDERAL BUREAU OF INVESTIGATION.   The FBI is responsible for counterintelligence in the United States; the CIA is responsible for it overseas. To the FBI, counterintelligence means catching foreign spies, or Americans working for foreign intelligence organizations, in the United States. This devolves on the FBI because of its general responsibility for law enforcement, but spies move in and out of the United States. When they are in another country, watching them is the responsibility of the CIA.

When the FBI catches spies, it thinks in terms of putting them in jail or, if they have diplomatic immunity, of expelling them from the country. When the CIA catches spies, it thinks in terms of turning them into double agents, that is, using them to spy on the government they have been working for. These are differing points of view with built-in potential for friction, and for many years the bureaucratic bad blood between the FBI and CIA was legendary. The feud was dampened under the leadership of Judge William Webster, who served first as director of the FBI and then as director of the CIA and who did not bring inherited bureaucratic bias to either job. But the interagency warfare resumed in 1994 as a result of the arrest of Aldrich Ames, a career CIA officer charged with spying for the Soviet Union and Russia over several years. The Ames case occasioned much finger-pointing over responsibility for lax counterintelligence procedures.

DRUG ENFORCEMENT ADMINISTRATION.   The Drug Enforcement Administration (DEA) is basically a police force, not an intelligence agency. It is not included in the intelligence community either in Reagan's executive order or in the statutory definition of the community in the 1993 Intelligence Authorization Act. But that act does authorize appropriations for DEA's intelligence and intelligence-related activities. These are mainly what one would expect in a police force—payment of informers (the CIA would call them human sources).

The CIA and the FBI are also in the counternarcotics intelligence business, as are the armed forces intelligence services. The CIA and the DEA overlap overseas; the FBI and the DEA overlap in the United States. Between the CIA and the DEA there is a difference in approach. Narcotics is all the DEA is interested in; it is only part (and sometimes a small part) of what the CIA is interested in. There is a more fundamental difference stemming from bureaucratic cultures: Cops think of informers as sleazeballs and stool pigeons; spies think of them as sources to be protected. Spies will back off from a prosecution that requires compromising sources; cops will not, at least not often.

TREASURY DEPARTMENT

The Treasury Department has a small intelligence unit in the office of the department's executive secretary. It has a much larger Office of International Affairs concerned with world monetary and economic questions, which have become more important as the volume of international currency movements has increased and as U.S. foreign economic interests have grown generally. Treasury attachés are assigned to major embassies to report directly on these matters, but the attachés are not part of the department's intelligence office and do not report to it, or through it. There is some overlap between State and Treasury in economic reporting, but generally the State Department's economic officers report on economics and Treasury attachés on money.

The Reagan executive order directs that collection by the Treasury Department, like collection by the State Department, be overt—in this case of foreign financial, monetary, and general economic information. Usually there is less reason for this material to be closely held than is the case with more sensitive political information. However, financial and monetary information can be sensitive, too—for example, when an attaché is predicting that a country's currency will have to be devalued or reporting something that the head of the central bank has told the attaché in confidence.

Mention should also be made of the Secret Service. Part of the Treasury Department, it conducts counterintelligence activities with respect to surveillance equipment that might be used against the president, the executive office of the president, and other officials under Secret Service protection.

The first-ever "counter-audio survey" (that is, de-bugging check) of the White House was done in 1965 during the Johnson administration. It took a ten-person team from State, the Secret Service, the CIA, the army, and the air force two months. One reason for the lengthy time was that White House wiring had never been mapped, and this had to be done to provide a basis for a continuing "counter-audio program." But even then there was no assurance that the White House was 100 percent clean. The survey included not only the White House proper but also the LBJ Ranch in Texas and extensions to homes and offices of officials and staff served from the White House switchboard.[15]

ENERGY DEPARTMENT

The Energy Department participates in the intelligence community through its Office of Intelligence. It is directed by the Reagan executive order to participate with the State Department in overtly collecting information about foreign energy matters. This includes data on foreign availability of energy supplies.

The Department of Energy is responsible for the U.S. facilities producing nuclear weapons, and it performs counterintelligence functions with respect to those facilities. There is an Office of Threat Assessment that concerns itself with terrorism. The department also contributes to governmentwide intelligence regarding nuclear proliferation. The department has no independent intelligence collection activities.

NOTES

1. P.L. 102-496, approved Oct. 24, 1992, sec. 702, amending National Security Act of 1947 (50 U.S.C. 401 et seq.) by adding a new sec. 3(6).
2. Benjamin Weiser, "Poland Helped U.S. Buy Soviet Weapons," *Washington Post*, Feb. 14, 1994.
3. Stansfield Turner, *Secrecy and Democracy: The CIA in Transition* (Boston: Houghton Mifflin, 1985), 129.
4. National Security Act of 1947, as amended (50 U.S.C. 403(a)), sec. 102(c)(2).
5. See Loch K. Johnson, "Smart Intelligence," *Foreign Policy* 89 (Winter 1992-1993), 53-69.
6. Patrick E. Tyler, "How the U.S. Cloaks a $24 Billion Budget," *Washington Post*, March 26, 1986.
7. Walter Pincus, "White House Labors to Redefine Role of Intelligence Community," *Washington Post*, June 13, 1994.
8. Ronald Kessler, *Inside the CIA: Revealing the Secrets of the World's Most Powerful Spy Agency* (New York: Pocket Books, 1992), xxvii.
9. Jeffrey Richelson, *The U.S. Intelligence Community* (Cambridge, Mass.: Ballinger, 1985), 41, citing *Time*, Feb. 6, 1978, 10.
10. Walter Pincus, "House Votes $28 Billion for Intelligence," *Washington Post*, July 21, 1994.
11. John Macartney, *Intelligence: What It Is and How to Use It*, 4. A former air force intelligence officer, Macartney is on the faculty of the National War College, Washington, D.C. This useful guide was privately published by the author.
12. Pincus, "White House Labors." See also George Lardner, Jr., "National Security Agency: Turning On and Tuning In," *Washington Post*, March 18, 1990. For a more extensive, detailed account of the NSA, see James Bamford, *The Puzzle Palace: A Report on America's Most Secret Agency* (Boston: Houghton Mifflin, 1982).
13. Pincus, "White House Labors." See also Tim Weiner, "Lost Titan Missile Carried 3 Satellites, U.S. Officials Report," *New York Times*, Aug. 4, 1993.
14. Executive Order 12333, sec. 1.12(c)(1).
15. National Security Files, National Security Action Memoranda, Box 5, Folder: NSAM 315—Communications Security Survey, Memo for Gordon Chase from James W. Clark, March 19, 1965. Lyndon Baines Johnson Library, Austin, Texas.

CHAPTER 4

Collection

"Even a blind hog finds an acorn once in a while."
—Arkansas proverb

You have to collect intelligence before you can do anything else with it. This chapter examines what the intelligence community collects, how the community goes about it, and the foreign policy risks and bureaucratic problems that arise. The chapter is concerned solely with "foreign intelligence," as in the National Foreign Intelligence Program (NFIP) discussed in Chapter 3. It does not address Tactical Intelligence and Related Activities (TIARA), which serve specialized military needs and rarely raise serious questions of national policy.

WHAT TO COLLECT

The decision about what to collect is called "tasking." Under the Intelligence Authorization Act of 1993, this decision is made by the director of central intelligence in the DCI's capacity as head of the intelligence community. As the act puts it, the DCI establishes "the requirements and priorities to govern the collection of national intelligence by elements of the intelligence community." In this the director has the assistance of the Community Management Staff, which had an authorized personnel strength of 161 people in 1993 to perform central management functions, such as tasking, for the whole community. Before the 1993 law tasking was done by the National Foreign Intelligence Board (NFIB), which is still the place where national intelligence estimates are coordinated (see Chapter 5).

Congress ordered the change in 1993 in an effort to strengthen the authority of the DCI and perhaps also in the hope that it would result in a more rational set of requirements than was produced by the interagency NFIB. More experience is required to determine if this change will have the intended result. The annual statement of the government's intelligence requirements, as prepared by NFIB, tended to be a catchall. It was described by a former DCI as "useless" as a guide to intelligence officers in the field. The trouble with it, he said, is that it covered everything, "because assistant secretaries are afraid to leave anything out." This is apparently sometimes literally true. One assistant secretary of state is said to have replied, "Everything," when he was asked what he would like to know.[1] Nevertheless, since intelligence is collected in the first place for the benefit of policy makers, it is reasonable to ask them what they need. If they say "everything," they have evaded the question, but they have also illuminated the problem.

There are two elements in tasking. One is requirements; the other is priorities. Decisions have to be made, and the decisions involve trade-offs. The capacity of the intelligence community is not infinitely elastic. It is finite. If you decide to collect A, you are not going to be able to collect B or C.

REQUIREMENTS

There are five kinds of requirements: (1) what the U.S. government really needs to know; (2) what it would be nice to know; (3) what some high official is merely curious about; (4) what nobody needs to know now but may need to know some time; and (5) requirements imposed indirectly by Congress. All of these, except possibly the last, are related to priorities and to capabilities (what the intelligence community calls "assets").

An example of the first kind of requirement is the precise status of North Korea's nuclear program. An example of the second kind is Chinese demographics. The first is more urgent and more specific. The second relates to an important subject, but because there is not much the United States can do about it anyway, it becomes less urgent. In a time of budget stringency, it may be postponed.

An example of the third kind of requirement is political corruption or other skullduggery almost anywhere. It is not always easy to tell the difference between solid information and gossip, and some intelligence officers don't try. The president is the most important customer of the intelligence community, and many presidents have been avid consumers of gossip, the more scandalous the better. Robert M. Gates took office as the director of the Central Intelligence Agency (CIA) in 1991 with the avowed objective of elevating gossip as a collection target. During the hearings on his nomination, he told the Senate Intelligence Committee that he wanted to introduce items agents "pick up on the cocktail circuit, the gossip that they hear," into intelligence reports before the "serious business." This, he said, would "clarify and give a liveliness to our reporting."[2]

Consider two examples of the fourth kind of requirement. In one case the requirement generates a proposal for a new satellite—very sophisticated and very expensive—which the National Reconnaissance Office wants to build and put into orbit without a clear idea of what it should look for. The argument is that "we won't know what's there until we find it." Or that "even if we don't find anything, we will have the capability to look for it in the future." Or, finally, "we need to keep intact the technical teams that build these things." This enterprise might or might not produce useful intelligence, but it will certainly cost a great deal of money. Another example is provided by the case of Somalia. In 1990 no one predicted that the United States was going to need to know about the factional politics of that country. In 1992-1993 the need became urgent. It makes sense to stockpile basic intelligence on obscure countries even when there is no foreseeable need for it. This does not take many people—perhaps one intelligence officer visiting for a few weeks.

The fifth kind of requirement is a fairly recent development. It arises from the propensity of Congress to make certain foreign policy actions contingent on certain findings by the president. There are several examples. Some have to do with nuclear or other weapons of mass destruction. If a country engages in a program to build these weapons or to export parts for them, it is not entitled to foreign aid or certain other benefits from the United States. The president must determine whether a given country is engaging in the proscribed activities, and he needs intelligence to help him decide. But these laws do not generate new intelligence requirements. This is something policy makers would want to know anyway. Other laws, mainly concerned with human rights, do put new tasks on the community. Countries that violate basic human rights are not entitled to most-favored-nation trade treatment and, in some cases, to other benefits. This creates a demand for intelligence that might not otherwise exist.

PRIORITIES

Priorities are more directly related to policy than are requirements. At one time there were requirements to monitor nuclear testing by both the Soviet Union and France, but the United States did not expect the French to use nuclear weapons against it and therefore the Soviet requirement was much more urgent. Large resources were devoted to the problem of identifying underground nuclear tests and distinguishing them from earthquakes. Requirements also drive priorities. The need to know about Soviet missiles drove development of the U-2, and the loss of the U-2 drove development of reconnaissance satellites.

As a practical matter, regardless of formal tasking, the intelligence community collects what it can get. Intelligence about Soviet missiles might have been a priority collection target, but if the National Security Agency (NSA) could not read the Soviet messages it was intercepting about missiles, it was not getting anywhere. At the same time, however, the intelligence community might have been producing reams of intelligence on low-priority African countries whose less sophisticated codes it could read. Similarly, the CIA's collection is limited by what its sources know. The agency may have a source in Country X who knows about, let us say, agrarian political movements. But that is not much help if the task is to collect about religious fundamentalists. Collection suffers while a source is being found. To avoid being put in this position, the CIA tries to develop sources that it does not need now but may need in the future. This extends in some cases to "stay behinds" who would report clandestinely and perform other chores if Americans had to leave the country.

To a considerable degree, a CIA station chief generates his own collection targets and priorities, often in consultation with the ambassador. Sometimes they are in response to queries from the White House or State Department. Sometimes this process is trapped in bureaucratic inertia. Targets may be pursued long after they have lost the importance that made them targets in the first place. In some countries in Latin America in the 1960s and 1970s, the CIA continued to try to infiltrate subversive groups long after those groups had lost whatever capacity they may have once had to cause trouble. It is not clear whether this resulted from failure of NFIB to keep its tasking up to date or from the CIA's tendency to keep on doing what it had been doing.

HOW TO COLLECT INTELLIGENCE

In terms of volume, most intelligence (75 to 90 percent) comes from open, or public, sources.[3] Quantification does not tell us anything about the relative value of open sources. This calls for a more difficult and subjective judgment. Open sources would not have made a timely discovery of missiles in Cuba or of nuclear tests in the Soviet Union and China. On the other hand, open sources did tell us that the shah of Iran was in a precarious position, but we were not paying attention or at least the Carter White House was not.

But the point remains: Most intelligence is not secret. It does not come from secret sources. It results from many people reading newspapers, magazines, books, and transcripts of foreign radio and television broadcasts. The CIA has one of the world's biggest libraries of current literature, including telephone directories and street and highway maps, as well as extensive collections of reference works, histories, biographies, geographies, and related materials. At one time a young officer in the American embassy in Moscow had the principal assignment of haunting book stores in as many cities as were then open to foreign diplomats and buying books. (The Soviet Union did much the same thing in the United States, where the Soviet embassy in Washington was a steady customer of the Government Printing Office.)

The Foreign Broadcast Information Service (FBIS), which is operated by the CIA, monitors foreign broadcasting stations from positions around the world and publishes daily reports. Anybody can subscribe. These reports are especially useful as a source of the texts of speeches by foreign leaders. They also contain reports of significant news events not covered by the international media.

Besides the CIA, many other agencies of the U.S. government maintain representatives in American embassies abroad, at least in the more important countries. These agencies, by no means all of which are members of the intelligence community, send back a constant flood of reports. Agricultural attachés report on crop conditions, farm markets, and prospects for exports of American farm products. Labor attachés report on foreign labor organizations and movements. Commercial attachés report on trade opportunities. None of these reports is generated by the intelligence community, but they are all highly relevant to policy makers who are trying to assess the situation in a foreign country. And they are in addition to reports from the State and Treasury departments and from sundry elements of Defense. Much of this is published. International organizations add to the flow. The International Monetary Fund and the World Bank publish mountains of economic statistics, for example.

A great deal of sound foreign policy can be made on the basis of public information. Rarely, if ever, do you need secret intelligence to make a judgment about the prospects for American trade with Country X, or whether Country Y is going to be able to make its foreign debt payments.

What is open collection in one country may be espionage in another. In the Government Printing Office in Washington, anybody can buy a telephone directory of the State Department. If you had tried to get such a directory of the Soviet Foreign Office before *glasnost*, you would certainly have excited the interest of the KGB. In many third world countries, information that is taken for granted as public in the United States is jealously guarded. Inquiries from foreigners about mineral surveys, or corporate sales or profits, or even the national budget are likely to arouse suspicion. But even after making allowances for these attitudinal, or cultural, differences, an intelligence agent can still learn a great deal without resorting to a cloak or a dagger.

Although most intelligence comes from open sources, most of the money is spent developing clandestine sources. These may be either technical or human.

TECHNICAL SOURCES

There are two primary technical sources of intelligence: photography (imagery in its more technically advanced forms) and eavesdropping. Both of these can be accomplished in a wide variety of ways. Photography can be a picture taken from hundreds of miles in space. Or it can be a tiny microfilm taken surreptitiously.

Eavesdropping produces signals intelligence (SIGINT) that includes several subcategories, depending on what signals are intercepted. SIGINT is generally considered the most reliable form of intelligence because the other party usually does not know he or she is being intercepted and therefore makes no effort at deception.

Not all eavesdropping produces SIGINT. Telephone wiretaps and electronic listening devices (bugs) planted in offices or homes produce human intelligence (HUMINT). The NSA does not do this; the CIA does (in the United States, the FBI).

Satellites involve no political risk, but eavesdropping does. So do some efforts to produce electronics intelligence (ELINT). By itself, political risk is not necessarily a reason not to use a particular method of intelligence collection. But the fact that a method is risky means that it involves a trade-off and a calculated decision. Is the intelligence that is likely to be obtained more valuable than the political (or sometimes the economic) price that is likely to be paid? This calculation is not easy because it involves assumptions about the likelihood of getting the intelligence and paying the price.

One of the ways that governments reduce the price is to conduct the operation under a cover that will provide *plausible deniability*. This is a euphemism for lying and getting away with it. Intelligence services generally attempt to disguise their activities so that if the activities come to light, the service and its government can deny any connection and be believed. There are degrees of plausible deniability. The optimum is the ability plausibly to deny any link between any part of the government and the activity in question. If this is not possible, it should appear that some low-level employee was acting without authority. The minion can be publicly repudiated, reprimanded, and fired—and privately given a raise and sent into hiding. At a minimum, the head of government or the chief of state must be kept totally apart.

AIRCRAFT AND PHOTOGRAPHY.   While flying inside the Soviet Union, a U.S. reconnaissance plane, the U-2, was shot down by a Soviet missile on May 1, 1960. The story of the U-2 shows how an urgent requirement led to revolutionary technological advance. It involves the miscalculation of political risks (or perhaps the failure to calculate them at all), but it is also a classic demonstration of the delicate balance that sometimes has to be struck between high-risk intelligence and uniquely valuable intelligence. It was the first major demonstration of the contradictions inherent in plausible deniability. It was the first step on the long journey to serious congressional oversight of the intelligence community. For all of these reasons, the story is recounted here in some detail even though it is more than thirty years old.

In the early 1950s the CIA got its first inkling of a secret Soviet missile development center at Kapustin Yar on the lower Volga River. The CIA wanted pictures. The air force—at least according to the CIA—said a flight couldn't be done.[4] The British did it using a World War II bomber that flew a route from Germany into the Soviet Union and down the Volga into Iran. When it landed, the plane was full of holes from Soviet antiaircraft fire, and the British refused to repeat the flight.

There then began a rivalry between the CIA and the air force that continues to this day, albeit in attenuated form. The CIA wanted a plane that could go high enough to avoid Soviet detection, or at least Soviet defenses. The air force wanted to build other characteristics into the plane so that it could also be used as a fighter. While this argument was in progress, the CIA went independently to Lockheed, which designed and produced the U-2 as a purely high-altitude reconnaissance aircraft. The U-2 made its first flight in 1956, and for four years it produced remarkable photographic intelligence of the Soviet Union.

The Soviets knew about the U-2 overflights of their country, but they were powerless to do anything about them because the plane flew at an altitude beyond the range of Soviet antiaircraft missiles. The American and Soviet governments engaged in a tacit conspiracy of secrecy. American boasts or Soviet protests would have had the same effect: The Soviet government would have been shown as impotent; it would have been humiliated and might have felt driven to take measures that neither government wanted.

During the fateful flight on May 1, 1960, a mechanical problem forced the U-2 to descend to an altitude at which a Soviet missile got close enough to disable the plane. The plane crashed near Sverdlovsk, 1,300 miles inside the Soviet Union. The pilot survived and was captured. The date was significant on two counts. It was a major national holiday in the Soviet Union, an occasion when a violation of Soviet sovereignty would be especially offensive. And it was fifteen days before the scheduled beginning of a round of high-level diplomatic activity that, it was hoped, would lead at least to a reduction in East-West tensions and possibly even to a nuclear test ban treaty. A four-power summit— the United States, the Soviet Union, Great Britain, and France—was to start in Paris May 16. This was to be followed by a meeting in the Soviet Union between President Dwight D. Eisenhower and Chairman Nikita Khrushchev.

The U-2 had taken off from Peshawar, Pakistan, and was due to land at Bodo, Norway. When it had not been heard from by the time it would have exhausted its fuel supply, the CIA concluded that it was down, but where and under what circumstances were unknown. Nor was anything known about the fate of the pilot, though the CIA had long presumed (and had so assured Eisenhower) that no pilot would survive a U-2 crash.

There was no immediate reaction from the Soviet government, but the National Security Agency had intercepted the conversations of Soviet air defense officers, and the United States knew that the Soviets knew that something had been flying over their territory. The quiet in Moscow could be taken as an indication that either (1) the plane along with the pilot had been so completely demolished that the Soviets were not sure what they had; or (2) they were still trying to decide how to handle the incident.

The U.S. government waited two days and then, through the National Aeronautics and Space Administration, released the cover story that had been prepared long before in broad outline and had been newly approved by President Eisenhower himself. The story said that a weather research plane from a base in Turkey had apparently gone down after the pilot reported difficulties with his oxygen supply. The story suggested that the pilot could have blacked out, and the plane could have gone a considerable distance off course. Search operations in northeastern Turkey were said to be under way.

Then on May 5 Khrushchev announced in the Supreme Soviet that an American spy plane had been shot down over Sverdlovsk, and confusion descended on Washington. Knowledge of U-2 flights (even of the plane's existence) had been so closely held that many officials who now had to be brought into the coverup literally did not know what they were talking about. When news of Khrushchev's speech first reached the upper echelons of the U.S. government, Eisenhower ordered that all public information be given out by the State Department and no one else. But then, succumbing to clamorous inquiries from the White House press corps, Eisenhower agreed that his press secretary, James Hagerty, could announce that NASA and State were investigating and would make their findings public. This sent reporters to NASA, which was instructed by Gen. Andrew Goodpaster, Eisenhower's staff secretary, to issue in memorandum form question-and-answer material it had received from the CIA in preparation for such a contingency.

Meanwhile, the State Department spokesman issued a statement substantially repeating NASA's earlier statement about a missing weather reconnaissance plane. But the new material from NASA included fictional details: a flight plan of 1,400 nautical miles over 3 hours 45 minutes at a maximum altitude of 45,000 feet and without reconnaissance cameras.[5] This violated one of the principles of successful lying: Don't say any more than you have to; if details start to unravel, the whole story may come apart. What contributed to its coming apart in this case was the fact that Sverdlovsk is 1,300 miles from the nearest Soviet border.

The next day the State Department spokesman laid the basis for even deeper trouble when he said, "There was absolutely no—N, O—no deliberate attempt to violate Soviet airspace. There never has been." The deeper trouble came the following day, May 7, when Khrushchev revealed more details. The Soviets had not only the plane but also the pilot, Francis Gary Powers. The U-2 had a built-in destruct mechanism that the pilot was supposed to activate just before he bailed out. In this case the plane was spinning upside down as it fell, and Powers could not reach the destruct switches. Even so, the U-2 was such a fragile thing (deliberately built light and thin to gain speed and altitude) that it was considered likely to be demolished on impact. Powers's U-2 was badly damaged, but there was enough left for the Soviets to know what they had. They shortly put the wreckage on public display in Gorky Park in Moscow. Worse, from the American point of view, they had some of the pictures it had taken, and Khrushchev showed these to the Supreme Soviet.

The CIA had given Powers a poisoned needle, one prick of which would produce almost instantaneous death. He had no instructions on whether to use it. That decision was his alone, but in any event the CIA was so sure that he would not survive a U-2 crash that he was left, as he put it, "completely unprepared." He did not even know the cover story. When he had asked what to do if captured, he had been told, "You may as well tell them everything, because they're going to get it out of you anyway." As a matter of fact, he did not tell them everything. He withheld or dissembled the technical details of the aircraft and the extent of his involvement in the program.[6] But at that time nobody in Washington knew what he told and what he left out. And Powers was at the disadvantage of not knowing what was being said in Washington. (The Soviets sentenced Powers to ten years imprisonment for espionage, but released him in 1962 in exchange for their spy Rudolf Abel. Powers was killed in 1977 in the crash of a helicopter that he piloted for a Los Angeles television station.)

Having been caught in a bare-faced lie with its first cover story, the U.S. government retreated to its fall-back position to preserve at least a shred of plausible deniability for the president. Khrushchev himself had left that option open when he told the Supreme Soviet, "I am quite willing to grant that the president knew nothing about the fact that such a plane was sent into the Soviet Union."[7] But this created a dilemma for Eisenhower. If he took this escape route, he could preserve something of the international position of the United States and of his relationship with Khrushchev, and he could probably salvage something of the summit. But then he would be admitting to the American people and to the world that he had not really been in charge of his own government, that he had not known what was going on in it. To an old army general, steeped in the military tradition of command responsibility (the diametrical opposite of plausible deniability), this would have been unthinkable and intolerable. Nor could he be sure how Khrushchev would react if Eisenhower did duck the responsibility. Maybe the door that Khrushchev seemed to leave open was really a trap. Maybe if Eisenhower walked through that door, Khrushchev would take it as a sign that the Americans could not be trusted.

Eisenhower spent that Saturday, May 7, at his farm at Gettysburg, while the State Department and CIA hashed over their multiple difficulties. Finally, they produced a statement that Eisenhower somewhat reluctantly approved over the telephone. In it the State Department attempted to do two things: (1) preserve the cover of deniability, and (2) turn responsibility for the affair back on the Soviets. The statement repeated that "insofar as the authorities in Washington are concerned, there was no authorization for any such flight as described by Mr. Khrushchev." But, the statement admitted, "it appears that in endeavoring to obtain information now concealed behind the Iron Curtain, a flight over Soviet territory was probably taken by an unarmed civilian U-2 plane."

The statement went on to complain of "the excessive secrecy practiced by the Soviet Union in contrast to the Free World." It referred to the U.S. Open Skies proposal of 1955, which was designed "to reduce mutual suspicion and to give a measure of protection against surprise attack" but "was rejected out of hand by the Soviet Union." [8] In 1955, the United States had proposed that it and the Soviet Union agree that each country could freely overfly the territory of the other. Now the State Department was implying that if the Soviet Union had agreed to this, U-2 flights would not have been necessary, and the present difficulty would not have arisen.

On Monday, May 9 the department returned to this theme: "It is unacceptable," said a statement to the press in the name of Secretary Christian A. Herter, "that the Soviet political system should be given an opportunity to make secret preparations to face the free world with the choice of abject surrender or nuclear destruction." Herter then went on to admit partial presidential responsibility while preserving a fig leaf of deniability:

> . . . [T]he President has put into effect since the beginning of his Administration directives to gather by every possible means the information required to protect the United States and the Free World against surprise attack and to enable them to make effective preparations for their defense. Under these directives programs have been developed and put into operation which have included extensive aerial surveillance by unarmed civilian aircraft. . . . Specific missions of these unarmed civilian aircraft have not been subject to Presidential authorization.[9]

The Soviet Union shot off a protest note to the American embassy in Moscow calling the State Department's statement "unprecedented in its cynicism." [10] In this unpromising atmosphere the four world leaders—Eisenhower, Khrushchev, Prime Minister Harold Macmillan of Great Britain, and President Charles deGaulle of France—assembled in Paris. Khrushchev laid down three conditions for Soviet participation in the conference: that the United States denounce the U-2 flights, that it promise not to repeat them, and that it punish those responsible. Khrushchev also withdrew the invitation to Eisenhower to visit the Soviet Union following the conference.

Eisenhower agreed to suspend the flights for the duration of his term in office (a matter of eight months) and renewed his Open Skies proposal. Khrushchev walked out, and the summit ended.

The Senate Foreign Relations Committee held hearings, of which a censored version was published at the time. (An unexpurgated version was published in 1982.)[11] Witnesses included Secretary of State Herter, CIA Director Allen Dulles, and Secretary of Defense Thomas S. Gates. They stripped a little more deniability from the president and spread a little more over themselves. In the version given to the committee, the president had approved *programs* of flights but not *individual* flights. The flight of May 1, it was said, was in the air without the knowledge of the president, the secretary of state, the acting secretary of state (the secretary being out of town), or the secretary of defense. In its innocence the committee took this as "an indication of how routine these flight operations had become." [12]

In point of fact, all of these people knew the flight was in the air, and Eisenhower had personally authorized it. This was a clear case of the executive branch misleading Congress. Officials would be prosecuted for this in later years in connection with other intelligence activities, but that time had not come in 1960. At least the committee was correct about the routineness of the flight. Eisenhower later said he had become "a bit careless with success" and "lulled into overconfidence." [13]

Indeed, Eisenhower had kept a tight rein on the U-2 from the beginning of the program, repeatedly denying authority for flights and occasionally approving flights with reluctance. The president is said to have viewed his role "chiefly in terms of weighing intelligence needs against diplomatic needs." [14] With some misgivings the president approved a flight for April 9. It did not get everything it went for, specifically pictures of a suspected new missile base at Plesetsk, six hundred miles north of Moscow. The CIA pressed for another flight. Eisenhower acceded but set an absolute deadline of May 1; he did not want the U-2 over the Soviet Union close to the summit. On May 1 the plane flew into history.

The executive branch witnesses frustrated the Foreign Relations Committee by refusing to tell the senators what the U-2 had been looking for that was so important. Without this information, the committee said in its report, it "cannot . . . come to any conclusion as to whether the importance of the information sought justified the risks which were taken." [15]

While they were in operation, the U-2 flights provided Eisenhower with convincing evidence that Soviet missile development was not proceeding as fast as some members of Congress charged, and they strengthened the president's determination to resist being drawn into an escalated arms race. But because the evidence was so secret, he could not use it beyond a tightly constricted inner circle. And so he could not use it to contradict the Democratic charges of a missile gap that played an important part in the 1960 election and evaporated shortly thereafter. Here was an example of a president allowing his party to suffer politically in order to protect an intelligence source. Later, as we shall see, it became more common for presidents to distort intelligence in order to gain an advantage for their party.

Although U-2s were not used again over the Soviet Union, they continued in service over other countries. A U-2 provided the evidence of Soviet missile sites in Cuba that set off the crisis in 1962. During the tense days of the resolution of the Cuban missile crisis, the CIA used an officer in Soviet military intelligence, Col. Oleg Penkovskiy, to supplement the information found by the U-2. The U-2 photographs provided the basis of questions to ask Penkovskiy, and Penkovskiy's reports led to better photographic interpretation. This is a remarkable example of how a human source can complement a technical source. In time, however, the Soviets found out what Colonel Penkovskiy was doing and executed him. [16]

Some officials in the CIA thought the lesson of the U-2 in the Soviet Union was taken too much to heart by the State Department. When the CIA wanted to overfly China from bases in Taiwan, Charles E. Bohlen, a former ambassador to the Soviet Union, demurred. As Ray S. Cline, who was chief of station in Taiwan and later deputy director for intelligence, recalled, Bohlen's objection was along these lines:

> You know, there's just an awful lot of intelligence that you guys can get, such as photography, that I'm happy to have if it's free, but I'd rather do without it than have any additional trouble over it.[17]

In a broader context Dean Rusk, secretary of state from 1961 to 1969, has expressed the same thought about some collection operations: "There were times when I vetoed a number of proposals for gathering intelligence because I would rather not have that particular information than to use the means that were being proposed to get it."[18]

The U-2 was succeeded by the SR-71 (for strategic reconnaissance), which could fly higher and a good deal faster. (Its last flight was across the United States in 68 minutes at an altitude of 80,000 feet.) With the SR-71, the United States resumed flights over portions of the Soviet Union and was also used over Libya, Nicaragua, Cuba, and other countries.[19] In 1990 the SR-71 was also retired, leaving the U.S. dependent on space satellites or conventional aircraft for aerial reconnaissance.

At least so far as Europe is concerned, the problem of aerial reconnaissance was greatly simplified in 1991 when the Soviet Union announced it would open its territory to aerial inspection. Thus, *de facto*, it accepted the concept of "Open Skies"—which Eisenhower had proposed and the Soviets had rejected in 1955. This opened the way to overflights by lower, slower planes to check on compliance with arms control agreements.

At the Senate Foreign Relations Committee hearings, Secretary of State Herter was asked if we had learned anything from the U-2 incident. He replied, "Not to have accidents."[20] In fact, two valuable lessons came from the incident. First, the doctrine of plausible deniability is most useful with respect to intelligence operations of limited scope. In the case of large operations, it is more likely than not to add to the embarrassment of failure. Second, diplomatic and intelligence needs must be balanced carefully by the president, a role Eisenhower understood. This balance involves more than diplomacy and intelligence. It involves the whole complex of American national interests, of which diplomacy and intelligence are only a part.

SATELLITE IMAGERY.   Satellites are the successors to reconnaissance aircraft. They are the spies in the sky (see Chapter 3). Satellites have gone beyond photography, so it is more accurate to speak of them as providing images. These images are made through converting radar and infrared signals into code that is then converted into pictures from which skilled interpreters can derive intelligence.

Satellites have neither the vulnerability nor the political risk of aircraft. Neither do they have the flexibility, and they are a great deal more expensive. They can cover the earth, but it is difficult to reprogram them quickly to cover new targets. The trade-off with aircraft was political risk versus value of intelligence. With satellites it is economic cost versus value of intelligence. The newer satellites cost more than a billion dollars, and they require considerable lead time to build and launch. Is this investment worthwhile in a time of budget stringency when we don't know what they are going to look for?

Satellite imagery has many uses broader than intelligence. It can make weather prediction more reliable. Natural resources can be surveyed (a sensitive point to some third world countries). The growth of crops can be measured, as can ecological damage.

CRYPTANALYSIS.   It is a tenet of cryptanalysis that any code can be broken. Success or failure in war or diplomacy often has turned on success or failure in breaking a code. In World War II the Allies gained enormous advantages through British success in breaking German codes and American success in breaking Japanese code.

The cryptanalyst begins work by collecting many messages (traffic), comparing them to each other, looking for patterns, and guessing what the patterns might mean. When enough patterns are discerned that are internally consistent and that still make sense when compared with other, similar traffic, the cryptanalyst is on the way to breaking the code. This is laborious, brain-wracking work. A good deal of the tedium has been taken out of it by computers, but computers have made it no less brain-wracking.

Computers are used not only to break codes but also to make codes. And they have made codes unbreakable. Modern codes are sent over radio transmitters broadcasting twenty-four hours a day. Sometimes the transmission is gibberish; sometimes it is a coded message. You need coded keys to tell when the messages start and end. In addition, of course, you need the codes to the messages themselves. And both sets of these codes are changed every day, so you can never accumulate much traffic. Theoretically, perhaps, the codes could be broken with enough supercomputers to try trillions of permutations. But the value of intelligence decreases rapidly with time, and even without this consideration, devoting so much valuable computer capacity to what might be no more than a theoretical exercise would be a gross misuse of resources. Thus, the only practical way to penetrate this traffic is to steal or buy the codes and related materials. Persons with access to these materials have a very valuable and salable commodity—if they are willing to betray their country and risk being executed or spending the rest of their lives in jail.

Even when intercepted messages cannot be read, valuable intelligence can be derived through traffic analysis. This is a technique for deducing information from the volume of messages and from their origin and destination. If the volume to or from a given point suddenly and significantly changes, the analyst can assume that a new activity has started or an old one has stopped. The analyst can then begin a search of other intelligence for further clues. If address and origin designators can be read, even if the message itself is unreadable, the skilled analyst can learn a good deal. Traffic analysis provided the first intelligence of the extent of the damage done to Hiroshima by the atomic bomb in August 1945. There was a total and prolonged cessation of messages originating there.

BASES AND PLATFORMS.   In order to acquire signals intelligence, you have to be in a position where you can intercept the signals. For this purpose

NSA has developed an extensive network of listening posts abroad. In some cases (the western Pacific is one) these listening posts are part of much larger military installations (those in the Philippines, for example). When these larger installations are closed for reasons unrelated to intelligence, NSA has to scramble for alternate arrangements. In some cases (Turkey, Iran), eavesdropping was the principal reason for a base's existence. The navy also had some overseas bases, the primary purpose of which was to track Soviet submarines by collecting underwater signals.

In addition, NSA operates a number of ships and aircraft as mobile listening posts. If we cannot penetrate a country, we can frequently listen to it from international waters or international air space beyond its borders. We can even provoke it into revealing things we want to know, and this is another source of political problems in foreign policy.

Tuning in on somebody else's radars yields electronic intelligence that enables engineers to devise measures to render those radars ineffective. These measures are known as electronic countermeasures (ECM). An aircraft with the proper ECM can neutralize the radar that controls antiaircraft fire. A ship can neutralize the radar that enables an enemy ship or shore station to know where the ship is. With the proper intelligence the other side can neutralize ECM through electronic counter countermeasures (ECCM). Presumably this process can go on indefinitely, or until one side becomes confused.

To collect electronic intelligence of this kind, one has to fly or sail close enough to the radar to pick up its signal, and one has to provoke the operators of the radar into turning it on. Efforts to do this have caused some of the most vexing of our post-World War II foreign policy problems.

All foreign military bases come with a political price tag. In the third world they have an economic price as well. Thus, the classic trade-off must be made. Is the intelligence worth what it costs? This decision ought to be made after deliberate consideration at the highest levels of the government. Rarely has it been made this way.

More frequently it is the result of parochial interagency squabbling. The intelligence community emphasizes the value of the intelligence acquired through a base. The State Department emphasizes the political cost of the base as a source of anti-Americanism and of friction with the local government. This can be offset to some extent by raising the economic price (that is, more foreign aid from the United States). But Congress complains about that. Most of the bases subject to these kinds of trade-offs were established in the 1950s, and many of them lost much of their usefulness with the end of the cold war at the end of the 1980s.

To make an informed judgment about this conflicted situation, a policy maker must know in some detail the intelligence picture—what we get from a base, how we might get it from some other source, how it fits in the totality of intelligence available to us. Until near the end of the 1970s, this kind of information was available only in the National Security Council, most of the members of which represented agencies that were interested parties. The intelligence collected was more valuable to some agencies than to others; some agencies got stuck with more of the price than others. This left the president and his national security adviser as the only people in the government who could strike a reasonable balance. Congress, which should have been part of the decision-making process, was inadequately informed. That was remedied following the establishment of the Senate and House intelligence committees in the mid-1970s, and the machinery is now in place for the decision-making process to work better. But the public still cannot be sure that the process does in fact work better because the public is still not a part of it.

Ironically, this improvement in the government's decision-making posture came only a few years before the end of the cold war removed the need for many of these decisions. But NSA is still collecting signals intelligence and will continue to do so. Several cases illustrate the dimensions of the problem.

In the 1970s, American policy in the eastern Mediterranean and the American foreign aid program in Turkey were hostage to NSA collection stations in Turkey targeted at the Soviet Union. Turkish military forces occupied part of the island of Cyprus after the Cypriot government was overthrown by a *coup d'état* in 1974. The Turkish action was doubly illegal. First, it was against international law. Second, it violated the conditions under which the Turks had received the American military equipment they used. The United States protested. Greece, with its close ethnic ties to the Cypriot population, protested more vigorously. Greek Americans took their case to Congress, which banned further military assistance to Turkey. Thus matters stood for several years. The Turks forced the closure of the American listening posts. Congress eventually restored military assistance to Turkey but informally linked funding levels by a mathematical formula to assistance to Greece. An uneasy calm returned to the eastern Mediterranean, and the Americans were allowed back onto their Turkish bases.

NSA also had bases in Iran. Among other things, they were collecting telemetry from Soviet missile tests. This ELINT (strictly, TELINT for telemetry intelligence) enabled the United States to determine many of the characteristics of the missiles. These listening posts were an important, unstated reason for American support of the shah of Iran prior to his overthrow in 1979. The stated reason, which was real enough, was geopolitical and involved control of the Persian Gulf. Close association with the shah was ruinous for America's image in the eyes of the Islamic fundamentalists who succeeded the shah and who closed the listening posts.

Air and sea collection platforms can pose even more acute problems. Aircraft skirting the edge of legality can get shot down. Several were. The crew of one RB-47 hit off the northern coast of the Soviet Union survived and was released by Chairman Khrushchev in a goodwill gesture to the incoming President Kennedy in 1961. These fliers were the lucky ones. The unlucky ones have not been heard of again.

Ships can be sunk, attacked, or captured. During the Six-Day Arab-Israeli War in June 1967, the Israelis bombed and strafed the *U.S.S. Liberty*, which was collecting signals intelligence in the Mediterranean. The attack killed 34 of the crew and wounded 171. The Israelis apologized for what they said was a mistake, though the ship was plainly marked with a large American flag. Egyptian radio charged U.S.-Israeli collusion, overlooking the fact that what was really going on was a crisis in U.S.-Israeli relations. The American embassy in Cairo did not even know the ship was in the neighborhood.

In 1968 the North Koreans captured the *U.S.S. Pueblo* with its crew and most of its eavesdropping equipment intact. At the time the *Pueblo* was in international waters on a mission that was regarded as so routine that it had not been cleared with the National Security Council. The Johnson White House thought the seizure was intended as a diversion during the Tet offensive that North Vietnam then had under way. If the seizure was in fact part of a larger communist strategy, failure to bring the *Pueblo*'s mission to the NSC was a particularly serious oversight. Several months later, after being tortured, the crew was released.

An incident with even wider repercussions occurred in the Gulf of Tonkin off the coast of Vietnam in August 1964. The U.S. destroyer *C. Turner Joy* reported that it had been attacked by North Vietnamese patrol boats while in international waters. The destroyer *Maddox* was sent to join the *Joy*, and two days later a second attack by the North Vietnamese was reported. Neither ship was damaged, but the Johnson administration used the incident to persuade Congress to pass the Tonkin Gulf Resolution, later described by Undersecretary of State Nicholas deB. Katzenbach as "the functional equivalent of a declaration of war." [21] Congress acted not knowing that the *Joy* was on a mission to provoke North Vietnamese coastal radar and that this mission coincided with a series of South Vietnamese hit-and-run raids against North Vietnamese coastal installations. Later investigation also raised serious questions about the scope of North Vietnamese attacks against the American ships and even whether the second attack had occurred at all.

HUMAN SOURCES

In spyspeak "human intelligence" has nothing to do with the mental capacity of people. It has to do with intelligence derived from human, as distinguished from technical, sources, although some HUMINT is collected by technical means (for example, a tap on somebody's phone or a bug in somebody's office). A good deal of human intelligence comes from unremarkable open sources—the bartenders and cab drivers that journalists love to quote or gossip from shops or coffee houses. But probably most of it is collected clandestinely and is reported confidentially. And most of this intelligence comes from paid informers ("agents," in spyspeak).

Most HUMINT is collected in foreign countries by the CIA and by the attaché services of the army, navy, and air force working under the Defense Intelligence Agency. Service attachés are mainly concerned with collecting intelligence about their counterpart services in the countries to which they are accredited. Especially in third world countries where the armed forces play an important political role, attachés report on plots, conspiracies, and incipient coups d'état—and sometimes try to influence them. But for most HUMINT, CIA is the preeminent agency.

RECRUITMENT OF AGENTS.   The phrase "working for the CIA" leads to a semantic quicksand. It is important to distinguish among various categories of people who do things for the CIA.

First, there are the intelligence officers and their supporting staff. These are the full-time career employees at the headquarters in Langley and the stations around the world. They may also be loosely called agents, but they are properly officers. There are many other kinds of agents.

Agents are the people overseas from whom officers receive intelligence. Most of them work part time because they have other jobs. If they are paid, they are said to be controlled, and the control is exercised by a case officer. These agents are called assets; they are like a bank account that can be drawn on in time of need.

Sources are people who do not have the formalized, or controlled, relationships of agents, but who are generally willing to tell an officer at least some of what they know. They do not really do anything for the CIA at all, though they may undertake a specific assignment incidental to their normal employment. For example, a station chief may ask a newspaper correspondent on a trip through the countryside to look for signs of agrarian unrest. This is something a good correspondent would do anyway. Sources are ordinarily not paid except perhaps for expenses.

One of the most difficult aspects of intelligence is the recruitment of agents—that is, finding someone who is willing to be a spy. People become spies for many different reasons, among them money, ideology, sex, blackmail, excitement, and vindictiveness. The first step in recruiting an espionage agent is to look at the group of people who are likely to have the information one wants—for example, a military staff, employees in the president's office or in a particular ministry, workers in a particular secret installation, members of a particular organization, especially members of an intelligence service. Then, among the target group, one looks for individuals who display some of the characteristics of vulnerability. They are perhaps in financial difficulties, or they have indicated some political sympathy for the United States, or they have a reputation for an active sex life (either heterosexual or homosexual), or they give some evidence of a grudge against somebody in their organization. Or one simply goes after a target of opportunity.

When an individual has been selected, he or she is cultivated very carefully by a CIA officer who does not reveal his or her CIA connection. The recruitment process may begin with contrived "casual" meetings at social events. It may continue through pursuit of common interests—music, tennis, golf, bridge, whatever. The developing relationship will provide opportunity for conversation over lunch or dinner or drinks during which the target's political attitudes or family or other problems can be probed ever so gently.

Targets who are selected because they appear to offer an opportunity for blackmail are put under technical and human surveillance. If suitable material for blackmail is produced, the material is carefully saved for future use, either by itself or as reinforcement for another pitch. Or if the surveillance produces nothing, it will probably be discontinued as fruitless.

Targets may be cultivated for years before the CIA decides either to land them or to abandon them. A decision to go ahead with the recruitment of someone is subject to approval by CIA headquarters in Washington, where the target's identity is considered in a broader context. If the target is in a particularly sensitive position, or if particularly sensitive negotiations are in progress with his or her government, further approval may be sought from the White House or the State Department. This will be at the level of the secretary or the national security adviser so as to protect the target's identity. If all signs are favorable and all clearances are in hand, a new officer is brought in, one who is a total stranger to the target, to make the final pitch. This is the most delicate moment.

If the target says yes, the CIA has recruited another spy. If the target says no, the CIA has really not lost very much except time and effort. The United States may suffer embarrassment in the form of a stiff diplomatic protest from the host government, but this does not necessarily become public. In any event, if the CIA has properly covered its tracks, the embarrassment will be short-lived.

The worst thing that can happen is that the target will say yes and mean no. In these cases the CIA has recruited a double agent and doesn't know it. The double agent works for both sides. He is spying on *us* at the same time we think he is spying on *them*.

The public record does not show the level at which the CIA's relationship with Panamanian general Manuel Antonio Noriega was approved, but the Noriega case illustrates another political hazard in agent recruitment: circumstances may change yesterday's asset into today's embarrassment. The CIA found Noriega useful for a good many years, until several things changed: Noriega's role in the Panamanian government, the volume of drugs transiting Panama, and U.S. policy. Thus, in 1989, the Bush administration felt impelled to mount a military invasion of Panama (which itself carried a political price) to capture Noriega and bring him to Miami, where he was convicted of drug charges in one of the most expensive criminal trials in American history.

It is impossible to calculate how many recruitment efforts are successful. Impressionistic evidence points to the conclusion that the percentage is fairly low. But in this respect, intelligence is like the oil business: one gusher will pay for a great many dry holes.

Notwithstanding all the effort put into recruitment, the most valuable agents are not recruited at all; they simply show up. These are the walk-ins—foreigners with knowledge of secrets who appear unannounced at an American embassy, or sometimes the State Department in Washington, and say, in effect, "I want to help you." Most people of this type who have come to public view in recent years were Soviet citizens, and most of them were motivated by ideology. Some were fed up with the Soviet system; some simply wanted to live in the West.

Some walk-ins are brought to the United States, where the CIA extensively questions them to learn what they know and to determine their bona fides. When their knowledge is exhausted, they are given new identities and established in an American community, maybe working at a trade or profession if they have one, maybe running a small business.

Some agents are left in place in whatever job they held before they were recruited or defected and they continue to report for years. Two of the most celebrated were Colonel Penkovskiy, an officer in Soviet military intelligence who was mentioned earlier, and Oleg Gordievski of the KGB (the powerful civilian organization in charge of state security). Gordievski was chief of the KGB *rezidentura* (equivalent to a CIA chief of station) in London when he defected in

1985. As an immediate consequence, Great Britain expelled twenty-five Soviet citizens for espionage (presumably those named by Gordievski). It was reported that Gordievski had been working for Western intelligence services for at least ten years, dating to a tour of duty for the KGB in Copenhagen in the 1970s.[22]

Many agents, whether recruited or walk-ins, serve a dual purpose or at least are in a position to do so. They not only report intelligence to the CIA. They also can be used on occasion to influence the policy of their government. Suppose a high foreign office or military official is a secret CIA asset. In the councils of his government, he can put forward arguments for the policy that the United States wants his government to follow. Some agents are recruited more for their influence than their intelligence value. (See Chapter 7.)

FOREIGN INTELLIGENCE SERVICES. In many countries the CIA assiduously cultivates the local intelligence service, which is frequently among its best sources. This was especially true during the cold war, when many governments made a particular effort to infiltrate or monitor local Communist parties. It is still true with respect to dissidents and insurgents of all types, and in some countries with respect to terrorists. Local intelligence services are also helpful in maintaining the security of embassies and other American installations.

This usefulness is not cost free. Especially in countries with authoritarian governments, the intelligence service and the police force are usually held in low public esteem. This bad image is likely to tarnish the United States if a close American relationship with the police or the intelligence service or the military becomes known. It is almost impossible to keep it totally secret. One reason is that the local services sometimes want their ties to the CIA known as a means of strengthening their own position within the country.

In some cases in the 1950s, the CIA established, or helped to establish, foreign intelligence services. This was the case with the Mossad in Israel, where there is now a monument to James J. Angleton, the long-time CIA counterintelligence chief who was instrumental in creating Mossad. (You wouldn't know this from looking at the monument, a plain stone with nothing but Angleton's name on it.) Mossad and the CIA collaborated in helping the shah establish SAVAK in Iran. The CIA also shared in the parentage of the Korean Central Intelligence Agency (KCIA) in South Korea.

SAVAK and KCIA accentuated the problem of image. Both had a reputation for heavy-handed brutality and torture. Both harassed antiregime nationals in the United States. Both were fertile sources of intelligence of dubious validity, especially in the case of Iran. But the shah made it clear that he did not want alternative sources cultivated, either by the embassy or the CIA. Three unfortunate consequences followed. The United States was caught in an embrace from which it could not escape. The Carter administration was surprised when the shah was overthrown in 1979. And the United States found its larger policy objectives in the Persian Gulf in conflict with its intelligence policy.

This last consequence is of broader application. American policy is to bring pressure (always political, sometimes economic) on governments to mitigate human rights abuses by their police and intelligence forces. Intelligence policy is to maintain close relations with those forces. Some argue that this is a more effective lever than overt pressure in mitigating abuses. It is also cogently argued that if you want to know what is going on in a country, you have to deal with the people who are involved, and sometimes they are not very nice people. But it also needs to be recognized that a political price is paid in terms of the American image.

As the intimacy of the intelligence collaboration increases, the image becomes more tarnished. This sharpens the dilemma for the United States. You very rarely get anything without giving something for it. You are lucky if you don't have to give more than money. Many foreign intelligence services want a quid pro quo in the form of shared intelligence from the United States or in the form of collaboration in covert actions.

In the case of South Africa, it seemed to be one thing to share intelligence on Soviet submarine and other ship movements around the Cape of Good Hope in exchange for information on Soviet and Cuban activities in Angola.[23] But it was quite something else to tip off the South African government on activities of the African Nationalist Congress, even, according to one report, to set up the arrest of ANC leader Nelson Mandela in 1962.[24]

Such associations became politically unacceptable in the United States. In the Anti-Apartheid Act of 1986 Congress enacted sweeping sanctions designed to distance the United States from the ruling regime in South Africa. One of these was a prohibition on "any form of cooperation, direct or indirect, with the armed forces of the Government of South Africa, except for activities which are reasonably designed to facilitate the collection of necessary intelligence."[25] Such excepted activities were to be reported to Congress.

These collaborations with foreign intelligence services raise another problem for the CIA. A station spends part of its time trying to establish a friendly working relationship with an agency of the host government and part of its time trying to penetrate that government. This is a fine line to walk without stumbling.

HUMINT vs. TECHINT

There is an ongoing argument in the intelligence community about the relative value of intelligence collected from human and from technical sources and about the relative effort that should go into collecting each. Historically, the CIA emphasized HUMINT so much that its officers serving abroad were rated on how many agents they recruited. One cannot be sure without access to closely held records, but such a policy must have led to the recruitment of some agents of dubious value. The CIA also has a system of rating agents, and those who are unproductive or unreliable are not retained. But rewarding officers according to the number of agents recruited could be counterproductive.

Budget figures are secret, but cost comparisons between HUMINT and TECHINT would be misleading even if they could be made. Each can do things that the other cannot. The real question is which is more appropriate for penetrating a given target. Cryptanalysis may be able to reconstruct a foreign cryptologic system, but that is doing it the hard way. A properly placed agent can steal the system and deliver it to you; that is doing it the easy way. A properly placed agent can also deliver missile test results, but TECHINT can get them sooner and more safely.

PROBLEMS OF COLLECTION

The sources of intelligence and the methods used to acquire it are possibly the most sensitive secrets of the intelligence community, and properly so. If a source or method is disclosed ("compromised" is the technical term), the other country can take steps to turn off that source or close that method. In most cases publication of the intelligence obtained from a particular source or by a particular method will alert the other country to a leak. Frequently this leak can be traced, with the result that future intelligence is lost.

Suppose that the United States is about to enter into an important negotiation with Country X. A high-priority collection target will be Country X's negotiating position—what it is willing to give up, what it will fight for to the bitter end, what it will insist on getting from the United States. Country X will carefully guard this information. Suppose U.S. intelligence is able to acquire this information notwithstanding. Some people (including, in times past, some members of Congress) argue that there is nothing secret about the information because Country X already knows it. This completely misses the point. What is secret is that the United States also knows it. If this is disclosed, then the information loses its value, and we will not get any more where it came from.

THIRD-COUNTRY TARGETS

In many places a good part of a station's work is directed not against the host government but against third countries. The Soviet embassy was always a target; the Chinese and Cuban embassies still are. So, occasionally, are other embassies or trading companies. Sometimes the host government cooperates in some of these activities; sometimes it looks the other way; sometimes it is genuinely ignorant.

During the cold war, the CIA and the KGB developed a symbiotic relationship. When the Soviet Union opened a new embassy, say, in Latin America, the CIA station immediately got more people, the better to watch the Soviets, who in turn, no doubt, were watching the Americans.

One former CIA officer tells of hiring a professional arsonist to set fire to the apartment of a Soviet military attaché so that CIA technicians could put a tap on the attaché's telephone during the ensuing confusion. But most of what they subsequently picked up were his conversations with his mistress; apparently he confined business calls to his office. In another case, the CIA had an apartment from which it could photograph people walking in the garden of the Soviet embassy. This sent it looking (without success, so far as is known) for somebody who could lip read Russian. In yet another case, the CIA opened a bakery shop across the street from a Soviet embassy; it hoped to use bread deliveries as a means of gaining physical access.

If such activities go awry, the potential for embarrassment is not so great as one might think. The CIA and KGB developed a considerable tolerance for each other's activities. Steps would be taken to counter a specific penetration, but each knew so much about the other that each was, to a considerable degree, hostage to the other. And third-country governments could usually be persuaded to look the other way. A former State Department official tells of a government telephone company's employees finding strange telephone lines going into the Soviet embassy. Following the lines led to the CIA. The president of the country, who was being paid by the CIA, insisted that the lines had to be removed, but there was no publicity.

COVER

The CIA finds it advantageous to operate abroad as something other than the CIA. Indeed, it would be impractical to announce you are from the CIA and expect to learn very much. "Cover," strictly speaking, refers to the spurious identification used by a CIA officer when he or she goes abroad. It may be "thin cover" (the American embassy, State Department, the Agency for International Development (AID), or some other foreign affairs agency), or it may be "deep cover" (any of a number of occupations outside the government, or a government agency not directly involved in foreign affairs).

Good cover must be natural, something that would explain the activities of the intelligence officer who is using it. In their ordinary day-to-day activities, journalists, professors, students, missionaries or other clergy, and some businesspeople can mingle in the local society and ask questions. These professions provided some of the favorite covers used by the CIA in its first thirty years. Protests from legitimate practitioners led to a drastic curtailment of this use in the 1970s.

Because of the nature of their jobs, people in these professions are likely to be well informed about things the CIA wants to know. They are people with whom the CIA likes to establish a relationship as sources—not necessarily as controlled, paid agents but simply as sources to whom an officer can turn from time to time for help and information. This does not mean that the CIA is using them as cover or that they are working for the CIA, but this is a distinction that is likely to be lost on people who are suspicious to begin with of the United States in general and the CIA in particular. It gets more confusing if, at the same time in the same country, a CIA officer is using a business as deep cover.

Secrecy is essential for nondiplomatic cover. In the first place, if the cover is compromised, the officer's usefulness is over. In the second place, the whole profession that was used for the cover is compromised and loses a good deal of its former effectiveness. If one visiting American professor is revealed to have been working for the CIA, then *all* visiting American professors are suspect. It is virtually impossible to maintain complete security in a large number of cases over a long period of time, and therefore the places the CIA can look for cover have tended to become more restricted.

Some government programs that are wholly concerned with foreign affairs have specifically been placed out of bounds. A long tradition, reinforced by the watchful eye of Sen. J. William Fulbright as long as he was in the Senate, has kept Fulbright scholars beyond the CIA's reach. The insistence of members of Congress, as well as the Kennedy administration, set Peace Corps volunteers apart in the early days of that program. That separation has since been formalized by a CIA policy against hiring or recruiting anybody who has worked in the Peace Corps in the last five years.

Sometimes the CIA creates its own cover in the form of a pseudo-legitimate business, or "proprietary." These generally have more to do with covert action than with collection and are treated in Chapter 7. But some of them serve both purposes. An example would be a newspaper or magazine published abroad. It would support or oppose causes, or slant the news, as determined by American objectives (covert action), but at the same time its editor would be free to go about collecting and reporting information.

One way for the CIA to use a newspaper, magazine, television network, university, business, or some other nongovernmental institution for cover is to reach an understanding with a high executive of the organization. A CIA officer is put on the organization's payroll (the CIA finds a way to reimburse the home office, sometimes through a proprietary), and the officer goes abroad to blend into a news bureau or other foreign operation. This arrangement involves a great deal of complicated paperwork, both with the institution's accounting department and with the Internal Revenue Service. This has been done with small businesses (a public relations-lobbying firm with overseas offices comes to mind). In a large organization the relationship is almost impossible to keep secret, so simpler, more informal arrangements are preferred.

The CIA's understanding with the institution's high executive may be that a specified officer will be issued credentials or will not be repudiated if he passes himself off as a representative of the Gadget Sales Corp. Or an officer may actually enroll, at the CIA's expense, as a graduate student in a university and then proceed to establish himself to do "research" in a particular country.

From the CIA's point of view, Americans living and working abroad provide a source—frequently a very good, well-informed source—of the kind of intelligence the CIA is looking for. The CIA has every reason to ask these Americans to share their information and insights with their own government.

But from the point of view of the Americans in question (and, indeed, from the point of view of American public policy), the matter is not that clear. Especially in the third world the suspicion that an American is either working for the CIA, or cooperating with it (many third world residents do not ordinarily make that distinction), can destroy the American's effectiveness in whatever he or she is trying to do. Of course, efforts are made to keep the cooperation secret, but they are not always successful.

Americans abroad have been linked to the CIA when there is no connection at all. Some of these stories are generated by local paranoia; some result from genuine misunderstanding; some are calculated disinformation spread by unfriendly foreign intelligence services. Whatever their source, the stories share one peculiar characteristic: the more vehemently they are denied, the more strongly they are believed.

The problem of cover poses a trade-off for the CIA and in a larger sense for the government. The more jobs that are put off-limits as cover, the more difficult it becomes for the CIA to do its job. Former DCI Stansfield Turner has gone so far as to suggest that "some agencies ought even to be required to establish new functions overseas that would provide good cover for the CIA." [26]

EMBASSY-CIA RELATIONS

An American embassy is a large tent. At the center sits the ambassador, and with him are the foreign service officers and staff from the State Department who perform the traditional functions of an embassy—political, economic, administrative, and consular. The tent also covers a host of other agencies—in the case of a large embassy, as many as fourteen. This, at any rate, was the count in Mexico City in the mid-1980s.[27] These agencies almost always include the U.S. Information Agency (USIA), the Agency for International Development (in countries with U.S. aid programs, that is, a great deal of the third world), and the Defense, Treasury, Agriculture, Commerce, and Labor departments. Always included, but almost never officially acknowledged, is the Central Intelligence Agency. All of these people are answerable to the ambassador, but they also report back directly to their own agencies in Washington, and it is on their own agencies that they rely for their next assignments and promotions.

To try to keep this group marching in the same direction, more or less in step, the ambassador has a group called the Country Team, which consists of the chief representatives of the principal agencies in the embassy—typically Defense, USIA, AID, CIA, and anybody else the ambassador wants. It usually meets with the ambassador once a week.

The ambassador also has a formidable array of legal powers. Under the law (22 U.S.C. 3927) and a succession of presidential orders going back to John Kennedy, the ambassador has "full responsibility for the direction, coordination, and supervision of all Government executive branch employees" in the country where he or she is serving. Further, the ambassador is to be kept "fully and currently informed with respect to all activities and operations of the Government within that country." And finally, "any executive branch agency having employees in a foreign country shall keep the chief of mission [ambassador] to that country fully and currently informed with respect to all activities and operations of its employees in that country." This clearly includes the CIA, and just as clearly it collides with the CIA's deeply ingrown penchant for secrecy of sources and methods.

The ambassador and the CIA are almost always dealing with some of the same people in the host country. All of these people may not be telling them the same thing. In some countries, especially in the third world, the CIA may be a popular target for demagogic attack, but at the same time officials may feel a particular ego gratification in dealing with the glamorous CIA instead of a run-of-the-mill embassy. They may also feel that it is more politically correct—or at least safer—to meet clandestinely with the CIA than openly with the ambassador. It has happened that the same foreign official has been a paid CIA asset at the same time he was an unpaid source of the ambassador. Both the CIA station chief and the ambassador need to be aware that influencing American foreign policy is a prime objective of most countries and that this must be taken into account in evaluating intelligence.

In the relationship between an ambassador and a station chief, there are many possibilities for confusion at best and conflict at worst. Some ambassadors are more assertive than others. Some station chiefs are more secretive, or more resistant to direction, than others. Most of the time an ambassador's authority (if he or she chooses to assert it strongly enough) is respected by the station chief. Many ambassadors do not insist on knowing everything unless they think they really need to know. The most sensitive thing is the identity of a CIA source. Some, perhaps most, ambassadors insist on knowing this if the source's identity would significantly affect the reliability of intelligence, or if the station chief and the ambassador are dealing with the same source. In those cases the ambassador is usually told. Some ambassadors don't want to know.

The total American operation in a country would probably have fewer glitches if there could be a total sharing of information and sources between the CIA and at least the senior political officers of the embassy. But the CIA is probably correct when it argues that this would endanger some sources. Source relationships are developed over a period of years and sometimes endure for years. Political officers come and go. Too many people would know too much sensitive information.

Many foreign service officers think the CIA relies too heavily on paid informers ("agents" or "controlled sources" in spyspeak). Many CIA officers think these agents produce better intelligence than the foreign service gets free. There is a danger that paid agents will tell the CIA what it wants to hear, or even make something up, so that their value as agents increases. The CIA keeps records on the reliability of the intelligence it buys. There are safeguards against its being fooled for very long, but the possibility is real.

There are further points of CIA-generated friction within an embassy, not all of them the CIA's fault. Although physically located in the embassy, the station is set apart by being segregated in especially secure quarters. Its officers are given some flimsy diplomatic cover, usually as members of the embassy's political section. The chief of station has perquisites rivaling, or in some cases exceeding, those of the ambassador. The station's allowances, including those for "representation" (the diplomatic word for entertainment), frequently exceed those of the embassy. The CIA may have better access than the embassy to the highest levels of the local government, and some ambassadors have been jealous of this access. One U.S. ambassador tells about a visit to his country by the DCI, who saw the president but not the ambassador.

CONCLUSION

Several collection problems have more to do with the efficient operation of the intelligence community than with serious questions of public policy or political control. The first of these problems revolves around tasking: what to collect. Because some intelligence is virtually unobtainable, the formal process of tasking can be unrealistic. Regardless of its directives, the community will collect what it can get. And what is collectible is not always useful or relevant.

It is hard to be selective in collecting certain types of SIGINT. If you are monitoring a radio frequency, you take what goes out over it. NSA has been compared to a giant vacuum cleaner sucking up everything in the sky so it can be sorted out later. The agency has miles of unprocessed tapes—enough, by one no doubt hyperbolic measure, to reach to the moon. They would certainly reach a long way.

The problem of cover continues, especially in third world countries that are paranoid about the CIA and have an exaggerated view of its capabilities. The more diversified the cover that the CIA uses, the more Americans overseas who will have their bona fides questioned. The more types of cover that are put off limits to the CIA, the more constricted it will be in performing its task.

It is the necessity for secrecy that justifiably makes the CIA so sensitive about protecting sources and methods. But experience amply demonstrates that the CIA cannot rely on secrecy being total. The need increases for high-level political consideration of the trade-offs involved in collection. There are political risks in hazardous techniques. There are quid pro quos of a different sort in some types of ELINT collection. How much are these techniques ruffling somebody else's feathers? What political or economic price is the United States paying, or might it have to pay, for collection bases or platforms?

Many of these risks vanished with the cold war, but they are likely to be revived in its aftermath. The intelligence community is an enormous bureaucracy, and the natural tendency of a bureaucracy is to look for things to do to keep busy (or to give the appearance of keeping busy) and thereby justify its continued existence. This gives a new challenge to those who oversee the community.

NOTES

1. Richard Harwood, "Agents Overshadowed by the Bureaucracy," *Washington Post*, Dec. 8, 1985.
2. Senate Select Committee on Intelligence, *Nomination of Robert M. Gates*, Hearings, 102d Cong., 1st sess., 1991 (S. Hrg. 102-799, vol. 1), 497-498.
3. Loch K. Johnson, *America's Secret Power: The CIA in a Democratic Society* (New York: Oxford University Press, 1989), 288, note 19; Harry Howe Ransom, *The Intelligence Establishment* (Cambridge, Mass.: Harvard University Press, 1970), 20; and Dean Rusk as told to Richard Rusk, *As I Saw It*, ed. Daniel S. Papp (New York: Norton, 1990), 553.
4. This account draws on an interview with Robert Amory. It was conducted by Joseph E. O'Connor on Feb. 9, 1966, as part of the Oral History Program of the John F. Kennedy Library. See especially pages 112-117. Amory was deputy director for intelligence of the CIA.
5. This account of American reaction to Khrushchev's May 5 speech draws heavily on Michael B. Beschloss, *Mayday: Eisenhower, Khrushchev and the U-2 Affair* (New York: Harper and Row, 1986), 47-52. See also John Prados, *Keepers of the Keys: A History of the National Security Council from Truman to Bush* (New York: William Morrow, 1991), 68.
6. Francis Gary Powers with Curt Gentry, *OperationOverflight* (New York: Holt, Rinehart, and Winston, 1970), 91-142.
7. Beschloss, *Mayday*, 61.
8. Ibid., 248-249.
9. Senate Committee on Foreign Relations, *Events Relating to the Summit Conference*, S. Rept. 1761, 86th Cong., 2d sess., 1960, 12.
10. Ibid., 13.
11. Senate Foreign Relations Committee, *Events Incident to the Summit Conference*,

Hearings, 86th Cong., 2d sess., 1960. Unexpurgated version in *Executive Sessions of the Senate Foreign Relations Committee (Historical Series)*, vol. 12, 1982, 248-404.

12. Senate Foreign Relations Committee, Report, *Summit Conference*, 23.
13. Beschloss, *Mayday*, 370.
14. Ibid., 238.
15. Senate Foreign Relations Committee, *Summit Conference*, 22.
16. Amory interview, Kennedy Library, 150-152.
17. Transcript, Ray S. Cline Oral History Interview by Ted Gittinger, Interview II, May 31, 1983, 36. Lyndon Baines Johnson Library, Austin, Texas.
18. Dean Rusk interviewed by Loch Johnson and Richard Rusk. Dean Rusk Oral History P, undated, 6. Richard B. Russell Memorial Library, Athens, Ga.
19. Patrick E. Tyler, "SR-71 Plane Roars Into Retirement," *Washington Post*, March 7, 1990.
20. Senate Foreign Relations Committee, Report, *Summit Conference*, 22.
21. Anthony Austin, *The President's War* (Philadelphia: Lippincott, 1974), 1-8.
22. The CIA arranged for Penkovskiy's story to be published posthumously under the title *The Penkovskiy Papers* (Garden City: Doubleday, 1965). See also Jerrold Schecter and Peter Derabian, *The Spy Who Saved the World* (New York: Macmillan, 1992). On Gordievski, see Michael Dobbs, "Top Soviet Agent in London Defects; Britain Expels 25," *Washington Post*, Sept. 13, 1985, and "KGB Defector Spied for West Since 1970s," *Washington Post*, Sept. 14, 1985. See also Christopher Andrew and Oleg Gordievski, *KGB: The Inside Story of Its Foreign Operations from Lenin to Gorbachev* (New York: HarperCollins, 1990).
23. Associated Press, "Officials Deny U.S. Gave Data on ANC to Pretoria Regime," *Washington Post*, July 24, 1986.
24. George Lardner, Jr., and David B. Ottaway, "CIA Linked to Mandela's 1962 Arrest," *Washington Post*, June 11, 1990.
25. P.L. 99-440, Sec. 322.
26. Stansfield Turner, "Intelligence for a New World Order," *Foreign Affairs* (Fall 1991): 159.
27. Pat M. Holt, "Mexico and Central America," in *The President, the Congress and Foreign Policy*, ed. Edmund S. Muskie, Kenneth Rush, and Kenneth W. Thompson (Lanham, Md.: University Press of America, 1986), 125.

CHAPTER 5

Analysis

God did not give man the gift of prescience. Intelligence analysts have been trying to provide for this oversight ever since.
—Richard Helms

The golden guess is morning-star to the full round of truth.
—Alfred, Lord Tennyson

Analysis is where intelligence and policy come together. The contribution of analysis to policy is the *raison d'etre* of intelligence. Analysis makes policy more informed. It clarifies choices, defines problems, sets the parameters of what will work, and fuels the debate.

The relationship between analysts and policy makers is full of tensions. There is a deeply held belief on both sides that analysis should be divorced from policy. But neither analysis nor policy making is carried on in a vacuum, and neither the analyst nor the policy maker begins with a clean slate.

The American policy-making process is disorderly, and intelligence is only one of many factors that influence it. There are many participants, all of them seeking to serve the national interest. But the national interest frequently looks different when viewed from the different perspectives of, say, the Pentagon, or the State Department, or the Treasury. In the felicitous phrase of Thomas Hughes, policy makers sometimes use intelligence the way a drunk uses a lamp post—that is, for support instead of illumination.[1]

This is the source of the tension. No matter how much the intelligence community may protest that it is aloof from policy, it is unavoidably a part of the policy-making process.

At the same time some policy makers, particularly in the White House or cabinet, distrust analysis because they think (sometimes with reason) that they know more than the analysts do. This may literally be the case. Some presidents and secretaries of state like to keep their own secrets, especially of their private talks with foreign leaders. Some, perhaps most, secretaries and presidents simply trust their own judgment more than that of intelligence analysts.

The question of bias in analysis is continuing and contentious. Some policy makers take bad news badly, and there is much ghoulish humor about shooting the messenger while ignoring the message. Even without overt pressure to conform to the party line, how much unspoken pressure do analysts feel? It would be extraordinary if they did not at least subconsciously try to please the boss, whether the president or the director of central intelligence (DCI). Are analysts themselves trying to influence policy by injecting their own bias into the process? What do analysts and policy makers really expect from each other?

THE ANALYTIC PROCESS

Intelligence analysis is the process of making sense (or trying to make sense) out of the vast amounts of data that the intelligence community generates every day. The result is the intelligence product. The product may be what is called current intelligence, or it may be analytical, estimative, or predictive intelligence.

Current intelligence is essentially a news report: "Our man in Timbuktu says the president is going to reshuffle his cabinet." Analytical intelligence explains, or attempts to explain, the nature, background, and significance of the reshuffle and what it means to the United States.

Some current intelligence does not require analysis. The preeminent example is the intelligence of an impending Japanese attack in 1941. There was no need to analyze this. The intelligence did not indicate the target anyway, only that an attack was imminent. What should have been done with it, but was not, was to distribute it promptly to the army and navy commanders in the Pacific. Most current intelligence is of lesser moment. A good deal of it is included in intelligence publications that are circulated to a select readership in the government. Some of these publications are like newspapers and magazines except that they are secret. *The National Intelligence Daily*, which was one of the most secret until its growing circulation led to a dilution of its contents, summarizes diverse reports.

Everybody who receives current intelligence puts his or her own interpretation on it. In analysis the intelligence community assesses not only all the current intelligence but also everything else that is known about a country or a subject, and it tries to come to an agreed estimate of the current situation and an agreed prediction of the future.

The basic analytic product is a National Intelligence Estimate (NIE) or Special National Intelligence Estimate (SNIE). Each estimate is signed by the DCI as the collective judgment of the intelligence community, an act which is usually the culmination of a long and tortuous process.

The process begins in the CIA's directorate of intelligence, which consists of analysts, researchers, and support personnel. At the top is the National Intelligence Council, which is organizationally removed from the CIA as part of the office of the DCI in his capacity as director of the intelligence community. The council has about fifty people—twelve national intelligence officers (NIOs), their assistants, and other staff concerned with evaluation. Draft estimates are frequently the subject of vigorous dispute. Once there is a draft, the process moves to the National Foreign Intelligence Board, where other members of the intelligence community are represented. These other agencies have generally been working on their own drafts of the NIE or SNIE in question. The chairman of the NFIB is the director of central intelligence, wearing his intelligence community hat. The CIA is represented by the deputy director. The objective of the board is to produce an estimate that represents a genuine consensus. If this is not possible, dissent is expressed in footnotes.

In 1993 this process was churning out almost one NIE a week, along with other reports. The number of NIEs was down from sixty to eighty a year during the Reagan administration, and some national intelligence officers wanted to reduce it further. In all, the CIA grinds out about a thousand intelligence assessments, research papers, and other documents a year.[2] In the opinion of one analyst, these other assessments are better than the NIEs, which he calls "almost useless because they tend to reflect the lowest common denominator." The analyst went further and said that if he were a policy maker, he doubted he would ever ask for an NIE. A survey of intelligence consumers by the Senate Intelligence Committee found "widespread disdain toward the value of the community's analytic work."[3]

Perhaps this judgment is overly harsh, but it reflects long bureaucratic combat. At the root of some of this combat is a built-in institutional bias. "An Air Force intelligence officer," David Halberstam has written, "will not . . . say that . . . bombing will not work."[4] Even if he has private doubts, such a statement would be heresy in the organization where he spends his days and probably hopes to spend the rest of his working life. This mindset—so ingrained it may be subconscious—is very much akin to the folk wisdom on Capitol Hill, where nobody expects a senator from Florida to vote against oranges or a senator from Iowa against corn and hogs.

Other elements of the intelligence community may not generate the strong and focused loyalties of the uniformed military services, but the same tendencies are at work. These are especially noticeable in the CIA in connection with areas where ongoing covert actions have given the agency an institutional stake in the outcome. Cuba, Central America, and Angola come to mind. The intelligence directorate of the CIA once had a major internal dispute over an intelligence estimate of Soviet activities in the third world. The problem was that the Soviet analysts did not know much about the third world, and the third world analysts did not know much about the Soviet Union; yet all sides were proceeding in good faith without noticeable bias.

This type of difficulty comes from overspecialization. The problem is compounded when there is a failure to share intelligence. The intelligence community is prone to compartmentalizing especially sensitive intelligence and limiting access to it. Once notoriously reluctant to share its intelligence, the National Security Agency (NSA) has become somewhat more forthcoming. The CIA's directorate of operations has not always told everything to the directorate of intelligence. Sometimes the directorate of operations does not recognize hot intelligence when it sees it.

Other problems are bureaucratic. Dissemination lists are out of date or not tailored to consumers. Compartmentation and nonrecognition were two of the factors that caused the CIA to be slow to grasp the significance of what it knew about the Banca Nazionale del Lavoro. The Justice Department caught this Italian bank making loans to Iraq through its branch in Atlanta at a time when such loans were illegal. The case provoked an investigation by the House Intelligence Committee, which declared itself "displeased to learn that not all of the information in the possession of the intelligence community had been provided in a timely manner to agencies charged with enforcing laws or regulations pertaining to banking practices." [5]

There is also a basic question of trust. Secretary of State Dean Rusk, as noted in an earlier chapter, felt constrained not to pass on the substance of his talks with Soviet foreign minister Andrei Gromyko. In hearings before the Pike committee in the House (see Chapter 10), Secretary of State Henry Kissinger was accused of withholding intelligence that might have made it possible to predict the 1973 Arab-Israeli War and also, when he was national security adviser, of keeping intelligence about Soviet violations of the SALT I arms control agreement not only from the CIA but also from Secretary of State William P. Rogers.[6]

In 1978 hearings before the Senate Intelligence Committee, McGeorge Bundy, national security adviser to Presidents John F. Kennedy and Lyndon Baines Johnson, discussed the importance of keeping the DCI and a limited number of his senior associates informed on negotiations "upon which they are likely to be asked for advice or comment."

> Now, that is a sensitive matter because the State Department, other officials from time to time, and Presidents quite often, wish to preserve the privacy of their diplomatic negotiations and you can get a situation in which it is a very important question of intelligence analysis whether this or that faction in an African country is of this or that basic persuasion, and the most reliable information on that available to the U.S. Government may well be in the hands of those who have talked as diplomats with representatives of those factions.
>
> If someone in the intelligence community does not have access to that perception, then necessarily the intelligence estimate lacks an element of information that will limit its value.
>
> Now, that is hard business and it involves trust, and when you don't have trust, it is very difficult to manage. In our time in the early 1960's we had a working arrangement with Mr. McCone, who was then the Director of the Central Intelligence Agency, that the President's private diplomatic communications to figures as different as Khrushchev, Nasser, the head of the Government of Israel, would be made available to an appropriate senior colleague of Mr. McCone so that the estimators would not be flying blind on important information available through other processes to the U.S. Government.[7]

Finally, the quality of the material that analysts are given to work with may be poor. For example, analysts might receive a fragmentary account, or even contradictory accounts, of a foreign cabinet meeting. Or the psychological profile of a foreign leader they receive might be put together by psychiatrists or psychologists who have never met the person.

USES AND MISUSES OF ANALYSIS

The question of bias, on the part of either the analyst or the policy maker, permeates the analytic process. Most public discussions of this problem focus on its more overt and political manifestations. Do policy makers in one way or another convey to analysts the expectation that they should be team players, that the analysis should support the policy? Or, conversely, do analysts consciously shape their analysis in a way to lead policy makers to a predetermined and desired conclusion? These questions were at the heart of the controversy over the nomination of Robert M. Gates to be DCI in 1991. Gates was a career CIA officer who had previously served as deputy director for intelligence, where he was in charge of analysis, and as deputy director of central intelligence. His critics, including some CIA analysts, charged that he tried to slant intelligence estimates to fit the Reagan administration's anti-Soviet views. After extensive hearings the Senate Intelligence Committee approved his nomination, and it was confirmed by the Senate November 5, 1991, by a vote of 64 to 31.

A more pervasive, subtle problem is bias that is unspoken and that may be unconscious. The question becomes one of semantics or psychology. Total absence of bias is rare. Persons displaying bias may deny it in all good faith. In truth, it exists in the eye of the beholder.

Consider the disparate reactions of members of the Senate Foreign Relations Committee to a 1981 briefing by the CIA on Central America and the Caribbean, an area loaded with ideological and political controversy. Three Democratic senators—Claiborne Pell, R.I.; Paul E. Tsongas, Mass.; and Christopher J. Dodd, Conn.—complained that the briefing "seriously violated" the agency's obligation of objective analysis and "bordered on policy prescription." Tsongas was described as so upset that he told the CIA briefer he considered the presentation "an insult" and walked out. But Sen. Jesse Helms, R-N.C., praised the briefing as "one of the best presentations I've heard." Reportedly, the briefing traced all the area's problems to Havana.[8] The evidence given to support this conclusion was sufficient for Helms, but too scanty for the Democrats. Or to put the matter more bluntly, the briefing fit Helms's preexisting bias and was at odds with the bias of the Democrats.

There is another moral to this tale: intelligence analysis on highly charged issues is going to make somebody—and probably somebody important—unhappy. The more Congress, as a recipient of intelligence analysis, is kept informed, the greater this probability is. But congressional involvement also provides a safeguard; it helps keep analysis honest. If the role of the DCI, as Richard Helms said, is to keep the game honest, then sharing data with Congress contributes powerfully to that end.

Chapter 4 noted that Congress has added to the tasks of collection through statutory provisions making various foreign programs contingent on presidential certification of one thing or another. These provisions also put a heavy burden on analysts. For example, Congress has required at various times that the president report on the status of certain foreign nuclear facilities, the intentions of certain governments with respect to manufacturing or acquiring nuclear explosives, and progress with respect to human rights in various countries. And Congress has made foreign aid dependent on the content of these reports.

The intelligence community would want to collect much of this intelligence anyway, but the judgment of analysts now becomes a more critical factor in important foreign policy decisions. Congress was specific about Pakistan: the president is required to certify annually that Pakistan does not have nuclear weapons; otherwise Pakistan cannot receive foreign aid. Richard J. Kerr, former deputy director of the CIA, has said that there was "an intelligence basis for not certifying from 1987 on." Yet the certification was regularly made, first by President Ronald Reagan and then by President George Bush, both of whom viewed Pakistan as indispensable in supporting the guerrilla war against Soviet occupation of Afghanistan.[9]

In August 1993 the Clinton administration invoked another law to restrict certain high-technology exports to China and Pakistan. On the basis of intelligence analysis, the administration determined that China had sold missile equipment to Pakistan.[10]

The intelligence community is under heavy pressure to verify compliance with arms control agreements or to find evidence of noncompliance. Some of the pressure comes from the executive branch; some comes from Congress. Some people want to find violations and are skeptical when they are told there are not any. Some people want to find compliance and are skeptical when they are told there are violations. The president is almost certain to come under political attack no matter what he certifies or fails to certify.

Finally, even if the final intelligence product is reasonably free of bias, leaks to the media (usually only of fragments) may give the impression of bias. Leaks are a weapon in the bureaucratic warfare of both the analytic and the policy-making processes. In the course of this warfare, an often irresistible temptation arises to give a favored journalist a salient fact to buttress one side or another of an argument.

The manipulation of secret intelligence through selective disclosure or through exaggeration is done more often by policy-making officials of the executive branch during disputes with Congress than by the intelligence community bureaucracy during the analytic process. But it is just as much a perversion of intelligence analysis as deliberate distortion of an NIE would be. Repeated manipulation of intelligence data by executive policy makers is at the heart of the continuing dispute between the legislative and executive branches over congressional access to information. Congress has largely won the war over access, but there are lingering pockets of resistance. And the congressional intelligence committees must be unremittingly persistent to be sure they are getting *all* the intelligence on a given point.

There is a residue of cynicism in both Congress and the media. Executive branch officials sometimes try to justify a policy with the argument that, "If you knew what we know about the situation in Country X, you would support the president's decision to invade it; but we can't tell you what we know because we have to protect intelligence sources and methods." When such statements are heard, many people on Capitol Hill and in the media at once conclude that the official has just made an assertion that is unsupported by the facts. The official is not protecting sources and methods but his or her boss. Although Congress now has access to the underlying information, the administration uses, or tries to use, secrecy classifications to keep Congress from exposing exaggerations and distortions.

On at least one occasion, the Bush administration deleted material from intelligence reports before the reports were sent to Congress. One of the reports Congress requires by law has to do with arms proliferation. In 1991 and again in 1992 this report declared it "highly probable" that China had not eliminated its biological warfare program despite having agreed to do so. That conclusion was deleted in those years but left in the report that was sent to Congress in January

1993 on Bush's last day in office. White House officials said the deletions reflected uncertainty about the truth of the statement. An intelligence official said the deletions were made to avoid controversy during congressional debate of most-favored-nation trade status for China.[11]

New digital technology has made it possible to construct fake photographs that never existed.[12] Years earlier the Nixon White House fabricated State Department telegrams that never existed. E. Howard Hunt, one of the leading players in the Watergate affair, told the investigating Senate committee that, while working in the White House in 1971, he had fabricated cables purporting to link President Kennedy with the 1963 assassination of Vietnamese president Ngo Dinh Diem. The purpose, according to Hunt, was to show complicity by a Catholic U.S. president in the assassination of a Catholic foreign president and thereby alienate the Catholic vote from the Democratic Party in 1972, when President Nixon would be running for reelection. Hunt leaked the phony cables to a writer for *Life* magazine, but they were not used.[13] (This Catholic connection seems far-fetched. Most Americans were probably not aware of Diem's religion. The American role in the overthrow of Diem has been fuzzy, but no one has seriously suggested an American role in his assassination.)

ANALYTIC PROBLEMS AND CONSUMER EXPECTATIONS

Imagine yourself an analyst in the intelligence service of a major foreign power. You have been assigned to produce a National Intelligence Estimate on the United States covering the short-term future (six to twelve months). You have the incomparable advantage of living in the United States and of having major library resources readily available. But the first morning you read the business pages of the newspapers to prepare to assemble your economic data, you will find sundry eminent and respected economists disagreeing with each other about both the condition and the future course of the American economy. You will find great uncertainty among American experts with respect to what Congress is going to do about taxes, or foreign aid, or health care, or—most importantly from your point of view—the defense budget. You can get polling data on everything from the president's job performance to the public's preferences in television programs to the outcome of the next election, but you don't know if you can trust the polls. Your country's intelligence service has been unable to penetrate the Federal Reserve Board, so you don't know whether interest rates are going up or down. Even if your service has penetrated the board, it may have found that the board itself doesn't know what to do about interest rates. You know that the weather is going to affect crops in the Middle West, but you don't know how this might relate to pending trade arrangements. Think, then, how much more difficult it is for American analysts dealing with a country much less open than the United States.

These analysts are under an almost irresistible temptation to hedge their bets. In the first place, they do not know what is going to happen. But they also are reluctant to go out on a limb. In order to cover their flanks, not to mention their rears, analysts tend toward worst-case scenarios. Former DCI Gates is fond of the old saying, "When an intelligence officer smells flowers, he looks around for a coffin."[14] So many policy makers have complained about the tendency of the intelligence community to cry wolf that they discount predictions of *coups d'état* and other foreign political disasters.

Policy makers expect intelligence to illuminate murky situations. That is, after all, the reason the American government spends vast sums of money to maintain the intelligence community. But these efforts do not always shed light. Some situations are naturally murky, and the best thing an analyst can do about them is to say so. The policy maker will then probably complain that the intelligence is not much help. In an effort to avoid this complaint, the analyst may find something in the intelligence that is not really there. This is a part of the intelligence-to-please syndrome that has nothing to do with bias.

There is a difference between secrets and mysteries. Secrets can be targeted for collection, and in many (but by no means all) cases, a good deal can be learned about them. Factories for making nuclear, biological, or chemical weapons are secret. With cleverness, persistence, the right technology, and luck, intelligence agencies can learn about those plants. The intentions of the governments of the countries where those plants are located are mysteries. Even if the United States penetrates their innermost decision-making councils (an exceedingly difficult thing to do in most cases), the chances are that it still won't know precisely what their plans are, or indeed if they have any. More mysterious still are the processes by which foreign governments make those plans. Of course, these are the things of most interest to policy makers.

Semantics form another formidable barrier to communication between analyst and policy maker. What is the difference between "possible," "conceivable," "probable," "likely," "unlikely," "improbable," "highly probable"? At one time the CIA's Office of National Estimates (forerunner of the intelligence community's National Intelligence Council) tried to standardize some of these meanings by quantifying them. Each member of the staff was asked to write down the numerical odds he or she ascribed to "serious possibility." The results ranged from 80-20 to 20-80. An effort was then made to compile a list of words that could be assigned more precise meanings. "Certainty" was 100 percent; "almost certain," 90 percent; "probable," 75 percent; "about even," dead center; "improbable," 25 percent; "almost certainly not," 10 percent; and "impossibility," 0 percent. This mathematical straitjacket was not adopted, but at least for a time there was a ban on the use of "possible" or "possibility" to imply likelihood.[15]

What is the difference between "few," "several," "many"? When the staff of the House Intelligence Committee reviewed U.S. intelligence performance in Central America, it complained about an intelligence briefing claiming that "lots of ships have been traced" from the Soviet Union, through various other countries, to Nicaragua when, in fact, there were "only a very few."[16] This prompted the Republican members of the committee to ask, "How many are 'many,' how few are 'few'?"[17]

Sometimes policy makers outrun the analysts with overblown statements not supported by the intelligence. Discussing his decision to send U.S. troops to the Dominican Republic in 1965, President Johnson said, "In this particular instance, a fact that has been emphasized all too little, I think, some 1,500 innocent people were murdered and shot, and their heads cut off." Upon more relaxed investigation, it became clear that the reason this had not been emphasized was that it had not happened. The president also said, "As we talked to our ambassador to confirm the horror and tragedy and the unbelievable fact that they were firing on Americans and the American embassy, he was talking to us from under a desk while bullets were going through his windows." [18] The ambassador in question, W. Tapley Bennett, later said to the Senate Foreign Relations Committee that he was not under his desk. "I would say," he diplomatically told the committee, "there has been some exaggeration that has crept into reported descriptions of various events."[19]

Intelligence analysts in these cases feel that if presidents (or sometimes secretaries of state) have been shown up as exaggerating, it is their own fault, and analysts sometimes take pleasure in helping to show them up. On the other hand, presidents and secretaries of state feel betrayed if the intelligence does not support them. Former DCI Gates has addressed the problem thus:

> When Secretary of State Alexander Haig asserted that the Soviets were behind international terrorism, intelligence analysts initially set out, not to address the issue in all its aspects, but rather to prove the secretary wrong—to prove simply that the Soviets do not orchestrate all international terrorism. But in so doing they went too far themselves and failed in early drafts to describe extensive and well-documented indirect Soviet support for terrorist groups and their sponsors. Far from kowtowing to policymakers, there is sometimes a strong impulse on the part of intelligence officers to show that a policy or decision is misguided or wrong, to poke an analytical finger in the policy eye. Policymakers know this and understandably resent it. To protect the independence of the analyst while keeping such impulses in check is one of the toughest jobs of intelligence agency managers.[20]

This kind of tension is not always (or perhaps even usually) the result of hyperbole by policy makers. Sometimes overriding national security considerations (as seen by a president) dictate a policy response with a thin, or even nonexistent, factual base. And with Congress increasingly privy to intelligence analysis, this puts a greater strain on the relations between policy maker and analyst. If the available intelligence does not support a policy, or is even contraindicative, and Congress knows this, at least some members of Congress are going to make life difficult for the policy maker. That is why policy makers have a greater interest in keeping Congress in the dark than does the intelligence community.

On at least two occasions, Secretary of State Henry Kissinger sought to restrict the flow of information from the CIA to the Senate Foreign Relations Committee. Members of the committee, prompted by staff, had asked the secretary questions based on items in the *National Intelligence Daily*. Kissinger was taken aback because he had not expected the committee to know about the subject matter and was not prepared to discuss it. Afterwards an apologetic William Colby, the DCI, informed the committee that it would no longer receive the *NID* but rather a lower level, less informative report. Both times this decision was reversed, but once only after Senate Majority Leader Mike Mansfield, D-Mont., a member of the committee, threatened to take the matter to President Gerald Ford.

The Ideal Product

Within the CIA there is tension between operations (that is, collection) and intelligence. The operations people are viewed (or view themselves) as the elite and resist sharing everything they know with the intelligence people. Training is heavily oriented toward operations. For years the CIA gave its officers no training in analysis. Then a segment on analysis was introduced into the junior officer training program. But beyond a course in formal logic, analysis is not something that lends itself to being taught. One assembles a great many facts (some of them conflicting) in some kind of coherent order and then determines where they logically lead. One must know enough about the subject to be able to recognize which facts are significant and which are not.

The trouble, of course, is that in a great many instances, the facts do not logically lead anywhere, or they may lead to several places, some of them inconsistent with others. It is this latter situation that produces the "on-the-one-hand-this-on-the-other-hand-that" analysis that drives policy makers crazy.

The ideal analysis is based on adequate, reliable intelligence, all of which points to one inescapable conclusion. The analysts' world is rarely so orderly. They rarely have all the intelligence they need, or think they need. Although the CIA has a way of rating the reliability of its sources, and over time every source will compile a track record, this is not foolproof and one can never be sure. So analysts almost inevitably have to guess. The guess is likely to be closer to the mark if they are experienced and well versed in the subject matter and have good instincts. But it is still a guess.

In the case of national intelligence estimates, clarity of analysis is handicapped by the process that is designed to produce the collective judgment of the intelligence community. Abba Eban, the former Israeli foreign minister, has described a consensus as meaning that "everyone agrees to say collectively what no one believes individually."[21] What Henry Kissinger called "constructive ambiguity" has its uses in diplomacy but not in intelligence.

It is a complaint of analysts that policy makers say, "Don't give us your analysis; just give us your facts"—by which they mean a prediction. But if the policy makers then skip the analysis and jump to the prediction, they are short-changing themselves. The road an analyst takes to get to a prediction is at least as important as the prediction itself. It is along this road that the analyst (and the policy maker who goes along for the ride) think through what the problem is when nobody knows what the answer is. Policy makers are more action oriented and tend to put this down as head-scratching. But they are unlikely to find the answer to a problem until they thoroughly understand the problem. One of the most valuable things intelligence analysis can do is to help policy makers understand a problem without an answer.[22]

There is a fine line between hedging predictions and covering all reasonable possibilities. Policy makers deserve to be told what the analyst's best estimate is and the level of confidence in that estimate. But policy makers ought also to be told of other possibilities and given alternative analyses.

CASE STUDIES

A review of selected case studies will illustrate the points made in the preceding section about the analytic process as well as about relations between analysts and policy makers.

SOVIET UNION

The Soviet Union vanished at the end of 1991, but during the cold war the intelligence community was under persistent attack with respect to its Soviet estimates. If the NIEs said the Soviet military was growing, American liberals smelled a plot to justify bigger Pentagon budgets. If the NIEs said the Soviet military was not growing, American conservatives smelled a coverup. Conservatives also tended to see the Soviet hand behind every anti-American movement in the third world, and they expected American intelligence to provide supporting evidence.

The intelligence community itself was of at least two minds about these issues, which were the subject of some epic bureaucratic struggles. In 1975, at the suggestion of the President's Foreign Intelligence Advisory Board, a competitive analysis of Soviet military strength was organized between the community's analysts (the A team) and a group of outside experts (the B team). The exercise was inconclusive. The Senate Intelligence Committee made its own review, which was also inconclusive.[23]

Sometimes similar disputes are carried on publicly at higher levels. In 1990 the director of the CIA, William H. Webster, told the House Armed Services Committee that the collapse of Soviet and Warsaw Pact military power was irreversible. This led Secretary of Defense Richard B. Cheney to complain that Webster was making it more difficult for him to generate congressional support for the president's defense budget.[24]

Two years later it was the Defense Intelligence Agency that upset Republicans in the Senate. The DIA director, Air Force Lt. Gen. James R. Clapper, Jr., told the Senate Armed Services Committee that the military capabilities of the former Soviet states were "in profound decline." This seemed to Sen. John W. Warner, R-Va., to be in "head-on collision" with President Bush's defense spending plans. But when Warner asked the general if his statement supported or conflicted with Bush's budget, committee chairman Sam Nunn, D-Ga., cut him off. "That's not the general's job," Nunn said.[25]

In 1989 Rep. Les Aspin, D-Wis., claimed that the Bush administration had withheld information about declining Soviet military expenditures, thereby interfering with congressional discussion of U.S. defense priorities.[26] This type of manipulation by a president becomes increasingly difficult as Congress gains increasing access to intelligence.

Throughout the cold war there was confusion and uncertainty about the size and performance of the Soviet economy. This subject was of considerable importance because it related to the underlying national strength on which Soviet military power rested and to the capability of the Soviet Union to sustain a prolonged war—or even, as it turned out, a prolonged defense buildup. The major difficulty lay in the absence of reliable data. The problem was not that the data were closely held by the Soviet government; in that case they could have been targeted for traditional espionage and found out, at least in part, sooner or later. The problem was that the data did not exist. After the breakup of the Soviet Union, it became clear that the Soviet government itself had been as much in the dark as everybody else.

A controlled, centrally planned economy (such as that which operated in the former Soviet Union) takes on an Alice in Wonderland quality in which the values of goods and services are not related to each other. Everything is worth what the government says it is. This both leads to, and disguises, distortions in the allocation of resources and in the measurement of economic performance. For example, you can count how many automobiles are being produced, but their selling price bears no relationship to their cost of production, so you don't know whether they represent economic growth or a drain on resources.

The intelligence community, mainly the CIA and to some extent the DIA, tried several ways to cut through this fog enshrouding the Soviet economy. It tried to estimate how much it would cost to produce comparable goods in the United States, and then it tried to translate those estimates back into Soviet terms. It tried to approach the question in terms of productivity: how many workers took how long to produce x units? But the intelligence community was always left with multiple uncertainties, among them the value of the ruble. It was not a convertible currency, and nobody had a clear idea of what it would be worth if it were convertible.

By 1990 the intelligence community, along with almost everybody else, was astonished by the rapidity and totality of the collapse of the Soviet Union. It was clear that whatever the truth about Soviet military strength, estimates of the Soviet economy had been wide of the mark and usually had substantially overstated Soviet economic performance. The Senate Foreign Relations Committee attempted to find out why. Sen. Daniel Patrick Moynihan, D-N.Y., asked rhetorically, "Would we have spent as much on our military during the 1980s if we had believed that the Soviet defense burden simply was not sustainable? I think not, and if I am correct, then the issue has been a momentous one for the state of the American economy." [27] The question can be asked another way: Would the Soviets have assumed such a burden if the United States had been spending less?

The committee assembled a distinguished group of academic economists and intelligence analysts. There was general agreement that the strength of the Soviet economy had been overestimated, but there was no agreement as to how this had happened.

CENTRAL AMERICA

Every kind of pressure was at work in the 1980s to influence intelligence analysis of Central America. The administration was passionately committed to a bitterly controversial policy. In pursuit of that policy, the CIA was deeply involved in a major covert action in Nicaragua, and the military was openly taking sides in a civil war in El Salvador. The foreign affairs bureaucracy was skeptical. Out of this witches' brew came the Iran-Contra scandal, but the Central American experience also illustrates many other problems of intelligence.

We shall consider Central America further in Chapter 7 in connection with covert action. Here we are concerned with intelligence analysis and estimates for that region. There was an unavoidable reciprocal relationship between the analysis and estimates, on the one hand, and, on the other, ideological commitment, covert action, military assistance, and human rights.

Nineteen seventy-nine was a critical year in Central America. The Sandinista revolution toppled the Somoza dictatorship in Nicaragua in July, and the president of El Salvador was overthrown by a military coup in October. From these two events flowed two civil wars that raged throughout the 1980s. American policy was to support the insurgents against the government in Nicaragua, the government against the insurgents in El Salvador.

With an almost religious fervor the Reagan administration believed that the Sandinista government of Nicaragua was an instrument of Soviet-Cuban ambitions to take over Central America. The administration viewed in the same light the insurgents opposing the government of El Salvador. From this it followed, in the administration's view, that the United States should unstintingly support the Nicaraguan Contras (the counter-revolutionaries trying to topple the Sandinistas) as well as the embattled Salvadoran government. Opponents of the policy argued that the administration's fear of Soviet-Cuban control of Central America was exaggerated, that all-out support of the Contras or the Salvadoran government might lead to overt American military intervention in an unpopular local war, and that the U.S.-backed Salvadoran government was brutal and authoritarian.

It is indicative of the changing importance that Washington attributed to El Salvador that the CIA had actually closed its station there in the mid-1970s but re-opened it a few years later. In 1980 the American ambassador to El Salvador, Robert E. White, was so dissatisfied with CIA performance that he insisted, over strenuous objections from CIA headquarters, that the station chief be replaced. The chief was close to the right-wing military socially, but he did nothing to carry out the task he had been given to infiltrate the presumed death squads. The House Intelligence Committee staff report on Central America quotes "an official" in El Salvador at the time to the effect that White imposed restrictions on contacts with the extreme right.[28] White says he banned "casual invitations" to a prominent rightist leader and ordered that contacts with the man be coordinated with the ambassador's office. This, he says, was part of an effort to put an end to a situation in which the embassy was speaking with "about seven different voices."[29] White also wrote that

> every administration enters office with its quota of ideologues. It is the job of the intelligence community to blunt uninformed zeal with sober, compelling and sustained analysis. In this basic responsibility the CIA failed. Instead of supplying objective reports that should have served as a basis for leading our country out of the Salvadoran morass, the CIA under William Casey put intelligence at the service of policy and provided justifications for ever-deeper involvement.[30]

Within the State Department the dispute over Nicaragua became so bitter that Elliott Abrams, the assistant secretary for Latin America, accused Francis J. McNeil, the deputy director of the Bureau of Intelligence and Research, of disloyalty. McNeil had questioned the effectiveness of the Contras and re-signed because of the dispute with Abrams. One anonymous official called this "a classic juxtaposition between the true believer [Abrams] and the dispassion-ate professional analyst [McNeil]." [31] As one of the results of the independent counsel's investigation of the Iran-Contra affair, Abrams subsequently pleaded guilty to two misdemeanor counts of withholding information from Congress. He was among those pardoned by President Bush on Christmas Eve 1992.)

Another analyst who resigned over Central America was John Horton of the CIA. Horton accused William J. Casey, then CIA director, of having an esti-mate on Mexico "rewritten over my dead body, so to speak" to make it support U.S. policy in Central America.[32] Another version, coming from within the CIA, has it that Casey rejected a good deal of shabbily written analysis, not because he disagreed with it but because it was badly written. The Horton paper had been the subject of controversy within the CIA before it got to Casey. Casey sent the estimate back with a handwritten note across the top—"This is a bunch of crap," a judgment in which others concurred. When the paper was rewritten, stating the same conclusions better, it went forward.

Later, writing in the *Washington Post*, Horton said, "I resigned as national intelligence officer for Latin America because of the pressure put on me by the director of central intelligence [Casey] to come up with a National Intelligence Estimate on Mexico that would satisfy him." Horton had formerly been the chief of station in Mexico. He wrote of the "natural tension" between intelli-gence officers and policy makers and added, "Sometimes [strong-minded offi-cials] don't care what the intelligence says so long as it doesn't get in their way. Attempts to squelch displeasing intelligence reports or judgments that don't back up an administration's policies have a nonpartisan provenance." [33] Casey was different from other DCIs in the active role he assumed in policy making. He had managed Reagan's 1980 presidential campaign. Reagan gave him cabi-net rank as DCI, the first and only DCI to have that status.

Shortly after taking office in January 1981, the Reagan administration is-sued a white paper, "Communist Interference in El Salvador." Based on docu-ments captured from guerrillas by government troops, the white paper traced a flow of arms purchased from Soviet allies (such as Vietnam, Ethiopia, and Bul-garia) through Nicaragua to El Salvador. This was its principal conclusion:

> It is clear that over the past year the insurgency in El Salvador has been progres-sively transformed into another case of indirect armed aggression against a small third world country by Communist powers acting through Cuba.[34]

Skeptics in Congress demanded proof and then were skeptical of the evi-dence that the administration produced. Rep. Lee H. Hamilton, D-Ind., was a member of the House Intelligence Committee in 1981 and served as its chair-man from 1985 to 1986. He later wrote:

> . . . [S]everal members of Congress, including myself, knew that U.S. intelli-gence did not support President Reagan's claim that Nicaragua's Sandinista government was shipping "a flood of arms" to communist guerrillas in El Salva-dor, but we were unable to respond to the president's assertions because the information was classified.[35]

Actually, there are ways for a congressional committee to respond to a situation of this kind. It can call the DCI to testify in a closed session. If the DCI does not present adequate supporting data, the committee, or its chairman, can say so publicly after the session, without saying what the data showed. If the administration continues to insist on its position, then either it is admitting that it is withholding information from Congress, or it is making the issue one of whom the public is to believe.

The House Intelligence Committee staff investigated the community's performance in Central America and found "overall competence . . . [but] occasional oversimplification and the suggestion of greater certainty than warranted by the evidence." [36] Even this mild criticism was released over the unanimous objection of the Republican members of the committee. A separate critique of the staff report said that it "makes a number of criticisms which are overstated, slanted, and do not reflect the careful analysis and judgment that we should expect from the Committee staff." [37]

As is hinted in both the staff report and the critique of it, there were differences not only about whether the analysis was biased but also about what bias is. These latter differences were much more profound and arose from disagreement over the policy itself. "Analytic thought and production decisions," the report stated, may occur in an environment "under pressure to reinforce policy—or perhaps to oppose it—rather than to inform it."

> Such pressure would not consist of deliberate efforts to suppress or distort evidence; rather, it would lie mostly in the natural incentives that cause time and talent to be devoted to providing welcome intelligence rather than to tackling questions that, although policy-relevant, seem thankless. The existence of any such environment, and its effect upon the health and effectiveness of the intelligence process, are impossible to identify with precision.[38]

The pressure on analysts was increased by a series of congressional requirements making continued U.S. assistance contingent on certain presidential certifications. These would, of course, have to be based in major part on intelligence.

In the case of Nicaragua, the Special Central American Assistance Act of 1979 provided that before releasing any assistance the president should certify "that the Government of Nicaragua has not cooperated with or harbors any international terrorist organization or is aiding, abetting, or supporting acts of violence or terrorism in other countries." [39] That provision became law May 31, 1980. President Carter waited until September 12 to make the certification, based, a White House statement said, on reports from intelligence agencies, American embassies in Nicaragua and neighboring countries, and "diverse information and opinions from all sources." The statement added that "the available evidence permits the President to make the certification required." It further added:

> The administration does not intend to abandon the vital Central American region to Cuba and its radical Marxist allies. To the contrary, the assistance made available by the President's certification will enable us to give effective support to those moderate and democratic Nicaraguans who are struggling to preserve

individual freedoms, political pluralism, the democratic process, and a strong, free enterprise participation in their economy.[40]

The CIA had found "a very high likelihood that such support activities ('training, transit, material, and arms') are occurring." [41] But Carter wanted to extend aid and found a way to do it.

In the case of El Salvador, the political pressures on the intelligence process were increased by the inability or unwillingness of successive Salvadoran governments to curb right-wing death squads, which were widely thought to be composed of members of the Salvadoran military. Democrats in Congress demanded tough American action. The Reagan and Bush administrations were more inclined to rely on behind-the-scenes pressure. This standoff led Congress to set standards and deadlines. Under this procedure military aid to El Salvador was to be suspended unless the president periodically certified to Congress that, in the words of a 1981 law, the government of El Salvador, among other things, "is achieving substantial control over all elements of its own armed forces, so as to bring to an end the indiscriminate torture and murder of Salvadoran citizens by these forces." [42]

Thus, the law created an atmosphere of pressure for evidence on which the president could certify that the required progress was in fact being made. Democrats in Congress complained not that intelligence analysis was skewed to support a certification but that President Reagan certified in the absence of sufficient evidence—as some members thought President Carter had done in the case of Nicaragua. In one case Sen. Christopher Dodd, D-Conn., called a certification "unwarranted";[43] and in another Sen. Patrick J. Leahy, D-Vt., said, "I cannot imagine how bad things would have to get before this administration would not certify that the conditions of the law had been met." [44]

State Department officials were cynical about the certification requirements, which they viewed as a congressional cop-out. Said Elliott Abrams, then assistant secretary for human rights:

> If Congress felt so strongly about human rights abuses, it could have simply cut off aid. But Congress didn't cut off aid, because it didn't want to risk being blamed, if the guerrillas won as a result, for "losing" El Salvador.

Deane Hinton, then ambassador to El Salvador, said the certification requirement was "a way for Congress . . . to be for and against something at the same time." [45] Abrams and Hinton have a point, but it does not take account of the fact that opinion was sharply divided in Congress, as it was in the country at large. Some members would have happily cut off aid and taken their chances on being blamed for the "loss" of El Salvador. Others would have happily given the administration whatever it asked for. Neither group had the votes to prevail. Certification was the compromise that resulted—wholly satisfactory to few, supported by many. That is the way the legislative process works, and it is what Abrams and Hinton missed.

In March 1993 Secretary of State Warren Christopher appointed two senior foreign service officers to investigate the performance of the State Department and the American embassy in El Salvador with respect to human rights. Had Congress been misled? Had human rights violations been covered up?

In July the panel reported its conclusion—namely, that "within the parameters of overall U.S. policy, the Department and Foreign Service personnel performed creditably—and on occasion with personal bravery—in advancing human rights in El Salvador." [46] The operative phrase is "within the parameters of overall U.S. policy." These parameters were shaped by conflicting requirements to which Foreign Service personnel uncomfortably adjusted as best they could.[47]

VIETNAM

The Vietnam War presents a rare case in which tactical intelligence had foreign policy consequences and in which the line between TIARA (Tactical Intelligence and Related Activities) and NFIP (National Foreign Intelligence Program) was extraordinarily blurred. Samuel A. Adams, the CIA's Vietnam intelligence officer, has described the mountains of intelligence he received—a stack of paper four or five inches thick every day.[48] Multiply that by ten years and add tactical field intelligence. Then consider the many people and organizations with different stakes in Vietnam outcomes. The wonder, perhaps, is not that there were controversies over intelligence but that there were not more of them.

One of the most celebrated controversies did not arise until 1982, seven years after the end of the war and nine years after the withdrawal of the last American troops. The popular CBS television program "Sixty Minutes" broadcast a segment entitled "The Uncounted Enemy: A Vietnam Deception." The program reported that at the behest of the U.S. military command in Vietnam, and specifically of Gen. William C. Westmoreland, the top U.S. commander, intelligence estimates of enemy strength were consistently understated, thereby giving the impression that the United States and its Vietnamese allies were doing better in the war than was in fact the case.

Westmoreland sued CBS and three individuals who had worked on the program for libel, asking $120 million in damages. The heart of the case, as well as of the program which gave rise to it, was the thorny problem of how the enemy should be counted. Some of the enemy—the "home militia" or "self-defense militia"—shifted roles constantly from guerrillas to civilians and back again. (The same phenomenon of role-shifting was part of the larger political problem in Vietnam.) In general, the CIA in Vietnam thought the home militia should be counted; the U.S. military thought they should not be. This is a question about which reasonable people can, and did, differ.

The military's counting system prevailed. In the period immediately preceding the Tet offensive, which started in January 1968, the military estimated enemy troops at 300,000—200,000 fewer than the CIA's estimate.

CBS charged that General Westmoreland had ordered omission of the home militia as part of an effort to deceive Washington policy makers, including President Johnson, and to advance the political argument that the war was being won.

After prolonged testimony in federal court in New York, the parties called it quits without a verdict. Instead, they issued a joint statement:

Now both General Westmoreland and CBS believe that their respective positions have been effectively placed before the public for its consideration and that continuing the legal process at this stage would serve no further purpose.

CBS respects General Westmoreland's long and faithful service to his country and never intended to assert, and does not believe, that General Westmoreland was unpatriotic or disloyal in performing his duties as he saw them.

General Westmoreland respects the long and distinguished journalistic tradition of CBS and the rights of journalists to examine the complex issues of Vietnam and to present perspectives contrary to his own.[49]

Vietnam presented other intelligence conundrums aplenty. The CIA repeatedly estimated that bombing would not halt supplies from the North; policy makers continued bombing, and supplies continued flowing to the South. The military insisted that the Cambodian port of Sihanoukville was a major transshipment point for supplying the South; the CIA just as adamantly insisted that this could not be so. When U.S. troops invaded Cambodia in 1970, evidence was captured to prove that it was so.

During most of the Vietnam period, Richard Helms was director of central intelligence, and Thomas L. Hughes was director of the Bureau of Intelligence and Research of the Department of State. Both have reported the absence of any pressure (from the president in Helms's case, from the secretary of state in Hughes's) to slant analysis. On the contrary, Helms has said that Johnson had a

> remarkable ability . . . when he finally realized that the facts were right and had been accurately presented and that his conception was wrong, to simply swallow and accept what you had told him and not refer to it any more. . . . This happened, for example, in connection with the amount of damage that the air bombardment of North Vietnam was accomplishing.[50]

Hughes has described his bureau's "complete freedom of choice of what to write about, how to write about it, and what conclusions to draw from it." He added:

> The secretary of state had repeated reason to know that INR analysis was unhelpful to the pursuit of policies on which the Administration had embarked, and that INR papers were often being used against arguments he was espousing. Never did this potentially embarrassing situation affect . . . INR's independent role.[51]

By and large, more slanting was done by policy makers than by intelligence analysts. During most of the Vietnam period, intelligence was simply irrelevant to policy. The policy makers' minds were made up.

IRAN

U.S. policy toward Iran illustrates the kind of bias that comes from fixed mindsets on the part of policy makers. The bias reached its most extreme form during the Carter administration (1977-1981), but the predicate was laid long before.

In 1953 a CIA-sponsored coup d'état overthrew a leftist nationalist prime minister in Iran. This enabled Shah Mohammed Reza Pahlavi to resume full control of the government (see Chapter 7). From then until 1979, when the shah was overthrown in turn by a radical Islamic revolution, a de facto alliance with Iran was one of the bedrocks of American policy in the area of the Persian Gulf. There were many reasons for this:

- The shah embarked on a series of policies to modernize (in American eyes, Westernize) his country.
- Iran enjoyed considerable oil wealth even before the sharp price increases of the 1970s, and it provided a good market for American exports, civilian as well as military.
- Iran was regarded as a solid anchor for the security of the Persian Gulf, through which flowed the large oil exports not only of Iran but also of Iraq, Kuwait, and Saudi Arabia.
- Iran provided bases from which the National Security Agency monitored Soviet missile tests and collected other signals intelligence.
- Iran generally projected a moderating, pro-Western influence in the region.

These considerations led to an inextricable intertwining of American interests with those of the shah. In the 1950s, the Israeli intelligence service (Mossad) and the CIA had helped to create the Iranian intelligence service (SAVAK). There were close arrangements between the CIA and SAVAK for the exchange of intelligence, especially for the flow from SAVAK to the CIA. The shah made it clear that he wanted SAVAK to be the principal source of American intelligence in Iran. The CIA and the embassy generally acquiesced in restraints on independent collection and reporting. They could scarcely have done otherwise. There is usually some room for testing limits, but when you are in another country, you have to play by its rules.

Meanwhile, all was not well in Iran. The shah's drive to modernization collided with the vested interests of powerful Iranian social groups that did not want the status quo disturbed. The collateral effects of modernization—women in Western dress, for example—collided with conservative Islamic religious beliefs. The shah dealt with these forces of resistance by oppression, not by political persuasion. Throughout 1978 the opposition grew, changed from riotous to violent, and became more radical. All of this was reported in the Western press.

In January 1978 police forcibly put down protest demonstrations by Moslems in the holy city of Qom. The loss of life was estimated at six by the police, at twenty by the dissidents. In the Moslem religion mourning is repeated at forty-day intervals. Thus, in February there were antigovernment riots again, this time in Tabriz, with up to 100 killed, 250 arrested, and 135 fires started. In May antigovernment riots occurred in thirty-four cities, including Tehran, as Moslems demanded strict adherence to Islamic law, including closing liquor stores and movie houses and requiring women to wear veils in public. In August 430 died in a movie house in Abadan when it was set afire and the doors locked. The shah changed prime ministers, abolished the post of minister of state for women's activities, restored the Moslem calendar, and closed gambling places. In September sporadic strikes began in telecommunications, banking, oil refining, and air transportation. This general turmoil got worse throughout the fall of 1978. Finally, on January 16, 1979, the shah left for Egypt. Thus, abundant information was available from public sources. The entries under "Iran" in the *New York Times* Index for 1978 take more than seven columns.

Meanwhile, back in Washington, as early as 1977, the National Security Council (NSC) staff had asked the CIA for a paper on Islamic fundamentalism. (The staff was concerned about Turkey, not Iran, but at least it was on the right subject.) When nothing was forthcoming, inquiries revealed that nobody at the CIA had studied the subject.[52] During 1978, the State Department's Bureau of Intelligence and Research did not even have a full-time Iran analyst.

In August 1978 the CIA published an Intelligence Assessment entitled "Iran After the Shah." Despite its title, the document asserted that "Iran is not in a revolutionary or even a 'prerevolutionary' situation." In September the DIA published an Intelligence Appraisal stating that the shah "is expected to remain actively in power over the next ten years."[53] At a press conference on December 12, President Carter said, "I fully expect the shah to maintain power in Iran and for the present problems in Iran to be resolved."[54]

Carter also expressed dissatisfaction with intelligence on Iran and in November asked the NSC, State, and CIA to "see how we could improve the quality of our assessment program and also, particularly, political assessments."[55] This set off a round of bureaucratic recriminations, in which the State Department blamed the national security adviser, Zbigniew Brzezinski, and the NSC staff blamed DCI Stansfield Turner.[56] In any event, on December 13 it was announced that the United States was beefing up the Tehran embassy political section for more reporting.

Intelligence analysis of Iran in the last year of the shah was wildly mistaken, but this is not the same thing as being biased. Policy makers tended to blame the intelligence producers, but the trouble was that the policy makers were impervious to the facts. Gary Sick, the NSC staff officer for Iran, later explained it like this:

> . . . [E]lements of the U.S. bureaucracy had themselves developed a vested interest in relations with the shah's regime, and they were not inclined to seek out problems or promote solutions that risked interfering with the pursuit of important but essentially parochial objectives. In each of these areas, whether it was commodity imports, educational exchange, defense procurement, petroleum production or international banking and finance, the overwhelming daily reality was that of business as usual, and neither Iranians nor Americans wished to see that disturbed. . . .
> . . . [T]here is no doubt that the immense responsibility of proclaiming a generation of U.S. policy bankrupt weighed heavily in the minds of those observing the ominous unfolding of events in Iran. . . .
> . . . [W]hat came to be known as the "intelligence failure" was not so much a failure of sources or observation or data as a structural inadequacy of the system itself to make the conceptual leap from chessboard to hurricane.[57]

Not only were consumers not asking the right questions; single-minded policy was creating an environment in which analysts were not encouraged to challenge conventional wisdom. Such an environment tends to cloud analytical initiative.[58]

Turner has gone further and charged the analysts with operating in their own closed society. In part because of the constraints of secrecy, he has written,

CIA analysts are disinclined to test their theories and conclusions on people outside the Agency. . . . [O]f more influence is an inherent reluctance in the CIA to go outside for second opinions. . . . CIA analysts, who live day by day in a rarefied atmosphere of secret information, tend to be patronizing of outsiders. . . . They are not viewed as having the same depth of background as the analysts.[59]

Cuba

The history of U.S.-Cuban relations provides many examples of the interplay of analysis and policy. Here we examine three: the Bay of Pigs, the missile crisis, and the forgotten Soviet brigade.

BAY OF PIGS.   In 1961, a little more than two years after Fidel Castro came to power in Cuba, President Kennedy gave the go-ahead to the Bay of Pigs operation on Cuba's South coast. The operation was a U.S.-sponsored invasion of Cuba by U.S.-trained and -equipped anti-Castro Cuban exiles. The exiles were trained at a secret base in Guatemala. They embarked for Cuba from Nicaragua. Kennedy had made it clear that although the United States would provide transport, neither the navy nor the air force would provide combat support.[60] The invasion was supposed to appear to be a purely Cuban operation. After the invaders established themselves, they were to proclaim a "Free Cuban Government," which the United States would then recognize and support.

For this plan to work, Cuban opposition had to be minimal. The CIA's intelligence assessments predicted precisely that and also held out the possibility of popular uprisings in support of the invaders. Neither of these things occurred. The invading forces were crushed in two days and felt betrayed by the lack of U.S. air and naval support, despite Kennedy's warning not to expect it.

Subsequent review found several things wrong with the decision-making process. One of them was the conjuncture of plans and analysis in the CIA. The agency's directorate of intelligence was not cleared for information about the plan; therefore, such analysis as was produced came from the directorate of operations, which had a self-interest in promoting the plan. Nor did the State Department's Bureau of Intelligence and Research know about it.

MISSILE CRISIS.   In the late summer of 1962, rumors began to circulate in Washington that the Soviet Union was either placing, or was about to place, offensive, nuclear-capable missiles in Cuba. The Kennedy administration denied the rumors, but Congress was sufficiently impressed that it passed a resolution expressing U.S. determination, among other things, "to prevent in Cuba the creation or use of an externally supported military capability endangering the security of the United States."[61]

Although the CIA was unable to find missiles in Cuba (and thought their presence there unlikely), it stepped up reconnaissance of the island and began a special daily intelligence report on Cuba August 29. While this was going on, John McCone, who had succeeded Allen Dulles as DCI, was in Europe. He was on his honeymoon, but this did not distract him from bombarding CIA headquarters with telegrams warning that the Soviets did have missiles in Cuba. U-2 photographs confirmed them in mid-October. McCone later said he had no hard evidence. "It was," he said, "wholly a question of judgment." [62] In other words, a hunch—or, in Alfred, Lord Tennyson's more elegant phrase, a "golden guess." It is significant of the independence of the NIE process, however, that even the DCI's hunch did not change the estimate.

A review of much declassified intelligence thirty years later showed that there was, in fact, evidence—some of it from the CIA's own agents—that was initially ignored at CIA headquarters. There were 2,000 to 3,000 reports of missiles in Cuba, but because many of them were shown to be false, none was heeded—a classic case of the boy crying wolf. The CIA had twenty-five agents in Cuba at that time. Their reports were also ignored until they began describing eighty-foot-long objects on flatbed trucks that could not turn street corners unless mailboxes and lamp posts were removed. [63]

Besides the missiles, the Soviets had considerably more other forces in Cuba than the CIA thought: 43,000 troops (instead of 10,000) as well as tactical nuclear weapons. These and other revelations at a conference in Havana in January 1992 led Robert S. McNamara, U.S. secretary of defense at the time of the 1962 crisis, to conclude: "The actions of all three parties [the United States, the Soviet Union, Cuba] were shaped by misjudgments, miscalculations, and misinformation." [64]

SOVIET BRIGADE.   In March 1979 Brzezinski asked for a review of intelligence about Soviet military forces in Cuba. To DCI Turner, this request fit a pattern: somebody in an intelligence agency had used secret data to conclude something the individual's superiors would not accept. The individual would then take the conclusion to Brzezinski's staff who, if it "fitted with the Brzezinski view of the world," would urge Brzezinski to urge Turner to investigate it. [65]

As part of the review in this case, the National Security Agency reported in mid-July that it had found what it called a Soviet combat brigade, which had been previously unreported, in Cuba. The head of NSA at this time was Adm. B. R. Inman. Admirals Turner at CIA and Inman at NSA did not get along. Turner thought NSA's use of the term "combat brigade" crossed the line between intelligence collection, which is NSA's proper role, and analysis, which is not NSA's job.

It did not take long for the NSA report to find its way to Sen. Richard B. Stone, D-Fla., who asked Secretary of Defense Harold Brown about it at a closed hearing of the Senate Foreign Relations Committee on July 17. Brown denied the report. Stone sent a letter about it to President Carter. Secretary of State Cyrus Vance, replying on behalf of the president, also denied it. The story leaked to the press but did not attract particular attention.

There the matter rested until the third week in August, when satellite photography confirmed the presence in Cuba of a Soviet armed forces unit of between 2,000 and 3,000 men with tanks, artillery, and armored personnel carriers. The intelligence community thought elements of the unit had been in Cuba for at least three years. Congress was in recess, but the State Department reported the substance of this finding to various members of Congress including Senator Stone and Sen. Frank Church, D-Idaho, chairman of the Senate Foreign Relations Committee. Candidates for reelection in 1980, Stone and

Church were both in a perilous political condition stemming primarily from their support in 1978 of the treaties relinquishing American control of the Panama Canal. Both, as it turned out, were defeated.

During the summer of 1979, the Senate Foreign Relations Committee also was considering the SALT II treaty with the Soviet Union for the further limitation of nuclear weapons. Cuba had been a sore point in U.S.-Soviet relations for twenty years and adding a new irritant was doubly dangerous for Democratic senators already in political trouble.

Church's reaction to the information he received from the State Department about the Soviet troops was to call a press conference in Idaho, where he was campaigning. He made the information public and demanded that the troops be removed. The affair escalated from that point into a domestic political issue as well as an issue in U.S.-Soviet relations. Domestically, opponents of SALT II, and of détente with the Soviet Union, raised a cry that the Carter administration should demand the withdrawal of all Soviet military personnel from Cuba, step up intelligence overflights, and increase military readiness. The Senate adopted a resolution that SALT II could not be ratified so long as Soviet troops were in a combat role in Cuba. The divisions between Brzezinski and the State Department were such that some press reports had Brzezinski siding with opponents of the administration. On the international front, the affair put new strains on U.S.-Soviet relations, and the Soviets found their suspicions reinforced that the whole thing was contrived by double-dealing Americans.

Then, in the middle of October 1979, McGeorge Bundy, who had been national security adviser during the 1962 missile crisis, confirmed that the Kennedy administration had agreed that a Soviet brigade could remain in Cuba at the same location where the one in controversy had been found in 1979. Robert McNamara, the secretary of defense in 1962 had testified to this effect to the Senate Armed Services Committee at that time.[66]

As a kind of postscript to the cold war, it was announced in Havana in September 1992 that Russia and Cuba had agreed that the brigade would be withdrawn. The withdrawal was completed July 6, 1993.

CONCLUSIONS ON CUBA.   This triptych of flawed intelligence has several lessons, in addition to those already mentioned, for both analysts and policy makers. The Bay of Pigs demonstrates the unwisdom of putting intelligence analysis in the sole hands of those conducting the operation. The CIA attempts to meet this problem by separating the covert action people in the directorate of operations from the analysts in the directorate of intelligence. There are some who think this separation is insufficient, but in the case of the Bay of Pigs, it was overdone. The directorate of intelligence was told nothing. In other cases it is not told everything.

An additional lesson from the Bay of Pigs is that policy makers should temper the analytic product with their own judgment. One of the reasons they got to be policy makers in the first place is that they are presumed to have good judgment. There were plenty of advance indications, unrelated to intelligence reports, that the Bay of Pigs was a bad idea. In fact, a powerful argument against it was made to President Kennedy by Sen. J. W. Fulbright, D-Ark., then chairman of the Foreign Relations Committee, who was not privy to the intelligence.[67]

The mistaken analysis that failed to warn of the missile crisis appears to have been no more than an error in judgment. The DCI, whose hunch was correct, did not try to ram it down the throats of his analysts. If he had been in Washington instead of on his honeymoon, overflights might have been ordered earlier. Whether the course of the crisis would have been any different if the United States had known about it earlier is an open question. And it seems unreasonable to expect even directors of central intelligence to forgo honeymoons.

The Soviet brigade has all the elements of a classic Washington story—bureaucratic rivalries, personal animosities, policy differences, live-or-die politics. At the heart of the story is the premature leak of intelligence and its use in both a policy dispute (the SALT II debate) and in a political context (Senate elections in Idaho and Florida). The leak would still not have mattered if there had been adequate institutional memory (or perhaps the inclination to use it) in either the Senate Armed Services Committee or the Defense Department. In both these institutions it was known that the existence of the brigade had been expressly agreed to in 1962, but nobody said so until the uproar had run its course.

CONCLUSION

Intelligence analysis is about making predictions, but it is more than that. It is about describing a foreign government, or political system, or society so that a policy maker can understand the limits of what might be expected from that country. Nevertheless, analysis is usually judged by a scorecard of how many times it has been right or wrong in predicting major events. This is somewhat unfair because, among other reasons, critics usually focus on mistakes in a search for ways to do things better. It is appropriate, therefore, to note here three spectacular analytic successes.

The CIA was surprised by the Arab-Israeli war in 1973 (as was Israel's Mossad, for that matter), but the CIA was right on target in anticipating the 1967 war. Similarly, in 1983 the entire intelligence community was pessimistic about the chances for accomplishing American objectives in Lebanon. The only argument was between the CIA (which rated the chances "bleak") and Defense (which rated them "nonexistent").[68] President Reagan sent the marines anyway, and the mission was a failure.

In 1991 the CIA was right again about the breakup of Yugoslavia. Policy makers paid no attention. The problem was too tough, especially in light of all the other things the United States had to deal with at that time.

So at worst, the CIA's record on intelligence analysis is mixed. The question is how to make it better.

Frustrated and annoyed by what struck him as a babel of competing voices from intelligence agencies, President Truman wanted intelligence *centralized*. So he got the CIA. A good case can be made for centralizing analysis in the CIA: it is the only part of the intelligence community without an institutional or bureaucratic stake in foreign policy. But the preponderance of opinion accepts the wisdom of the old adage about two heads being better than one.

James R. Schlesinger has been both DCI and secretary of defense. He is one of many who have stressed the desirability of competitive analysis—that is, analysis done by a number of people who have different points of view and who argue with each other about different interpretations.[69] This is indeed how the system is supposed to work, but there are practical and institutional limitations.

The practical limitation is numbers: only so many people can be involved. The institutional limitation is how the participants engage in the process. If the product is a lowest-common-denominator consensus, or if it is a statement loaded with dissenting footnotes that do not argue the point, then it is useless. It is equally useless, or worse, if it is regarded by participants as a marketplace for bureaucratic trade-offs. Former DCI Turner has pointed out that the Defense Intelligence Agency respects the uniformed services' aversion to analyses that might upset their programs in Congress; State and CIA, in turn, overcompensate for Defense Department bias.[70]

But when the system works, competitive analysis provides a safeguard against unchallenged acceptance of conventional wisdom. It provides a framework in which a devil's advocate can play a starring role. Competitive analysis is also a safeguard against bias, either that imposed from the top or that insinuated from below.

Analysis is not the sole prerogative of the intelligence community. It is one of the major responsibilities of the State Department's ambassadors and foreign service officers, and some of them are very good at it. The most prominent example of this perhaps is the long telegram George Kennan sent from Moscow in 1947 that became the basis for the policy of containment. The policy endured for more than forty years and was crowned with success in the breakup of the Soviet Union. It was built on a masterful analysis of the dynamics of the Soviet system. The gist of Kennan's argument was that if Soviet expansionism was prevented, internal changes would eventually make the Soviet bloc less aggressive.[71] Kennan wrote with the insights gained from years of study of the Soviet Union but without any of the secret data that we now think of as "intelligence."

In truth, the Foreign Service's reporting function overlaps with the CIA's collection function and with the intelligence community's analytic function. This unavoidably has led to tension in embassies and in Washington. In good circumstances it produces creative tension and informative competitive analysis. In bad circumstances it produces bureaucratic bickering.

There is general agreement that the independence of analysts must be preserved, but this does not mean separation from policy makers. On the contrary, analysts from Sherman Kent in 1949 to Robert Gates in 1991 have commented on the desirability of locating analysts and policy makers in physical proximity to each other. This facilitates understanding by analysts of what is important to policy makers and by policy makers of the problems of analysts.

The congressional intelligence committees have made some useful critiques of intelligence analysis in specific cases. It would probably be even more useful if Congress came to view itself, and came to be viewed by the community, as a consumer of intelligence on a par with, say, the National Security Council.

Most analytic products are more highly classified than they need to be. Some legitimately need to be secret because they cite secret intelligence as supporting evidence. Some need to be secret because we do not want a prediction of political disaster in Country X to become a self-fulfilling prophecy. Or we do not want the U.S. intelligence community's view of a foreign situation to influence developments there. But a great deal of analysis is classified because of bureaucratic inertia: the intelligence community has an institutional tilt toward secrecy. And even some information that ought to be secret could be edited for public consumption (the bureaucratic term is *sanitized*). This would inform public discussion, even as analysis now informs policy making.

NOTES

1. Thomas L. Hughes, *The Fate of Facts in a World of Men: Foreign Policy and Intelligence-Making* (New York: Foreign Policy Association, 1976), 24.
2. Charles R. Babcock, "An Opening to the Heart of the Process," *Washington Post*, Oct. 4, 1991.
3. Cited in Loch K. Johnson, "Smart Intelligence," *Foreign Policy* 89 (Winter 1992-1993): 53-69.
4. David Halberstam, *The Best and the Brightest* (New York: Random House, 1972), 359.
5. House Permanent Select Committee on Intelligence, *Pursuant to Clause 1(d) of Rule IX of the Rules of the House of Representatives*, H. Rept. 102-1082, 102d Cong., 2d sess., 1992.
6. Frank J. Smist, Jr., *Congress Oversees the United States Intelligence Community, 1947-1989* (Knoxville: University of Tennessee Press, 1990), 193, 202.
7. Senate Select Committee on Intelligence, *National Intelligence Reorganization and Reform Act of 1978*, Hearings, 95th Cong., 2d sess., 1978, 73.
8. Associated Press, "3 Senate Democrats Criticize Briefing by CIA on Caribbean," *Washington Post*, Dec. 23, 1981.
9. See Seymour M. Hersh, "A Reporter at Large: On the Nuclear Edge," *The New Yorker*, March 29, 1993, 56-73, especially 57, 60.
10. Daniel Williams, "U.S. Punishes China Over Missile Sales," *Washington Post*, Aug. 26, 1993.
11. R. Jeffrey Smith, "China May Have Revived Germ Weapons Program, U.S. Officials Say," *Washington Post*, Feb. 24, 1993.
12. William J. Mitchell, "When Is Seeing Believing?" *Scientific American*, February 1994, 68-73.
13. Senate Select Committee on Presidential Campaign Activities, *Presidential Campaign Activities of 1972*, Hearings, 93rd Cong., 1st sess., September 24 and 25, 1973, Book 9, 3668-3673, 3732-3734.
14. Benjamin Weiser, "CIA Nominee Remains an Enigma to Many," *Washington Post*, Sept. 16, 1991.
15. Sherman Kent, *Reminiscences of a Varied Life: An Autobiography* (San Rafael, Calif.: The Printing Factory, 1991), 263-264.
16. House Permanent Select Committee on Intelligence, Staff Report, *U.S. Intelligence Performance on Central America*, Committee Print, 97th Cong., 2d sess., 1982, 8.

17. Rep. C. W. Bill Young in *Congressional Record*, daily ed., October 1, 1982, E4631.
18. *Public Papers of the Presidents of the United States: Lyndon B. Johnson, 1965*, news conference, June 17, 1965, Book II, 678.
19. Senate Foreign Relations Committee, *Nomination of William Tapley Bennett, Jr., to Be Ambassador to Portugal*, May 3, 1966, 28. Unpublished transcript in National Archives.
20. Robert M. Gates, "The CIA and American Foreign Policy," *Foreign Affairs* 66 (Winter 1987/88): 221.
21. Quoted by Robert M. Gates in *The Future of American Intelligence*, an address to the intelligence community, December 4, 1991, 14. CIA release.
22. For an elaboration of these points, see Senate Intelligence Committee, *Nomination of Robert M. Gates*, Hearings, 102d Cong., 1st sess., 1991, vol. 1, 539-642.
23. Senate Select Committee on Intelligence, *The National Intelligence Estimates A-B Team Episode Concerning Soviet Strategic Capability and Objectives*, Committee Print, 95th Cong., 2d sess., 1978. See also Cecil V. Crabb, Jr. and Pat M. Holt, *Invitation to Struggle: Congress, the President, and Foreign Policy*, 4th ed. (Washington, D.C.: CQ Press, 1992), 182.
24. Patrick E. Tyler, "Cheney Finds CIA Director Is No Comrade in Arms," *Washington Post*, March 6, 1990.
25. George Lardner, Jr., "Republics' Procurement of Arms Said to Plunge," *Washington Post*, Jan. 23, 1992.
26. R. Jeffrey Smith, "Aspin: U.S. Suppressing Data on Cuts," *Washington Post*, Nov. 17, 1989.
27. Senate Foreign Relations Committee, *Estimating the Size and Growth of the Soviet Economy*, Senate Hearing 101-1112, 101st Cong., 2d sess., 1990, 4.
28. House Intelligence Committee, *U.S. Intelligence Performance on Central America*, 12.
29. Robert E. White, statement to author, March 13, 1992.
30. Robert E. White, "Renewal in El Salvador," *Washington Post*, Jan. 16, 1992.
31. John M. Goshko, "Reagan-Era 'Tough Guy' on Latin America Policy," *Washington Post*, Oct. 8, 1981.
32. Joanne Omang, "Analyst Says He Quit CIA When Casey Altered His Report to Support Policy," *Washington Post*, Sept. 28, 1984.
33. John Horton, "Why I Quit the CIA," *Washington Post*, Jan. 2, 1985.
34. Text in *New York Times*, Feb. 24, 1981.
35. Lee H. Hamilton, "The Costs of Too Much Secrecy," *Washington Post*, April 13, 1992.
36. House Intelligence Committee, *U.S. Intelligence Performance on Central America*, 1.
37. "The House Permanent Select Committee on Intelligence Staff Report on Central America," Extension of Remarks of Hon. C.W. Bill Young, *Congressional Record*, daily ed., October 1, 1982, E4631-E4632.
38. House Intelligence Committee, *U.S. Intelligence Performance on Central America*, 1.
39. P.L. 96-257, approved May 31, 1980, 94 Stat. 422.
40. "Economic Assistance to Nicaragua," *Weekly Compilation of Presidential Documents*, September 15, 1980, 1712.
41. House Intelligence Committee, *U.S. Intelligence Performance on Central America*, 7.
42. This phraseology is from the International Security and Development Cooperation Act of 1981 (P.L. 97-113, approved December 29, 1981). Subsequent laws had comparable provisions.

43. See *Congressional Quarterly Weekly Report*, January 29, 1983, 217-219.
44. Lou Cannon and Charles Fishman, "Reagan to Seek Additional Aid for Region," *Washington Post*, July 21, 1983.
45. For Abrams and Hinton quotes, and much more, see Mark Danner, "The Truth of El Mozote," *New Yorker*, December 6, 1993, 50-133, at 97-98.
46. U.S. Department of State, *Report of the Secretary of State's Panel on El Salvador*, July 1993, 1.
47. See Danner, "The Truth of El Mozote," 106-124.
48. Transcript, Samuel A. Adams Oral History Interview, September 20, 1984, by Ted Gittinger, Interview 1, 42. Lyndon Baines Johnson Library, Austin, Texas.
49. Text in *New York Times*, Feb. 19, 1985.
50. Richard Helms, interviewed by Paige Mulhollan, April 4, 1969, 12-13. Lyndon Baines Johnson Library, Austin, Texas.
51. Thomas L. Hughes, "The Power to Speak and the Power to Listen: Reflections on Bureaucratic Politics and a Recommendation on Information Flows," in *Secrecy and Foreign Policy*, ed. Thomas M. Franck and Edward Weisband (New York: Oxford University Press, 1974), 17.
52. Benjamin Weiser, "CIA Nominee Remains an Enigma to Many," *Washington Post*, Sept. 16, 1991.
53. House Permanent Select Committee on Intelligence, Staff Report, *Iran: Evaluation of U.S. Intelligence Performance Prior to November 1978*, Committee Print, January 1979, 6-7.
54. Press conference, December 12, 1978; text in *Weekly Compilation of Presidential Documents*, December 18, 1978, 2226.
55. Press conference, November 30, 1978; text in *Weekly Compilation of Presidential Documents*, December 4, 1978, 2103.
56. Seymour M. Hersh, "Brzezinski Is Said to Have Rejected Warnings about Problems in Iran," *New York Times*, Dec. 21, 1978.
57. Gary Sick, *All Fall Down: America's Tragic Encounter with Iran* (New York: Random House, 1985), 38-42.
58. House Intelligence Committee, *Iran*, 8.
59. Stansfield Turner, *Secrecy and Democracy: The CIA in Transition* (Boston: Houghton Mifflin, 1985), 116.
60. There has been some confusion over the firmness of Kennedy's decision not to use U.S. forces. The record indicates Kennedy himself was firm. The confusion arose because (1) the Cubans did not want to believe what they were being told by the White House, and (2) they might have been getting less categorical statements from lower level U.S. military and CIA officials. See Peter Wyden, *Bay of Pigs: The Untold Story* (New York: Simon and Schuster, 1979), 161; and Arthur M. Schlesinger, Jr., *A Thousand Days: John F. Kennedy in the White House* (Boston: Houghton Mifflin, 1965), 262-264.
61. P.L. 87-733, approved October 3, 1962, 76 Stat. 697.
62. Thomas L. Hughes, *The Fate of Facts in a World of Men: Foreign Policy and Intelligence-Making* (New York: Foreign Policy Association, 1976), 44.
63. Eric Schmitt, "Once More Unto the Brink: Cuban Crisis Relived," *New York Times*, Oct. 20, 1992.
64. Associated Press, "During Cuba Crisis, U.S. Faced A-Arms with 40-Mile Range," *New York Times*, Jan. 14, 1992; and Martin Tolchin, "U.S. Underestimated Soviet Force in Cuba During '62 Missile Crisis," *New York Times*, Jan. 15, 1992. See also Anatoli I. Gribkov and William Y. Smith, *Operation ANADYR: U.S. and Soviet Generals Recount the Cuban Missile Crisis* (Chicago: Edition Q, 1994).

65. Stansfield Turner, "Foreword," in David D. Newsom, *The Soviet Brigade in Cuba* (Bloomington: Indiana University Press, 1987), vii.
66. This account draws heavily on Newsom, *The Soviet Brigade in Cuba*.
67. See Schlesinger, *A Thousand Days*, 251-252; and Wyden, *Bay of Pigs*, 120-152.
68. Senate Intelligence Committee, *Nomination of Robert M. Gates*, 566.
69. See his statement before the Senate Intelligence Committee, February 20, 1991. Unpublished transcript.
70. Stansfield Turner, "The Pentagon's Intelligence Mess," *Washington Post*, Jan. 12, 1986.
71. See "X" (Pseudonym for George Kennan), "The Sources of Soviet Conduct," *Foreign Affairs* 25 (July 1947): 566-582.

CHAPTER 6

Counterintelligence

*J. Edgar Hoover never took orders from an attorney general, rarely
from a president, only occasionally from God.*
—Former high-ranking official in the State Department

Counterintelligence is unique in the intelligence community because it is
where foreign intelligence goes domestic. It is where the techniques of espionage collide most directly with the restraints of the U.S. Constitution. It is
where distinctions clearly drawn in concept are easily blurred in practice—between loyalty risks and security risks, subversion and dissent, treachery and
patriotism, orthodoxy and nonconformity. It is where the cold war impinged
most directly on American life.

The purpose of counterintelligence is to keep the other fellow from doing
to you what you are trying to do to him. In the technical jargon the purpose "is
to discover hostile foreign intelligence operations and destroy their effectiveness." It includes counterespionage (efforts to penetrate a hostile intelligence
service), countersabotage, and countersubversion.[1]

Counterintelligence is basically concerned with protecting the government's secrets. An important part of this work is penetrating foreign intelligence services so that we know what techniques they use against us. A penetration might also identify foreign agents working against us (some of whom
might be people we thought were working for us). Although complicated, this
is still a finite task. But include the number of secrets the government has, the
number of people who have access to them, bureaucratic friction within and
between intelligence agencies, and the frenzy of the cold war, and you have the
recipe for a witch's brew of hysteria, demagoguery, and confusion.

PROTECTING SECRETS

The government has a method for identifying the material that it deems
worthy of protection. It calls this method "classification." Surprisingly, in a
government where so much emphasis is put on openness and public access,
these rules have not been enacted by Congress after public debate but have been
proclaimed by a succession of presidents after private consideration. The version that has been in effect since 1982 is contained in Executive Order 12356,
National Security Information, issued by President Ronald Reagan.[2]

The order defines national security information as "information that has been determined pursuant to this Order or any predecessor order to require protection against unauthorized disclosure and that is so designated" (Sec. 6.1 (c)). This information is classified in three levels in descending order of sensitivity: Top Secret, Secret, and Confidential. The level of classification depends on the degree of damage unauthorized disclosure "reasonably could be expected to cause . . . to the national security." In the case of Top Secret information, this damage must be "exceptionally grave." In the case of Secret, it must be "serious." And in the case of Confidential, it must simply be "damage" (Sec.1.1(a)). All of these criteria are totally subjective. The executive order gives no hint of guidance to the official who is trying to decide whether a document should be classified and if so at what level. There is a further level of classification not mentioned in the executive order. It is based on codewords and arises from the intelligence community's penchant for compartmentation. The classification is used to limit the distribution of intelligence based on particularly sensitive sources. Such intelligence is classified, say, TOP SECRET HULAHOOP, or SECRET PANDORA, or whatever the codeword is. (Hulahoop and Pandora are fictitious but illustrative.) To get access to this national security information, you have to be cleared not only for Top Secret but also for Hulahoop; not only for Secret, but also for Pandora.

The executive order not only provides no standards for distinguishing between "exceptionally grave" and "serious" damage; its definition of national security information subject to classification is truly all-embracing. The order sets forth ten subjects, as follows (Sec. 1.3.):

1. Military plans, weapons, or operations.
2. "The vulnerabilities or capabilities of systems, installations, projects, or plans relating to the national security." (This is broad and vague at the same time. What does it mean?)
3. "Foreign government information." (This is not as ridiculous as it sounds. Elsewhere (sec. 6.1(d)) "foreign government information" is defined as being information either supplied by, or developed in conjunction with, a foreign government on the understanding that it will remain confidential. Thus, on inspection, this requirement is quite reasonable: if you learn something in confidence, you should hold it in confidence.)
4. "Intelligence activities (including special activities [that is, covert action]), or intelligence sources or methods."
5. "Foreign relations or foreign activities of the United States." (A catch-all phrase if there ever was one.)
6. "Scientific, technological, or economic matters relating to the national security."
7. Government programs for safeguarding nuclear materials or facilities.
8. Cryptology.
9. A confidential source.
10. "Other categories of information that are related to the national security and that require protection against unauthorized disclosure as determined by the President or by agency heads or other officials who

have been delegated original classification authority by the President." (In this paragraph, the drafters of the executive order are saying, in effect, "if we forgot anything, you can use this authority to make up for it.")

This question now arises: who within the government has authority to determine that a particular piece of information is so important to national security that it ought to be protected at one of the three classification levels? The higher the classification, the fewer the number of officials who have authority to impose it. These officials are designated in writing, by the president or by selected agency heads who have themselves been designated by the president.

In 1993 there were 5,661 people in the federal government who had the legal authority to say a document contained classified information. This was the smallest number since the issuance of the Reagan order in 1982. Of the total, 1,361 were authorized to classify at the Top Secret level, 3,218 at the Secret level, and 1,082 at the Confidential level.

These officials classified a total of 245,951 documents in fiscal 1993. Of these, 18,145 were Top Secret, 129,820 were Secret, and 97,986 were Confidential.

Most classified documents are derivative—that is, they do not contain original information and are classified because they restate, or otherwise refer to, information that has already been classified in a previous document. In fiscal 1993, derivative classification was given to 6,162,737 documents (Top Secret, 695,740; Secret, 4,476,493; Confidential 990,504). Thus, the government's hoard of secrets (new and derivative classifications) increased by 6,408,688.[3]

This is a minor fraction of the total, which is counted in hundreds of millions of pages, some of them forty years old or more. The rate of growth has been diminishing. Since 1972, there has been a program of systematic review for declassification of documents as they become thirty years old; certain intelligence and cryptologic records are not reviewed until they are fifty years old. In 1993, 9.0 million pages were so reviewed, and 6.6 million were declassified.

Most classified documents originate in four agencies. In order of volume classified in 1993, they are Defense, Justice, CIA, and State, but when derivative classifications are added, Defense and CIA have more than the others.

To oversee this system, the Reagan executive order established the Information Security Oversight Office, which is charged with reviewing agencies' classification practices. Do they classify documents at the proper level? Are they conscientious about declassification review? Do they have adequate internal programs for safeguarding classified information? The director of the office is given broad authority to review pertinent agency regulations and guidelines and to conduct on-site reviews of agency operations.

By the spring of 1994, a number of proposals for change were emerging from discussions in both the executive branch and Congress. The Clinton administration was working on a new executive order to replace the one issued by President Reagan, and both congressional intelligence committees were considering legislative action. In June 1993 Les Aspin, the secretary of defense at the time, and DCI Woolsey had appointed a Joint Security Commission to review security requirements and procedures. Headed by Washington lawyer Jeffrey H.

Smith, the commission reported in February 1994 its recommendations to simplify classification categories, give new attention to the security of information systems, and revise personnel security standards.[4]

PHYSICAL SECURITY

There are elaborate rules for protecting the physical security of this mountain of classified documents. The higher the level of classification, the more elaborate the rules become.

Measures to increase the physical security of documents make it more difficult to use them. Sign-in, sign-out procedures for entering or leaving offices become more complicated. Offices and files acquire more, and more sophisticated, locks. Rooms are de-bugged, or swept for listening devices, and then the procedure is repeated, even though the room has been secured under constant watch. Telephones, electric typewriters, and computers are viewed with grim suspicion: they are all subject to penetration, so much so that in some cases they become virtually useless. A document can't simply be thrown away; it has to be burned or shredded under the supervision of an armed guard. Briefcases are inspected when the users of the documents leave the secure area. All of this may not cause paralysis, but it does cause inefficiency.

Some of these procedures are directed against electronic penetration of offices and conference rooms. When, and if, these penetrations occur, they are rarely publicized. A notable exception is the new American embassy in Moscow, which was found to be honeycombed with listening devices in 1985 while it was still under construction. Anecdotal evidence suggests that other penetrations may have occurred more frequently than has been admitted. After Attorney General Robert F. Kennedy visited Poland in the summer of 1964, it was discovered that the American embassy offices, in Ambassador John Moors Cabot's phrase, were "terribly bugged." This gave Cabot some wry comfort. It meant that the Polish government must have learned that Kennedy had managed to irritate the embassy as much as he did the government.[5] (Kennedy went to Poland despite the Polish government's refusal to invite him. He attracted huge throngs, whom he twice addressed from the top of Cabot's ambassadorial limousine, damaging the roof. He was an hour late to an official dinner at the embassy. Both Kennedy and Cabot were from Boston, but the culture gap between them was wide and deep. Cabot was a proper Bostonian who had been long schooled in the proper ways of the Foreign Service.)[6]

The procedures for physical security are also designed to guard against theft or careless loss of classified documents. For this purpose the procedures are a nuisance—overdone, misdirected, and ineffective. Missing documents usually have not been stolen by foreign spies or snooping reporters but misplaced or taken by Americans who have approved access to them.

One of the most damaging cases of espionage against the United States was carried on for years by a navy spy ring headed by John A. Walker, Jr. The ring consisted of Walker, his brother, his son, and a friend—all members of the uniformed navy. From 1968 to 1985 they sold navy codes to the Soviet Union. They simply walked away from navy code rooms carrying the material they wanted. This might not have been detected at all if the leader's ex-wife had not gotten mad enough at him to call the FBI.

A similar but less serious case involved Randy Miles Jeffries, a messenger for a reporting firm that provided stenographic transcripts of congressional committee hearings, including those dealing with classified defense matters. In December 1985 Jeffries telephoned the Soviet embassy with an offer to sell. He got a call back from an FBI agent impersonating a Russian (complete with accent) and was arrested after meeting with the undercover FBI agent.[7]

PERSONNEL SECURITY

As the Walker and Jeffries cases suggest, the protection of classified information has less to do with the physical security of documents than with the trustworthiness of the people entrusted with the documents.

There are three aspects of personnel security. One is ensuring, as far as possible, that the people who are given access to secrets will keep secrets and will be discreet and responsible. The second is watching for evidence that they are not reliable. The third is looking for and watching the foreign intelligence officers who might be trying to tempt them.

WHO GETS ACCESS?   The government certifies that an individual is sufficiently reliable to be trusted with its secrets by bestowing on him or her a security clearance. This figurative anointment follows an investigation, the rigor of which depends on the level of classification of the information for which clearance is granted. The highest levels of clearance require a full field investigation by the FBI. This usually takes weeks, sometimes months if the individual has lived abroad or changed jobs often. In a full field investigation, the FBI talks to almost everybody it can find who has ever had anything to do with the person being investigated—former teachers, classmates, roommates, neighbors, employers, employees, colleagues, relatives, members of the clergy, ex-spouses (or girl- or boyfriends). School, police, and credit records are consulted. The results are reported, including details of personal habits, but are not evaluated. The evaluation is made, and the security clearance is issued or withheld, by the security office of the individual's employing agency, sometimes by the head of the agency, even a member of the cabinet or the president himself.

Members of Congress are presumed to have been cleared when they were elected. They are not further investigated, though the FBI kept files on some of them during the reign of J. Edgar Hoover. Congress is rightly obsessed with the equality of its members. Rules of both houses provide that every member is entitled to see all the files of every committee. This has caused some executive branch officials to swallow hard before revealing certain sensitive information; but at least as far as the intelligence committees are concerned, the sharing of such information has been surrounded by enough safeguards that it has not been a problem (see Chapter 10). Congressional staff members are investigated in the same way as employees of the executive branch. Staff clearances are issued or withheld by the employing committee or member on the basis of the FBI reports. In the case of the Senate Intelligence Committee, the FBI reports are also sent to the DCI, who can raise a question but cannot exercise a veto.

Besides the FBI, some agencies have their own security investigators, and so there are notable overlaps. Multiple security offices have created multiple bureaucratic interests in perpetuating the system. These have given birth to requirements that persons holding security clearances, especially top secret clearances, be reinvestigated at intervals. These requirements have at least as much to do with protecting the job security of the investigators as with protecting the national security of the United States. A serious reinvestigation of John Walker might well have revealed his espionage at an earlier stage. After Walker's arrest, he told the FBI that he had forged his last security clearance.

Serious reinvestigation would certainly have led to earlier action against Aldrich H. Ames and his wife, Rosario, who pleaded guilty in April 1994 to charges of spying for the Russians. Over a period of nine years, beginning in 1985, Ames gave the KGB and its successor agency (the SVRR) the names of Russian agents working for the CIA. At least ten Russians and one East European were executed as a consequence. In return, Ames received approximately $2.5 million. Ames was sentenced to life in prison with no possibility of parole. The government agreed to a lesser sentence for Mrs. Ames, the terms of which were to be determined depending on Ames's cooperation with the government during extensive questioning that began after his sentence. The incentive for this arrangement, from the Ames's point of view, was the welfare of their son, who was five years old at the time of their arrest. The incentive from the government's point of view was the information that Ames could provide, as well as his life-time imprisonment. An additional incentive for the government was to avoid a trial. There was the ever-present threat of the disclosure of more secrets in court, and a conviction was not assured.

The evolution of this case revealed a scenario in which all parties—the Ameses, the Russians, the FBI, and the CIA—violated basic rules of espionage and counterintelligence. Ames, a career CIA officer, was made chief of the Soviet counterintelligence branch in 1984 after his return from a tour in Mexico City. There he met Rosario de las Casas, cultural attaché of the Colombian embassy and a paid CIA agent. They were subsequently married in Washington, D.C. (The CIA's first mistake: why did it acquiesce in a marriage between one of its officers and a foreign national whom it knew to be unreliable? If she would sell out to the CIA when she was working for Colombia, she would sell out to somebody else.)

Beginning in about 1985, the CIA noticed that its agents in the KGB were disappearing. When the CIA began to try to track who might have known the identity of these agents, it discovered two hundred people. (Second mistake: this is far too many people to know the real identity of a foreign agent, as distinguished from the agent's cryptonym.)

Ames was in the CIA station in Rome from 1986 to 1989. On his return to CIA headquarters, he went on a spending spree—$540,000 in cash for a house in Arlington, Virginia, a Jaguar, credit card charges of $5,000 a month. (First mistake by Ames.) This spending was called to the CIA's attention, and the agency asked Ames about it. He said his wife had inherited money. The CIA's Bogotá station reported it could not find her father's will, and the CIA let it drop. (Third mistake.)

By 1991 the CIA was suspicious enough to transfer Ames to a less sensitive job in counternarcotics, but it did not cut off his access to classified documents in his old office. (Fourth mistake.) Ames even took the documents home with him. (Second mistake by Ames. Fifth mistake by CIA: carelessness in checking what leaves the headquarters building.)

Meanwhile, the Russians were sending Ames written instructions about what they wanted and even written statements of how much they were paying him. (Big mistake by Russians to put this in writing. Bigger mistake by Ames to keep it in his house, where the FBI eventually found it.) As is discussed further below, the Ames case also reverberated throughout the intelligence community, reigniting bureaucratic animosities.

The risk of a secret being revealed increases more than proportionately with the number of people who know it. As the sign in the office of a former Mafia figure said, "Three can keep a secret if two are dead." [8] The moral for intelligence services is to make secrets accessible to no more people than necessary. Security clearances should be limited.

Nobody knows the number of people who have authorized access to classified information, but it is very large. In 1985 military personnel, Defense Department civilians, and military contractor employees with some kind of security clearance totaled 4.3 million people.[9] And, of course, there were a large number in other agencies.

In the aftermath of the Walker spy case, the Defense Department in general and the navy in particular reduced the number of people holding security clearances. At the time the reductions were ordered, 900,000 of the navy's 1,010,000 uniformed personnel and civilian employees held some level of clearance. Within a month this number was reduced by 19 percent.[10] But experience with such reduction programs indicates that they tend to be transitory. In any event, the security failure in the Walker case was not the result of too many people having clearances; it was the result of the wrong people having them. As long as the navy is going to use codes for its communications, *somebody* is going to have to be cleared to handle the codes.

Surely, one would think, something that is potentially known to 4 million people cannot be very secret. But the secrets the government is really trying to protect are not potentially known to that many, or even to almost that many. The higher the level of classification, or the more sensitive the compartmented classification, the harder it is to get a security clearance. There are two standards for weeding people out. One has to do with personal reliability; the other with the need to know. This latter standard becomes stricter as the information becomes more sensitive. It does not matter how reliable you may be; if you do not need the information protected by a particular codeword-compartmented classification in order to do your job, you are not cleared for access to that classification.

At least that's the way the system is supposed to work. Trying to limit either the amount of information that is classified or the number of people with access to it is a losing battle. This is particularly true of the number of people with access. In many areas of the government, congressional staffs prominent among them, an exotic security clearance is a mark of prestige and much sought after, even if rarely used. This kind of pressure is hard for some supervisors to resist. And among defense contractors, consulting firms, and think tanks, a security clearance is literally the staff of life—no clearance, no contract, no job.

In keeping with this principle, the CIA compartmentalizes intelligence— that is, officers operate in compartments separated from each other, and each is privy only to the intelligence that is directly related to his or her current assignment. This reduces the number of people who know any given fact, and thereby it reduces the possibility of exposure.

But it also reduces the possibility of an officer relating one piece of intelligence to another piece. Excessive compartmentation sometimes hinders operational efficiency. Analysts may not see all of a picture. Some collection programs or covert actions may work at crosspurposes.

At the beginning of the cold war in the late 1940s, the question of who got a security clearance was muddied by a wave of public excitement engendered by spy scares and concern over the devious and underhanded techniques of Communist and Soviet subversion. Superpower rivalry between the United States and the Soviet Union was transformed into ideological war between democracy and communism. The fervor of this war was increased by the Soviet Union's acquisition of nuclear weapons earlier than most people in the West had thought possible and by the revelation that this acquisition had been aided by espionage. The level and character of public alarm reminded some of the atmosphere of Salem, Massachusetts, during the witch hunts of the seventeenth century. The distinguished dramatist Arthur Miller even wrote a successful play (*The Crucible*) calling attention to this parallel.

Just when the government was trying to improve the security of employees who dealt with secrets, Congress and the public began to demand procedures to ensure the loyalty of all employees. Loyalty review boards in all agencies attempted to enforce an earlier version of political correctness. There is a difference between security and loyalty. A security risk is somebody who talks too much (because he or she likes to gossip), or drinks too much, or is simply careless or irresponsible. A loyalty risk is somebody who is likely to betray his or her country. All loyalty risks, by definition, are security risks, but not all security risks are loyalty risks. Counterintelligence is interested in guarding against persons who are security risks and who also have access to classified information. Of no counterintelligence interest is a person, regardless of ideology or personal habits, who has no access to classified information.

In the late 1940s the House Un-American Activities Committee held a series of heavily publicized hearings in which it blurred these distinctions almost to the point of obliteration. Established in the 1930s, the committee originally devoted itself to searching out Nazis and Nazi sympathizers. After World War II it hunted Communists. Among other things, it uncovered the case of Alger Hiss, a State Department official who was subsequently convicted of perjury for denying his involvement in a pre-World War II Communist group. This was the case that first brought Richard M. Nixon, then a young Congressman from California, to public attention. From 1950 until the Senate finally reined him in with a vote of censure in 1954, Sen. Joseph McCarthy, R-Wis., spread terror throughout the government with reckless charges of communism and other security risks in the State Department and other agencies. Under its long-time director, J. Edgar Hoover, the FBI acquired a reputation for snooping into the personal lives of people it was investigating. Hoover surreptitiously fed data from his supposedly confidential files both to the Un-American Activities Committee in the House and to McCarthy in the Senate.

The hysteria engendered by McCarthyism lingered for a generation. One could not confidently say it had been put to rest until a new wave of espionage cases in the 1980s failed to revive it.

LOOKING FOR SPIES.   A foreign intelligence service tries to learn U.S. secrets the same way the U.S. intelligence community tries to learn foreign secrets—that is, through human sources and technical means. It is to guard against technical penetrations that the United States takes the elaborate physical security precautions described above. These are generally effective, at least as far as is known publicly. The elaborate bugging of the new American embassy in Moscow and occasional bugging of other installations appear to be exceptions.

Human sources offer foreign intelligence services more rewarding targets. These sources are among the many Americans in and out of the government who have passed security investigations and have been cleared for access to the nation's secrets. Some security breaches occur inadvertently—perhaps through careless talk in a public place, an ill-considered remark in a press conference or a speech in Congress. Some occur systematically. These involve Americans who have been recruited by foreign intelligence services and who report to those services on a more or less regular basis. Such Americans become agents of foreign intelligence services in the same way that certain foreigners become agents of the CIA. The most damaging security breaches come from Americans who seek out a foreign service and volunteer to supply it with secrets.

Security investigations and other precautions, no matter how careful, are less than 100 percent effective, and the question arises of how to supplement or reinforce them. Every agency in the intelligence community has its own security staff that watches to see that prescribed procedures are followed. But the Federal Bureau of Investigation is the lead counterintelligence agency. Espionage and related acts are crimes, and the FBI is the federal government's principal law enforcement agency.

The efficiency of counterintelligence would be enhanced if it concentrated on doing less better. Give most attention to the few types of information foreign intelligence agencies most want to learn: technical data (a great deal of this is available in open sources, and its acquisition is entirely legal; some, including data relating to nuclear and other advanced weapons, is highly classified); codes and cryptologic devices; the United States' own intelligence sources and methods; and diplomatic plans and negotiating positions.

The Americans who know about these things (a tiny fraction of those who have security clearances) form the pool of targets of foreign intelligence services. They are also the ones of greatest interest to the FBI.

Most of the people in this group go about their jobs in an unremarkable way and are good at what they do. They may be a small percentage of the total who have security clearances, but there are still too many for all of them to be watched (not to mention the legal problems that such surveillance would entail). How can one of them be picked out of the pack? This depends on dumb luck, the alertness of colleagues, and possibly an agency's own security office.

There are some telltale signs to look for. One is a change in lifestyle, with spending beyond what his (almost all have been men) salary would support. Have his children started going to expensive private schools? Has he changed from a Ford to a Mercedes Benz? Maybe a rich uncle died, but maybe he's being paid by somebody else.

Conversely, evidence of financial difficulty is also a danger signal. Has he suddenly acquired family obligations that he cannot meet—aged parents, huge medical bills, an expensive divorce? Is he desperate to find an outside source of money?

Another tipoff is frequent leave for short trips where there has been no pattern of this in the past. Where is he going and whom is he meeting? If he is going to Vienna or Mexico City, favored by Russians for clandestine meetings, be especially vigilant.

Has there been a sudden, marked interest in the office in matters that are not directly related to his work and in which he has not previously shown much interest? Finally, can one discern a sudden drop in morale in his approach to his job? Has he been denied a raise or promotion or coveted transfer? Is he bearing a grudge? Counterintelligence officers should be asking these questions and closely heeding the answers.

In response to the rash of spy prosecutions in the 1980s, the Senate Intelligence Committee appointed a distinguished panel of outside experts to recommend improvements in counterintelligence. The panel was headed by Baltimore businessman Eli S. Jacobs, and it made thirteen legislative proposals. Some have been enacted—for example, authority for the National Security Agency to provide special financial assistance to former employees. Other proposals would give the FBI access to bank and credit card records.

Former employees no longer have access to documents. If they turn into spies, they must rely on their memories, which can be very damaging. This was the case with Ronald Pelton, who worked for NSA from 1965 until 1979 and then fed his recollections to the KGB from 1980 until he was arrested in 1985. He might never have been caught if a Soviet defector had not told the CIA that the KGB was getting material from a former NSA employee. The defector did not know the employee's name, but his revelation started an FBI search that eventually led to Pelton.

Unless a spy is caught with incriminating documents in his possession, or in the act of passing information to a foreign agent, it is difficult to prosecute him successfully without his cooperation—that is, unless he is willing to discuss his activities with FBI agents. A surprising number of spies admit their espionage when confronted by the FBI. It is to avoid being caught in the act that so many transfers take place outside the United States. Vienna was favored by the Soviet Union.

If the suspect is uncooperative, it may be impractical to prosecute him; the most persuasive evidence against him may not be admissible in court. Erich Bloch, a foreign service officer who had served in Berlin and Vienna, provides a case in point. Bloch had been under investigation since at least 1989 after he had reportedly been seen (or photographed, in one version) passing a suitcase to a KGB officer in Paris. By 1990, when he was assigned in Washington, he was put on leave, his $80,000-a-year salary was suspended, and the State Department began proceedings to fire him. The FBI was said to be keeping Bloch under surveillance but without results.

The media immediately joined the FBI in the Bloch watch, and television crews descended on the Washington neighborhood (near the Chinese embassy) where he lived. He was shown going to the supermarket trailed by camera crews, sound technicians, reporters, and, presumably, FBI agents. But he remained silent.

The supposition was that the FBI had become frustrated by Bloch's noncooperation and by its inability to secure more evidence and had leaked the story in the hope that publicity might bring matters to a head. It did not. Bloch tried to resign from the Foreign Service, but the State Department insisted on firing him, and it also canceled his pension, which would have been something more than $50,000 a year. A year later the Justice Department was still interviewing potential witnesses in Europe. In 1993 a news item from Chapel Hill, North Carolina, reported that Bloch had been arrested for shoplifting groceries from the supermarket where he worked as a cashier.[11] The moral for a spy is: if you don't say *anything*, you're going to make it very much harder for them to convict you, but they can still cause you a lot of trouble.

Another case that illustrates how counterintelligence works—and sometimes doesn't work—is that of Edward Lee Howard. First, the CIA did not even know Howard had defected until it was told by a KGB defector. Second, the case demonstrates that it is difficult to catch a clever spy even after you know about him. Among other reasons, the spy's techniques for evading surveillance are becoming more sophisticated. When he realized he was under suspicion, Howard used the techniques he had been taught by the CIA (he reportedly ranked first in his class in countersurveillance) to elude the FBI and eventually make his way to Moscow.

Howard, then twenty-nine, was hired by the CIA in 1981 and slated for assignment to Moscow. He and his wife, Mary, were trained as a team. It was intended that Howard would handle U.S. agents in place in Moscow, and he was fully briefed on methods of operating in that city, then tightly constricted. But before Howard's departure, the Soviet division of the CIA began having second thoughts about him because of his past record of drug use and heavy drinking and questionable results of a polygraph examination. At first the CIA intended to reassign him to a less sensitive position, but after further consideration, it decided to fire him in 1983. This action violated a principle of counterintelligence: Don't give somebody who knows a great many secrets (especially somebody with an apparently unstable personality) a reason to hold a grudge.

By answering a help-wanted ad, Howard got a job with the New Mexico legislature. Over the next couple of years, he made several trips to Europe. In the summer of 1985, Col. Vitaly Yurchenko of the KGB defected to the CIA. Yurchenko talked of a former CIA officer (the only one, he said, whom the KGB had ever had) who had told the KGB about the CIA's Moscow operations. Yurchenko knew this person only as "Roger," but the CIA quickly identified Howard and sent the FBI to New Mexico. As his CIA trainers had taught him,

Howard left the FBI watching the wrong exit from his house.[12] He eventually made his way to Moscow.

WHEN A SPY IS CAUGHT.   The first impulse, especially in the Department of Justice, is to throw the spy out of the country if he has diplomatic immunity or to throw him in jail if he does not. But there may be reasons to do something else.

If he has diplomatic immunity, the technical term for throwing him out of the country is to declare him *persona non grata*. That is a nice all-purpose phrase, and you don't even have to say with any specificity why his *persona* is *non grata*. You can simply say he was engaging in activities incompatible with his diplomatic status. That might mean he is spying, or that he is accumulating too many parking tickets, or that he has done something else you don't like. But it almost always carries a diplomatic price. If the spy in question were a Russian, the State Department could be sure that a person of equivalent rank would be expelled from the American embassy in Moscow. Other countries might back off from current negotiations important to the United States, or raise difficult questions about access to bases, or simply engage in petty harassment of Americans. None of these considerations justifies tolerating espionage, but some of them may justify temporizing with it briefly.

If the spy does not have diplomatic immunity, thought has to be given to what his trial will be like. The evidence might convince the Justice Department, but will it convince a jury? More importantly, can all of the evidence be presented to a jury? The most damning parts may have been obtained illegally and therefore may be inadmissible in court. Or if they are admissible, they may compromise a source or a further investigation. The Justice Department also has to face the prospect that the defense lawyer will demand all the department's data concerning his or her client—even material that the department does not intend to use as evidence. National security could be damaged more by disclosure of some of this data than it would be protected by the conviction of this particular defendant.

There are other considerations regardless of diplomatic immunity. Two benefits might be obtained by delaying action against the suspects while keeping them under surveillance. Such a tactic might lead to their accomplices and to a wider network of spies. It might also provide an opportunity to turn them into double agents.

THE CIA AND THE FBI

When the Central Intelligence Agency identifies a foreign spy, or potential spy, overseas, it notifies the FBI of that spy's prospective arrival in the United States. Upon arrival, the spy becomes the responsibility of the FBI. If the spy later moves abroad again, responsibility passes back to the CIA. This arrangement has given rise to bureaucratic warfare of truly epic proportions with fallout affecting operations.

There are historical reasons for the division of labor between the FBI and CIA. The FBI is a law enforcement organization, and many of the activities of foreign intelligence agencies in the United States are illegal. Americans who provide classified information to foreign agencies are committing a crime. The CIA is an intelligence organization. At the time it was created, in 1947, it was explicitly denied "police, subpoena, law-enforcement powers, or internal security functions." [13]

One source of CIA-FBI friction is old-fashioned bureaucratic jealousy. The FBI was in business long before the CIA, and for almost fifty years it was headed by Hoover, the legendary bureaucratic in-fighter, turf-protector, and empire-builder. During World War II, Hoover persuaded President Franklin D. Roosevelt to authorize FBI operations in Latin America. After World War II, Hoover had ambitions to head a worldwide intelligence network and did not gracefully see that field preempted by the CIA. The FBI abandoned its foreign activities with some world-class footdragging. When Hoover died in 1972, nineteen American embassies still had legal attachés, the euphemism for FBI agents overseas. These agents were supposed to concentrate on law enforcement (for example, looking for stolen cars in Mexico or fugitives in any country), but few outsiders were confident that all their activities were so mundane.

Another source of CIA-FBI friction stems from the agencies' different functions. The CIA is interested in collecting intelligence. How to penetrate a foreign intelligence service is always on the minds of CIA officers. When they find a foreign intelligence officer trying to penetrate the U.S. government, their first thought is how to take advantage of this situation. Is there a way to convert the foreigner into a double agent ("double him up," in spyspeak)? Is there a way to persuade the foreigner to defect—through threat, cajolery, blackmail, bribery, or appeal to higher motives? Can the situation be manipulated so that we learn more from the spy than the spy is learning from us? The CIA, in short, is inclined to watch an attempt at foreign espionage or penetration develop and try to take advantage of it.

Not so the FBI. All the FBI's instincts run strongly to putting crooks in jail, whether they be bank robbers or spies. The FBI sometimes refrains from arresting known spies while keeping them under surveillance in the hope that they will lead to their confederates. But it has different objectives and a different agenda than does the CIA.

Geography usually determines which agency has control over a particular defector. Foreign intelligence officers who defect abroad almost necessarily make first contact with the CIA. In the United States they might go to the FBI. There are institutional differences in the agencies in how they treat defectors. Some defectors have been in contact with both agencies. Those who have been willing to talk about their experience have said they were generally treated better by the FBI, which they found to be more understanding than the CIA of the emotional stress that a defector is under.[14]

Within the CIA, there is wrangling among the counterintelligence staff, the Office of Security, and the Office of Russian and European Affairs (formerly the Division of Soviet Affairs). The function of the counterintelligence staff is to penetrate foreign intelligence services and to debrief defectors. The Office of Security is supposed to protect the agency against penetration, and the Russian office is supposed to recruit agents to work against the former Soviet Union.[15] As is discussed further below, there was a period in the 1960s and 1970s when the counterintelligence staff effectively took over the functions of the Office of

Security and precluded recruitment by the Soviet division. During this period, the CIA frequently rubbed the FBI the wrong way by labeling the FBI's Soviet sources as Soviet plants.

These bureaucratic rivalries, which had been dampened somewhat, burst forth anew as the aftermath of the Ames spy case reverberated throughout the intelligence community, Congress, and the White House. Nobody looked good in the Ames case, but the CIA looked the worst of all, and its rivals hurried to move in on what had been the CIA's turf. Congress was insisting that the FBI be given a larger role in the CIA's internal counterintelligence functions. In the summer of 1994, FBI director Louis Freeh traveled to Moscow, where he opened an FBI office, something that only five years before would have been unimaginable to both the Russians and the CIA. The stated purpose was to help the Russians deal with a growing crime wave, but the symbolism was overwhelming.

FOREIGN INTELLIGENCE SERVICES

Hostile foreign intelligence services are at once the sources of the main threat and the target of the principal effort. Friendly or neutral services pose a different, and in some respects, more complicated problem.

DEFENSE AGAINST FOREIGN SERVICES

The first task in watching foreigners thought to be engaging (or seeking to engage) in espionage is to decide whom to watch.

All spies (or intelligence officers, to use the dignified term) working outside their own country have a cover to disguise their real occupation. All major embassies in Washington have an intelligence section, though it is not called that. In the former Soviet embassy it was called the *rezidentura*, and its chief was called the *rezident*. All major embassies also have service attachés who are concerned with military intelligence. This is quite parallel to the organization of American embassies abroad, with the CIA station, the chief of station, and the service attachés. Many foreign consulates in major cities other than Washington also have intelligence components, as do major missions to the United Nations in New York.

In addition, some countries utilize unofficial cover for some of their intelligence officers. Some governments, notably the five permanent members of the U.N. Security Council (the United States, Russia as the successor to the Soviet Union, the United Kingdom, France, and China), can nominate a limited number of their own citizens to high positions in the U.N. Secretariat. This was sometimes used as intelligence cover by the Soviet Union, but at least one Soviet who defected while assigned to the United Nations was more diplomat than spy. Arkady Shevchenko, who had been a senior official of the Soviet Ministry of Foreign Affairs, was undersecretary general of the United Nations when he defected in the 1970s and began a three-year relationship with the CIA supplying information about the internal workings of the Soviet government and its arms control policies.[16]

Other officers of foreign intelligence services are in the United States under a variety of private or semi-official cover—in journalism or business, academia, or government purchasing missions. Some come on a short-term basis as tourists or members of delegations or performing groups of one kind or another. Again there is a parallel to the unofficial cover used by the CIA overseas.

Finally, there are intelligence officers who are in the United States with false identities and false documents, and under false pretenses. These are the so-called illegals. They are given elaborate "legends" (that is, cover stories), which they mold their lives to fit. They may be here for years before they actually engage in espionage. In the meantime they establish themselves as members of the community and acquire jobs that will perhaps give them access to information of interest or put them in a position to commit sabotage (for example, work in a defense plant). Col. Rudolf Abel of the KGB lived for nine years in a Brooklyn apartment ostensibly as an artist and photographer, while he was directing the activities of a network of Soviet illegals in the United States. Betrayed by a defector, Abel was convicted of espionage and sentenced to thirty years, but in 1962, after five years in prison, he was exchanged for U-2 pilot Francis Gary Powers (see Chapter 4).

A classic example of an illegal was Eli Cohen. The Israeli intelligence agency Mossad sent Cohen to Argentina in 1959 to establish himself as an Arab nationalist under the name of Kamil Amin Taabet. Cohen moved to Damascus in 1961 and quickly became a prominent political figure with wide contacts in the Syrian government. From a clandestine radio transmitter in his home in Damascus, he sent Israel detailed political and military intelligence for four years. The transmitter was his undoing. The Syrians traced it, caught Cohen in the act of broadcasting, and hanged him in the Damascus public square.[17]

Intelligence officers assigned to embassies or consulates have diplomatic passports and diplomatic immunity. They can be expelled from the country, but they cannot be arrested. Those with unofficial cover and illegals can be arrested, prosecuted, and, if convicted, sent to jail or worse.

The deeper a spy's cover, the more difficult identification becomes. Unless an illegal does something stupid, it is almost impossible to identify him or her. Most such identifications come from defectors, which is one reason defectors are so valuable.

But there are some clues. The FBI looks at biographic data supplied by the CIA and relies on the State Department for reports of patterns of activity and interests of particular individuals. Sometimes the FBI also relies on physical surveillance and even wiretapping. Surveillance is expensive (it requires large amounts of manpower), but the FBI does a great deal of it on diplomats from the former Soviet bloc as well as other countries. Wiretapping of embassies is illegal under the 1961 Vienna Convention on Diplomatic Relations and is not admitted. (The United States is not the only, and perhaps not even the principal, transgressor of the Vienna Convention.)

One of the priorities of foreign intelligence officers in the United States is to recruit Americans to do their work for them. Those in American intelligence agencies or in other sensitive positions are preferred, but for technical data in public sources, any American who knows where to look for specified information is acceptable. Journalists, librarians, academics, and researchers fit this category.

The effort at recruitment proceeds much as described in Chapter 4 with respect to intelligence sources. A crucial point comes when money changes hands for the first time. One common way of leading into this casually is for the foreign intelligence officer to overcompensate his recruitment target for some minor service. The foreign officer may have asked his target to get some books for him. The books are for sale to the general public, but the foreigner finds it inconvenient, he says, to go to the specialized book store where they are available. The foreigner then reimburses the target for more than the cost of the books—"something for your trouble." The next time the foreigner pays for a specific research job—still material in the public domain, but edging closer to forbidden material of even greater interest. When the relationship reaches the point where the payment is for something illegal, the foreigner has the source hooked because now the source is subject to blackmail—unless, of course, the source has been operating throughout under instructions from the FBI. In this case it is the foreigner who is subject to deportation if he has diplomatic immunity, or arrest if he does not.

Counterintelligence services depend not only on electronic and physical surveillance of suspected foreign spies (ELSUR and FISUR in FBI jargon); they also depend on the cooperation of targeted Americans. If these Americans report the contacts and if they are willing to continue to deal with the foreign intelligence officer who is trying to recruit them, they may become part of an elaborate scheme orchestrated by the FBI. The purpose would be, at a minimum, to catch the foreigner red-handed; or, better, to be led to others in a network; or, best of all, to convert the foreigner into a double agent. To maintain the credibility of a double agent with his foreign service, something has to be given to him. The information given is called a "throwaway." Its content is carefully chosen and is sometimes the subject of bitter dispute within the U.S. government. In the best of all situations, it can be disinformation—false information that deliberately misleads the other government. (The British had great success in doing this with German spies whom they captured in Great Britain during World War II.)[18] While this is going on, of course, the American who was the original target of recruitment has himself been acting as a double agent.

PENETRATION OF FOREIGN SERVICES

The effort to penetrate foreign intelligence services proceeds much as the effort to recruit any clandestine source, described in Chapter 4. When successful, this effort produces a defector—a foreign intelligence officer who decides he would rather work for you than for his own service. Despite strenuous efforts by intelligence services to identify and cultivate potential defectors, most defectors are self-motivated. They simply appear. Frequently, they want protection, usually in the form of asylum, but sometimes they volunteer to defect in place—that is, to convert themselves into double agents.

The first contact may be made any number of ways. Some defectors go to an American embassy abroad. One went to the home of the CIA station chief. Another left a note on the seat of an American diplomat's car while it was parked on a street in Vienna. In the United States they go to the State Department or the FBI.

However the initial contact is made, standard operating procedure calls for the United States to be receptive. In one case, when a defector said he had to be out of the country where the defection took place in two hours, the CIA not only met this deadline but also produced a false passport for him.

After immediate security considerations are taken care of, the first priority is establishing the defector's bona fides. Is he genuine, or has he been sent by his service to spread disinformation? Or worse, is he a potential mole, sent to burrow into the CIA or other agency and reach a position where he can report its innermost secrets and frustrate its best laid plans?

These are the worst nightmares of any intelligence service, and a mild case of paranoia is a job requirement for a good counterintelligence officer. There is a fine line between due prudence and such pervasive skepticism that every defector is seen as part of a plot.

If the CIA is satisfied that a defector is genuine, the question arises: does he cross over—that is, make a clean break with his past—or does he defect in place? It is much safer for a defector to make a clean break. He will be taken to Washington, established in a safe house where his creature comforts will be attended to, and interviewed (debriefed, in the jargon) at length, sometimes over a period of months. He will be handsomely paid, given a new identity, and found a job or established in a business.

If he defects in place, he returns to his old job, usually with a mental list of things the CIA would like for him to learn. He is told how to contact the CIA when he has something to report. The relationship continues if he is reassigned from one country to another. As his career advances, his value to the CIA increases. But he and his case officer must act with the utmost circumspection because a defector in place is in great danger. The price of getting caught is very high.

GUARDING AGAINST PENETRATION

If planting a mole, or getting a defector-in-place, in a foreign intelligence service is the intelligence equivalent of a home run in baseball, then keeping moles and defectors-in-place out of your own service is the equivalent of pitching a no-hit game. The problem is that it's easier to keep score in baseball than in intelligence. You can never be sure when you've shut the other team out, or when it has hit a home run.

The CIA's Soviet operations were disrupted for ten years or more during the 1960s and 1970s when the counterintelligence staff and a portion of the Soviet division became obsessed with the idea that spurious defectors were assaulting the agency. Ironically, the obsession was fed by a defector—Anatoly Golitsyn, who walked away from the KGB *rezidentura* in Helsinki in 1961 into the arms of the CIA. Taken to Washington, Golitsyn shortly won the confidence of James J. Angleton, CIA chief of counterintelligence from 1954 to 1974. To refresh Golitsyn's memory, Angleton made available to Golitsyn voluminous CIA files on Soviet intelligence.

Golitsyn then destroyed Angleton's confidence in most of the CIA's Soviet sources. He further identified—erroneously, it turned out after more careful investigation—alleged moles in the intelligence services of Canada, France, and Norway. Several American officers had their careers ruined, as did officers in allied services. At least one Soviet trying to defect was turned back to the KGB. The CIA's Soviet division was effectively precluded from recruitment, because any Soviet source would be, in Angleton's eyes, a plant. A volunteer defector, Yuri Nosenko, was declared by Golitsyn to be a phony and was questioned under brutal conditions in solitary confinement for five years.

Finally, CIA director William Colby fired Angleton, released Nosenko, and thoroughly reorganized counterintelligence.[19] One of Colby's reforms was to limit the assignment of officers to counterintelligence to five years, a measure designed to stop the onset of paranoia before it went too far.

During the depths of the cold war, visiting Soviets who had no connection with espionage frequently asked for asylum in the United States or in other countries. This commonly happened in connection with touring groups of ballet dancers or musicians or athletes, sometimes members of U.N. groups or persons attending scientific or academic conferences. In every case they had to be checked out as thoroughly as possible to determine if this was a means selected by the KGB to infiltrate an illegal.

The most celebrated modern moles were actually a quintet of British subjects who victimized their own intelligence service—Kim Philby, Guy Burgess, Donald Maclean, Anthony Blunt, and John Cairncross. They were recruited by the KGB while they were at Cambridge University in the 1930s, joined British intelligence thereafter, and did their most damaging work in the 1950s. At one time Philby was the British intelligence liaison with the CIA, a position that enabled him to give the Soviets American as well as British secrets. On the verge of being found out, Burgess and Maclean escaped from Great Britain to Moscow in 1951. Philby fled to Moscow from Beirut in 1964. He died in the Soviet Union in 1988 at the age of 76. Blunt died in London in 1983 at the age of 75. Cairncross was identified as the fifth man in 1990 by the defector Oleg Gordievski. He was given immunity by the British government after he admitted spying.

"FRIENDLY" FOREIGN SERVICES

In terms of international relations, three kinds of foreign intelligence services operate in the United States. There are hostile services, of which the KGB of the former Soviet Union was the preeminent example. Following the breakup of the Soviet Union, the KGB was itself broken into two agencies of the Russian government—the SVRR (Foreign Intelligence Service, corresponding to the U.S. CIA) and the MBRF (Federal Counterintelligence Service, similar to the U.S. FBI). Like the KGB, the SVRR operates in the United States, and it is still hostile. Other hostile services of prime concern are those of Cuba and the People's Republic of China. At the other extreme are friendly services, of which the British are the preeminent example. Also in this category are Canada, Australia, New Zealand, and most of the countries in the North Atlantic Treaty

Organization (NATO). Then there is an in-between category of countries whose governments are friendly, or at least ostensibly so, but whose intelligence services may not be. Preeminent in this group is Israel. Others are South Korea, Pakistan, and Taiwan. Iran was in this group prior to the overthrow of the shah in 1979, at which time it moved into the hostile category. Iraq is another country that moved from in-between to hostile with a change in the political climate.

This in-between group presents a particularly sticky political problem. Not only are there cases of outright espionage, but also and more commonly there are activities directed against their own nationals in the United States. These activities include efforts at recruitment, harassment of exiles, and sometimes murder.

Third world countries regularly complain about U.S. intervention in their affairs. In fact, however, governments as well as opposition groups in the third world seek American support. Some authoritarian third world governments use their intelligence services to silence, intimidate, or otherwise neutralize exile and other groups carrying on propaganda in the United States. Most U.S. activities of these intelligence services violate American law in one way or another. Yet there are incentives for the American government to look the other way. There are reasons not to jeopardize bilateral relations with the governments in question. The United States has (or had) military base rights or intelligence gathering facilities in some of the countries. Restrictions on foreign intelligence services in the United States would certainly be followed by restrictions on American agencies abroad.

ISRAEL. The Israeli Mossad is one of the world's premier intelligence services. It has unparalleled sources almost all over the world, but especially in the Middle East. It has a capacity for covert action that the CIA and SVRR might well envy. It has an extensive intelligence-sharing relationship with the United States. The CIA's James Angleton had a great deal to do with the establishment of Mossad in the early days of the state of Israel, and a monument to Angleton was erected in Israel after his death. Angleton remained the focal point of CIA contact with Mossad throughout his career at the CIA. His interest was in the intelligence potential of Jewish émigrés from the Soviet Union: whether any of them was a KGB plant, and whether any was a potential source for Mossad and the CIA. It was Mossad that delivered to the CIA in Europe a copy of Nikita Khrushchev's 1956 speech denouncing Stalin, one of the cold war's greatest intelligence coups.

Notwithstanding this record of collaboration, U.S.-Israeli and CIA-Mossad relations were shaken in 1985 with the arrest outside the Israeli embassy in Washington of Jonathan Jay Pollard, a civilian counterintelligence analyst for the Naval Investigative Service. Pollard later pleaded guilty to taking part in an espionage conspiracy and was sentenced to life imprisonment. His wife, Anne Henderson-Pollard, pleaded guilty to receiving embezzled government property and to being an accessory after the fact in the possession of classified government documents. She was sentenced to five years. Pollard sold the Israelis classified documents that measured ten feet by six feet by six feet. The Israeli embassy rented an apartment in Northwest Washington where a secretary worked weekends to copy documents Pollard delivered on Friday afternoons and picked up Monday mornings.

The Pollard case severely strained U.S.-Israeli relations. The Israeli government apologized, but its cover story that the Pollard affair was a rogue operation lacked plausibility. The matter was complicated by the fact that Pollard was Jewish. In a letter written from prison to the *Jerusalem Post,* Pollard asserted "an absolute obligation" to help Israel and complained of being abandoned both by the Israeli government and the American Jewish community.[20]

In the aftermath of the Persian Gulf War of 1991, during which Israel was attacked by Iraqi Scud missiles, the American section of the World Jewish Congress called Pollard's sentence "far harsher" than that of anyone else convicted of spying for friendly or neutral governments.[21] Pollard himself appealed his sentence on the ground that its harshness violated a plea bargain he had made with the government, but he lost in the U.S. Court of Appeals for the District of Columbia. The Israeli government, supported by Jewish groups in the United States and Canada, took up the case with appeals first to President George Bush and then to President Bill Clinton. Bush left office without taking action. In March 1994 Clinton approved a recommendation of the Justice Department to deny clemency.[22]

KOREA.   The Korean Central Intelligence Agency (KCIA) mounted a multimillion dollar campaign to influence U.S. policy toward Korea. This was, in fact, a covert action directed against the United States and especially the U.S. Congress. American policy was pro-Korean anyway and had been since the Korean peninsula was divided along the 38th parallel following World War II. The U.S. Central Intelligence Agency even played a key role in establishing the KCIA in the early 1960s. During the late 1960s and continuing into the 1970s, the KCIA embarked on a program designed to ensure that the United States continued to support not only Korea but the Korean regime then in power, that American foreign aid continued at a high level, and that it was delivered through favored channels. There were secret campaign contributions and attempts to bribe members of Congress as well as congressional staff.

The Senate Intelligence Committee concluded in 1978 that one of the difficulties in coping with activities of this kind lay in the fragmentation of the U.S. government's own counterintelligence agencies. The FBI was too preoccupied with the Soviet Union. Relevant intelligence usually came to the attention of the CIA and the State Department incidentally to the collection of other intelligence and then was not shared with other agencies.[23]

CHILE.   The Chilean intelligence service went so far, in 1976, as to blow up a former Chilean ambassador, and an American along with him, as their car passed almost across the street from the Chilean embassy in Washington. The hit man was an American agent who confessed and implicated Chilean intelligence.

The Chileans for their part raised the question of whether the CIA was responsible. Chilean president Gen. Augusto Pinochet spun a fanciful hypothetical scenario in which the CIA infiltrated DINA, the Chilean intelligence service, and then pulled off the assassination to make Chile look bad.[24] The FBI agent who broke the case did not support this version. He did say that others could have warned the bureau in advance but did not.[25]

IRAN.   SAVAK, the Iranian intelligence service, was a cooperative creation of the CIA and Mossad after the CIA helped restore the shah to power in 1953. At the insistence of the shah, SAVAK became almost the only source of American intelligence in Iran, and this was perhaps the main reason why the United States was so poorly informed when the shah was overthrown in 1979.

At the same time, SAVAK was operating in the United States almost without restraint. During the 1970s, there were a large number of Iranian students in American universities, and many of them were opposed to the shah's regime. SAVAK sought to identify them so that reprisals could be taken against their families in Iran or against the students themselves when they returned to Iran. Some were also pressured to become SAVAK agents or informants.[26]

The United States felt constrained from curbing SAVAK's activities by considerations of foreign policy. Iran allowed the United States to operate a number of bases in Iran for the collection of signals intelligence against the Soviet Union. And in broader geopolitical terms, the United States saw Iranian hegemony over the Persian Gulf as a stabilizing factor.

CIVIL LIBERTIES

Spying is intrusive by definition. A great deal of counterintelligence is spying on spies or suspected spies and is carried on in the United States. Some of the techniques impinge on rights guaranteed by the First and Fourth amendments to the Constitution. The pertinent provision of the First Amendment guarantees "the right of the people peaceably to assemble." The Fourth Amendment, which is the more important so far as counterintelligence is concerned, reads in its entirety:

> The right of the people to be secure in their persons, houses, papers, and effects, against unreasonable searches and seizures, shall not be violated, and no Warrants shall issue, but upon probable cause, supported by Oath or affirmation, and particularly describing the place to be searched, and the persons or things to be seized.

The authors of this amendment did not know what a telephone is, but they made it illegal to tap one. They did not know what electronic listening devices are, but they made it illegal to install them surreptitiously. They also made it illegal to enter a house or office surreptitiously and to steal or copy documents (although they didn't know what copying machines are either). The FBI regularly does all of these things in its efforts to catch foreign spies. A good deal of the history (and controversy) of counterintelligence in the United States since the early 1970s involves efforts to balance national security and individual rights. Most of these efforts have come down to subjecting law enforcement activities to judicial oversight through the requirement of search warrants.

Both Presidents Lyndon B. Johnson and Richard Nixon had the idea that much of the popular opposition to their policies in Vietnam must be Soviet-inspired, and they pressed both the FBI and the CIA to provide supporting evidence. This put the CIA on especially shaky legal ground because its basic statute prohibits it from engaging in domestic functions.

The FBI had no such statutory constraint; its only limitation was in the Constitution, but that was one that Director Hoover took lightly out of long habit. The FBI's counterintelligence work was always confused by lack of a clear distinction between ideological anticommunism and workaday espionage. Hoover himself had begun his career in the Justice Department in the days of the anticommunist raids of Attorney General A. Mitchell Palmer at the end of World War I. The legality of those raids was questionable under the Fourth Amendment as well as the due process clause of the Fifth and Fourteenth amendments ("no person shall be . . . deprived of life, liberty, or property, without due process of law"). Hoover was a thinly disguised ally of Sen. Joseph McCarthy. For him, and for the bureau that he molded in his image, there was never very much difference between leftists and communists on the one hand and agents of the Soviet Union on the other.

The bureau infiltrated and otherwise harassed organizations that espoused liberal ideas but had nothing to do with the Soviet Union. The CIA was reported to have maintained intelligence files on at least 10,000 Americans.[27] No link was ever found between the Soviet Union and opposition in the United States to the Vietnam War.

Hoover died in 1972. Many of the bureau's abuses of civil liberties were revealed in the intelligence investigations of the 1970s and as a result of disclosures under the Freedom of Information Act. The bureau's targets included members of Congress, among them Sen. Wayne Morse, D-Ore., an especially acerbic critic of the Johnson administration's Vietnam policies. In 1967, after Morse and seven other senators asked President Johnson to halt bombing of North Vietnam, an FBI report discussed "possible communist and subversive influences" on Morse and the others. When Morse inserted letters in the *Congressional Record* from ninety-three people opposing the war, Johnson directed the FBI to "seek derogatory information" on the letter-writers. Jake Jacobsen, who had been a lawyer in the Johnson White House, defended these actions as not having as much to do with Morse as with the people who wrote to him, because "some of the things they seemed to say might be subversive."[28]

After a period of some confusion following Hoover's death, President Carter (1977-1981) appointed William H. Webster, a federal judge in St. Louis, as director of the FBI. Also during the Carter administration Congress passed the Foreign Intelligence Surveillance Act of 1978 (P.L. 95-511, approved October 25, 1978, 50 U.S.C. 1801). This act seeks to bring the judicial process into surveillance. (Hitherto surveillance had been done only on the authority of the attorney general.) The act establishes a special court consisting of seven U.S. district judges, designated by the chief justice from different circuits and serving overlapping terms of seven years each. The court's sole function is to hear applications for electronic surveillance. There is an appellate court of three judges, designated by the chief justice from district or circuit courts, and a further appeal can be taken to the Supreme Court. Since the special court meets in secret, the government is the only party that knows there is anything to appeal, and the appellate procedure in effect gives the government three chances to get what it wants.

Nevertheless, the government must meet certain standards. All applications, which must be approved by the attorney general before they even get to the court, must include the identity or description of the target; the facts and circumstances justifying the belief that the facilities are being used by a foreign power; minimization procedures to limit the acquisition, retention, and dissemination of information produced by the surveillance; a detailed description of the information sought and the type of communications or activities involved; a certification from the president's national security affairs adviser or an official of comparable rank that the information sought is important intelligence, along with the reasons therefore, and that it cannot be reasonably obtained "by normal investigative techniques"; the means of surveillance and whether physical entry is required; the period of surveillance; and the coverage of each device to be used.

Court orders authorizing surveillance are limited to ninety days (or one year if the only target is a foreign power). Unintended acquisitions of communications wholly within the United States are to be destroyed unless the attorney general determines that they represent a threat of death or serious bodily harm.

Each year in April the attorney general must submit a report to the Administrative Office of the U.S. Courts and to Congress of the total number of applications for orders and extensions of electronic surveillance and the total number granted, modified, or denied. These reports are not made public. The congressional intelligence committees were required to review the act's operations annually for five years and report their recommendations, if any. The committees expressed general satisfaction. As the Senate committee put it after the fifth year, "[T]he number [of surveillances] involved is not excessive, . . . such surveillances of U.S. persons are not capricious, and . . . the requirements of the Act are being met." It was also noted that no application had been rejected, though at least one had been modified.[29]

The act inserts an additional layer of approval of electronic espionage and sets additional standards, but the public is dependent on the vigilance of the secret court and the congressional intelligence committees for assurance that the standards are being met.

Meanwhile, change came slowly to the FBI. Directors came and went, but the legacy of J. Edgar Hoover survived in the bureaucratic culture.

Whereas in the 1960s and 1970s, the FBI concentrated on establishing a link between the Soviet Union and opponents of U.S. policy in Vietnam, in the 1980s it directed its attention to finding foreign ties of opponents of Reagan's policies in Central America.

Americans newly returned from Nicaragua were aggressively interviewed by FBI agents. Webster told Congress that the interviews were related to foreign counterintelligence investigations, but Rep. Don Edwards, D-Calif., chairman of the House Judiciary Subcommittee on Civil and Constitutional Rights and himself a former FBI agent, said "they have the odor of harassment."[30] Between 1985 and 1987, American groups opposed to the Reagan-backed Nicaraguan Contras reported more than fifty break-ins in which files were rifled, but cash and expensive equipment were left untouched.

And then there was the affair of the Committee in Solidarity with the People of El Salvador (CISPES), a group opposing Reagan policies in El Salvador. From 1983 to 1985, the FBI infiltrated CISPES chapters and wiretapped its members' phones. The CISPES affair spawned 178 spinoff investigations, involved 59 FBI field offices, and generated files on 1,330 groups and 2,375 individuals. The Senate Intelligence Committee called it a "serious failure in FBI management." The committee said the investigation "was initiated primarily on the basis of allegations that should not have been considered credible; it was broadened beyond the scope justified even by those allegations; and it continued after the available information had clearly fallen below the standards required by the applicable guidelines." [31]

Sen. David L. Boren, D-Okla., chairman, and Sen. William S. Cohen, R-Maine, vice chairman, of the Intelligence Committee, demanded that the information be removed from FBI files. Instead of destroying the files, the FBI sent them to the National Archives, a step that inexplicably satisfied CISPES. As late as 1991, a federal judge in Chicago ruled that the FBI had violated a consent decree settling an earlier case and that the Chicago field office of the FBI had continued its CISPES activities after the Justice Department had instructed it to close its investigation.[32]

CONCLUSION

Working in counterintelligence is like walking through an endless hall of mirrors. You are never sure if something is what it seems to be.

People betray their country for a variety of reasons. The most common are ideology, money, sex, and spite. The public record does not disclose every instance of betrayal nor necessarily the real motive. At least in the last decade of the cold war, it appears that most defectors from the communist world were motivated by ideology, most from the United States by money (perhaps an ironic commentary on communism and capitalism).

Whatever the motive, most defections were self-generated. Soviet defectors sought out Americans (or, in some cases, British) offering help; Americans sought out Soviets, shamelessly peddling the information with which they had been entrusted. The end of the cold war took a good deal of the ideology out of international relations (though communism persists in Asia). The demise of the Soviet Union sharply restricted the market for those who seek to sell secrets. Whether the Chinese will be willing to take up the slack remains to be seen.

There remain other countries interested in learning selected American secrets. Some of these countries, especially those with oil wealth, are able to pay handsomely.

The need for counterintelligence continues. Performance will never be perfect. But there are some things that could be done to make it better.

First, too much information is classified and at too high a level. The standards for classification are subjective and overly broad.

Second, too many people have access to too many secrets. The rules about compartmenting information are sensible, but in practice the compartment walls tend to crumble.

Third, the intelligence community is conducive to the development of an atmosphere of trust among the people who work in it. Rules are bent and signs of questionable procedures are ignored. Members of the Walker spy ring could walk out of navy code rooms carrying material to deliver to the Soviets, and nobody paid attention. Aldrich Ames flouted the rules even more egregiously at the CIA. Maybe this can never be stopped, but aggressive leadership by management might make it less likely.

NOTES

1. Senate Select Committee to Study Governmental Operations with Respect to Intelligence Activities (Church Committee), Final Report, *Foreign and Military Intelligence*, Book 1, S. Rept. 94-755, 1976, 163, 620.
2. 47 *Federal Register* 14874-14884, April 6, 1982.
3. Statistics are from Information Security Oversight Office, *1993 Report to the President*.
4. Joint Security Commission, *Redefining Security*, a report to the Secretary of Defense and the Director of Central Intelligence, Washington, D.C., 1994.
5. John Moors Cabot, recorded interview with William V. Moss, January 27, 1971, John F. Kennedy Library Oral History Program, 23.
6. See Arthur M. Schlesinger, Jr., *Robert Kennedy and His Times* (New York: Ballantine Books, 1978), 707-708.
7. Ruth Marcus, "Jeffries Pleads Guilty to Spying Count," *Washington Post*, Jan. 24, 1986.
8. Curt Gentry, *J. Edgar Hoover: The Man and the Secrets* (New York: W.W. Norton, 1991), 497.
9. Ruth Marcus, "Spy Charges Lead to Cuts in Navy Security Clearances," *Washington Post*, July 26, 1985.
10. Ibid.
11. "Former Envoy Is Charged with Stealing Groceries," *New York Times*, Jan. 13, 1993.
12. Walter Pincus, "The CIA Agent Who Sold Out," *Washington Post*, May 30, 1986.
13. National Security Act of 1947, sec. 102(d)(3), 50 U.S.C. 403.
14. Ronald Kessler, *Spy vs. Spy: Stalking Soviet Spies in America* (New York: Charles Scribner's Sons, 1988), 186; and Charles R. Babcock, "Case Turns Spotlight on CIA's Handling of Soviet Defectors," *Washington Post*, Nov. 6, 1985.
15. Tom Mangold, *Cold Warrior: James Jesus Angleton, the CIA's Master Spy Hunter* (New York: Simon and Schuster, 1991), 313-314, quoting former DCI William Colby.
16. See Arkady Shevchenko, *Breaking with Moscow* (New York: Knopf, 1985).
17. This story is told in gripping detail in Zwy Aldouby and Jerrold Ballinger, *The Shattered Silence: The Eli Cohen Affair* (New York: Coward, McCann and Geoghegan, 1971).
18. See J. C. Masterman, *The Double-Cross System in the War of 1939 to 1945* (New Haven: Yale University Press, 1972).
19. Mangold, *Cold Warrior*. See also David Wise, *Molehunt: The Secret Search for Traitors That Shattered the CIA* (New York: Random House, 1992).
20. Howard Kurtz, "Pollard Letter Asserts 'Obligation' to Spy," *Washington Post*, Feb. 11, 1987.
21. Howard Kurtz, "Gulf War Spurs Support for Pollard," *Washington Post*, May 5, 1991.

22. Ruth Marcus, "Clinton Denies Clemency to Israeli Spy Pollard," *Washington Post*, March 24, 1994.

23. Senate Select Committee on Intelligence, *Activities of "Friendly" Foreign Intelligence Services in the United States: A Case Study*, news release, June 22, 1978; Tad Szulc, "Inside South Korea's C.I.A.," *New York Times Magazine*, March 6, 1977; Michael J. Glennon, "Liaison and the Law: Foreign Intelligence Agencies' Activities in the United States," *Harvard International Law Journal* (Winter 1984).

24. Edward Cody, "Pinochet Cites CIA in Attack," *Washington Post*, May 8, 1987.

25. Adela Gooch, "FBI Agent Honored in Letelier Case," *Washington Post*, Sept. 26, 1989. See also John Dinges and Saul Landau, *Assassination on Embassy Row* (New York: Pantheon Books, 1980).

26. See Mansur Rafizadeh,*Witness: From the Shah to the Secret Arms Deal, An Insider's Account of U.S. Involvement in Iran* (New York: William Morrow, 1987).

27. Seymour M. Hersh, "Huge CIA Operation Reported in U.S. Against Antiwar Forces, Other Dissidents in Nixon Years," *New York Times*, Dec. 22, 1974.

28. Associated Press, "FBI Investigated Wayne Morse over Vietnam War Opposition," *Washington Post*, July 17, 1988.

29. Senate Intelligence Committee, *The Foreign Intelligence Surveillance Act of 1978: The First Five Years*, S. Rept. 98-660, 98th Cong., 2d sess., 1984, 8, 23.

30. Howard Kurtz, "FBI Probing Nicaragua Visitors," *Washington Post*, May 12, 1987.

31. Senate Intelligence Committee, *The FBI and CISPES*, S. Print 100-46, July 1989.

32. American Bar Association, *National Security Law Report*, November 1991.

CHAPTER 7

Covert Action

The CIA has committed every crime there is except rape.
—Walter Bedell Smith, former director of central intelligence

Covert action is the most controversial, troublesome part of intelligence. It is the part that is most likely to get the country, or the administration, in trouble if it fails. It might also save trouble if it succeeds. Covert action was an important weapon of the cold war, but it has broader applications. In some periods the United States has used it a great deal; in some periods very little. This chapter takes a look at covert action—what it is, how it works, who decides, and what problems can result.

WHAT IT IS

Covert action is an activity designed to produce a result in a foreign country without the role of the United States being evident. The American role should be so well concealed that it cannot be uncovered by investigatory techniques and can be plausibly denied. This is a short, informal, but workable definition. Technical or legal definitions have become steadily more complicated.

When Congress first addressed the question in 1974, it did not mention covert action at all but simply referred to CIA "operations in foreign countries, other than activities intended solely for obtaining necessary intelligence." [1] Two years later a committee headed by Democratic senator Frank Church of Idaho defined covert action "as clandestine activity designed to influence foreign governments, events, organizations or persons in support of U.S. foreign policy conducted in such a way that the involvement of the U.S. Government is not apparent." [2] An executive order by President Ronald Reagan in 1981 used the following definition:

> activities conducted in support of national foreign policy objectives abroad which are planned and executed so that the role of the United States Government is not apparent or acknowledged publicly, and functions in support of such activities, but which are not intended to influence United States political processes, public opinion, policies, or media and do not include diplomatic activities or the collection and production of intelligence or related support functions. [3]

135

The executive order's reference to "special activities" is a euphemism for "covert action."

Congress wrote a more detailed definition in the Intelligence Authorization Act of 1991, which remained the controlling legal definition in 1994:

> As used in this title, the term "covert action" means an activity or activities of the United States Government to influence political, economic, or military conditions abroad, where it is intended that the role of the United States Government will not be apparent or acknowledged publicly, but does not include—
>
> 1. activities the primary purpose of which is to acquire intelligence, traditional counterintelligence activities, traditional activities to improve or maintain the operational security of United States Government programs, or administrative activities;
> 2. traditional diplomatic or military activities or routine support to such activities;
> 3. traditional law enforcement activities conducted by United States Government law enforcement agencies or routine support to such activities; or
> 4. activities to provide routine support to the overt activities (other than activities described in paragraph (1), (2), or (3)) of other United States Government agencies abroad.

One reason these definitions have gotten longer and more complicated is that Congress has become more insistent that covert actions be reported to the congressional intelligence committees. Both Presidents Reagan (1981-1989) and George Bush (1989-1993) resisted these reporting requirements. Congress therefore felt compelled to speak with increasing specificity. The exceptions in the 1991 act also reflect recognition of a number of fuzzy areas. As will be developed more fully in the following section, some traditional diplomatic activity is designed to bring *sub rosa* influence on a foreign government.

However defined, covert action is the United States doing something that it does not want other people to know about. Under an executive order issued by President Jimmy Carter in 1978, the CIA is the only agency authorized to conduct covert action (except the armed forces in time of war) without special dispensation from the president.[4] The same order expressly prohibited assassination: "No person employed by or acting on behalf of the United States Government shall engage in, or conspire to engage in, assassination." This prohibition was repeated verbatim in the Reagan order in 1981. The Reagan order also repeated Carter's designation of the CIA as the sole covert action agency.

Since 1947 when the CIA was created, successive administrations have professed to find statutory authority for covert action in an obscure phrase in the agency's basic charter. The CIA is given the duty "to perform such other functions and duties related to intelligence affecting the national security as the National Security Council may from time to time direct."[5] Congress has acquiesced in this interpretation.

It is worth noting that it took from 1947, when the National Security Act was passed, to 1978, when Carter issued his executive order, to produce even guidelines governing covert action, and these guidelines were mainly in response to Church committee revelations about past assassination plots. These plots targeted Cuban leader Fidel Castro, Patrice Lumumba, the premier in the

Congo (now Zaire), and Col. Abdul Kassem, the prime minister of Iraq. The CIA was also associated unclearly with the assassins of Gen. Rafael Trujillo, dictator of the Dominican Republic, President Ngo Dinh Diem of Vietnam, and Gen. Rene Schneider, commander of the Chilean army. There is no proof that the CIA ever engaged in assassination, though as William Colby, a former director of central intelligence (DCI), remarked, "It wasn't for want of trying," especially with respect to Castro.[6]

HOW IT WORKS

Covert action embraces a range and variety of activities limited only by the imagination of those who plan them. Within any given action there may be an almost infinite range of gradations.

Most covert actions are small, inexpensive, and in many cases unexceptional. Some qualify as covert actions mainly because the CIA has had the money for them and the State Department has not. The living expenses of a foreign ruler in exile and of his entourage have been paid—and not lavishly. In one case the ruler in question was from a poor third world country and had been driven from his homeland by an aggressive foreign power. He had been, and continued to be, friendly to the United States. The secret funds to support him were thought to be justified both as gratitude for past favors and as a down payment for future favors in the (probably remote) contingency of his return to power.

In a somewhat similar case the CIA supported the leader of an irregular foreign military force that had been defeated while fighting in a larger U.S.-sponsored covert action. This man would have qualified for overt U.S. assistance in resettlement as a refugee, and some of his followers did come to the United States under those conditions. But the CIA felt a special responsibility to the leader.

In another case the CIA prevented the breakup of an international conference by paying the hotel bills of a key, but impecunious, third world delegation that otherwise would have had to go home. Although the purpose of the conference was to settle a dispute to which the United States was not a party, the State Department very much wanted the conference to succeed. Keeping it alive was deemed an appropriate use of CIA funds. It is not clear whether the beneficiaries of this largess were aware ("witting" in spyspeak) of the source of their help. In any event the conference failed.

There have also been covert actions for the physical protection of foreign leaders whom the United States particularly wanted to remain in power. In such cases the CIA has supplied communications equipment and has given how-to-do-it tips to the leader's security guards. In at least one instance the leader was assassinated anyway.

As a precondition of any covert action, Congress has required that the president find it to be "important" to the national security. There is room for argument as to whether some individual cases meet that test, but the test itself does not mean very much. It is characteristic of presidents that they think almost anything they want to do in foreign affairs is "important" to the national security. Congress has occasionally used other formulations. Words such as "vital" or "essential" are thought to provide a sterner test than "important," but the distinction has escaped most presidents.

PROPRIETARIES

A proprietary is a commercial company owned and operated by the CIA and used to perform services for the agency. The services are of a nature, or are needed in a volume, that would arouse suspicion if the agency sought to procure them from established firms. Using a proprietary makes it possible to bypass government procurement regulations (the CIA is exempt from a good many of these anyway) and provides flexibility as well as security. The proprietary serves as a cover that would not be available if the agency tried to do these things itself. Security is enhanced to the degree that a proprietary is able to serve the public as well as the CIA.

Air transportation is a prominent example. For many years, especially during the secret war in Laos, a firm called Air America flew CIA personnel and equipment throughout the Far East. Southern Air Transport operated mainly in Latin America. The CIA has also created proprietaries in the fields of journalism and finance. Sometimes the purpose has been to provide cover for collection; sometimes, to facilitate plans for covert action.

Typically the proprietaries are incorporated by front individuals in Delaware. One DCI once bragged to the Senate Foreign Relations Committee that most proprietaries returned a profit to the U.S. Treasury. But the closeness with which proprietaries are controlled and the secrecy in which they operate provide many opportunities for loose accounting at best and fraud at worst. The people who are responsible for these things in the CIA insist that there are strict controls and that funds could not be improperly diverted without the knowledge of many people (which in itself is a safeguard). The congressional intelligence committees likewise insist they are vigilant (though some members confess to private doubts). But the public has to take these assurances largely on faith.

Closely related to commercial proprietaries are phony foundations created to serve as "cut-outs" while posing as legitimate grant-making institutions. (A cut-out is an individual or an organization that stands between an intelligence service and the recipient of its funds. A cut-out also may stand between the service and one of its agents.) Numerous such foundations have existed at one time or another. In addition, the CIA has sometimes augmented the funds of independent foundations with the understanding that these supplementary monies would be used for specific grants.[7]

The number of proprietaries is a tightly held secret. Sometimes it is hard to tell if a foundation, for example, is a 100 percent CIA proprietary or if it is only being used as a channel for funds and carries on other programs unrelated to intelligence. In the latter case it is an instrument of covert action but not a proprietary, and some of its directors and officers may not be witting.

In 1991 Congress authorized the Defense Department to establish proprietaries to provide cover for intelligence collection activities abroad, which is different from covert action. The proprietaries are operated by the Defense

Intelligence Agency. No proprietary may be established after December 31, 1995.[8]

PROPAGANDA

For the straightforward dispersing of information about foreign policy, the United States has the U.S. Information Agency. The propaganda that is a tool of covert action is always untraceable and sometimes untrue.

MEDIA.   Many covert actions involve subornation of the foreign media. A journalist is paid to write an editorial supporting or opposing a given proposal, or to slant a news story or broadcast. Usually the journalist is receiving a retainer, or other regular payments, from the CIA. The CIA frequently has used this technique to influence foreign elections (for example, Italy in 1948 and Chile in 1964 and thereafter) or to influence debates abroad over foreign policy issues of importance to the United States (on nuclear weapons, disarmament, or policy toward the former Soviet Union, for example).

Another technique is to subsidize an established newspaper or magazine, the owners or editors of which are generally supportive of U.S. objectives. The CIA can do this directly (through a cash payment to help meet expenses) or indirectly (through the purchase of advertising). Sometimes the CIA underwrites the cost of an advertiser buying more ads than he or she normally would. For years the CIA drummed up (and paid for) advertising in *El Mercurio*, one of the leading newspapers in Santiago, Chile. The purpose was to keep a democratic voice alive. During the radical regime of Salvador Allende (1970-1973), Agustin Edwards, owner of *El Mercurio* (and of much more in Chile) lobbied in Washington for an anti-Allende policy at the same time his paper was receiving CIA subventions. But Edwards was conservative; he would no doubt have done the same thing even without CIA payments.

A higher level of covert intervention is to do your own publishing. For a time the CIA published the English-language *Daily American* in Rome. The paper was read mainly by American and British tourists. It is hard to see what benefit the paper was expected to bring to the United States, let alone how it was important to the national security. Perhaps it provided convenient cover. *América Latina Mas Alla de Sus Fronteras* (Latin America Beyond Its Borders) was different. During the 1950s, North American intellectuals complained recurrently that Latin America had no high-grade Spanish-language publication about international affairs (along the lines of *Foreign Affairs* in the United States) nor any money to start one. Presto! There appeared *America Latina Mas Alla de Sus Fronteras*, a quarterly journal with well-written articles by well-known Latin American leaders and scholars. Alas, it had a short life. Its true parentage was not revealed until later. The CIA also funded *Encounter*, an anticommunist intellectual magazine that was published in Europe after World War II.

At one time the CIA operated a news syndicate in London called Forum World Features. The syndicate had two functions: to place articles in English-language papers published abroad and to act as a conduit for payments to foreign journalists working for the CIA. Forum World Features was a Delaware corporation. At one time or another, its board of directors included Richard Mellon Scaife, a Pittsburgh banker, and John Hay Whitney, ambassador to Great Britain in the Eisenhower administration and later publisher of the *New York Herald Tribune.*[9]

The CIA was also thought to be the hidden sponsor of the Inter-American Press Association, an organization of Latin American and U.S. newspapers that was active in the 1950s and 1960s. One of its principal objectives was to promote freedom of the press.

This technique of covert action does not stop with newspapers and magazines. It extends to books. The Church committee found that the CIA had sponsored, produced, or otherwise subsidized more than 1,250 books published abroad, a number of them in English. Some were reviewed and sold in the United States. Some were written on contract by professors at well-known universities and published as the author's scholarly work. Most, perhaps all, in this category were legitimate scholarship, but they were tainted by hidden sponsorship.

The CIA's hidden use of foreign media—whether newspapers, magazines, books, or radio and television—contributes to a phenomenon known as *blowback.* This occurs when an American news organization unwittingly picks up something that the CIA has planted in a foreign publication and reports it in the United States as an example of foreign opinion. This problem is discussed further in the next section.

DISINFORMATION.   Disinformation is spyspeak for false or misleading information. Various techniques are available for its dissemination. A journalist might be paid to write or broadcast a false story, or an unwitting journalist might be persuaded to do so innocently. Anonymous handbills might be circulated, or graffiti or posters put on walls (especially common in the third world). Gossip might be spread by word of mouth.

Disinformation can have various purposes. One is character assassination, either as part of a political campaign or in order to drive an individual from public life or from a particular position. Character assassination was once engaged in by the CIA but was reportedly abandoned sometime prior to 1975.[10] Other kinds of disinformation are rumors, gossip, or false reports concerning the political plans or other policy intentions of a foreign government or opposition party. (For example, taxes are going to be raised, or import quotas established, or the currency devalued. Company X is going to close a plant or lay off a thousand workers. A political deal is about to be made or broken.)

Some of this activity resembles a *provocation*—an action designed to provoke a response that will provide an excuse for government repression or will enable the government to identify the otherwise anonymous leaders of an opposition group. The person who carries out such an action is an *agent provocateur.* The technique was developed to a high art by the Soviet Union, but it was also used by other European governments against local Communist parties, left-wing groups, and, sometimes, labor unions.

The line between disinformation and more or less legitimate political debate is a fine one. Democratic politicians like to set up a straw man whom they can then proceed to destroy. An entire speech might be constructed against the evils of unilateral disarmament when nobody has suggested such a thing. What makes disinformation different is that it is spread clandestinely by a foreign power, whereas political debate, no matter how shallow, is open and homegrown.

Sometimes the American media have been used by the U.S. government to spread disinformation. One of these cases involved the Libyan regime of Muammar Gadhafi, who was a special irritant to the Reagan administration. The U.S. Navy and Libyan forces came to blows over the definition of international waters in the Gulf of Sidra off the Libyan coast. In addition, the Reagan administration held Gadhafi responsible for sundry terrorist activities. One of these was the bombing of a West Berlin nightclub in April 1986. Two U.S. servicemen died. Later that month U.S. planes carried out bombing raids against Libya. In addition to such overt military retaliation, Libya was the target of repeated proposals for covert action, not all of which were approved, and none of which was successful. One such proposal that was approved by President Reagan in the summer of 1986 called for a disinformation program designed to play on Gadhafi's presumed paranoia. The plan was to combine "real and illusionary events" and to suggest pending American moves in support of an imaginary anti-Gadhafi movement inside Libya. The authors of the plan hoped that Gadhafi would be driven to increase pressure against the army, which in turn would be driven to rebel and overthrow him.

The disinformation first appeared in the *Wall Street Journal* on August 25, 1986. A front-page story reported that the Reagan administration was completing plans for "a new and larger bombing of Libya." The White House called the story "authoritative." Other newspapers and television networks picked up the story, but as reporters tried to learn more, the story began to disintegrate. By October the broad outline of the truth emerged: the whole thing had been made up by the Reagan White House.[11]

The press was furious, feeling that it had been deceived, but neither President Reagan nor Secretary of State George Shultz saw anything wrong in what had been done. "Our position," Reagan explained, "has been one in which we would just as soon have Mr. Gadhafi go to bed every night wondering what we might do." Secretary Shultz concurred, "If I were a private citizen . . . and I read that my government was trying to confuse somebody who was conducting terrorist acts and murdering Americans, I'd say, 'Gee, I hope it's true.' "[12] An anonymous "senior administration official" offered this justification:

> You must distinguish between the audiences, you must distinguish between deception and disinformation. . . . Col. Gadhafi should have some doubt as to what we are doing or might do. But in no way, in carrying out that general policy of the president's, has the White House or anybody suggested or done anything to provide disinformation to the American media.[13]

The administration seemed to be saying that it was possible to mislead Gadhafi, through a story in a prominent American newspaper, without misleading the American people, who make up most of the newspaper's readership.

On the basis of a quick investigation, the staff of the Senate Intelligence Committee split a different hair: the committee staff director absolved the administration of deliberately attempting to plant false stories about Libya in the

U.S. news media, but did not address the question of whether the administration had encouraged the dissemination of an inaccurate story.[14]

Sen. Richard Lugar, R-Ind., chairman of the Foreign Relations Committee, and Sen. Sam Nunn, D-Ga., ranking Democrat on the Armed Services Committee, both used the adjective "stupid" to describe the plan. Nunn added that it was also "inept." [15] There was a further point that apologists for the operation did not take into account. Whatever one might think of the propriety of the American government deceiving the American people, there was no reasonable possibility that such an elaborate hoax could be maintained after the original *Wall Street Journal* story set off the Washington press corps in full cry after details. When the story unraveled, as it inevitably would, then Gadhafi would no longer be deceived either, and the whole covert action would collapse. The net result would be a loss of credibility by the U.S. government. Finally, it should be noted that this was strictly a White House operation; the intelligence community was not involved.

Another covert action plan against Libya (which did not come to fruition either) used a particularly sophisticated kind of disinformation involving third countries. Sudanese intelligence services set up what appeared to be a cell of antigovernment plotters and established contact with Libyans who had been attempting to overthrow Sudanese president Jaafar Nimeri. The idea was that Libyans would be lured into attacking Sudan, thereby providing a pretext for a counterattack against Libya by Egyptian air forces. The U.S. Air Force would help secretly with AWACS radar planes and refueling. The plan fell apart when American participation was revealed prematurely.[16]

Third country disinformation was also used in the CIA's campaign in the early 1970s to undermine the Chilean government of President Allende. In this case the object was to give an exaggerated impression in Chile, especially among the armed forces, of Cuban efforts to infiltrate the Chilean military. Phony reports of these efforts were surreptitiously passed to Chilean officers in third countries in the expectation that the officers would report them back to Santiago, where they would be taken as fact.[17]

The Reagan administration's Strategic Defense Initiative (SDI) or Star Wars program of missile defense gave rise to disinformation that deceived both the Soviet Union and the U.S. Congress. In theory, the defense system would work by firing missiles that would intercept and destroy incoming missiles. The program was bitterly controversial in the United States, and Congress constantly fought over how much to appropriate for it. The program was equally controversial with the Soviet Union, which made its abandonment a key goal of arms control negotiations.

In 1993 it was revealed that SDI tests conducted in 1984 had been rigged to make the program look more successful than it was. As a result of these false tests, Congress appropriated more money to continue the program, and the Soviet Union spent more money to counter the program than it otherwise would have. This additional Soviet spending was sufficiently burdensome, in one estimate, to hasten the Soviet Union's collapse by five years. Even before that, in the view of Robert C. McFarlane, President Reagan's national security adviser during part of the Star Wars program, SDI drove the Soviet Union to serious arms control negotiations.

On the other hand, Les Aspin, who was chairman of the House Armed Services Committee during a part of the same period, has criticized the program. He said that conducting such a program today without informing Congress would be illegal. And an anonymous nuclear physicist who had worked on Star Wars said that the program was characterized by "secrecy, greed, self-deception, deception of the Congress and actually even of the president." [18]

Purists might argue that the rigged SDI tests are not an example of covert action since neither the CIA nor any other intelligence agency was involved, but that is a semantic quibble. The basic purpose was to deceive Congress in order to get more appropriations; deception of the Soviet Union was an afterthought. This may be unfair, but the basic point is undiminished: disinformation, as often as not, is a Catch-22; the United States cannot deceive other people without deceiving its own.

Soviet disinformation against the United States frequently took the form of blaming the CIA for every bad thing that happened, or of setting the CIA up as a straw man to blame for bad things that had not happened yet. When Indian prime minister Indira Gandhi was assassinated in 1984, Tass (the Soviet news agency) and *Pravda* (the Soviet Communist Party newspaper) carried stories hinting at CIA complicity. Some of these were picked up in the Indian press. The year before, communist-oriented Indian papers published a purported cable from Jeane Kirkpatrick, then U.S. ambassador to the United Nations, outlining a strategy for breaking up India into smaller countries. This disinformation had a short life when the cable was proved to be a forgery.[19]

Another piece of Soviet disinformation has proved hardier than most. During the 1980s, the KGB circulated in Latin America stories that North Americans buy Latin American babies and orphans for body parts and organ transplants. A similar story resurfaced in Guatemala in the spring of 1994 and caused mob attacks on some Americans there.

Anti-American propaganda, especially against the CIA, is made more effective by a predisposition in the third world to believe it. Thus, when the CIA is blamed for a coup, even one that did not come off, it is hard to tell whether the CIA is taking a bad rap, or the story is true, or the story's origins are indigenous or inspired abroad. As long ago as World War I, the Allied powers successfully targeted American public opinion to generate support for America's entry into the war. The instrument was a disinformation campaign spreading stories of German atrocities against Belgian babies. These tales were not what precipitated American participation in World War I, but they created a climate of opinion less unfavorable to participation.

The possibility of another kind of disinformation arose in the aftermath of the cold war when some material from KGB, Communist Party, and other files began to become available to scholars in Moscow. Russians even offered to sell some of this material to Western authors. (The file on Kim Philby, the British intelligence officer who secretly worked for the KGB, was priced at $50,000.) Some Western historians wondered: were all the former Soviet files legitimate, or were some fabricated?

Finally, disinformation, or at least gross deception, has been used in more elaborate covert actions directed against the United States. In an effort to create tension between Egypt and the United States in 1954, Israeli intelligence used

Egyptian Jews to place bombs at American facilities in Egypt. Egypt executed two local Jews, and an Israeli intelligence agent also died.[20]

In 1985 Congress ordered the State Department to make a public report on "Soviet and Communist disinformation and press manipulation with respect to the United States."[21] The report, which was sent to Congress in August 1986, recommended establishment of an Office of Disinformation, Analysis and Response. Subsequently renamed the Office of Active Measures Analysis and Response, it became a part of the State Department's Bureau of Intelligence and Research. ("Active measures" is what the KGB called covert action.) With the collapse of the Soviet Union in 1991, the office was abolished and such of its functions as remained relevant were distributed among other offices in the bureau.

STAY BEHINDS.   In countries where political changes may make a continued U.S. government presence impossible, the CIA establishes friendly local residents as "stay behinds"—that is, people who would remain after the Americans leave. The purpose is partly for intelligence collection, partly for possible covert action. The stay behinds are provided with radios and other equipment.

In the early days of the cold war, a considerable network of stay behinds was organized in Western Europe to provide an underground resistance in case of a Soviet invasion or other communist takeover.[22] Less elaborate arrangements have been made in some third world countries with uncertain political futures.

FINANCING FOREIGN ORGANIZATIONS

To further its covert purposes abroad, the United States sometimes finances foreign organizations—political organizations, political parties, and labor unions and other groups.

POLITICAL ORGANIZATIONS.   A covert action may furnish propaganda materials to an organization for its use in a country—antigovernment materials to an opposition group, progovernment materials to a government group. In a country with an authoritarian government, antigovernment propaganda has to be distributed covertly. This can be dangerous, not only for the indigenous organization but also for the CIA officers involved, even when they have diplomatic immunity. In Ethiopia in 1983, a CIA officer, under cover as a commercial attaché, was apprehended inside the home of a member of an Ethiopian opposition group to which he had been supplying antigovernment propaganda. The circumstances of his discovery suggest that the government had infiltrated the opposition. Detained for more than a month, he suffered a fractured skull, chipped vertebrae, and dislocated shoulders under torture. The CIA at first knew only that he had disappeared. The agency mounted a frantic search that ended when Israeli intelligence reported that he was being held by Ethiopian security police. He was released only after the strongest, but secret, protests from the United States. The officer, the station chief, and the deputy station chief were all expelled from Ethiopia. The United States expelled two Ethiopians stationed in Washington.[23]

Sometimes covert action has meant funding an organization that served no purpose other than as a counterweight. In the late 1940s, the CIA put up the money for the Congress of Cultural Freedom in Paris. Acting through the AFL-CIO, the CIA also heavily subsidized noncommunist labor unions in Western Europe during this period.

POLITICAL PARTIES.   A simpler kind of covert action designed to influence foreign politics is the financing of political parties. Christian Democratic parties were the vehicle of choice for many years both in Europe and Latin America. Christian Democrats offered a liberal, and frequently a viable, alternative to communism. In addition, Christian Democracy is an international movement and therefore provides an abundance of cut-outs. As noted earlier, a cut-out is a way to disguise the source of the funds and to make the funds more difficult to trace.

Probably no type of covert action has a higher potential for backfiring than direct intervention in another country's elections. With the first credible charge of foreign interference, the intended beneficiary is ruined. It is therefore of the utmost importance that the American hand be concealed. The purpose of the cut-out is to aid in that concealment. Sometimes two or even more cut-outs are used. Christian Democratic parties have a loose international network that makes it easy to channel funds from a party in one country to a party in another. The funds then arrive in the target country as an expression of fraternal Christian Democratic solidarity, not as a form of foreign intervention. To make the operation even more secure, the funds may move in stages: (1) from the CIA to a handful of wealthy Americans known for their support of liberal causes; (2) then to a third-country Christian Democratic Party; (3) finally, to the ultimate recipient. The beneficiary may win an election in blissful ignorance of the real source of some of his campaign contributions. In fact, in Chile in 1964, he probably did.

In particular cases where foreign policy objectives have been thought to require an all-out effort, the CIA has combined all of these techniques, along with some others. In Chile in 1964, in addition to what has been described, it supported the mobilization of many interest groups, including labor, students, business, and the professions. Editorials and news stories were planted in third country publications and then reported in Chile as representative of foreign opinion. (Some of them were also inadvertently reported in the United States, another example of blowback.) Agricultural commodities supplied to Chile under the foreign aid program (P.L. 480) were turned over to local Christian Democratic parties for distribution; in this way the Christian Democrats received the political credit. This was the same technique once used in the United States by big city political bosses who sent baskets of food or coal to deserving party members at Christmas or perhaps in other times of need. The CIA spent $3 million, or about $1 per Chilean voter in the 1964 elections. In the U.S. election the same year, the major party candidates together spent about 50 cents per voter.[24]

The Institute of Political Education, which operated in San José, Costa Rica, in the early 1960s, was an effort to institutionalize the covert propagation of democracy. Major funding for the institute was provided by the CIA through a foundation in New York. The institute presented itself as jointly sponsored and funded by a coalition of leading democratic parties in Latin America—principally, Acción Democrática in Venezuela, the Liberal Party in Colombia, the National Liberation Party in Costa Rica, the Liberal Party in Honduras, APRA (*Alianza Popular Revolucionaria Americana*) in Peru, and the MRL (*Movimiento Revolucionario Liberal*) in Bolivia.

The purpose of the institute was to train young political leaders in the nuts and bolts of party organization and electoral processes. Its major project was the democratization of the Dominican Republic following the assassination of longtime dictator Gen. Rafael Leonidas Trujillo in May 1961. The chosen instrument for this purpose was Juan Bosch and his Dominican Revolutionary Party (PRD, after its Spanish initials). Bosch was installed as the president of the institute, and an entire class was filled with PRD workers. The group returned to the Dominican Republic in 1962, and Bosch was duly elected president, but in September 1963 he was overthrown.

In 1983 Congress eliminated much of the incentive for these covert contortions when it adopted a recommendation of the Reagan administration and established the National Endowment for Democracy, a private, nonprofit organization financed by appropriated funds. The endowment makes grants to institutes sponsored by the Democratic and Republican parties, as well as to the AFL-CIO and the U.S. Chamber of Commerce. The grants are for foreign activities to strengthen democratic political parties and processes. Private contributions are also received, and the connection with the U.S. government is sufficiently tenuous that the activity can be carried out publicly.

The Agency for International Development (AID), which administers the foreign aid program, also has assumed some of the foreign political work once done by the CIA. In 1990, for example, Congress provided AID with $10 million for a "Transition to Democracy" project in South Africa. The project gave the Inkatha Freedom Party and the African National Congress "infrastructure support" for such things as office and communication equipment and items needed for publication and distribution of pamphlets.

LABOR UNIONS AND OTHER GROUPS.   Political parties, of course, are not the only organizations that influence events in foreign countries. In many countries labor unions play an important role. An early covert action was to finance noncommunist unions in Western Europe at the start of the cold war. Subsequently, third world unions received help on a selective basis.

The U.S. government's principal instrument for promoting trade union development in Latin America has been the American Institute of Free Labor Development (AIFLD), a joint enterprise of the AFL-CIO and U.S. business. Most of AIFLD's funding has come overtly through the U.S. foreign aid program. There have been repeated indications, however, that AIFLD has been used at least as a funnel for covert funds destined for electoral activity in Latin America. In 1985 labor union officials in El Salvador said AIFLD had promised them $150,000 that never arrived. The reason apparently was that the United States decided that the right wing did not represent as big a threat as had been thought. The previous year Salvadoran unions had received $200,000 to pay political workers during a presidential election campaign.[25]

Any pressure group promoting a cause congenial to U.S. foreign policy is a candidate for covert support. Sometimes the inspiration to organize such a group is part of a covert action. Sometimes the support is nothing more than a typewriter or mimeograph machine for the group's office. These efforts can grow. The United States' involvement in Angola started with not much more than a mimeograph machine for an anticommunist group, but it ended with underwriting a civil war.

AGENTS OF INFLUENCE

An agent of influence is a foreigner who is under American control and who is in a position to influence a foreign government, organization, or institution. The agent might be the president (or monarch) of the country. It might be the foreign minister's (or somebody else's) wife or mistress. It might be anybody in a policy-making position or anybody who can influence somebody in a policy-making position. It might even be a person in a position to influence public opinion. Many agents of influence are foreign journalists. The role of an agent of influence in covert action is to try to persuade the foreign government, organization, or institution to adopt the particular policy or course of action favored by the United States.

There are two kinds of covert actions in which agents of influence are used. The more numerous kind is routine and ongoing. The agents are generally well briefed on U.S. foreign policy as it affects their country, and their job is to see to it that their country's actions are compatible with that policy and, if possible, to advance it. The agents might be expected, for example, to have their country on the same side as the United States in the United Nations or other international organization. They must be careful, of course, not to be so vocal or active as to acquire a reputation as too pro-American; that would impair their effectiveness and possibly cost them their jobs.

There are fuzzy areas where distinctions are hard to make. If a foreign official is paid by the CIA to speak up for the U.S. position in a cabinet meeting, he is an agent of influence. But if he speaks up for the United States because that is how he perceives his own country's national interest, he is simply a friend. Maybe he is a friend who is also an agent.

The other kind of covert action is larger and is specifically targeted. The purpose may be to influence the action of the target country's Congress or Parliament on an issue of concern to the United States. Such an issue might be ratification of a treaty, action on trade legislation, or even action on an internal issue affecting American interests—for example, tax policy, land reform, or rules for foreign investment. In such cases a covert action uses as many agents of influence as are available in or outside the government. Many case officers and cut-outs are required under centralized coordination and direction, usually by the chief of station. Sometimes an active propaganda or lobbying campaign is mounted in the country in question.

It is readily apparent that agents of influence can also be collection agents (see Chapter 4). If the CIA hires, bribes, blackmails, seduces, or otherwise persuades foreigners to feed it information to which they are privy, most of the time those same foreigners can be used to influence others with whom they come in contact. If the collection agent is a janitor who brings the CIA the contents of wastebaskets, this person has no influence. If the collection agent is the secretary of an official, the official may or may not listen to the secretary's suggestions, but the secretary can still report on what the boss is doing. But if the agent is an official, then obviously the agent is a gold nugget both for collection and influence (unless, of course, he or she is a double agent).

Agents serve this dual role in many organizations outside of governments. Over the years in many countries the CIA has devoted a great deal of time and effort to infiltrating organizations—usually those that it regards as subversive but sometimes those that are simply of more than ordinary influence. The object has been, first, to find out as much as possible about the organization in question—its sources of financing, its process of making decisions, its ties with other organizations, and its strengths and weaknesses in general. The object has also been to influence the organization's decisions and actions, to aid and abet them if they are favorable to American foreign policy objectives and to sabotage them if they are not.

Whether you are dealing with a country's foreign office or a ragtag group of guerrillas out in the jungle, it is a good idea to have more than one agent. This has sometimes made the CIA the butt of jokes ("that two-bit gang doesn't have but ten members, and five of them are being paid by the CIA"), and doubtless the CIA has sometimes had more agents than it really needed. But multiple agents are prudent insurance against a variety of risks. They make it easier to spot an agent who has been doubled because the agent's reports will be at variance with others. They make it easier to spot an agent who is exaggerating his or her reports in the hope of extracting more money from the CIA. If one agent is compromised, you still have others.

During the cold war, the CIA tried mightily to infiltrate Communist parties around the world. That target is of less interest since the breakup of the Soviet Union and the disappearance of the Soviet Communist Party, but it continues to be relevant, especially in the Far East, as long as the Chinese Communist Party plays its dominant role there. *Sendero Luminoso* (Shining Path), a radical Maoist revolutionary group in Peru, is of great interest, as are terrorist organizations in general, especially those associated with radical Arab states or movements.

There are two ways to infiltrate a group, an organization, or a government office. One way is to find somebody who is already a part of it and who can be persuaded, by whatever means, to report to you on its internal activities and also to try to influence those activities on your behalf. The other way is to send somebody under your control to join the organization. If the organization is engaged in illegal or shady activities, this is likely to take a long time because the outsider trying to join will not be admitted until he establishes himself as trustworthy. Some terrorist organizations are said to require, as a test of membership, that an applicant shoot and kill somebody at random on a city street. This is a test that few people are sufficiently motivated to attempt.

As a rule, the CIA's primary reason for the placement of agents in organizations or governments is the collection of intelligence. If the agency were to set out to recruit or infiltrate agents of influence for a particular covert action, the process would be so time-consuming that the action would be over before the agents were in place. An exception is paramilitary operations for which units are recruited and trained after it is decided to undertake the operation.

MILITARY AND PARAMILITARY FORCES

A foreign country's military forces can be used indirectly to carry out a covert action directed against that country. A typical example occurs when a foreign army is inspired or encouraged to carry out a coup d'état against its own government. The CIA may not be involved at all. The inspiration may come directly from the ambassador, who may tell a general, "If you do this, the United States will recognize your government immediately. We'll enter into a foreign aid program, and we'll send the navy to keep the former government from counterattacking." This violates the Carter and Reagan executive orders making the CIA the sole agent of covert action, but most of the examples of this kind occurred before those orders were issued. In any event, it is usually called diplomacy. Jefferson Caffery, a distinguished career foreign service officer who held many ambassadorial posts in the mid-twentieth century, once told a visiting Senate delegation that he had been in nine revolutions and had managed four of them. It is doubtful if modern ambassadors are as active as Caffery; certainly none is so frank.

Encouragement of foreign military coups is deliberately indirect and ambiguous. The CIA does not like to leave a paper trail. Its officers speak and write in circumlocutions. This leaves room for doubt and dispute over whether a coup is, in fact, American-inspired. It is the job of American military attachés to know what the foreign military forces are up to and what their leaders are thinking. An attaché has done his job extraordinarily well when a foreign officer confides in him that a coup is planned. How the American reacts at that moment may determine what message the plotters think they have received from the U.S. government about American policy. This, in turn, may determine whether the coup goes ahead or is aborted. The message the plotters think they receive may be different from the message the American thinks he is sending. His words may say, "don't," but his body language, either deliberately or inadvertently, may say, "go".

This kind of fuzziness is one reason many people, especially in the third world, see CIA involvement where none exists. Another reason is that there are plenty of cases where it did, in fact, exist. A review of some of these cases shows the variety of techniques and circumstances.

MOB ACTION.   Military force is not always necessary; sometimes mob action will do. In 1951, under the leadership of Mohammed Mossadegh, the Iranian Majlis (Parliament) passed a law nationalizing the British-owned Anglo-Iranian Oil Company, and Mossadegh's popularity became so great that Shah Mohammed Reza Pahlavi appointed him prime minister. During the next two years, Mossadegh pushed through further nationalist measures, and as his power increased, the shah's declined. In August 1953 the shah tried to remove Mossadegh from office but was himself forced to flee the country when mobs took to the streets in support of Mossadegh.

At this point the CIA and its British counterpart, MI6, turned things around, and the mobs demonstrated in support of the shah. (Large sums of cash in small bills were available to encourage these demonstrations.) This time it was Mossadegh who fled, and the shah returned to rule Iran until he was forced to flee a second, and final, time in 1979.[26] The British motivation in this was to reclaim their oil company; the American motivation was to stop a potential trend to nationalization of foreign oil companies in the Middle East.

It is indicative of the difference in the American and British approaches to covert action that the American role in the overthrow of Mossadegh is mentioned frequently; the British role, rarely. One former British intelligence officer has written that MI6 had a great deal more to do with ousting Mossadegh than did the CIA. MI6, he says, planned the coup for two years: "All that the CIA contributed . . . was that when they saw which way the wind was blowing, they affixed portraits of the Shah to their cars and drove around Tehran with horns sounding and headlights flashing!" [27]

EXILES.   In 1954 President Jacobo Arbenz Guzmán of Guatemala was overthrown by a band of exiles who invaded the country from Honduras. Arbenz had taken office three years earlier with a reformist program that included land redistribution. His government, which expropriated 225,000 acres owned by the United Fruit Company, drifted steadily to the left and received some arms from the Soviet bloc.

The CIA found a Guatemalan army officer, Col. Carlos Castillo Armas, who had escaped from jail and gone into exile in Honduras after leading an unsuccessful revolt against Arbenz. Castillo Armas rounded up a small group of other exiles, and the CIA supplied him with some former U.S. Air Force planes with American civilian pilots. The invasion of Guatemala was launched in June 1954. After initial problems it eventually succeeded (with the help of more American planes), and Castillo Armas became president of Guatemala on July 8.[28]

During the fighting, such as it was, the CIA used a disinformation technique known as *snuggling*. A rebel radio announcer mimicked the voice of the government spokesman, and the CIA used the frequency next to the government station, so that many listeners thought they were hearing the government when in fact they were hearing the rebels.[29]

There was an unfortunate side effect of the short-lived revolution when the rebel air force sank a British merchant ship under the mistaken impression that it was carrying gasoline to the government. (It was in fact carrying cotton.)

The Guatemalan affair would not have been possible without the exiles. Exiles or refugees have also played important roles in other covert actions—for example, in Cuba and Afghanistan. There is a fine line between using such groups to accomplish American purposes abroad and dealing with them as parts of the American body politic. The United States is the country of first choice for most exiles. Some think of themselves as refugees and then as immigrants and eventually as Americans. Others retain a dream to return some day to their homeland; they have an abiding hatred for the government that drove them into exile and a burning desire to see it overthrown (preferably with their help). These exiles are eager to influence U.S. foreign policy to this end, and they provide a reservoir of potential recruits for CIA-sponsored paramilitary forces.

(The Cuban community centered in Miami is a notable example.) Even immigrants who become thoroughly Americanized retain emotional ties to their homelands and form influential foreign policy lobbies. Polish Americans and Greek Americans are two of many examples that could be cited.

CUBA.   Fidel Castro came to power in Cuba on New Year's Day 1959 as a new kind of Latin American revolutionary—young (thirty-two), charismatic, leftist. He promptly embarked on a program of revolutionary change that involved imprisonment or liquidation of agents of the old regime as well as expropriation of foreign businesses, most of them American. If he was not already a communist in 1959 (as many thought), he shortly became one.

By 1960 the Eisenhower administration despaired of getting along with Castro, and the president authorized the covert action program that eventually came to be known as the Bay of Pigs. The Castro revolution produced an abundance of Cuban exiles, most of whom made their way to Miami, where they constituted a noisy ethnic anti-Castro lobby. The Eisenhower program called for clandestinely organizing a number of these exiles into a brigade-size military force, equipping them, training them at a secret base in Guatemala, and supporting them in an invasion of Cuba to be launched from Nicaragua. (Note that without the earlier success of the covert action in Guatemala, other arrangements would have had to be made for training for the Bay of Pigs.)

These plans were well advanced by January 1961, when John F. Kennedy succeeded Dwight D. Eisenhower as president. After some hesitation Kennedy gave the go-ahead for the Bay of Pigs invasion. He made it clear that he would not permit the direct involvement of American forces. Without such direct American help the invasion was a disastrous failure. Members of the invading force who were not killed were captured. They were later ransomed for $53 million worth of food and medicine.

Castro thereupon became an obsession for both the Kennedy administration and the Cuban exiles. Between 1961 and 1965, there were at least eight plots to kill Castro.[30] One of them was a contract with the mafia. The CIA also stretched its imagination for other dirty tricks that, if they would not remove him, would at least embarrass him. One of the more ingenious of these was a powder to be sprinkled on his boots. If it worked, its fumes would make his beard fall out, thereby destroying the macho image which is so important in Latin America. It did not work.

The exiles, for their part, did not rest. In the years immediately following the Bay of Pigs, the exiles had help from the CIA, mainly in the form of supplies and technical assistance, for a series of mosquito-bite raids on the Cuban coast and other harassing activities. Under the Johnson administration, which succeeded Kennedy in 1963, the CIA involvement was phased out, but the exiles were only slightly deterred. In one respect they broadened their activities, directing harassment and sabotage operations against perceived pro-Castro elements in the United States and in third countries. The exiles also formed the talent pool from which the Watergate burglars were drawn in 1972.[31]

The Bay of Pigs came less than a year after the U-2 incident (see Chapter 4). The U-2 provided the first significant impetus toward congressional oversight of the intelligence community. The Bay of Pigs gave it another push. The Senate Foreign Relations Committee again held hearings in executive session, but no report was issued.[32] When the hearings were over, Sen. Homer E. Capehart, a Republican member of the committee from Indiana, remarked that he had seen Boy Scouts better organized.

NICARAGUA.   The regime of President Anastasio Somoza was overthrown in July 1979 by indigenous opponents with no significant help from abroad. Somoza went into exile (he was later assassinated in Paraguay), and the victorious rebels began trying to consolidate their revolution. They called themselves Sandinistas, after César Augusto Sandino, who had conducted a guerrilla war against the U.S. Marine occupation in the 1920s and 1930s. Sandino was murdered in 1934 when he went to a presumed peace conference with the father of the Somoza who was deposed in 1979. Nicaragua had spent all of the intervening forty-five years under the domination of the Somoza family.

The Sandinistas shortly exhibited a leftward, authoritarian bent and established close relations with the Soviet Union and with Cuba (which had many advisers and a foreign aid program in the country). The Sandinistas also had ties with guerrilla forces attempting to overthrow a right-wing government in El Salvador. All of this alarmed the Reagan administration, which took office in the United States in 1981 and which soon set in motion plans for covert action against the Sandinistas.

The chosen instrument in these plans was the large number of Somocista exiles in Miami and Honduras as well as some anti-Sandinista groups remaining in Nicaragua. In the beginning the American objective was to interdict the flow of arms from Nicaragua to the Salvadoran rebels. (Nicaragua was simply a transfer point; the arms originated in Cuba or in the European Soviet bloc. Some of them were American and had been captured by communist forces in Vietnam.) But the American objective soon broadened to putting pressure on the Nicaraguan government as well.

Perhaps inevitably, the American activities leaked to the press, and vigorous political controversy ensued. The controversy increased when it was disclosed that the CIA had overseen the mining of Nicaraguan harbors as a means of enforcing an undeclared but de facto blockade. Congress responded by passing a succession of laws forbidding activity designed to overthrow the Nicaraguan government.

Thus was set the scene for what became the Iran-Contra scandal, possibly the most arrogant, egregious misuse of executive power in American history. The details of that scandal have been amply documented elsewhere and need not be repeated here beyond the bare facts.[33] These are that the Reagan White House, and especially the staff of the National Security Council, refused to accept the congressional decision to halt anti-Sandinista activities. At the same time, some arms sales were secretly made to Iran (at a time when such sales contravened U.S. policy) in the hope of securing the release of Americans held hostage by Moslem extremists in Lebanon. Proceeds of the arms sales were diverted through secret Swiss bank accounts to support the Nicaraguan Contras. This scheme began to unravel when an aircraft flying an illegal mission to supply the Contras was shot down, and the Sandinistas captured a surviving American crew member.

In 1989 the incoming Bush administration in Washington arranged a political truce in both the United States and Nicaragua. Elections held in Nicaragua in 1990 were won by anti-Sandinista forces, but there was little political reconciliation, and the economy went into a deep slump.

LAOS.   In Laos dissident internal groups were used as a tool of covert action. The United States' involvement in Laos, beginning in the 1950s and ending in 1975, was related to its larger concerns over Vietnam. The involvement basically took the form of clandestine support of Meo tribesmen in northern and northwestern Laos; the tribesmen were encouraged to resist inroads by Vietnamese and Laotian communists. By the late 1960s, this resulted in a medium-sized war in which the United States was a principal but unacknowledged player. The CIA station in Vientiane had more than 100 officers as well as a branch office across the river in Thailand. (The figure of 100 came from a confidential source in the CIA; published estimates have the station at "about" 400 officers.)[34] Air America, a CIA proprietary disguised as a commercial airline, provided logistical support. Light planes, flown by U.S. Air Force pilots in civilian clothes, served as spotters for Meo artillery fire. In the end this covert action failed, and Laos came under communist domination. The Meo suffered heavy casualties.

IRAQ.   U.S. support of the Kurds in Iraq is analogous to U.S. support of the Meo in Laos: it was shortlived, it was given for extraneous reasons, and it was ineffective. During the early 1970s, the United States responded to appeals from its friend the shah of Iran and covertly supplied arms to Kurds in northern Iraq. Seeking independence from Iraq, as they had been for a long time, the Kurds were a force for instability in the country. Promoting instability in Iraq suited the purposes of the shah, who was also concerned that the Iraqi regime had given sanctuary to certain Iranian exiles.

In 1975 Iran and Iraq settled their boundary dispute over access to the Persian Gulf. As part of the settlement, Iran agreed to stop helping the Kurds in Iraq; although the United States was not involved in the Iran-Iraq agreement, it also abandoned the Kurds.

In the aftermath of the Persian Gulf War in 1991, the Kurds rose against a weakened Iraq but to no avail; an Iraqi campaign of suppression against them was stopped only by vigorous allied intervention. The allies, led by the United States, established a protected zone for the Kurds north of the thirty-sixth parallel and provided, quite overtly, substantial food, medicine, and other relief assistance. By the fall of 1992, the Kurds had a rudimentary self-government in place, American protection and assistance, but no international recognition.

ANGOLA.   Until 1975 Angola was a Portuguese colony on the southwest coast of Africa with an area bigger than Texas and California combined and a population less than metropolitan Los Angeles. Angola became independent with three factions fighting for control: the Marxist Popular Movement for the Liberation of Angola (MPLA, after its Portuguese initials), the centrist National

Front for the Liberation of Angola (FNLA), and the rightist National Union for the Total Independence of Angola (UNITA). The United States initially gave covert assistance to the centrist FNLA, while the Soviet Union helped the MPLA and South Africa helped UNITA. The American involvement started small but grew rapidly, and in early 1976 Congress ended it. Congress would probably not have known about it at all without passage of the Hughes-Ryan amendment to the foreign aid bill in 1974. The amendment required all covert actions to be reported to certain committees.

Angola became an example of almost all the problems, complexities, and contradictions of covert action. It was the subject of Congress's first specific prohibition of a covert action. Later it was the subject of the first public congressional debate over whether an aid program should be overt or covert. There was open lobbying on both sides, and Congress was treated to the bizarre spectacle of the principal Angolan rebel hiring a Washington public relations firm to press his case for covert aid. Through it all the United States remained Angola's biggest trading partner, annually importing $1.1 billion worth of oil produced by the Gulf (later Chevron) Oil Corporation in an Angolan field guarded by Cuban troops.

Without U.S. aid the FNLA dropped out of the picture. The MPLA formed a government but was unable to consolidate its hold on the country, even with the assistance of several thousand Cuban troops whose presence added a further complicating factor. When the Reagan administration took office in 1981, the only anticommunist force in Angola was UNITA, led by Jonas Savimbi and supported by the Republic of South Africa.

Under heavy administration pressure, Congress voted in 1985 to repeal the ban on aid to Angola, and Savimbi finally got the aid the following year. In December 1990 MPLA and UNITA agreed to a cease-fire and to elections, which were held under U.N. supervision in September 1992. UNITA lost and initially refused to accept MPLA's victory, but in December UNITA agreed to join a government of national unity and to include its forces in a new unified army. The agreement was short lived. By January 1993 Savimbi's forces were again in the field attacking government positions. The warfare continued despite repeated talk of new cease-fire agreements, and in September 1993 an exasperated U.N. Security Council imposed an oil and arms embargo against UNITA. Negotiations resumed in December 1993 with no result by the summer of 1994.

AFGHANISTAN.   Afghanistan was the focus of the CIA's all-time biggest covert action program. Authoritative figures have not been published, but informed estimates of its price tag run as high as $3 billion—$2 billion in arms and $1 billion in supplies and equipment—over nine years.[35] This was a large amount of money for a large program, one so large that it ceased being covert long before it was over.

When the Soviet Union sent troops into Afghanistan in December 1979 to strengthen a shaky pro-Soviet government, unexpectedly strong local opposition was aroused. Anti-Soviet Afghans poured across the borders into Iran and Pakistan. Those in Pakistan became the instrument by which the Soviets in Afghanistan were eventually defeated a decade later.

To give its invasion of Afghanistan a fig leaf of respectability, the Soviet Union portrayed it as a response to a call for help from a fraternal government. The Brezhnev doctrine, named after Soviet premier Leonid Brezhnev, held that "socialist" governments anywhere in the world would not be allowed to fall. But for the Carter administration, the invasion signaled the end of what was left of U.S.-Soviet détente. Carter asked the Senate to suspend consideration of SALT II, the second strategic arms limitation treaty. Carter also authorized the U.S. covert action program in Afghanistan.

Typically, the program started small. The initial objective was not to drive the Soviets from Afghanistan but only to harass them. This was in accordance with the initial assessment in Washington that the Soviets could sustain their occupation of Afghanistan indefinitely at an acceptable cost. In the beginning the arms used in the program were mainly light weapons from China, some donated by the Chinese, some purchased by the CIA. Saudi Arabia also supplied some funds. The program on the ground was managed by Pakistan's Inter-Services Intelligence (ISI). Pakistanis organized the Afghans, trained them at bases in Pakistan, and even on some occasions accompanied them on their forays back into Afghanistan.

Then in about 1984 a combination of factors led to a major escalation in the scope and tempo of the program. In Washington President Reagan and his DCI, William Casey, were viscerally more predisposed to covert action than were President Carter and his DCI, Stansfield Turner. To counter the Brezhnev doctrine, Reagan had put forth his own doctrine: the United States would help any groups resisting, or seeking to overthrow, communist governments. In the field the United States was having more success than had been anticipated, and a new intelligence source was providing specific information about Soviet war plans. After considerable internal debate the Reagan administration decided to give the Afghans more sophisticated weapons as well as more sensitive intelligence about Soviet movements.[36]

This greater activity brought to the surface problems that had always been in the program. One was the perennial problem of the accountability of funds; with more funds there were more reports of graft. The cosponsors of the program had diverse objectives. They agreed only on expelling the Soviets; in other respects they had widely different agendas. The Pakistanis had a geopolitical interest (they share a common boundary with Afghanistan), but they also had a religious interest (promotion of Islamic fundamentalism, which was among the last things the United States wanted). The Saudis, who followed a different branch of Islam, also were not happy with the prospect. The Afghan rebels split along more or less the same lines, and there was friction over which group got how much help. Independently, an Iranian program trained a large number of Afghan refugees to be guerrilla fighters. Some of them turned up years later fighting underground against established governments in Algeria, Egypt, and Tunisia.[37]

Notwithstanding these difficulties, the program worked. The Soviet occupiers encountered mounting troubles in what came to be referred to as their Vietnam. With their country beset by even greater problems at home, they threw in the towel in 1988 and completed their withdrawal in 1989.

The American-Pakistani-Saudi-Chinese covert intervention ended with the Soviets' exodus, but peace did not return to Afghanistan. On the contrary, the differences between the guerrilla factions became even more marked as the various groups fought among themselves. It was reported in December 1992 that these internecine battles had caused more destruction in Kabul than the fourteen-year war against the communists.[38]

Unlike contemporaneous covert actions in Nicaragua and Angola, the covert action in Afghanistan was backed by Congress. More than once Congress appropriated more money than the executive branch had requested. Sen. Orrin Hatch, R-Utah, then a member of the Intelligence Committee, even made a secret trip to Beijing to solicit more aid from the Chinese.

The program lost its covertness for two reasons. One was its size. Even in a place as remote as northwest Pakistan and Afghanistan, an operation this big cannot be concealed indefinitely. The second reason was the weaponry. The rebels used modern weapons from the United States. If they were captured, the Soviets would know that they could only have come from the United States. Before the Reagan administration's decision to send sophisticated arms, the rebels' weapons could have come from any number of places—and did.

Long after the program in Afghanistan lost its secrecy, the U.S. government preserved the hands-off fiction. This was one way to keep the operation from presenting a direct challenge to what was then the Soviet Union. If the Soviets chose to accept it as a challenge, they could do so—and escalate the situation into a major superpower confrontation, which neither country wanted. On the other hand, if the Soviets chose to ignore the thinly disguised American hand, as in fact they did, confrontation could be avoided. As in the U-2 case, each superpower knew that the other knew what was being done, and each chose to ignore it.

Some unintended consequences of the Afghan operation remained in 1994. The United States became concerned that Stinger shoulder-fired, heat-seeking antiaircraft missiles, which had been supplied (after some soul-searching) to the guerrillas, might fall into the hands of terrorists who would use them against civilian aircraft. Therefore, the CIA started trying to buy them back, sometimes in black markets for twice their original value. There was also concern about possible next targets of Islamic fundamentalists who had received arms and training as Afghan rebels.[39]

Covert Actions That Did Not Happen

Mention should be made of suggestions and plans for covert action that never came to fruition because they were disapproved by higher political authority. Some of these plans lie buried in unmarked graves. Others, those described in this section, have come to public attention in one way or another.

INDONESIA. A military coup d'état in 1965 turned into an anticommunist revolution that eventually left perhaps as many as 250,000 dead. The CIA was first said to be behind it. Then the coup was said to be self-generated but the CIA was said to have furnished the names of 5,000 persons to be killed. Finally, archives in the Lyndon B. Johnson Library revealed the truth. Although the United States had yearned for a change in government in Indonesia, it had despaired of bringing one about. When the coup happened, it caught the entire U.S. government, including the CIA, by surprise. One Suharto emerged as the army commander, and the American mission in Jakarta did not even know who he was. (Indonesians are given to using only one name, and there were several high-ranking Suhartos.)[40]

GREECE.   In 1967 the American embassy in Athens, strongly urged on by the CIA station, recommended a $100,000 covert program to finance an opposition party in prospective elections scheduled for July. The recommendation was disapproved by the White House, but a military coup in April made the question moot. The CIA was accused of being behind the coup, but the weight of the evidence is that the agency was not directly involved.[41]

LIBYA.   Among the several covert action plans directed against the Libyan regime of Col. Muammar Gadhafi was one involving use of several hundred Libyan soldiers who had been captured in Chad. Libya conducted a long campaign of harassment against its southern neighbor Chad in the 1980s, and it was thought that some of the Libyan troops involved could be turned against Gadhafi. The troops in question were trained in Chad and then flown to Zaire, where some of them decided they wanted to go home. The remainder were taken to a refugee camp in Kenya from which they eventually dispersed.[42]

GRENADA.   Alarmed by evidence of Cuban penetration of Grenada, a tiny island in the Caribbean, the Reagan administration in 1981 proposed a plan to use economic pressure to destabilize the Grenadan government. The Senate Intelligence Committee reacted so adversely that the plan was scrapped.[43] Two years later, in 1983, Reagan ordered American troops to seize the island. They did so, and withdrew after overseeing a change in government and the departure of some Cubans, most of whom were building an airfield. The American foreign aid program subsequently paid to finish the airfield that the Cubans had started.

WHO DECIDES COVERT ACTION?

More often than not, proposals for covert action originate in the bureaucracy—in the State Department, the CIA, the Pentagon, or the National Security Council staff—and sometimes they are so much a part of the policy-making process that nobody can say with confidence who first suggested a given action. It simply emerges from a consideration of a problem: life would be easier if Party A won a forthcoming election, or if Minister B were not so stubborn, or if Country C's military could be persuaded to do X. Once covert action is suggested as a possible option, the CIA is asked to produce a plan to implement it.

The plan then follows a fairly standardized route that has changed over time in detail but not in general outline. It is considered by an interagency committee, which has had a number of names over the years as well as a shifting membership. It always includes high-level representatives of the State and Defense departments, the CIA, and the NSC staff. Sometimes the committee has included representatives of the White House, the intelligence community, and the Justice Department. This interagency committee is the crucial element. If the committee rejects a proposal, it is rarely heard of again (though some hardy perennials keep turning up from time to time, perhaps in modified form). Committee approval of a proposal usually sets a covert action in motion. Theoretically, the committee is acting on behalf, and with the authority, of the NSC, but the NSC does not always know what the committee is doing. Sometimes this is because the council delegates the decision, sometimes because it is trying to shield the president so that his responsibility can be denied if the operation goes sour.

The committee is a reflection of its members and particularly of the strength of character (or lack thereof) of its chairman. During the Nixon and Ford administrations, Henry Kissinger—first as national security adviser and then as secretary of state—was chairman of the committee and was its dominant figure. The committee frequently acted by telephone, and in one stretch from April 1972 to December 1974, it approved nearly forty covert actions without a single meeting.[44]

However the decision is made in the executive branch, there then comes another step, added since Congress got serious about oversight in the mid-1970s. The president is required to make a "finding" that the proposed action "is necessary to support identifiable foreign policy objectives of the United States and is important to the national security of the United States." The finding must be in writing unless the requirement for action is so urgent that time does not permit. Even in those cases a written record is to be made contemporaneously and reduced to a written finding as soon as possible but in no more than forty-eight hours. The finding must specify any government entity, other than the CIA, that is authorized to participate and the rules under which it does so. The finding must also state whether any third party, not under the control of the U.S. government, is expected to participate. Finally, no finding may "authorize any action that would violate the Constitution or any statute of the United States."[45]

The finding is to be reported to the congressional intelligence committees "as soon as possible" and before the start of the covert action. There are two exceptions. If the president determines "that it is essential to limit access to the finding to meet extraordinary circumstances affecting vital interests of the United States," the finding may be reported to a more select group: the chairmen and ranking minority members of the intelligence committees, the Speaker and minority leader of the House, majority and minority leaders of the Senate, and "such other member or members of the congressional leadership as may be included by the president." Second, if the finding is not reported in advance, the president "shall fully inform the intelligence committees in a timely fashion and shall provide a statement of the reasons for not giving prior notice." The president also has to explain why he has chosen to limit access.[46]

If the intelligence committees, or the smaller group of congressional leaders receiving the report, have no objection to the proposed covert action, it proceeds. If they do object, it may proceed anyway, but the committees have several options to continue the argument. They may express their objections so forcefully to the DCI at the time he presents the finding that he goes back to the president with a recommendation that the action be abandoned. Or the committees can take up their objections directly with the president. As a former chairman of the House Intelligence Committee has said, it is easier for Congress than for the bureaucracy to say no to the president.

Of course, if the committees are not told until after the action has been started, they have no chance to block it. The House Intelligence Committee reported in 1988 that there had been only one instance of prior notice to the leadership group instead of to the full committee.[47] (Obviously not included were the multiple failures to give notice related to Iran-Contra.) One House committee source has estimated that the House Intelligence Committee caused the modification or abandonment of six proposed covert actions over a period of six years during the Reagan administration.

These provisions were among the legacies of the Iran-Contra affair. They were enacted in 1991 only after prolonged controversy between the Senate Intelligence Committee and President Bush. They are part of the Intelligence Authorization Act for Fiscal 1991.

PROBLEMS OF COVERT ACTION

Covert action causes the most dramatic foreign policy problems, of course, when it fails. It has been fashionable to point to the Bay of Pigs as perhaps the most spectacular example. Yet the recovery of the American image after the Bay of Pigs was equally spectacular. The landing in Cuba took place in April 1961. In December, only eight months later, President Kennedy was greeted by wildly cheering crowds on a visit to Bogotá. In January 1962 the United States was able to put together a vote in the Organization of American States to ostracize the Castro regime.

More important problems of covert action arise when the action is not kept covert. Secrecy becomes more difficult as the size of the operation increases. This is especially the case if military or paramilitary forces are involved. These forces mean people, and people talk. They talk less if they are well disciplined and highly motivated, but the more people, the greater the likelihood that at least one will talk.

As military and paramilitary operations increase in size, they become more complicated, increasing the possibility that something will go wrong and the whole enterprise will unravel. The end of the Iran-Contra operation began when a single American survived an airplane crash. The danger of compromise is less if the action is being carried out in remote parts of the world. The covert action in Laos was on a very large scale, but it was kept secret for years because there was no one else there to notice.

Large operations without military or paramilitary forces are less prone to disclosure, mainly because they typically involve money instead of people. Some sizable political action operations have remained secret for considerable periods. But even in these cases, small operations are more likely to go undetected than big ones.

There is a paradox about covert action: success feeds on itself and ultimately leads to failure. The success of the operation in Iran to overthrow Mossadegh in 1953 laid the predicate for the attempt to overthrow Arbenz in Guatemala in 1954, which encouraged the Bay of Pigs attempt in 1961 to overthrow Castro—a dismal failure. One Washington wag at the time remarked that the policy makers forgot that Cuba was surrounded by water.

There is another problem. Repeated covert actions require the maintenance of a group of skilled, motivated people with a high *esprit de corps*. Such people will look for things to do to demonstrate their technical expertise. Strong and disciplined leadership is required to control them, to tell them no, to keep them idle for substantial periods of time. This is especially the case when they are suggesting to the political leadership that "we could remove this problem you find so troublesome."

COST-BENEFIT ANALYSES

The consideration of whether to undertake a covert action requires cost-benefit analysis. The cost component of this analysis includes the economic costs, which can be quantified and expressed in dollar terms, and the political costs, which are intangible, frequently indirect, and not quantifiable. The benefit component includes the same factors.

Except when large-scale military or paramilitary forces are involved, the economic costs are rarely significant. A major political covert action, such as the 1964 Chilean election, may cost several millions of dollars and still be a small percentage of the CIA's total budget. The economic benefits also are rarely significant. Covert action is a political tool, used for political, not economic, purposes.

One major exception is when a covert action reverses a government's economic policy. The anti-Mossadegh coup in Iran was partially motivated by the desire to reverse Mossadegh's nationalization of the Anglo-Iranian Oil Company and (so far as the United States was concerned) by the desire to lay to rest the specter that a policy of petroleum nationalization would spread throughout the Middle East. The economic benefits, therefore, were immediate and very large for the British; for the Americans they were indirect. To the extent that the Iranian coup did in fact inhibit nationalization elsewhere in the Middle East, these indirect American (and to some extent British) benefits were huge. This cause-and-effect relationship is arguable; what is not arguable is that no other nationalizations occurred until 1973 (in Libya and Saudi Arabia).

It is the political costs and benefits that weigh most heavily in the equation and that are also most difficult to calculate. The most obvious political cost is: what happens if the action fails? There are two kinds of failure. A covert action may fail with the U.S. involvement undisclosed. In this case the political cost to the United States is minimal, if anything. Or the action may fail with the U.S. hand revealed. In this case the political cost is at least national embarrassment and at most a major setback for foreign policy.

Other political costs must be paid in any case. Frequently foreign groups (a political party, labor union, or group of army officers, for example) are asked to participate in covert actions, sometimes at considerable risk. Afterwards the groups in question think the United States owes them something. Where, they ask, is the quid pro quo? And they may not be satisfied with what they get out of the action, or what the United States offers them later. So the United States is subject to a kind of reverse blackmail.

Finally, there is a political and frequently an economic cost even if the covert action is successful. "What do we do if we win?" Sen. J. W. Fulbright, D-Ark., asked President Kennedy in arguing against the Bay of Pigs. Fulbright foresaw a de facto Cuban government that would be little more than an American puppet. Supporting the puppet would involve the United States in an endless morass of Cuban politics and intrigue, not to mention a near open-ended commitment to economic assistance and reconstruction.

The other side of the equation is the political benefits. These are sometimes substantial, though they are equally difficult to calculate. One of the CIA's earliest covert actions was aimed at defeat of the Communist Party in the Italian elections of 1948. It can be argued that the communists would have been defeated anyway, but this is speculative. At that time (and for many years thereafter) there was no example of a Communist Party being dislodged from power after once achieving it. So the political benefit of the covert intervention in Italy in 1948 was very great, and the cost was small.

The case of Iran in 1953 is more problematic. There followed twenty-six years of a pro-American government under the shah, but the shah's own shortcomings led to his succession by a rabid anti-American government. That, of course, could not have been foreseen in 1953. The disaster that overtook the American position in Tehran in 1979 was unrelated to the anti-Mossadegh coup; it was, rather, the consequence of the failure to assess correctly events in Iran in 1977 and 1978. By most conventional measurements, the 1953 covert action was cost effective and successful, but a question remains: Would a more tolerant, cooperative policy toward Mossadegh have produced different results, possibly more difficult in the short term but more satisfactory in the long term?

When that question is asked about Guatemala in 1954, with Arbenz substituted for Mossadegh, the answer is less speculative. The political cost of overthrowing Arbenz has been forty years of instability, civil unrest, and undisciplined military forces. The political benefit was very short term with the removal of Arbenz. The economic costs in Guatemala have been high because the United States has felt impelled to pour in foreign aid. There was one economic benefit: a threat was removed from the extensive holdings of the United Fruit Company (as well as other American investments).

The cold war was an important factor in the covert actions discussed in this chapter. All of them had an anticommunist or anti-Soviet element, which weighed heavily on the benefit side of any equation. Finally, one other aspect of covert action should be mentioned. The failure to keep so many covert actions covert helped the CIA acquire a grossly exaggerated reputation in the third world. There is a widespread predisposition to believe anything bad about it and to attribute to it powers that it does not possess. People's willingness to believe bad things about the CIA was a godsend for various KGB programs of disinformation. Their willingness to accept its near-omnipotence saddled it with guilt for every unpopular thing that happened.

This popular mindset has been a source of dismay and frustration to many Americans working or traveling in the third world, but in one sense, it is not entirely a bad thing. "Let people think we can do anything," this line of thought goes. "Let them be a little scared of us. They will be less apt to cross us, more apt to cooperate with us."

SECONDARY EFFECTS

Once the CIA has trained people in the dirty tricks of covert action, it never knows how they are going to use this know-how after they have served the agency's purpose. Cubans who received CIA training were suspected of conducting their own freelance anti-Castro operations after the United States had stopped. This problem is less acute with Americans who make intelligence a career, who are highly motivated and well disciplined. But even among this group, there are those who wander into unapproved channels. The Watergate burglars whose break-in of Democratic National Committee offices during the Nixon administration led to President Nixon's resignation were guided by CIA veteran (and Nixon White House aide) Howard Hunt and included Cubans who had received CIA training. In another case Edwin P. Wilson sold his CIA skills and connections to the Libyan government and was sentenced to thirty-two years imprisonment on multiple weapons-smuggling charges.[48]

The problem is greater with respect to foreign dissidents who have their own reasons for carrying on a vendetta. The Cuban exiles who were trained for the Bay of Pigs and other escapades are a case in point; they have pulled off many wholly unauthorized actions against Cuba. Honduran commandos trained by the CIA later engaged in killing and torturing people suspected of helping Salvadoran rebels. The CIA wanted them to stop help going to the rebels but not to kill and torture.[49] People who received antiterrorist training in Lebanon perpetrated a terrorist act themselves: they set off a car bomb that killed eighty persons, but not the one at whom it was aimed.[50]

Finally, there is the question of the effectiveness of covert action. David A. Phillips, who was a CIA practitioner of covert action for many years, concluded that "most of our mistakes occur when we attempt to persuade foreigners to do something which the United States wants more than they do."[51] Richard Bissell, the one-time head of covert operations, remarked that "there have been many short-term tactical victories but very few lasting successes." William G. Miller, the Church committee's staff director, commented:

> The committee's review of covert action tends to support Bissell's view. It appears that where covert action programs are consistent with declared American foreign policy supported by the Congress and the people, there has been a significant measure of long-term success; where there was a contradiction between the public rhetoric of our policymakers and open programs such as AID and the Peace Corps and the secret actions undertaken, there is a record in all too many instances of ultimate failure and damage to overall U.S. interests.[52]

SHOULD WE DO IT?

Almost all covert action is dirty tricks, some dirtier than others. Almost all is illegal. At a minimum, it is intervention in the affairs of another sovereign state, and this is contrary to the Charter of the United Nations, among other treaties. At a maximum, covert action may involve bribery, burglary, or other serious crimes. Assassination has been ruled out by executive order. Legislation has ruled out actions "that would violate the Constitution or any statute of the

United States" and actions "intended to influence United States political processes, public opinion, policies, or media." [53]

Some Americans find covert action distasteful per se, and more find aspects of it so. Does this kind of sneaky activity really reflect the kind of country we want to be? Or is it something that the exigencies of world politics demand?

The level of covert action has gone up and down dramatically since 1947. There were times in the 1950s when covert action accounted for almost half of the CIA budget. The Church committee counted 900 major covert actions between 1961 and 1975, but by 1975 covert action was accounting for a minuscule fraction of the budget, and it dropped even more in the Carter administration (1977-1981). Covert action expanded dramatically in the Reagan years (1981-1989), especially when the flamboyant William Casey was DCI (1981-1986). Thereafter it declined again.

Various people who have studied the matter have recommended that a capacity for covert action be maintained but used with great restraint. [54] One of the troubles with such a recommendation is that when the capacity exists, somebody is tempted to use it. Either the covert action operatives become restless and devise assignments, which they persuade policy makers to adopt, or the policy makers see covert action as a quick fix for a problem. Yet the record shows periods, principally under Presidents Ford and Carter, when covert action was indeed used sparingly. The reluctance to abandon covert action entirely is based on uncertainty whether some contingency will arise to require it. The argument in favor of abandoning covert action is that when its end is legitimate, there are other ways to achieve it (though admittedly some of them are more difficult). If the end is not legitimate, we ought not to try to achieve it anyway.

A word needs to be said about the legislative stricture against attempts to influence "United States political processes, public opinion, policies, or media." This is a refinement of the original 1947 law that prohibited domestic operations by the CIA, but it is particularly relevant to covert actions dealing with the foreign media. As has been noted, a common form of covert action has been to insert articles in the foreign media. Sometimes Americans (usually academics) have been paid to write books for foreign publication. Such a book may express a point of view that the United States, through the CIA, is trying to promote overseas. Or it may contain straightforward information about a complicated situation, and this, too, may serve the American purpose. The author may be (usually is) honest in his facts and opinions. But the book is still unattributed propaganda that would lose credibility if its true provenance were known. Sometimes portions of these materials have been picked up unwittingly by American media or commercial publishers and reprinted in the United States. Since this is inadvertent (at least in most cases), the original publication cannot be called an "attempt" to influence U.S. opinion, but it clearly has that effect to some degree. The only way to be sure this does not occur is to stop publishing matter under false pretenses abroad. The purpose of the U.S. Information Agency is to engage in straightforward, aboveboard attempts to influence foreign public opinion, and that ought to be enough. (USIA is also prohibited by law from distributing its material in the United States, but since USIA material is labeled as such, it does not have the problem of blowback.)

FOR WHAT PURPOSE?

As noted earlier, the law requires that a covert action support "identifiable foreign policy objectives of the United States" and be "important" to the national security. This is not helpful in defining purposes. For the Reagan administration the identifiable foreign policy objective of aiding the Nicaraguan Contras was to keep communism from making further inroads in the Western Hemisphere, and this was "important" to the national security. Many people agreed with the objective of keeping communism out but did not view Nicaragua as a credible threat. When Congress ordered aid to the Contras stopped, the president did not mount a public campaign to reinstate his policy. Instead, he continued the policy in secret in defiance of the law.

This is precisely the major problem of covert action: the propensity of presidents to use it to avoid domestic political controversy. Other examples abound, many of them not involving military force. The Nixon administration never made any secret of its dislike for the Allende administration in Chile. A substantial number of Americans also disliked Allende's politics, but they were not willing to support a series of dirty tricks to throw him out. How influential those dirty tricks were in the Allende overthrow remains controversial; a respectable school of thought holds that Allende self-destructed, but the truth is lost in the fogs of history. One writer has succinctly stated the problem as follows:

> ... [I]n Chile before the coup of 1973, U.S. officials drew a fine distinction between covertly supporting opposition groups, which was the U.S. purpose, and aiding a coup, which was not. Yet in the chaos of Santiago that fine distinction could not hold. Thus, the lesson history drew from Allende's overthrow is not that his experiment failed on its own terms but that the CIA overthrew him.[55]

At the same time that the Reagan administration was illegally aiding the Nicaraguan Contras, it was carrying out a similar program of aid to the Afghan rebels with the general approbation of Congress and the public. If covert action is appropriate at all, it is appropriate only for policies that enjoy widespread public support. It ought not to be used to avoid public debate; the problem is that as long as covert action is an option for presidents to use, presidents will be tempted to use it for precisely that purpose. Greater vigilance on Capitol Hill has made the wrongful use of covert action by the executive branch more difficult. Whether it has become impossible remains to be seen.

NOTES

1. Sec. 662 of the Foreign Assistance Act of 1961, as amended in 1974. 22 U.S.C. 2422.
2. Senate Select Committee to Study Governmental Operations with Respect to Intelligence Activities (hereafter cited as the Church committee), *Foreign and Military*

Intelligence, S. Rept. 94-755, Book 1, 94th Cong., 2d sess., 1976, 131.

3. Executive Order 12333, *United States Intelligence Activities, Federal Register,* December 8, 1981, 59953-59954.

4. Executive Order 12036, *United States Intelligence Activities, Federal Register,* January 26, 1978, 3674-3692.

5. Sec. 102(d)(5) (50 U.S.C. 403) of the National Security Act of 1947, as amended.

6. Quoted in John Ranelagh, *The Agency: The Rise and Decline of the CIA* (New York: Simon and Schuster, 1986), 336.

7. Many CIA-sponsored foundations are listed in Sol Stern, "A Short Account of International Student Politics and the Cold War, with Particular Reference to the NSA, CIA, etc.," *Ramparts: A Muckraker's Guide to 1968 and Other Horrors,* 1969, 87-97.

8. Intelligence Authorization Act, Fiscal Year 1991, P.L. 102-88, approved August 14, 1991, sec. 504.

9. Nicholas M. Horrock, "CIA Infiltration of Press Overseas Viewed as Influencing News Received by Americans," *New York Times,* Feb. 9, 1976.

10. See statement of David A. Phillips to Church committee, December 5, 1975, Hearings, vol. 7, *Covert Action,* 56.

11. See Bob Woodward, "Gadhafi Target of Secret U.S. Deception Plan," *Washington Post,* Oct. 2, 1986; and "State Department Plan Urged Libya Coup," *Washington Post,* Oct. 5, 1986.

12. "Shultz Defends Administration Efforts To 'Make Gadhafi Nervous,' " *Washington Post,* Oct. 4, 1986.

13. "Reagan: Gadhafi Should 'Go to Bed . . . Wondering What We Might Do,' " *Washington Post,* Oct. 3, 1986.

14. Lou Cannon, "Administration 'Hurt,' " *Washington Post,* Oct. 4, 1986.

15. Dan Phillips, "Deception Effort against Gadhafi Hit," *Washington Post,* Oct. 6, 1986.

16. See Patrick E. Tyler, "U.S. Aborted 1983 Trap Set for Libyan Forces," *Washington Post,* July 12, 1987.

17. See Gregory F. Treverton, *Covert Action: The Limits of Intervention in the Postwar World* (New York: Basic Books, 1987), 134-135.

18. See Stephen S. Rosenfeld, "Star Wars: Scandal *And* Coup?" *Washington Post,* Aug. 20, 1993; Robert C. McFarlane, "Consider What Star Wars Accomplished," *New York Times,* Aug. 24, 1993; Tim Weiner, "General Details Altered 'Star Wars' Test," *New York Times,* Aug. 27, 1993; and R. Jeffrey Smith, "3 'Star Wars' Tests Rigged, Aspin Says," *Washington Post,* Sept. 10, 1993.

19. William Claiborne, "Moscow Seen Continuing Propaganda," *Washington Post,* Nov. 8, 1984.

20. Ze'ev Schiff, "Israel Breaks the Rules," *Washington Post,* Dec. 8, 1985.

21. Foreign Relations Authorization Act, Fiscal Years 1986 and 1987, P.L. 99-93 (99 Stat. 405, approved August 16, 1985). Sec. 147.

22. See William Colby and Peter Forbath, *Honorable Men: My Life in the CIA* (New York: Simon and Schuster, 1978), 81-85. See also Clare Pedrick, "CIA Organized Secret Army in Western Europe," *Washington Post,* Nov. 14, 1990.

23. See Patrick E. Tyler and David B. Ottaway, "Ethiopian Security Police Seized, Tortured CIA Agent," *Washington Post,* April 25, 1986.

24. Treverton, *Covert Action,* 18.

25. See Robert J. McCartney, "The $150,000 Election Campaign Headache," *Washington Post,* March 26, 1985; and "Duarte Sees Party Gaining in Salvadoran Election," *Washington Post,* March 28, 1985.

26. The Mossadegh story is told in detail in Kermit Roosevelt, *Countercoup: The Struggle for the Control of Iran* (New York: McGraw-Hill, 1979). Roosevelt was the CIA officer in charge of the operation. See also William A. Dorman and Mansour Farhang,

The U.S. Press and Iran: Foreign Policy and the Journalism of Deference (Berkeley: University of California Press, 1987), 50-62; and Jonathan Kwitny, *Endless Enemies: The Making of an Unfriendly World* (New York: Congdon and Weed, 1984), 160-178.

27. Anthony Cavendish, *Inside Intelligence* (Palü Publishing Ltd., 1987), 129-130.

28. See David Wise and Thomas B. Ross, *The Invisible Government* (New York: Random House, 1964), 165-183. See also Richard H. Immerman, *The CIA in Guatemala: The Foreign Policy of Intervention* (Austin: University of Texas Press, 1982).

29. Treverton, *Covert Action*, 16.

30. Ibid., 24.

31. See Warren Hinckle and William W. Turner, *The Fish Is Red: The Story of the Secret War against Castro* (New York: Harper and Row, 1981).

32. An expurgated version of these hearings was published in 1984. See *Executive Sessions of the Senate Foreign Relations Committee (Historical Series)*, Vol. 8, Pt 1., 87th Cong., 1st sess., 1961 (made public April 1984), 313-384, 387-449, 503-539, 571-627.

33. See, for example, the materials developed by two congressional committees awkwardly named the House Select Committee to Investigate Covert Arms Transactions with Iran and the Senate Select Committee on Secret Military Assistance to Iran and the Nicaraguan Opposition. The committees published thirteen volumes of joint hearings under the general title, *Iran-Contra Investigation* (Washington, D.C.: Government Printing Office, 1987) plus several volumes of supporting documents. Their joint report, *Iran-Contra Affair*, is H. Rept. 100-433 and S. Rept. 100-216, 100th Cong., 1st sess., November 1987. The report of the independent counsel appointed to investigate the affair is also available: United States Court of Appeals for the District of Columbia Circuit, *Final Report of the Independent Counsel for Iran/Contra Matters*, three volumes (Washington, D.C.: Government Printing Office, 1993). See also Theodore Draper, *A Very Thin Line: The Iran-Contra Affairs* (New York: Hill and Wang, 1991).

34. Loch K. Johnson, *America's Secret Power: The CIA in a Democratic Society* (New York: Oxford University Press, 1989), 67.

35. David B. Ottaway, "What Is 'Afghan Lesson' for Superpowers?" *Washington Post*, Feb. 12, 1979.

36. See especially Steve Coll, "Anatomy of a Victory: CIA's Covert Afghan War," *Washington Post*, July 19, 1992.

37. Youssef M. Ibrahim, "Arabs Raise a Nervous Cry over Iranian Militancy," *New York Times*, Dec. 21, 1992.

38. Associated Press, "Uzbek Militia, Once Kabul's Ally, Battles Islamic President's Forces," *New York Times*, Dec. 10, 1992.

39. Thomas W. Lippman, "Aid to Afghan Rebels Returns to Haunt U.S." *Washington Post*, July 26, 1993; and Molly Moore, "CIA Falters in Recovery of Missiles," *Washington Post*, March 7, 1994.

40. H. W. Brands, "The Limits of Manipulation: How the United States Didn't Topple Sukarno," *Journal of American History* (December 1989).

41. See Laurence Stern, "Bitter Lessons: How We Failed in Cyprus," *Foreign Policy* (Summer 1975): 34-78.

42. See "U.S. Flies Libyan Rebels from Chad," *Washington Post*, Dec. 9, 1990; and "Plan to Train Anti-Gadhafi Fighters Fails," *Washington Post*, March 13, 1991.

43. Patrick E. Tyler, "U.S. Tracks Cuban Aid to Grenada," *Washington Post*, Feb. 27, 1983.

44. House Select Committee on Intelligence, *U.S. Intelligence Agencies and Activities: The Performance of the Intelligence Community*, Hearings, 94th Cong., 1st sess., 1975, Pt. 2, 827.

45. These requirements are spelled out *in extenso* in Sec. 503(a) of the National Security Act, as amended by Sec. 602 of the Intelligence Authorization Act, Fiscal Year 1991. (P.L. 102-88, approved August 14, 1991.)
46. Ibid.
47. House Intelligence Committee, *Pursuant to Clause 1(d) Rule XI of the Rules of the House of Representatives* (Annual Report), H. Rept. 100-1115, December 27, 1988, 15.
48. See Peter Maas, "Selling Out: How an Ex-CIA Agent Made Millions Working for Qaddafi," *New York Times Magazine*, April 13, 1986.
49. See Reuter, "U.S.-Trained Squads Executed Suspects," *Washington Post*, Feb. 14, 1986.
50. Bob Woodward and Charles R. Babcock, "Antiterrorist Plan Rescinded after Unauthorized Bombing," *Washington Post*, May 12, 1985, and "Sen. Leahy is Probing Some CIA Operations," *Washington Post*, May 13, 1985.
51. Church committee, Hearings, vol. 7, *Covert Action*, 56.
52. Ibid., 6.
53. Intelligence Authorization Act for Fiscal Year 1991, P.L. 102-88, approved August 14, 1991. Secs. 503(a)(5) and 503(f).
54. See, for example, the Report of the Commission on the Organization of the Government for the Conduct of Foreign Policy (the Murphy Commission, after its chairman, Robert Murphy), June 1975; Testimony of David A. Phillips, president, Association of Retired Intelligence Officers, Church committee, December 5, 1975; *The Need to Know*, The Report of the Twentieth Century Fund Task Force on Covert Action and American Democracy (New York: Twentieth Century Fund Press, 1992).
55. Treverton, *Covert Action*, 9.

PART III

Mechanisms of Public Control

There are three institutions through which public control of secret activities can be effected in the United States. One is the media—press, radio, television—which perform an indispensable function of informing and enlightening the public, and the government as well. The second is the president and the apparatus that is gathered about him in the White House. The third is the Congress.

For the sake of typological completeness, two more may be listed: the public, through the electoral process, and the intelligence community itself, through internal controls. However, before the electoral process can work, something has to happen in one of the other institutions to propel an issue into the political arena. And although there are more cases than meet the public eye in which the intelligence community's internal controls have squelched ill-advised schemes, no institution in a democracy should be trusted to police itself.

Chapter 8 examines the tense, symbiotic relationship between the media and the intelligence community. The media try to learn what the community is doing; the community tries to manipulate the media. An intelligence operation can be ruined by publicity. When the media learn of such an operation, they face agonizing decisions over where the public interest lies. The media serve not only as a channel of information to the public; they are sometimes a channel between different parts of the government.

Chapter 9 looks at the role of the president. There are an array of lesser agencies to help the president meet his intelligence responsibilities—the National Security Council, the President's Foreign Intelligence Advisory Board, and a variety of interagency committees and working groups. But in the end this aspect of the government reflects each president's individual predilections and personal working habits. The system goes most seriously awry when a president succumbs to the temptation to use the intelligence community (usually the CIA) as his personal handmaiden, when he resorts to covert action as much to avoid controversy at home as to achieve a result abroad.

Chapter 10 reviews the role of Congress in intelligence oversight. This is a role that grew from almost nothing in the beginning to full-blown oversight committees in each house. The creation of these committees has been a large step forward in making the intelligence community more responsive to the public will, but the committees necessarily do much of their work in secret. Congressional oversight was initially resisted by the intelligence bureaucracy, but it has come to be accepted and is even seen by some in the community as a protection against political pressures. The congressional intelligence committees did not prevent the Iran-Contra scandal during Ronald Reagan's second term as president, but it is asserted that they learned enough to prevent a repetition. The rest of us can only hope so.

CHAPTER 8

The Media

*There always has to be a certain distance between high public offi-
cials and newspapermen. I wouldn't say a wall or a fence, but an air
space, that's very necessary.*

—Walter Lippmann

The relationship between the government and the media is at once symbiotic and conflictual, even adversarial. This is inherent in a free, democratic society. Such a relationship even exists in some countries that are neither free nor
democratic. The popular characterization of the press as the "fourth estate"
stems from eighteenth-century prerevolutionary France (neither free nor democratic), where the term was used to describe the special relationship of the press
to the Estates General, in which the other three estates (the nobility, the clergy,
and the general populace) were formally represented. A few years later a special
status for the press was cemented into the U.S. Constitution through the First
Amendment guarantee that "Congress shall make no law . . . abridging the freedom of speech, or of the press." The Founding Fathers had taken special pains to
construct a federal government with tension between the three branches. This,
some thought, was the particular genius of the Constitution. The First Amendment ensured that the same tension would exist between the press (later including radio and television) and the government.

The tension is given a special quality by the symbiosis and conflict in the
relationship. The relationship is symbiotic because each party has something
the other wants and needs. What the media have that the government wants is
a channel of communication to the public. This is crucial to the government. It
is what makes the office of president such a "bully pulpit," in Theodore Roosevelt's phrase. The president uses the media to seek public support for his administration's policies. Members of Congress use the media to acquire the public recognition that is all-important for politicians.

There are many stories, some of them apocryphal, some of them unfortu-
nately not, of the lengths to which members of Congress will go to obtain publicity. The probably mythical remark of a member to a reporter—"I don't care
what you say about me; just spell my name right"—has been raised to the level
of folk wisdom through endless repetition. When the Senate approved the
United Nations Charter by a vote of 89 to 2, a reporter asked Sen. William
Langer, R-N.D., why he voted no (along with California Republican Hiram

Johnson). "Every newspaper in the country will print the names of those who voted against it," Langer is said to have replied. "Nobody will print the names of the 89 who voted for it." (Langer was an unreconstructed isolationist who just did not like the United Nations, but he was also enough of an individualist that this explanation of his vote is in character.) The destructive and irresponsible witch-hunting tirades of Sen. Joseph R. McCarthy, R-Wis., in the 1950s were motivated at least as much by a demagogic lust for publicity as by ideological alarm over communism.

What the government has that the media want is information. Every day in many ways the government takes countless actions that affect the lives of the people and therefore make news. Some of these actions are humdrum and of interest to only a few people—for example, a new interpretation by the Internal Revenue Service of an obscure provision of the tax code. This will not make the network evening news, but somewhere in Washington there is a publication that will report it. Many government actions affect many, perhaps most, people immediately and directly; people are either better off or worse off as a consequence. The nation might even be in a war, large or small. All of these things are news, and news is the reason the media exist.

That is the symbiosis. The conflict comes from the different interests of the government and the media in how news is presented and interpreted. In simplest terms the government wants the news presented in a way that reflects credit on the government. To this end the government tries mightily to influence, if it cannot control, what flows through the channel that the media provide between the government and the public, because this is what shapes public attitudes toward government. In the fashionable phrase of the 1990s, the government seeks to put a spin on the news. The media view these efforts as directed toward distortion and concealment; they consequently believe it is their job, even their responsibility, to disclose these efforts.

Nowhere is this contradictory relationship of simultaneous symbiosis and conflict more acute than with respect to the intelligence community. Intelligence agencies necessarily deal in secrets. They shun the glare of publicity as though it were a deadly virus. Journalists, on the other hand, understand intellectually the need for secrecy, but all their instincts recoil from it. And there is an enormous perhaps unbridgeable chasm between what intelligence officers and journalists conceive legitimate secrets to be.

At the same time the media and the intelligence community are trying to use each other as the source of information, or perhaps of some other favor. When a reporter has lunch with an intelligence officer, neither can be sure who is interviewing whom.

Jim Hoagland, Pulitzer-prize-winning correspondent and *Washington Post* columnist, has written perceptively of the

> difficult issues journalists confront when they come into contact with the shadow worlds of intelligence and espionage, where agendas and identities are by definition hidden and every contact involves the question: Who is manipulating whom?
>
> Journalist and spy should in theory react to each other like cat and dog. The former wants to expose everything to the light of day, seven days a week. The latter's craft is concealment. When their paths cross, however, their con-

tact is often more like cat and mouse. Each probes the other for information, intention and, ultimately, advantage.[1]

Indeed, good reporters try to cultivate sources in intelligence services as assiduously as intelligence officers try to cultivate sources in some other country's foreign office. Intelligence services try to co-opt reporters, their papers, their magazines, their networks, so that what is reported as well as what is not reported serves the intelligence agencies' purposes.

The U.S. Constitution, reinforced by decisions of the U.S. Supreme Court, has given the media broad, almost unlimited, freedom. With that there comes responsibility, not only to deal carefully with legitimate questions of national security but also to serve as a watchdog of the government and of its secret activities.

This was well expressed by Justice Potter Stewart in his concurring opinion in *New York Times Co.* v. *United States* (403 U.S. 713, decided June 30, 1971). In this landmark case the Supreme Court rejected efforts by the Nixon administration to suppress publication of Pentagon papers about U.S. involvement in Vietnam. Stewart began by pointing out that the Constitution gives the president "enormous power in the two related areas of national defense and international relations" and that this power is "largely unchecked by the Legislative and Judicial branches." He continued:

> In the absence of the governmental checks and balances present in other areas of our national life, the only effective restraint upon executive policy and power in the areas of national defense and international affairs may lie in an enlightened citizenry—in an informed and critical public opinion which alone can here protect the values of democratic government. For this reason, it is perhaps here that a press that is alert, aware, and free most vitally serves the basic purpose of the First Amendment. For without an informed and free press there cannot be an enlightened people.

On the CIA headquarters building is the Biblical quotation, "Ye shall know the truth, and the truth shall make you free" (John 8:32). Justice Stewart was saying that unless people know the truth, they cannot be free; and at times they must rely mainly, if not entirely, on the media. The media are an important public watchdog. Although not a part of the government, they play an important role in the public oversight of secret activities.

COLLECTION OF NEWS AND INTELLIGENCE

The CIA collects intelligence; the news media gather news. Those two things are not very different. The principal difference in practice is that some of the CIA's methods would be illegal or unethical if used by the media. But both intelligence officers and news reporters make their rounds of government officials and informed citizens of a foreign country asking questions about matters of interest. They then report what they have learned—intelligence officers in confidence to CIA headquarters, news reporters publicly in print or on the air.

Since they are not in competition with each other (as one TV network is with another), it is natural that the CIA and the news media should compare notes and exchange information from time to time. And this is one of the ways the relationship starts down a slippery slope. It is acceptable for the CIA to use journalists, or for journalists to use the CIA; but it is not acceptable for journalists to allow themselves to be used.

JOURNALISTS AS AGENTS

From time to time there is a cry in Congress, or even in the media, for statutory or other restrictions on the CIA's relations with the media. In the first place it would be extraordinarily difficult to write such restrictions beyond dealing with an employer-employee relationship. But more to the point, it is not the CIA's responsibility to regulate this relationship; it is the journalist's. The journalist's responsibility just to say no is not limited to the intelligence community; it is governmentwide. It is equally inappropriate for a journalist to write an article for the U.S. Information Agency as it is to report for the CIA. The First Amendment guarantees journalists freedom from government control; this implies a heavy responsibility not to submit to government control, or even to government manipulation. A more difficult problem is that journalists don't always know when they are being used.

A member of almost any other profession—in academia, the clergy, business, or something else—can refuse to have any knowing contacts with the CIA. He or she will not lose very much, if anything, by such a policy. A foreign correspondent who follows such a policy is in danger of losing a great deal.

When looking into the murky world of intelligence, one rarely can be entirely sure of anything. It appears, however, that the CIA used the media in the 1950s, 1960s, and early 1970s much more than it has since. One estimate in 1977 was that more than 400 American journalists had secretly carried out assignments for the CIA in the preceding twenty-five years.[2] Another study said the CIA had contracts with "some three dozen" American journalists in 1973. Of these, five worked for general circulation news organizations, and thirty were stringers (journalists who are not regularly employed by a publication but receive ad hoc assignments for which they are paid piece rates), freelance writers, or full-time correspondents for small publications.[3]

As director of central intelligence (DCI), George Bush formally announced in February 1976, "Effective immediately, the CIA will not enter into any paid or contractual relationship with any full-time or part-time news correspondent accredited by any United States news service, newspaper, periodical, radio or television network or station." In the same statement Bush said, "The CIA has no secret or contractual relationship with any American clergyman or missionary. This practice will be continued as a matter of policy."[4]

At that time it was reported that fifty American journalists were employed by the CIA or maintained relations with it. In April it was reported that the CIA intended to keep about half of them.[5] This was, of course, inconsistent with what Bush had announced in February.

In 1977 Stansfield Turner, Bush's successor as DCI, took another whack at the problem. He made it CIA policy not to use nonjournalist staff of U.S. news organizations to conduct intelligence activities "without the specific, express approval of senior management of the organization concerned." He added that the CIA would not "use the name or facilities of any U.S. media organization to provide cover for any Agency employees or activities."[6]

A nettlesome problem that was not addressed by either of the policy statements concerns freelancers, those individuals who write or broadcast first for one media outlet and then for another but who are employed by none. Is it o.k. if they undertake simultaneous or sequential reporting assignments for a newspaper and the CIA? And how does one define *freelancer* anyway? Does the term include a person who has full-time local employment in, say, Geneva, but who occasionally undertakes an assignment for an American outlet?

A good deal of anxious discussion could be avoided by returning to the principle that the media have a responsibility to say no to the CIA. In the case of freelancers, it is up to the news organization that buys their work to assure itself that the freelancer in question is not working part-time for an intelligence service. It would assure itself of this with respect to one of its employees; it should do no less with respect to those whose work it uses *ad hoc*. (This is not foolproof. If an intelligence service is determined to penetrate a major news organization, it can no doubt do so; but it will also no doubt find this has not been worth the trouble.)

As the cold war was ending, a new chief of the KGB, Yevgeny Primakov (the first civilian to hold that job), echoed George Bush of fifteen years earlier. In October 1991 Primakov told a press conference in Moscow that he was opposed to the practice of using journalists as cover for intelligence agents and would try to stop it. At the same time it was announced that the Soviet newspaper *Izvestia* was reducing its foreign staff from forty to fifteen.[7]

Whether they were paid or had other formal relations, foreign correspondents for years made it a regular practice to seek out the station chief and include him in their rounds. The station chief is well informed on the political situation in the country. Much of his information is unclassified, and he was glad to share it with the correspondent. If he knew the correspondent well, he might even share some low-level classified information on an off-the-record or background basis. The station chief's motivation was a desire to find out what the correspondent knew and also to influence what he or she reported. (Among other motives, the station chief did not want the correspondent to send a story counter to what the station was reporting. This would certainly trigger an inquiry from headquarters as to who was right.) In order to influence what the correspondent reported, the station chief might very well be selective in the information he shared. Despite these little games, these exchanges of views were generally mutually beneficial. But then the CIA found that station chiefs were becoming so well known to the media that their cover was wearing thin. So these contacts were ended.[8]

There are less innocent and more subtle aspects to the relationship. Is it o.k. for a correspondent to ask questions, planted by the CIA, in an interview with a foreign official? Is it o.k. for the correspondent then to repeat off-the-record answers to the CIA when the correspondent does not report them in his or her newspaper? Is it o.k. for the correspondent to act as an intermediary ("cut-out") between a CIA officer and a clandestine source? There are many gradations. Every correspondent has to make his or her own decision where to draw the line. There is no unanimity as to where the line should be, but it is generally well short of active collaboration.

CHARGES OF COLLABORATION

In at least two cases journalists have sued each other over charges of collaboration. In one case the alleged collaboration was with the CIA; in the other it was with the KGB.

The first case involved Kennett Love of the *New York Times* and Jonathan Kwitny of the *Wall Street Journal*. While based in Cairo, Love covered the coup against Prime Minister Mohammed Mossadegh in Iran in 1953 and the aftermath continuing into 1954. Love has consistently denied that he was aware of CIA involvement in the coup, much less that he was a part of it.

In fact, both the shah's government and the American embassy in Tehran complained to *Times* editors in New York about Love's coverage of less favorable aspects of the shah's regime, and the shah twice ordered Love's visa cancelled. The *Times* in those days discouraged investigative reporting, and when Love did become aware of the CIA's role, he was discouraged from following up on it.[9]

In 1960 Love was a press fellow of the Council on Foreign Relations in New York and wrote a paper about the events in Iran in those years. He later gave a copy to Allen Dulles, by then the ex-DCI, and it was preserved in Dulles's papers, which are at Princeton University. There it was retrieved by Jonathan Kwitny of the *Wall Street Journal*. It is quoted at length in Kwitny's book, *Endless Enemies*, a merciless critique of U.S. policy in the third world. Kwitny strongly implies Love's complicity in the CIA-backed coup.[10]

Love sued Kwitny for both libel (seeking $5 million in damages) and copyright infringement. He prevailed with respect to the copyright.

The second case involves *Time* magazine and Dusko Doder, former Moscow bureau chief of the *Washington Post*. In 1985 KGB colonel Vitaly Yurchenko defected to the American embassy in Rome. During the CIA debriefings that followed, Yurchenko was the source of several leads that resulted in major espionage cases. One lead, which did not pan out, involved Doder. Yurchenko reportedly said that Doder had accepted $1,000 from a KGB officer while traveling with a Russian woman South of Moscow. Three months after his defection in Rome, Yurchenko excused himself during dinner with a CIA companion in a Washington restaurant, walked up Wisconsin Avenue to the new Soviet embassy, and undefected.

The FBI failed to find any evidence to substantiate Yurchenko's report about Doder. FBI director William Webster took the matter to Benjamin Bradlee, then executive editor of the *Post*. After investigation Bradlee concluded the report was groundless. All parties did agree that during his tour in Moscow, Doder, a native of Yugoslavia who spoke fluent Russian, had developed first-rate sources. The American embassy even thought he had one in the KGB, which raised the question of who was using whom. But all of Doder's stories in the *Post* checked out, even some that had been denied by the embassy and State Department.

Nothing was heard of this case publicly until December 1992, when *Time* magazine published a story about it. The story said that "Yurchenko's allegation that Doder took money from the KGB cannot be proved." It also raised these questions:

Did the KGB co-opt Doder? Or was it the other way around? Certainly he owed his scoops to leaks from the Soviet government, and his stories often reflected the views of his sources. But then, many reporters—whether they cover the Kremlin, the White House or city hall—echo their sources' views and are given inside information as a result.[11]

Doder, no longer with the *Post* and living in Belgrade, filed a libel suit in London, seeking unspecified monetary damages and an injunction against repeating the allegations.[12] The suit was pending in early 1994.

Journalists as Go-Betweens

During the Cuban missile crisis in October 1962, John Scali, the ABC reporter covering the State Department, was used by the KGB as a channel of communication to the American government. This highly unusual arrangement violated all the rules of journalism, but the circumstances were themselves so highly unusual that it did not attract much comment. The Soviet in question was Alexander Fomin, head of all KGB operations in the United States. Fomin and Scali had been occasional lunch companions (as had Fomin and many other correspondents), and Fomin initiated the missile crisis contact.

The crisis burst upon the world on Monday, October 22, 1962, when President John F. Kennedy announced the presence of Soviet missiles in Cuba, demanded their withdrawal, and instituted a quarantine (a word thought to be less bellicose than blockade) of the island. On Friday, October 26, Fomin and Scali met, at Fomin's request, at the Occidental Restaurant near the White House (a favorite also of Richard Helms when he was DCI). Fomin proposed a deal: the Soviets would remove their missiles under UN inspection and promise not to reintroduce them. The United States would publicly promise not to invade Cuba. Scali took the proposal to Roger Hilsman, director of the State Department's Bureau of Intelligence and Research. Hilsman took it to Secretary Dean Rusk, who took it to the informal Executive Committee that was managing the crisis in the White House. Then Rusk gave Scali a note saying that the Americans thought this could be worked out but that time was short. He told Scali to tell Fomin that the reply came from "the highest levels" (a phrase usually used as a circumlocution to mean "president").

That same night Scali and Fomin met again, this time in the coffee shop of the Statler Hilton Hotel (now the Capital Hilton) less than a block from the Soviet embassy. Fomin tried to introduce the idea of UN inspections of Florida as well as Cuba, but he did not press the matter and rushed off. The next morning a new message arrived from Soviet chairman Nikita Khrushchev, raising new conditions. Rusk called Scali and asked him what he could learn. Scali got to Fomin and accused him of a double cross. Fomin pleaded a cable delay; the Soviet embassy at that moment was expecting yet a new cable. Scali duly reported this to the White House, this time seeing the president himself.[13]

The matter was resolved substantially on the basis Fomin first suggested to Scali. (In a side agreement, unpublicized until years later, the United States promised to withdraw missiles from Turkey.) Scali later left ABC to serve as U.S. ambassador to the United Nations.

In this case the KGB used an ABC correspondent as a knowing and willing go-between to deal with the United States. In another case ABC complained that Shin Bet, the secret Israeli internal security service, impersonated an ABC crew without the network's knowledge or consent. That incident occurred in the West Bank in 1988 when, according to ABC, Shin Bet agents posed as an ABC crew to lure an Arab out of his house and arrest him.[14]

WHO USES WHOM?

Washington Post reporter Bob Woodward tells about a briefing he received from the CIA before a trip to Libya in 1984. Woodward asked what questions he should ask Libyan leader Muammar Gadhafi. With a straight face the briefing officer suggested Woodward ask, "I understand you are full of sleeping pills—you look drugged. Do you have trouble sleeping?" Woodward describes his reaction after the briefing:

> I had received valid information, I thought, a rather carefully calibrated intro-
> duction, but I also had a lingering feeling that this master covert operator had
> been planting a seed. He had overdone it slightly, painting the Libyan leader a
> little too much a loon. As I reviewed the conversation and my notes, I realized I
> couldn't tell whether I was being 'fed.' As facts or analysis, it seemed honest,
> straight, certainly helpful. But I couldn't get rid of the notion that the suggested
> question to Qaddafi had other purposes.[15]

Woodward experienced the same uncertainty about CIA information on another occasion as well. A CIA official told him on background that DCI William Casey was considering making a request to Saudi Arabia for money for the Nicaraguan Contras after Congress cut off U.S. funds. "It had to be clear to him that I would publish this," writes Woodward, "but it was not clear to me whether what I was being told was a trial balloon or whether I had been told in the hope that publication would sabotage the possibility of asking the Saudis for help."[16]

Surprisingly, correspondents seem not to get very much help from their employers on how to handle relations with intelligence services. An informal survey did not reveal any policy guidelines laid down by management other than rules of general application, such as don't take any money. But what if the money is for expenses to supplement niggardly allowances from the correspondent's home office? One correspondent about to leave for an overseas assignment had a suggestion from his managing editor that it might be a good idea to have a talk with the CIA director. The correspondent did so, did not learn very much, and was not approached to do anything.

The CIA is (or was) interested in journalists not only as sources of intelligence; it was interested in journalism as deep cover for its own officers. It even gave some of these officers training in journalism so that they would know how to behave when using that cover. At one time some newspapers (the *New York Times* being one) accredited some CIA officers as stringers.[17] This is not quite the same thing as using journalists as sources, but it is bad journalism and bad public policy nonetheless.

THE MEDIA AND SECRETS

Some of the most agonizing decisions in newsrooms are over whether a "secret" is properly a secret. When responsible government officials, or government officials in positions of responsibility (these are not necessarily the same thing), say that publication of a given story would damage the national security, are they reflecting a sober assessment, or are they engaging in special pleading? Except over a very narrow band of information (war plans, for example), there is no agreement on what ought to be secret, nor is it likely that there ever will be.

Journalists thrive on openness. Not only does the intelligence community thrive on secrecy; it is itself a closed society. The journalistic approach is, when in doubt, publish. The intelligence approach is, when in doubt, classify.

An executive order of the Reagan administration prohibits classification of information "in order to conceal violations of law, inefficiency, or administrative error; to prevent embarrassment to a person, organization, or agency; to restrain competition; or to prevent or delay the release of information that does not require protection in the interest of national security." [18]

This is a splendid statement of policy, but if an official in one of the foreign affairs or intelligence agencies wants to prevent publication of a fact that is embarrassing (or worse), his (or her) imagination is almost always equal to the task of finding a reason rooted in national security. The media, which are skeptical both by instinct and training, usually tend to play down the national security reasons and play up the other reasons. This is another source of tension between the media and the intelligence community.

Leaks: Who, What, Why?

A leak is a piece of confidential information that is published. It does not necessarily have anything to do with intelligence or with national security. It may be what went on in a closed congressional committee meeting about a purely domestic subject such as taxes. It may be what one Supreme Court justice said to another. It usually, but not always, comes from an anonymous source.

Whatever their source, leaks regularly drive presidents and other high officials into paroxysms of frustration and indignation. President Kennedy once exhorted his staff to find a leaker and bring him into Kennedy's presence so that he, Kennedy, could have the pleasure of firing the miscreant himself. After investigation the staff timidly reported to the president that he was the guilty party, having committed the indiscretion at lunch with Philip Graham, then publisher of the *Washington Post*. President Lyndon B. Johnson had such a phobia about leaks that he would refuse to appoint someone to a job if news of the impending appointment leaked prematurely. Johnson was suspected of sometimes leaking the news himself after he had changed his mind about an appointment and was looking for an excuse to back out of it.

President Ronald Reagan once announced that he was "up to my keister with leaks" and ordered polygraphs of the whole State Department. The president changed his mind about this folly when Secretary of State George Shultz said he would resign if the president persisted. When Henry Kissinger was President Richard Nixon's national security adviser, he once became so upset over a leak about the secret U.S. bombing of Cambodia that he ordered wiretaps on several of his own staff. Later Kissinger reflected on this:

> In retrospect, I think our reaction—no doubt, my reaction—was excessive. You see, most of the leaks—if you are philosophical about it—go away. I mean, they're unpleasant, but so what? If you ignore them, most of them are not of that huge significance.[19]

This hysteria about leaks is not confined to presidents. The House of Representatives mounted a full investigation to find out where Daniel Schorr, then a CBS correspondent, got the report of the committee investigating the intelligence community (see Chapter 10). But to no avail. Years later the Senate even appointed a special counsel to run down the source of leaks from the Senate Judiciary Committee about Anita Hill's charges of sexual harassment against Supreme Court nominee Clarence Thomas, but again to no avail.

The media are as zealous as the CIA in protecting their sources. Some reporters have gone to jail on contempt-of-court charges in defense of that principle.

There are two broad kinds of leaks: those that are the result of journalistic enterprise and those that are initiated by the leaker. The first comes about because reporters know there is a story developing. An international conference is in progress or is being planned. What is going on inside it? What is the state of U.S. policy planning for it? The reporter who asks enough questions of enough people is likely to find out more than the State Department wants him or her to know, though it will mainly be State Department officials who have passed along the information. No single official will have told the reporter very much, but a good reporter can piece together a lot of scraps. Sometimes reporters are not sure there is a story, but they see a tip and suspect an iceberg may be under it. When Eugene Hasenfus was captured in Nicaragua after surviving an airplane crash on an illegal mission to aid the Contras, he turned out to be the tip below which lay the iceberg of Iran-Contra.

Most stories based on leaks originate with the leaker, that is, with a government official who is breaking the rules (unless the leaker is the president or a member of the cabinet, who makes the rules). Sometimes the leak is only a fragment, a tip or a lead that the reporter must develop independently. Sometimes the leak is the whole story.

Leakers have a variety of motivations, some mischievous, some commendable, some neutral. Leaks have become a weapon of bureaucratic warfare. Suppose State and the CIA, on one side, and the Defense Department and Defense Intelligence Agency (DIA), on the other, are at loggerheads over a major national intelligence estimate. There are likely to be leaks about the softheads at State and CIA or the hardnoses at Defense and DIA. The object of the leaks is to alert the media, the public, and Congress that a row is brewing and that one side needs help. Or perhaps the object is to warn opponents that the leaker means business. If you want to know where a leak comes from, look for whose interests it advances. This will usually lead you to the guilty office, but pinpointing the individual culprit is more difficult.

USES OF LEAKS

The government uses leaks to shape, or at least influence, the way news is presented. It also uses backgrounders, those conversations that are not leaks but that impart facts and opinions on a nonattributable basis. Dean Rusk had a select group of State Department correspondents in for drinks and background talk on Friday afternoons when he was secretary of state. As backgrounders became more common, the sources' disguises became thinner. An anonymous "senior official"—sometimes further identified as speaking with a German accent—always traveled with Henry Kissinger when he was secretary. A "senior official" has usually been on the secretary of state's or the president's plane ever since.

Leaks are sometimes trial balloons. A trial balloon is a proposal made anonymously to see what reaction it provokes. If the reaction is negative, the proposal can be quietly forgotten, and the president is never identified with it. If the reaction is favorable, the president can embrace the proposal publicly. A variant of this technique is to float a number of trial balloons presaging drastic actions that are not, in fact, intended. Then, when a more modest action is taken, it seems less drastic than it would have otherwise.

For example, when the Johnson administration was planning a major increase in U.S. troops in Vietnam in the summer of 1965, there were rumors all over Washington of impending tax increases and mobilization of military reserve forces. When neither of these things happened, the presidential decision to reinforce troops already in Vietnam did not look like such a big escalation.

Leaks can be the work of a whistle-blower who wants to throw light on an activity for which light is fatal. These leaks can be made to Congress as well as to the media. An anonymous naval officer tipped off the Senate Foreign Relations Committee that there was something spurious about the report of North Vietnam's attack on destroyers in the Gulf of Tonkin. (See Chapter 4.)

Leaks not concerned with whistle-blowing are made to Congress in a search for allies in bureaucratic or policy wars. If the navy and air force are competing for a new airplane, you can be sure that both services plus the prime contractors will be patrolling the corridors of Capitol Hill. And as this process plays itself out, some classified performance characteristics are almost certain to find their way into the public domain.

The danger of leaks is an excuse commonly used in the executive branch to avoid sending sensitive information to Congress. Often that excuse is a cover for the real reason: the executive has been doing something it does not want Congress to know about. Or a leak would reveal something that weakens the case for a particular policy of the administration.

A survey in the mid-1980s found that congressional leaders did in fact leak more regularly than executive officials, 52 percent to 37 percent, but there are no data as to who leaked what.[20] No members of the intelligence committees were included in the sample. Nor were any staff included, either from Congress or the executive branch. This is a serious omission, because the staff are the means of transmission for many leaks. This does not mean that the staff are less trustworthy. It means that members of Congress use the staff to do their leaking and other disagreeable chores. There is a joke on the Hill that that is why they pay the staff so much.

A somewhat later survey by the staff of the Senate Intelligence Committee produced an opposite result. It found that in the first six months of 1986, there were 147 disclosures of classified information in eight leading newspapers. Of these, 98 were attributed to anonymous executive branch sources, 17 to military, nongovernment, or foreign sources, and 13 to Congress. In 19 cases the stories were so vague that the type of source could not be determined.[21]

Cynics on the Hill think that sometimes the executive branch sends information to Congress so that the executive branch can leak it and then blame Congress. This is thought to happen also in internecine disputes within the executive branch. One might call it a kind of sophisticated disinformation. Oliver North charged that members of Congress gave *Newsweek* classified information about the hijacking of the cruise ship *Achille Lauro* in the Mediterranean in 1985. *Newsweek* thereupon revealed that its source was not a member of Congress but Oliver North himself. This is one of the few examples of the media revealing the source of a leak, and it was done in extraordinary circumstances.[22]

Leaks are almost never made to the whole press corps. Among other reasons, this would make it more difficult for the source to remain anonymous. After receiving a leak, a reporter must consider several matters: the source; the source's motivation; the accuracy of the story, especially if it contains unflattering information; why that particular reporter was chosen. If the reporter is satisfied that the information is accurate, the leaker's motives become of secondary importance. The media doesn't really care if the national security adviser and the secretary of state are using leaks to carry on a feud. The feud itself is a good story. Zbigniew Brzezinski, President Jimmy Carter's national security adviser, complained that the State Department used leaks against him:

> There were people outside [the White House], particularly in the State Department, who used the press simply as a way of making certain that I did not overshadow the Secretary of State. . . . They were reacting to . . . my greater role . . . by leaks or by suggestions to the press designed to discredit me.[23]

Yet Cyrus Vance, who was secretary of state at the time Brzezinski was national security adviser, said he never leaked, that leaking was "one of the most corrosive practices that goes on in Washington."[24]

One technique by which the government seeks to manipulate the media is to impart information off the record or on background. (Off the record means that none of the information imparted can be used. Background means that the information can be used, but the source cannot be identified.) Either way, the object is to give the government's side of the story. Especially when the subject matter is intelligence, the facts can be checked independently only with great difficulty if at all. For the conscientious reporter, this presents a serious problem: how much credibility should be given to the information? It is fair to say that less credibility, by a wide margin, is given in the 1990s than in the 1960s. One reporter explains why: "I believe it's my job to assume that they may very well be lying and misrepresenting because all of my experience suggests they probably are."[25]

So far as the intelligence community is concerned, the object of off-the-record and background briefings is rarely to float a trial balloon or to plant a particular story. Instead, it is to shape the coverage of a developing story or of a story yet to come. Or it may be simply to gamble on looking good later. If you predict, off-the-record, a coup in Country X and the coup happens, some columnist is going to pat you on the back afterwards. The CIA was so adroit at shaping coverage while it was planning the coup in Guatemala in 1954 that when its plans leaked in explicit detail, *Time* magazine scoffed that the revelation was "fanciful . . . less of a plot than a scenario . . . master-minded in Moscow and designed to divert the attention from Guatemala as the Western Hemisphere's Red problem child." [26] Throughout most of the 1980s, the CIA tried mightily, and with markedly less success, to convince the media of communist threats in Nicaragua and El Salvador.

Some reporters dislike off-the-record and background briefings. Some even suggest, from time to time, that they be boycotted, but this is hard to do in a competitive media environment. The briefings do occasionally serve a constructive purpose for the media: they may provide a starting point to work on a story.

Foreign intelligence agencies also try to use the U.S. media to promote their particular points of view. The foreign editor of a prominent magazine tells of being approached by Mossad, the Israeli intelligence service, with an offer to share intelligence on terrorism in the Middle East. The offer was accepted, but nothing was ever printed because it could not be independently confirmed. Mossad's purpose was to spread its version of terrorist activity. KGB officers, under various covers, used to seek out American correspondents and give them morsels of news, sometimes Soviet disinformation, sometimes legitimate. It was not always easy to tell the difference.

TO PRINT OR NOT TO PRINT

A news organization's instinct is to print or broadcast a story—any story—when it is satisfied that the story is true. Usually it does so but not always. Sometimes it suppresses a story or parts of one. These are always agonizing decisions.

When a paper or a network has a sensitive story about foreign policy or defense or intelligence, it customarily informs the government agency principally concerned. This gives the agency a chance to comment (a further check on accuracy) and also to show cause why the story should not be printed or broadcast.

If the argument is to be successful, it has to be very strong and rooted in the national security. A pro forma argument is sure to be brushed off. The media are more skeptical of appeals to national security than they used to be. The *New York Times* knew about U-2 overflights of the Soviet Union but did not print the story. The *Times* did print a story about the impending Bay of Pigs invasion of Cuba, but only after watering it down to remove all references to the CIA. The *Times* also reduced the play it gave to the story from a four-column to a one-column headline. The caution by the *Times* suggests that a good rule would be: when in doubt, print. Some people (including President Kennedy) thought the original story would have led to cancellation of the enterprise and would have saved great national embarrassment.[27]

Another story that was printed but only after long delay involved the *Glomar Explorer*, a ship built for the CIA by Howard Hughes's Summa Corporation in Los Angeles. The ship's mission was to raise a Soviet submarine from the floor of the Pacific Ocean 750 miles west of Hawaii. The weather in that part of the Pacific restricted operations of this type to a few months a year. During its first season, the *Glomar* operated in total secrecy and with the promise of great success.

But then there was a burglary of Summa's offices. Besides $70,000, the thieves took a box of documents, including a memo describing *Glomar*. The CIA pressed the FBI, which alerted the Los Angeles police, to get the memo back. The *Los Angeles Times* printed parts of the story on page one February 7, 1975. DCI William Colby persuaded the editor to move the story inside the paper after the first edition and not to follow up. The same day he persuaded the *New York Times* to put the story inside (it appeared on page 30) and to kill it after the first edition. For more than a month Colby went from one newspaper office and television network to another with the same plea: the *Glomar* could give the United States an enormous intelligence coup but only if the Soviets did not get there first to destroy the evidence.

Finally on March 18, 1975, columnist Jack Anderson reasoned that the story was so widely known in the press corps that somebody was going to use it and so Anderson did. Others then followed.[28] The CIA then abandoned the project because of the prospect of armed Soviet opposition if it were resumed. Recovered while the *Glomar* was working were the bodies of several Soviet sailors. They were given a decent burial at sea, and a videotape was made of the ceremony. After the cold war ended, DCI Robert Gates delivered the tape to Moscow.

Perhaps the most celebrated publication of an intelligence leak involved the so-called Pentagon Papers, a voluminous documented history of the evolution of U.S. policy in Southeast Asia and of how it led to involvement in the Vietnam War. The study was prepared in the Pentagon, and it included much highly classified material. Daniel Ellsberg, who had helped compile the study as a Defense Department official, gave a copy to the *New York Times*.

There followed an internal debate in the *Times* over what to do with the material. Lawyers for the *Times* were divided; most of the editors favored publication. When the first story appeared in June 1971, the Nixon administration demanded that publication cease and that the papers be returned to the Defense Department. The administration also sought, and got, an order from a federal court for the *Times* to cease publication of the series. The *Times* refused to return the papers but complied with the court order pending appeal. Meanwhile, the *Washington Post*, which was not under a court order, published more of the papers. The administration then got a court order against the *Post*, which joined the *Times* in its appeal. The Supreme Court sided with the newspapers. Erwin Griswold, who argued the government's case before the Court as solicitor general, later admitted that the Nixon administration had overreacted and that the material in the Pentagon Papers was not harmful to national security.[29]

During the Reagan administration, the print media and the CIA clashed again over disclosure of sensitive information. Ronald Pelton, a former employee of the National Security Agency, was arrested in 1985 on espionage charges. The case involved, among other things, a secret project to tap Soviet underwater cables in the Sea of Okhotsk off the coast of Siberia. Codenamed Ivy Bells, the project had long since been compromised, but NSA was so jealous in guarding whatever shred of secrecy might remain that it objected to any reference to the project in Pelton's trial. Nevertheless, the *Washington Post* had the story and spent weeks in the spring of 1986 haggling, both internally and with the Reagan administration, over how much, if any, of the story to print.

The Justice Department turned down a plea from DCI William Casey to seek a prior restraint order against the *Post* (citing the Pentagon Papers precedent, among other reasons). Casey then threatened to prosecute the *Post* if it published the story. Casey thereby, no doubt inadvertently, moved the issue from one story's problematic effect on national security to a constitutional confrontation over freedom of the press. The *Post* ran a story on the threat while holding temporarily the story on Ivy Bells. The story reporting the threat to prosecute also had the *New York Times*, the *Washington Times*, *Time*, and *Newsweek* on the Casey hit list. NBC reported part of the story May 19, and the *Post* printed its version May 21. The uproar subsided.[30]

The statute that Casey threatened to use against the press in the Ivy Bells case sets criminal penalties for publicizing information concerning signals intelligence.[31] The government did successfully prosecute Samuel Loring Morison, a navy intelligence analyst, for supplying *Jane's Defence Weekly* with three secret satellite photographs of a Soviet nuclear-powered aircraft carrier under construction. Morison also worked part-time for *Jane's* (a British publication reporting on military forces worldwide), a dubious arrangement from the point of view of both naval intelligence and *Jane's*.

CONCLUSION

There are two principal ways in which the media perform their oversight role. The first, of course, is through publicity. Publicizing a covert action in advance is almost a sure way to kill it. In addition, simply increasing public understanding is a useful function.

The second way is through the media's relationship with the congressional intelligence committees. This is not the leaker-leakee relationship that the intelligence community once feared. It is at once more subtle and more aboveboard. One acute observer has commented on the "significant external influence" that the press has exerted on the House and Senate intelligence committees. "The print media," this writer says, "especially the *New York Times* and the *Washington Post*, have framed the issues and played a crucial role as agenda setters for these committees."[32]

The press sets the agenda for Congress as a whole perhaps more than is generally realized. Congress tends to react to this morning's headlines. So, in some circumstances, does the White House. A dramatic example is the *New York Times* story on December 22, 1974, which revealed past CIA abuses (see Chapter 10). This single story led to the following events: (1) appointment by

President Ford of the Commission on CIA Activities within the United States (popularly known as the Rockefeller Commission after its chairman, Vice President Nelson Rockefeller); (2) unprecedented public release of DCI William Colby's executive session testimony before the intelligence subcommittees of the Senate Appropriations and Armed Services committees; (3) subsequent (and more searching) investigations by the Church committee in the Senate and the Pike committee in the House; and (4) eventual creation of the permanent intelligence committees in both houses.

The press and the intelligence committees tend to work together in ways that are rare with respect to the press and executive agencies. One experienced Washington reporter commented that creation of the committees made the intelligence community easier to cover: there are more people who are willing to talk to you. In addition, the committees can get answers from the community when reporters cannot. It was a reporter from the Associated Press who gave the House Intelligence Committee a copy of *Psychological Operations in Guerrilla Warfare*, a manual that turned out to have been written by the CIA for the Nicaraguan Contras. It made a good story for the AP and a good investigation for the committee.[33]

The government tries to limit the media's oversight role through co-optation, and it works in ways that are manifold and subtle. Most reporters resist most of the time, but it is a rare journalist who resists all the time. Some occasions are more difficult than others. If one of the Sunday television talk shows tries to put balance in a program by matching a critical expert from, say, academia with a cabinet officer, the secretary may refuse to appear. The secretary knows that the network is relying on his or her name to boost the show's ratings. If the network has to choose between a public figure and an outside critic, it will almost always take the public figure at the expense of a balanced discussion. Thus does the government influence the way television presents public issues.

Another tool of co-optation is the appearance of sharing secrets. Classified briefings (at least the first two or three) have a certain glamor—entrance through a door with a combination electronic lock, security warnings over a podium, earnest young officers (the only people who ever call reporters "sir" or "ma'am"). It's a heady experience, until the reporters realize much later that they haven't really been told very much.

There are social enticements: invitations to White House dinners for visiting foreign dignitaries, or possibly more intimate groups with the president, the first lady, and a few colleagues. Three times a year the media invite high officials to elaborate dinners of their own. The press engages in an unseemly competition over whose invitation the secretary of state, or secretary of defense, will accept—and this gives the secretaries a chance to play favorites. Walter Lippmann described the problem thus:

> The most important forms of corruption in the modern journalist's world are the many guises and disguises of social climbing on the pyramids of power. The temptations are many; some are simple, some are refined, and often they are yielded to without the consciousness of yielding. Only a constant awareness of them offers protection.[34]

It is in this milieu that reporters are liable to slip into a pattern in which access to high government officials becomes more important than substance. This has it backwards. No reporter for a major newspaper or television network has cause to worry about access to anybody. Every official in Washington, up to and including the cabinet, is happy to provide access almost on demand.

On his retirement March 14, 1967, Lippmann advised the National Press Club to have carved on its portals: "Put not your trust in princes." [35] It would be good to have it carved over the U.S. Senate and House of Representatives as well.

NOTES

1. Jim Hoagland, "Of News Sources and Spies," *Washington Post*, June 25, 1991.

2. Carl Bernstein, "The CIA and the Media," *Rolling Stone*, Oct. 20, 1977, 55-67.

3. Stuart H. Loory, "The CIA's Use of the Press: A 'Mighty Wurlitzer,'" *Columbia Journalism Review* (September/October 1974): 9-18.

4. Quoted in Nicholas M. Horrock, "CIA to Stop Enlisting Agents from the Press and the Church," *New York Times*, Feb. 12, 1976.

5. David E. Rosenbaum, "CIA Will Keep More than 25 Journalist-Agents," *New York Times*, April 27, 1976.

6. Quoted in Loch K. Johnson, *America's Secret Power: The CIA in a Democratic Society* (New York: Oxford University Press, 1989), 187. On a broader scale this book provides a thoughtful discussion of CIA-media relations, 182-203.

7. Michael Dobbs, "KGB Spy War with U.S. Falls Victim to Glasnost," *Washington Post*, Oct. 3, 1991.

8. Stansfield Turner, *Secrecy and Democracy: The CIA in Transition* (Boston: Houghton Mifflin, 1985), 101.

9. William A. Dorman and Mansour Farhang, *The U.S. Press and Iran: Foreign Policy and the Journalism of Deference* (Berkeley: University of California Press, 1987), 50-62.

10. Jonathan Kwitny, *Endless Enemies: The Making of an Unfriendly World* (New York: Congdon & Weed, 1984), 160-176.

11. Jay Peterzell, "A Cold War Tale," *Time*, December 28, 1992.

12. "Former Post Reporter Sues *Time*," *Washington Post*, Feb. 12, 1993. See also Howard Kurtz, "Ex-Post Correspondent Disputes Report of KGB Ties," *Washington Post*, Dec. 20, 1992; Howard Kurtz, "Journalists Pen Protests to *Time*," *Washington Post*, Jan. 17, 1993; and Michael Dobbs, "Ex-Post Reporter's File Fails to Back Defector," *Washington Post*, Feb. 26, 1993.

13. Arthur M. Schlesinger, Jr., *A Thousand Days: John F. Kennedy in the White House* (Boston: Houghton Mifflin, 1965), 825-828. Dean Rusk as told to Richard Rusk, *As I Saw It*, ed. Daniel S. Papp (New York: W.W. Norton, 1990), 238.

14. Glenn Frankel, "ABC: Israeli Agents Posed as Its Crew to Arrest Arab," *Washington Post*, July 7, 1988.

15. Bob Woodward, *Veil: The Secret Wars of the CIA 1981-1987* (New York: Simon and Schuster, 1987), 328.

16. Ibid., 329.

17. Bernstein, "The CIA and the Media," 60.

18. Executive Order 12356, April 2, 1982, sec. 1.6(a).

19. Quoted in Martin Linsky, *Impact: How the Press Affects Federal Policymaking* (New

York: W.W. Norton, 1986), 199.

20. Ibid., 136. For data on the design and conduct of the survey, see 227-231. For detailed results, see 234-242.

21. Mark Lawrence, "Executive Branch Leads the Leakers," *Washington Post*, July 28, 1987.

22. *Washington's Art of the News Leak: An Interview with Joseph Laitin*, Woodrow Wilson Center Report, September 1990, 10.

23. Quoted in Linsky, *Impact*, 136.

24. Ibid., 201.

25. Ibid., 206.

26. Quoted in Gregory F. Treverton, *Covert Action: The Limits of Intervention in the Postwar World* (New York: Basic Books, 1987), 64-65. See also Richard H. Immerman, *The CIA in Guatemala: The Foreign Policy of Intervention* (Austin: University of Texas Press, 1983).

27. Peter Wyden, *Bay of Pigs: The Untold Story* (New York: Simon and Schuster, 1979), 153-155; James Reston, *Deadline: A Memoir* (New York: Times Books, 1991), 333-334.

28. William Colby and Peter Forbath, *Honorable Men: My Life in the CIA* (New York: Simon and Schuster, 1978), 413-418.

29. See Reston, *Deadline*, 336-338; and Erwin Griswold, "Secrets Not Worth Keeping," *Washington Post*, Feb. 15, 1989. See also *New York Times Co. v. United States*, 403 United States, 713, 1971.

30. Woodward, *Veil*, 448-463.

31. 18 U.S.C. 798. Specifically, the statute forbids publishing any classified information concerning codes, ciphers, or cryptographic systems, devices used for cryptographic or communications intelligence purposes, communication intelligence activities, or information obtained from communications intelligence.

32. Frank J. Smist, Jr., *Congress Oversees the United States Intelligence Community, 1947-1989* (Knoxville: University of Tennessee Press, 1990), 19. See also Johnson, *America's Secret Power*, 220-221.

33. Ibid., 241.

34. Quoted in Ronald Steel, *Walter Lippmann and the American Century* (Boston: Little, Brown, 1980), 572.

35. Ibid., 582.

CHAPTER 9

The President

The Buck Stops Here.
—Sign on President Harry S. Truman's Desk

The buck stops here with me.
—John Poindexter, national security adviser to
President Ronald Reagan

The Constitution could not put it more plainly or simply: "The executive Power shall be vested in a President of the United States of America" (Art. II, Sec. 1). Those words make the president the unquestioned head of the executive branch of the U.S. government and of all its parts, from the tiny Washington National Monument Society to the huge Department of Defense.

The American presidency is frequently referred to as the most powerful office in the world, but many (perhaps most) presidents are exasperated by the sluggishness, or even the unresponsiveness, of the massive bureaucracy over which they preside. A possibly apocryphal story has John Kennedy pointing to the rows of buttons on his telephone and his desk and saying to a visitor, "You see all those buttons? I can push every one of them and nothing will happen." Lyndon Johnson once complained in scatalogical terms (this is not apocryphal) that "some [expletive] assistant secretary of the treasury can make a speech directly contrary to my economic policy and I can't do anything about it." (This was a bit of typical Johnson hyperbole. Although presidents may not be able to do much about mid-level civil servants, they can do plenty about assistant secretaries, such as firing them. But the point stands, despite the hyperbole.)

No part of the executive branch poses a bigger challenge to a president's management skills than the fractious foreign affairs bureaucracy. The hard core of this bureaucracy is the National Security Council (NSC) staff, the Department of State, the Department of Defense, and the Central Intelligence Agency. Paradoxically, it is in the area of foreign affairs that the president's constitutional powers are greatest. He is the commander-in-chief of the armed forces, and he is the voice of the United States in dealing with other nations. This is a source of recurring struggle with Congress, but the advantage is generally with the president unless he makes some crippling mistake.

There is a further paradox in the difficulty of presidential management of the foreign affairs bureaucracy: no part of the government is more thoroughly professionalized, but none is more adept at dragging its feet. The career officers of the Foreign Service in the Department of State, the officers of the army, navy, air force, and marines in the Department of Defense, and the intelligence officers of the CIA are all devoted to following, and staying within, the chain of command, which leads, ultimately, to the White House. But all of these services are also closed societies. Foreign service officers spend much (in some cases most) of their careers abroad in the artificial diplomatic ghettos of capital cities. Military officers spend their careers in the even more artificial society of military bases. Intelligence officers are almost necessarily limited to talking to each other. This culture is characteristic of groups that are resistant to change. It also is typical of groups with fierce institutional loyalties. Such loyalties are at the bottom of many unseemly bureaucratic squabbles.

In contrast, presidents and the people whom they bring with them to the White House have spent their lives in politics. This is a milieu that could scarcely be more different from the close-knit societies described in the preceding paragraph. These differences are the ingredients of a culture clash.

A widely reported story in Washington early in the Clinton administration had a new young female staffer passing a general as one entered and one left the White House. "Good evening," said the general. The staffer sniffed, "We don't talk to generals." This is an extreme example. It may not be true. But it is illustrative of the White House's distrust of the bureaucracy, a distrust that is never far below the surface and is sometimes pervasive.

Jimmy Carter and Ronald Reagan are two very different personalities, and they presided over two very different administrations. But they both got to the White House by campaigning against the government that they wanted to head. That is not a good way to win friends among the people on whom you must rely to carry out your program. In the period between the election and the inauguration of both Carter and Reagan, bureaucrats all over Washington were making private jokes about how they would show these new presidents a thing or two about how the government really works. In the case of Reagan, the problem was complicated by the new president's heavy ideological approach. The incoming Reagan team even went so far as to notify the State Department that all officers holding presidential appointments were expected to be gone by the day after the inauguration. If interpreted literally, this edict would have shut out every career foreign service officer. Even if interpreted to include only those senior officials in policy-making positions, the order, if obeyed, would have seriously disrupted the conduct of routine business.

The secretary of state, secretary of defense, and director of the CIA are caught in the middle of the cultural clash. They are the president's appointees. Their loyalties are to him. They are expected to manage, and they want to manage, their departments so as to carry out the president's program with the least amount of friction. The career services of State, Defense, and CIA, over which these appointees preside, are perfectly willing to carry out the president's program. In addition, they want to keep the president out of trouble—if for no other reason, because when the president is in trouble in foreign affairs, the country is in trouble. So they point out unsuspected difficulties. They counsel restraint. They may also, subtly and gradually over a period of time, co-opt their secretary, so that he is representing their department to the White House as much as he is representing the White House to their department. If all of this works, it can lead to a fruitful relationship, but rarely to a smooth one, especially if the career services of State, Defense, and CIA have different agendas.[1]

PRESIDENTS AS MANAGERS

Historians and political scientists speak of "strong" presidents and "weak" ones, but these terms are relative within a very small universe. From Washington to Clinton, only forty-one people have been president. All of them have been strong personalities; otherwise, they would not have become president. Each has had his individual style, and this has been reflected in how he has managed his office and the government sprawled beyond it. We are concerned here with how the presidents from Truman to Clinton have dealt with the intelligence community and the foreign affairs agencies generally.

There are two crucial sets of relationships in executive branch oversight of the intelligence community: (1) that between the president and the director of central intelligence (DCI), and (2) that between the DCI and the other principal players in national security policy—the secretaries of state and defense and the national security adviser. These relationships depend importantly on personalities, especially those of the president and the DCI. The framework has changed over time as the intelligence community has become larger and more bureaucratic. The development of oversight mechanisms in Congress added an unrelated and sometimes hostile instrument of control, this one more formal than the lines running between the president and the community.

PRESIDENT HARRY TRUMAN (1945-1953)

President Truman never left any doubt as to who was in charge. Once asked if he agreed with something Secretary of State Dean Acheson had said about the Middle East, the president replied sharply, "You got it backwards, The secretary agrees with what I've said about the Middle East." In the midst of the Korean War, Truman fired Gen. Douglas MacArthur, an immensely popular war hero. Truman seems to have paid little attention to the CIA. He viewed it as his personal information service and an adjunct of the National Security Council.

In his memoirs President Truman described the policy-making process as follows. The CIA presented the NSC with an estimate of the effects of a proposed policy. This estimate represented the judgment of the CIA and "a cross section of the judgments of all the advisory councils of the CIA": the State Department, the Federal Bureau of Investigation, the director of intelligence of the Atomic Energy Commission, and G-2, A-2, and ONI (that is, army, air force, and navy intelligence). "The Secretary of State," Truman wrote, "then makes the final recommendation of policy, and the President makes the final decision."[2]

Probably few other participants in the process would have presented it in those terms. The creation of the CIA was widely deplored throughout the foreign policy agencies of the government. Dean Acheson, who was undersecretary of state at the time, wrote in his memoirs, "I had the gravest forebodings about this organization and warned the President that as set up neither he, the National Security Council, nor anyone else would be in a position to know what it was doing or to control it." [3] (Acheson came to support the CIA's intelligence collection but remained distrustful of its analysis, possibly because he thought he knew more than the analysts.) The CIA's "advisory councils," as Truman called them, were so jealous of the new boy on the block that they shared intelligence reluctantly if at all.

Truman stayed above the bureaucratic frictions. He was happy with the results he was seeing. "Here, at last," he wrote, "a coordinated method had been worked out, and a practical way had been found for keeping the President informed as to what was known and what was going on." [4] DCI Walter B. Smith (1950-1953) brought the bureaucracy more or less to heel, the president got what he wanted, and that was all that mattered.

President Dwight Eisenhower (1953-1961)

Eisenhower brought military management style to the White House. Everything was staffed out and brought to the president for a yes or no decision. It was said of John Foster Dulles, who was secretary of state during most of the Eisenhower presidency, that he carried the State Department around in his hat. At times he made the department's bureaucracy seem almost irrelevant.

At the CIA John Foster's brother Allen led the spooks through their greatest years. Allen Dulles was perhaps the most activist DCI until William Casey came along in the Reagan administration forty years later, but unlike Casey, Dulles served a president who kept a firm grip on things. Eisenhower involved himself closely in the management of the U-2 (see Chapter 4) and also in the CIA-sponsored coup d'état in Guatemala (see Chapter 7). Early in the Guatemalan affair the U.S.-backed rebels lost a number of aircraft, and the question arose as to whether to supply more planes or to let the coup fail. Eisenhower himself made the decision to go ahead with more planes and later recalled it like this:

> I said to Mr. [Allen] Dulles . . . before I made this decision I said "What are the chances that this will succeed?" Well, he said he thought about twenty percent. I told him later, "If you'd have said ninety percent, I'd have said no, but you seemed to be honest." [5]

It was during the Eisenhower administration that the doctrine of plausible deniability took root, but for Eisenhower, this was not so much a standard procedure as it was a presidential option. As one writer has put it, Eisenhower "would deny something if he considered it politic or beneficial to do so, but if he had to, he would also own up rather than blame subordinates." [6]

President John Kennedy (1961-1963)

Kennedy represented an abrupt change in style. Eisenhower was the last president born in the nineteenth century; Kennedy was the first born in the twentieth. In World War II Eisenhower commanded the invasion of Europe; Kennedy commanded a PT boat. Eisenhower had the military's ingrained respect for channels. Kennedy had none. He dismantled many of the committees that Eisenhower had established to filter decisions to the president. Especially in the early months of his administration, he had a disconcerting habit of telephoning State Department desk officers directly. Charles E. (Chip) Bohlen, a distinguished senior foreign service officer, former ambassador to the Soviet Union, and Kennedy friend, recalled that "once . . . the president asked me in these words, 'What's wrong with that goddam department of yours, Chip?' and I told him that he was." [7]

Kennedy made McGeorge Bundy head of the NSC staff and thereby laid the groundwork for the future rise to prominence of the national security adviser. By making Robert McNamara secretary of defense, he shook up the Pentagon bureaucracy. He felt betrayed by the CIA in the Bay of Pigs affair in 1961. (See chapters 5 and 7.) After waiting a decent interval, he replaced Allen Dulles as DCI with John McCone, who had served as chairman of the Atomic Energy Commission in the Eisenhower administration. McCone will probably be best remembered as DCI for his early intuition that Soviet missiles were in Cuba, contradicting the judgment of CIA professionals. But he is remembered with great respect by career officers. As another consequence of the Bay of Pigs, Kennedy revitalized the President's Foreign Intelligence Advisory Board, which had been established by Eisenhower.

Perhaps the biggest impact of the Kennedy administration on the intelligence community was the preoccupation with counterinsurgency, special operations, and covert action. This was accompanied by a vendetta against Cuba after the failure of the Bay of Pigs. A public safety element was included in foreign aid. Among other things, the public safety program trained foreign police forces to deal with riots and more serious insurgencies. (Congress acquiesced in the program's beginning but later decreed its end when the program identified the United States too closely with foreign police brutality.) The army established its elite special operations forces, the Green Berets, specialists in unconventional warfare. The president's brother, Attorney General Robert Kennedy, was a driving force in the emphasis on counterinsurgency and in none of it more than in his ceaseless, obsessive demands for covert action against Cuba.

PRESIDENT LYNDON JOHNSON (1963-1969)

Johnson was more interested in domestic than in foreign policy. His considerable successes in domestic affairs (civil rights, the Great Society) were overshadowed by his failure in foreign policy (Vietnam), a failure which ruined his administration. Like Kennedy, he tended to be a hands-on manager. During the crisis in the Dominican Republic in the spring and summer of 1965, a State Department official described the president as the "acting Dominican desk officer." Later he personally involved himself in the selection of bombing targets in Vietnam. Johnson left Rusk and McNamara in place at State and Defense, replacing McNamara only in the last year of his administration with Clark Clifford. Bundy left the NSC job in 1966 and was followed by Walt W. Rostow. Rostow was a veteran of the Office of Strategic Services (OSS), and the intelligence community found him easy to work with.

McCone left the CIA after a little more than a year of the Johnson administration, by all accounts because he was generally dissatisfied with his relationship with the president. There was no big disagreement between the two; there was simply no rapport. McCone later contrasted the work habits of Kennedy and Johnson:

> President Kennedy used to insist that he sit down with me alone for an hour or so a week to review a lot of things, both current and prospective. He was always anxious to know what we thought might be the danger spot down the road in six months or a year. . . . President Johnson only wanted to see me when I had something particularly I wanted to tell him. His door was always open, but he wasn't inclined to want to sit for a general review." [8]

McCone told Richard Helms he felt he did not have any impact and did not have sufficient influence.[9] Johnson replaced McCone with Adm. William F. Raborn, Jr., "an unfortunate choice," in McCone's view.[10] Raborn had previously run the navy's Polaris submarine missile program. One story has it that Johnson told his staff he wanted a Texas admiral who had voted Democratic in 1964. Raborn had the misfortune to arrive at about the same time as the Dominican Republic crisis erupted in April 1965, and he never quite got control of his job. A part of Raborn's problem may have been that Johnson made clear to others (if not directly to Raborn) that Raborn had been selected because Johnson thought he could handle Congress but that the president would rely on Helms, Raborn's deputy DCI, to manage the agency. In fact, Johnson told Helms to go everywhere Raborn did, and when Raborn resigned in 1966, Johnson made Helms his successor.

Helms later described Johnson's attitude toward the CIA:

> Mr. Johnson gave me such a free hand . . . that I do not believe he really had the faintest idea how the Central Intelligence Agency was organized, or how the intelligence community was organized. He expected me to produce the goods. When I produced them, which I think I did with regularity, he never asked any questions about where they came from.[11]

Formal NSC meetings fell into disuse during the Johnson administration. The president preferred to manage foreign policy through Tuesday lunches with Rusk, McNamara, Helms, and Rostow. And he preferred to manage the CIA through Helms.

PRESIDENT RICHARD NIXON (1969-1974)

Nixon arrived in the White House with a world view that was already well formed, with the benefit of having observed the national security apparatus at close range as vice president during the Eisenhower administration, and with a more than ordinary distrust of the career foreign service. Whereas Johnson's administration was ruined by foreign policy failures, Nixon's considerable foreign policy successes (the diplomatic opening to China, the SALT I arms control agreement, the Vietnam peace agreement) were ruined by his domestic failures (Watergate).

Nixon appointed his long-time friend William P. Rogers, who had been attorney general in the Eisenhower administration, to be secretary of state and made Henry Kissinger his national security adviser. With Nixon's acquiescence, if not support, Kissinger set about usurping the job of the secretary of state until, in the last year of the Nixon administration, he formally held both jobs.

Like Johnson, Nixon did not know much about the intelligence community, nor did he seem to care. Early in his administration he asked for a briefing on covert action, which went on for about two hours and exhausted his interest. He did not trust the CIA, suspecting that it underestimated Soviet military strength. Kissinger demanded raw data, instead of the analytic product, and was especially fascinated by intercepts coming from NSA.

At the start of the Nixon administration in 1969, newly installed National Security Adviser Henry Kissinger brought word to DCI Richard Helms that the president wished him to leave NSC meetings as soon as he had finished his briefing so as to avoid any appearance that the DCI was involved in policy. As it turned out in the first such meeting, when Helms finished, Nixon invited everybody to lunch, and Helms never left, then or in later meetings. (Helms had forehandedly complained to Melvin Laird, the new secretary of defense, about his prospective exclusion, and Laird had persuaded Kissinger that it was a bad idea.)[12] The irony of this anecdote is that Helms was one of the more rigid DCIs in keeping the CIA out of policy while the Nixon-Kissinger fastidiousness was probably rooted in the feeling that Allen Dulles had been too much involved in policy when he was DCI (and Nixon was vice president) during the Eisenhower administration (1953-1961).

In the summer of 1972, a group operating on behalf of the Nixon reelection campaign broke into the offices of the Democratic National Committee in the Watergate Office Building in Washington with the purpose of planting telephone bugs and rifling files. Nixon tried to divert the FBI from its investigation of this break-in by pleading a connection to the Bay of Pigs. For this purpose presidential assistant H. R. Haldeman, on behalf of the president, told Helms to ask that the FBI stop its inquiries in Mexico related to the source of the Watergate burglars' funds. Helms went so far as to send his deputy, Gen. Vernon Walters, to remind L. Patrick Gray, the acting FBI director, of the CIA-FBI agreement not to impinge on each other's sources without notice. In fact, as Helms explicitly told Haldeman, there was no connection between Watergate and either the Bay of Pigs or the CIA. After the 1972 election Nixon removed Helms from the CIA and sent him to Iran as ambassador.

These events were occurring contemporaneously with the supersecret Track II operation designed to topple President Salvador Allende in Chile. As a consequence of his role in protecting the CIA from involvement in the Watergate coverup, Helms lost his job as DCI. As a consequence of his role in protecting the secrecy of Track II, he was prosecuted for misleading Congress. In the first instance Helms resisted what he regarded as improper presidential attempts to manipulate the CIA for domestic purposes. In the second, he served the same president in what he regarded as appropriate covert action abroad.

To replace Helms at CIA, Nixon appointed James R. Schlesinger, who attempted a major reorganization of the agency, something that did not sit well with the bureaucracy. Nixon shortly shifted Schlesinger to Defense and made William Colby, a CIA careerist, DCI.

There were more White House shenanigans with the intelligence community during the Nixon administration. As public protests and demonstrations against the Vietnam war mounted, President Nixon became increasingly convinced that domestic radicals, encouraged from Moscow, were a threat to national security. Tom Charles Huston, a former army intelligence officer on the White House staff, put together a plan for authorizing unprecedented domestic spying. Restraints would be secretly removed from communications intercepts, physical break-ins and surveillance, mail openings, and other intrusive measures. The plan received the blessing of the principal intelligence agency chiefs and was approved by the president, but even FBI director J. Edgar Hoover balked when he looked at it a second time. The president thereupon rescinded his approval of the Huston plan.

PRESIDENT GERALD FORD (1974-1977)

Ford became president when Nixon resigned in August 1974 under the insupportable burden of Watergate. Ford's unenviable job was to bring the country together after a decade of divisiveness, controversy, and scandal. He brought Brent Scowcroft in as national security adviser, leaving Kissinger as secretary of state. Watergate was behind him, but the CIA's troubles seemed to grow daily with new revelations of past misdeeds. Congress passed legislation requiring that certain committees be informed of covert actions. Ford appointed a commission headed by Vice President Nelson Rockefeller to investigate and try to restore public confidence in the CIA but to no avail. Congress started its own investigations, led in the Senate by Frank Church, D-Idaho, and in the House by Otis Pike, D-N.Y.

It was Colby's job as DCI to steer the agency through trying times. He got high marks on Capitol Hill but not in the White House. In early 1976 Ford replaced him with George Bush.

PRESIDENT JIMMY CARTER (1977-1981)

Carter was unable to persuade the Senate to confirm his first choice to be DCI—Theodore Sorensen, who had been Kennedy's White House counsel. He then nominated Adm. Stansfield Turner, his contemporary at the Naval Academy.

The Carter administration's foreign policy machinery did not work smoothly. Secretary of State Cyrus Vance and National Security Adviser Zbigniew Brzezinski had sharply differing views of the Soviet threat and carried on a running feud, with Turner sometimes in the crossfire. Vance resigned on principle in the spring of 1980 because he disapproved of the U.S. mission to try to rescue hostages in Iran. Carter appointed Sen. Edmund Muskie, a Maine Democrat, to succeed him.

The intelligence community was also more than ordinarily disputatious. Admirals Turner at CIA and Inman at NSA did not get along, each accusing the other of grabbing for power. There was friction between the CIA and the Defense Intelligence Agency. But relations between CIA and State were good, and even relations between the CIA and the FBI improved. (Turner and FBI director Webster had known each other at Amherst.)

The greatest turmoil was at the CIA. Turner wanted to put more emphasis on collection from technical instead of human sources. Given the improvement in technical collection capabilities, a good argument could be made for moving in this direction; but Turner, the outsider, clashed with the clandestine operators in the Directorate of Operations, the insiders. The clash was intensified by Turner's program of staff reductions and reorganization.

Under Turner covert action reached probably its lowest point in the agency's history—a continuation of a trend that had been in progress since at least the late Nixon era. In the White House Brzezinski was a covert action enthusiast, but few of his proposals survived review. Reversal of the downward trend began in the last year of the Carter administration as the United States responded to the Soviet invasion of Afghanistan.

One other point of particular note: the CIA was dead wrong in not foreseeing the fall of the shah of Iran in 1979.

PRESIDENT RONALD REAGAN (1981-1989)

Reagan was the most committed, and the least engaged, of the post-World War II presidents. His commitment was strongly ideological; he sought to promote an image of America as "a shining city on a hill." But he had little knowledge of, and less interest in, how the government worked, and he happily left this to others. Reagan's first secretary of state, Alexander Haig, who served from January 1981 to July 1982, developed an aggressive policy against the Soviet Union and its surrogates abroad and against liberal foreign service officers in the State Department. Haig was succeeded at State by George Shultz, who brought a greater sense of balanced moderation. Reagan's first DCI, William Casey, was obsessed with both policy and covert action. During Reagan's first term, the intelligence community budget increased by as much as 17 percent a year, a good deal of which was for covert action. Casey was the most politicized of all DCIs and the only one to be given cabinet rank. There are a good many people in Washington who believe that Shultz, either tacitly or explicitly, traded off Central America to Casey and the Republican right wing in return for a free hand in other areas. However this may be, Casey reigned supreme in Central America. He fell ill with a brain tumor shortly after the Iran-Contra scandal began to unravel and died before he could be questioned about it.

To succeed Casey, Reagan chose FBI director William Webster, who swung the pendulum 180 degrees away from Casey's involvement in policy. He was deliberately aloof, as befits a judge. He also made some progress toward ending the long-running feud between the FBI and the CIA, but the differences are so deep in the two bureaucratic cultures that Webster's peacemaking began to erode after he left.

PRESIDENT GEORGE BUSH (1989-1993)

Bush was so engrossed in foreign policy that at times he almost gave the impression of being bored with domestic affairs. Before becoming Reagan's vice president, he had served as ambassador to the United Nations, as chief of the U.S. Liaison Office in China (before that office was upgraded to an embassy), and as DCI. Congress found him generally more cooperative when he was DCI than when he was president. The Senate rejected one of its own—former senator John Tower, R-Tex.—as Bush's first nominee to be secretary of defense, but Bush then assembled a close-knit team to manage the foreign affairs agencies.

For secretary of state Bush appointed James Baker III, a long-time personal friend. Baker had been White House chief of staff in the first Reagan administration and secretary of the treasury in the second. For secretary of defense, after Tower was rejected, Bush chose Dick Cheney, then a Republican member of Congress from Wyoming who had been chief of staff in the Ford White House. To fill the position of national security adviser, the president brought back Brent Scowcroft, who had held the same job under President Ford. And Bush kept Webster at the CIA. When Webster left in 1991, the president nominated Robert M. Gates, a career intelligence officer who had been on the NSC staff. The nomination was controversial, but later Gates's critics admitted he had done well in pushing the agency to adjust to the end of the cold war.

The process of making foreign policy in the Bush administration was briskly efficient and was carried on without much regard for the career bureaucrats. The president himself was heavily and personally engaged, setting a new standard for presidential telephone conversations with foreign leaders.

President Bill Clinton (1993-   )

Clinton, unlike Bush, regarded foreign policy as a distraction from his domestic agenda. His appointments to the foreign policy agencies were foreign affairs professionals rather than career civil servants. Warren Christopher, the secretary of state, had been deputy secretary to Vance and Muskie during the Carter administration. Les Aspin, the secretary of defense, had been chairman of the House Armed Services Committee. He had trouble making the transition between the different milieus of Capitol Hill and the Pentagon and was eased out after less than a year. To replace Aspin, Clinton chose retired admiral B. R. Inman (former head of NSA, former deputy DCI under Casey). But Inman changed his mind and withdrew before his nomination even went to the Senate. Clinton then nominated, and the Senate confirmed, Deputy Defense Secretary William Perry, who had served as deputy under secretary for research and engineering in both the Ford and Carter administrations. R. James Woolsey, who followed Gates at CIA, had held a number of jobs in the arms control field. The national security adviser, Anthony Lake, had been chief of the State Department policy planning staff in the Carter administration.

INTELLIGENCE AS A MANAGEMENT PROBLEM

When the Central Intelligence Agency was created in 1947, it was conceived as a small, easily manageable group responsible directly to the president. In the House of Representatives a single, closed hearing was held by what was then the Committee on Expenditures in the Executive Departments. This committee, which has since been transformed through a congressional reorganization into the Committee on Government Operations, had jurisdiction at that time over organizational matters in the executive branch. The hearing held on

June 27, 1947, convened in such great secrecy that the witnesses were identified not by their names but by letters. For example, Gen. Hoyt Vandenberg, then director of the Central Intelligence Group (see Chapter 2), was identified as "Mr. A," Allen Dulles was "Mr. B," and so on. The transcript of the hearing was preserved and was published in 1982 under the joint imprimatur of the House Committee on Government Operations and the House Intelligence Committee.

Dulles had been the principal OSS representative in Switzerland during World War II. He was later the DCI under President Eisenhower, but he was present in the House hearing room in 1947 as one of those who had planned the proposed permanent CIA. The following exchange took place between Dulles and Republican representative J. Caleb Boggs of Delaware:

> Mr. Boggs. In view of your experience, sir, would you contemplate that this Central Intelligence Agency, to set it up, would require a lot of personnel here in the United States? Would it develop into a large bureau, or how large a bureau would it develop into, in operations in the United States?
>
> Mr. B [Dulles]. I do not believe in a big agency. I know I was happier in Switzerland when they could not send anybody to me from the United States than I was after the frontier opened up; and I did a lot of work because I was not bedeviled with administrative problems. I could do better with 10 people than I could with 50. On the evaluation side there, you require a certain number of people. On the side of collecting business information, I should think that a couple of dozen people throughout the United States could do it, two in New York, one in Chicago and one in San Francisco.
>   You ought to keep it small. If this thing gets to be a great big octopus, it should not function well. Abroad, you will need a certain number of people, but it ought not to be a great number. It ought to be scores rather than hundreds.[13]

In December 1946, six months before Dulles's appearance before the House committee, the staff of the Central Intelligence Group, predecessor of the CIA, "numbered approximately 1,816," according to data published years later by the Church committee.[14] Under the CIA this number sharply increased, but it is, and always has been, secret. It is characteristic of executive branch witnesses before Congress to underestimate the size (and expense) of proposed new agencies but rarely as grossly as Dulles did in 1947. Dulles was possibly carried away by his nostalgia for wartime Switzerland and by a desire not to arouse suspicions in a conservative House committee. But his answer reflected (although it overstated) the prevailing view: the CIA was to be essentially a service staff for the president.

Although the CIA was never the cozy little group hypothesized by Allen Dulles before the House committee, the intelligence community as a whole in its early days was small compared with what it later became. The CIA, which was the elite agency of the community, had several other characteristics that importantly influenced its role in the government and its relationship with the White House. Originally and for some time thereafter, it had a high proportion of veterans of the OSS. This was a cohesive group with a high esprit de corps, qualities that came from shared experiences of risk, danger, and accomplishment. And it was ingrown because of the secrecy that necessarily surrounded it. During its formative years, the CIA was headed by Walter B. Smith, the general who had been Eisenhower's chief of staff during the liberation of Europe in World War II, and by Allen Dulles, the intelligence icon of the OSS in Switzerland.

During most of the Truman and Eisenhower administrations, the CIA operated more or less as had been intended—as personal support for the president. But at the same time it was venturing farther into covert activity and engaging in more hazardous collection. The agencies in the community were also proliferating. The National Security Agency was established in 1952; the Defense Intelligence Agency, in 1961. With the coming of the space age in the 1950s, the Defense Department began very secretly to develop reconnaissance satellites. This expansion brought with it new problems of management, of what the armed forces call command and control. But the most sensitive activities, those with the highest potential for public political backlash, were those of the CIA.

As noted in earlier chapters, many of these activities were of arguable value from the point of view of their long-range effects on American foreign policy, but none caused particular controversy at the time—none, that is, until the U-2 came crashing down in the Soviet Union in May 1960. (See Chapter 4.) This misfortune had several effects (unrecognized at the time) on the system of management and oversight of the intelligence community.

First, it brought into sharp focus the dilemma inherent in the doctrine of plausible deniability. When Eisenhower acknowledged responsibility for the U-2, he so shattered the doctrine that it was not revived until a quarter of a century later, when the Reagan White House was desperately grasping for straws in the Iran-Contra scandal. Second, the U-2 incident marked the end of the era of quiet intelligence and the beginning of a period of noisy public debate, fueled by exposés and public failures. Third, it marked the beginning of a transition from management of the intelligence community as an old-boy network responsive to the whims and desires of the president to a structured, impersonal management in which Congress plays a role. The U-2 was the first of a series of shattering events that led, over the next fifteen years, to the establishment of the congressional intelligence committees.

PRESIDENTIAL TOOLS OF OVERSIGHT

Several agencies help the president oversee intelligence activities—the National Security Council, the President's Foreign Intelligence Advisory Board, and the Office of Management and Budget.

THE NATIONAL SECURITY COUNCIL

In creating the CIA, Congress put it under the National Security Council and provided that it would carry out its duties "under the direction of" the NSC. The members of the NSC are named in the law as the president, the vice president, and the secretaries of state and defense. (Additional members were named originally but have been dropped from the NSC in various reorganizations.) Gratuitously, the act provides that the chairman of the Joint Chiefs of

Staff "may" attend meetings of the NSC "subject to the direction of the president" in his role as principal military adviser, and the Director of National Drug Control Policy "may" attend, also in an advisory role and "subject to the direction of the president." The president may, of course, invite anybody he wishes, and presidents frequently do.

The DCI is another official who, by law, "may . . . attend and participate" in NSC meetings. DCIs regularly do so to provide intelligence briefings. The DCI is the council's official intelligence adviser, just as the chairman of the Joint Chiefs of Staff is the council's official military adviser, though neither has a vote.

But that doesn't make any difference because the NSC is whatever the president wants it to be. The president is the only member who matters. The other members matter in the sense that they have important jobs, but the president is the only one whose vote counts. The NSC is his creature. It will do his bidding, or he will bypass it or find other people to appoint as members. Thus, to say, as the National Security Act does, that the CIA operates under the direction of the NSC is a bit of congressional window dressing. The CIA was set up to operate under the direction of the president, who can, and does, use the NSC as his instrument to control it.[15]

Covert action has been the biggest management problem. It is complicated by the doctrine of plausible deniability, which implies that there is no management. The idea that the United States should engage in covert action was inspired by the developing cold war. At first it was no more than a formless idea without a target, the notion that somewhere there must be circumstances in which it would be useful for the United States to engage in clandestine psychological or political activities. Adm. Roscoe H. Hillenkoetter, who was DCI from 1947 to 1950, thought that congressional authorization would be necessary for the initiation of what was then called "psychological warfare," as well as for the expenditure of funds for that purpose.[16] More than forty years later the White House and Congress argued bitterly over whether Congress should be notified of covert actions. Not even the most radical member of Congress ever suggested, however, that congressional approval was necessary for covert action. History would have been markedly changed in unpredictable ways if Hillenkoetter's view had prevailed in 1947.

Although the relevant agencies agreed that a mechanism for covert action was desirable, nobody wanted to be in charge. Secretary of Defense James Forrestal and the military services thought that covert psychological warfare should be in the State Department and be managed by a triumvirate of an assistant secretary of state, the DCI, and a military representative. Secretary of State George Marshall would have none of this, arguing that if such activity was exposed as under State Department sponsorship, it would embarrass the department and discredit American foreign policy. Nor did the military have enthusiasm for the task. Both State and the military wanted to maintain control but without operational responsibility.

The CIA got the job more or less by default. It also had the biggest reservoir of experience as a consequence of the OSS service of many of its employees. Thus, there was established something called the Special Procedures Group in the CIA's Office of Special Operations.

The NSC's first policy paper, NSC-1/3, approved covert intervention in the Italian election in 1948 to prevent a communist victory. Later in 1948 other NSC papers established broader programs of covert action worldwide.[17] The Special Procedures Group was replaced by the Office of Special Projects, which soon became the Office of Policy Coordination. It was in the CIA, but its director was named by the secretary of state and its policy guidance came from State and Defense.

This was not an effective system of control. Activities proliferated but without political backlash because they did not come to public attention. In April 1951 the NSC dealt with the situation by creating a subcommittee called the Psychological Strategy Board, which was charged with directing psychological warfare programs.

This was basically the structure that President Eisenhower found when he took office in 1953. Under Eisenhower there was more tinkering with the mechanisms for managing covert action. Viewed as inadequate, the Psychological Strategy Board was replaced in September 1953 by the Operations Coordinating Board, whose members were at the deputy secretary level. Still unsatisfied, the NSC two years later established the "Special Group," or 5412 Committee, as it came to be called after the NSC directive that created it for the specific purpose of reviewing covert action projects. This committee has gone through various transmutations and name changes—the 303 Committee, the 40 Committee—but since 1955 it has been the basic instrument through which the NSC and the president have managed covert action.

PRESIDENT'S FOREIGN INTELLIGENCE ADVISORY BOARD

Another Eisenhower innovation was the President's Board of Consultants on Foreign Intelligence Activities, created by Executive Order 10656 on February 6, 1956. The board was the result of the development of the U-2 and of Eisenhower's interest in the application of technology to intelligence. Its first chairman was Dr. James R. Killian, president of the Massachusetts Institute of Technology, and in its early years its work was related to technical questions. One of the original members was Joseph P. Kennedy, the father of the future president.

In the aftermath of the Bay of Pigs, President Kennedy gave the board a broader focus and renamed it the President's Foreign Intelligence Advisory Board (PFIAB). He kept Killian as chairman and added Clark Clifford as a member. (Joseph Kennedy had long since resigned.) Later Clifford was named chairman.

In the Kennedy administration the board concerned itself with procedures in the intelligence community and with how mistakes were made. Writing in 1991, Clifford described an active board:

> We made 170 formal recommendations to President Kennedy in the space of only twenty-nine months, most relating to intelligence activities within the Department of Defense, the rest in the Department of State and the CIA. He approved 125 of these recommendations, disapproved two, and deferred action on the rest. At the time of his death [November 22, 1963] eighty-five of the 125 approved recommendations had been implemented; the rest were completed

under President Johnson, and we continued to make recommendations at about the same pace throughout Johnson's tenure.[18]

When Clifford testified on this subject (among others) to the Senate Intelligence Committee in 1978, his recollection was different. Kennedy always met with the board himself, but after that

> the board went rapidly downhill. It didn't amount to very much under President Johnson. It amounted, I think, to less as time went on. And I noted with some concern later on that it looked as though it had become the repository place for political appointments to maybe pay off political debts of some kind, which I thought was unfortunate because at one time it did a real job.[19]

The point about using the board for political appointments is confirmed by other evidence. When former DCI George Bush was vice president, the suggestion was made to him that the board be abolished. "Forget it," Bush is said to have responded. "It's the most popular appointment we have."

Jimmy Carter abolished the board, but Ronald Reagan revived it and appointed, among others, Anne Armstrong, John Connally, and Peter O'Donnell, all from Texas and prominent in the Republican Party. Armstrong and Connally had at least been exposed to intelligence, she as ambassador to Great Britain, he as secretary of the navy and secretary of the treasury. Other Reagan appointees included former ambassador Clare Boothe Luce, Washington criminal lawyer Edward Bennett Williams, former Diner's Club executive William O. Baker, Alfred S. Bloomingdale of the department store, and entrepreneur Ross Perot. More relevant to the board's work were physicist John Wheeler, former State Department official David Abshire, and Adm. Thomas Moorer, former chief of naval operations.

Another Reagan appointee was Martin Anderson, a senior member of the White House staff and Stanford University economist. After being reelected in 1984, Reagan reshuffled the board, firing Anderson and ten others and appointing four new members, including former ambassador to the United Nations Jeane Kirkpatrick. Anderson has attributed these changes to a devious plot involving Mrs. Armstrong and DCI William Casey. In Anderson's version Mrs. Armstrong, the chairman of the board, felt she did not receive sufficient respect from some members and that the board was too big with twenty-one members. Casey simply felt it was getting in his way (other DCIs have had the same feeling) and made common cause with Armstrong. Letters changing the membership of the board were written. Casey and Armstrong managed to get these letters onto Reagan's desk by sending them through National Security Adviser Robert McFarlane, thus bypassing the established channel through the White House chief of staff. Anderson's conclusion:

> It is impossible to say for certain that if the old PFIAB was in place the Iran-Contra affair would not have happened. As later testimony before Congress would bear out, Casey and Poindexter and [NSC staff member Oliver] North would probably have had no more compunction about misleading the board than they had about misleading anyone else. But a large, vigorous board would have made it more likely that the skullduggery would have been discovered much, much earlier.[20]

President Clinton appointed to the Foreign Intelligence Advisory Board Zoë E. Baird, after she failed to become attorney general, and Vernon E. Jordan, who helped manage Clinton's transition team between the election and inauguration. But Clinton made Adm. William J. Crowe, former chairman of the Joint Chiefs of Staff, chairman. After Admiral Crowe was named ambassador to Great Britain in March 1994, Clinton replaced him at PFIAB with Les Aspin, the former chairman of the House Armed Services Committee and the former secretary of defense. Warren B. Rudman, who was once a member of the Senate Intelligence Committee, became vice chairman. Following the arrest and guilty plea of CIA officer Aldrich Ames on espionage charges, Aspin and Rudman set out to use PFIAB as the vehicle for a major study of the intelligence community. The study reportedly would include not only the security lapses that made the Ames case possible, but also the broader question of the role of intelligence in the post-cold war world.

Clinton also abolished the Intelligence Oversight Board that had been established by President Ford (Executive Order 11905, February 18, 1976). The principal duty of this three-member board had been to receive and forward to the president reports from inspectors general of the intelligence agencies.

Those who work in senior positions in the intelligence community are of mixed views about the usefulness of the Foreign Intelligence Advisory Board. One suspects that this depends in part on their experience with it. The board can usually (not always) get the attention of the president. It can therefore be helpful to an intelligence agency in its bureaucratic or policy struggles. Or, conversely, it can be a problem for an agency.

The board only meets every month or two for a couple of days each time. Under Reagan, the board had as many as twenty-one members. This was not only unwieldy; it made the intelligence community nervous about security. Bush cut it down to six. He made former senator John Tower chairman, possibly as consolation for not having been confirmed by the Senate to be secretary of defense. The other members included such intelligence professionals as B. R. Inman, former director of NSA and former deputy DCI, and Lew Allen, another former director of NSA. Another Bush appointee was William Hyland, editor of *Foreign Affairs* and formerly of the NSC staff. After Tower was killed in a plane crash in April 1991, Inman became chairman and the board's activity increased.

How much difference PFIAB makes depends largely on the president and on whom he appoints to the board. Kennedy was interested, among other reasons, because he had been badly burned by faulty advice about the Bay of Pigs. According to Clifford, during the Kennedy administration the board brought about a great many changes in the way the intelligence community did things. We do not know if those were big changes or little changes. Since big changes would probably have been apparent, they were most likely small, which is not to say they were unimportant. Johnson and Nixon paid less attention to the board, and, as noted, Carter abolished it. One account has it that this was at the behest of DCI Stansfield Turner, who saw the board as a way around him directly to the president. Turner says it was because establishment of the congressional intelligence committees made the board dispensable. (Some other DCIs have found the board a helpful friend at court in interagency disputes.) Reagan loaded the board with his political friends and then paid little attention.

Because of his previous experience as DCI, Bush knew more about intelligence than any other president, and he took the board seriously. It is said he would even take time out from his failing reelection campaign to read memos from the board. (This might have been one of the things wrong with his campaign; on the other hand, he might have found the board's memos a welcome relief.)

THE OFFICE OF MANAGEMENT AND BUDGET

The Office of Management and Budget (OMB) within the executive office of the president prepares the federal budget and coordinates, on behalf of the president, the work of all agencies of the executive branch with a view to ensuring that what they are doing is consistent with the president's program. OMB is a powerful management tool, but as an instrument of intelligence oversight, presidents have been disinclined to use it.

Even in connection with the budget, where ordinarily OMB has the last word next to the president himself, the office seems not to have been very influential. One former director says it controls big items but not small ones. A former CIA case officer says he kept three budgets, which he described as "audience oriented."

OMB could perform a signal public service, as could the congressional intelligence and appropriations committees, by insisting that the intelligence community spend only appropriated funds. This would mean that the receipts of proprietaries would go into the Treasury (which is supposed to happen anyway). There would be no more passing the hat among friendly foreign governments. And Congress would have to repeal the ill-advised statute authorizing the DCI to accept gifts and bequests. Sometimes money is the only control OMB and Congress have, and it is a mistake to give it up.

THE NSC AND IRAN-CONTRA

What made the Iran-Contra affair possible was not inadequate supervision of the intelligence community. It was inadequate supervision of the NSC staff. If proof were needed that the NSC is whatever the president wants it to be, such proof is provided by Iran-Contra. (For a detailed discussion of the Iran-Contra scandal, see Chapter 7.)

The National Security Act of 1947 envisioned that the National Security Council would be the watchdog of the CIA. The members of the NSC are all ex officio and are named in the act. Throughout the period of Iran-Contra, those members were President Ronald Reagan, Vice President George Bush, Secretary of State George P. Shultz, and Secretary of Defense Caspar Weinberger. This is what each of them ex post facto said his position was:

Reagan did not know about it.
Bush did not know about it.
Shultz was opposed.
Weinberger was opposed.

So how could Iran-Contra happen when half the NSC members were opposed to it, none was in favor of it, and the only one who counted (the president) did not even know about it? It is conceivable, though unlikely, that Reagan did in fact know about it, and that his claimed lack of knowledge was the exercise of plausible deniability. If so, it would be the most plausibly any presidential knowledge ever got denied.

Reagan's memory was notoriously fuzzy, but it was clear and consistent at least with respect to diverting Iranian arms sales proceeds to the Contras. Never was it more clear than in a letter he wrote to his good friend, former senator Paul Laxalt, R-Nev., when the question arose in the 1994 Virginia senatorial campaign of Lt. Col. Oliver North, who had been a prime mover in Iran-Contra from his position on the NSC staff. Said Reagan:

> . . . I am getting pretty steamed about the statements coming from Oliver North. I never instructed him or anyone in my administration to mislead Congress on Iran-Contra matters or anything else. And I certainly did not know anything about the Iran-Contra diversion.[21]

The independent counsel appointed to investigate Iran-Contra matters concluded that "President Reagan was apparently unconcerned as to the details of how his policy objectives for contra support were being carried out by subordinates who were operating virtually free from oversight or accountability."[22]

With respect to Bush, the independent counsel concluded: "The criminal investigation of Bush was regrettably incomplete." Then the independent counsel went on to say:

> Bush acknowledged that he was regularly informed of events connected with the Iran arms sales, including the 1985 Israeli missile shipments. These statements conflicted with his more extreme public assertions that he was "out of the loop" regarding the operational details of the Iran initiative and was generally unaware of the strong opposition to the arms sales by Secretary of Defense Weinberger and Secretary of State George P. Shultz. He denied knowledge of the diversion of proceeds from the arms sales to assist the contras. He also denied knowledge of the secret contra-resupply operation supervised by North.[23]

It seems clear that Iran-Contra was the brainchild of the NSC staff, which not only conceived the operation but carried it out. DCI William Casey was involved, but we do not know how much because Casey was hospitalized for a brain tumor shortly after the affair became public and died without ever being questioned about it.

The NSC staff is the instrument of the NSC through which the council carries out its duties, including supervision of the intelligence community. But the staff is no longer a staff. It has become an entity in itself, almost a separate department of the government. This change dates from the arrival of Henry Kissinger to head the staff at the beginning of the Nixon administration. The position of national security adviser gives the president someone to ride herd, on his behalf, on the foreign affairs agencies—someone he trusts, someone who is loyal to him, someone who is not answerable to anybody else and does not have to be confirmed by the Senate. The president needs an assistant like this.

But in the Reagan administration, matters were reversed. The staff began running the president. President Reagan governed with very loose reins. He had an activist staff at the NSC and a policy-oriented DCI. His relationship with the NSC is epitomized in the following exchange between John Poindexter, the national security adviser, and John W. Nields, Jr., chief counsel to the House Iran-Contra Committee:

> Mr. Nields. I think you have already testified to this, that over the five-and-a-half years that you worked for this president, that you came to know him and what he wanted and what his policies were?
>
> Mr. Poindexter. Yes. That is correct.
>
> Mr. Nields. And when the issue of what has been referred to as the diversion [of arms sales proceeds to aid the Contras] was brought to you, I think you testified that based on your five-and-a-half years, you knew how he would want that decision to be made?
>
> Mr. Poindexter. Yes. That is correct.
>
> Mr. Nields. And you felt, therefore, that you could make the decision yourself without bringing it to him?
>
> Mr. Poindexter. And, more importantly, I think—well, as importantly, I thought I had the authority to do that. . . .
>
> Mr. Nields. But, admiral, didn't the diversion proposal raise really two issues: One of them was what did the president favor? . . . But didn't it raise a second issue? . . . That is the question of whether he would want to be told or whether he would want to be shielded from responsibility for a politically embarrassing decision? Didn't it present that second issue, too?
>
> Mr. Poindexter. I suppose it did.
>
> Mr. Nields. And my question to you is this. Based on your five-and-a-half years of experience with him, what led you to believe that he would want deniability as opposed to responsibility for an embarrassing political decision?
>
> Mr. Poindexter. That was a personal judgment on my part.[24]

So the tail came to wag the dog. In forty years between Harry Truman and Ronald Reagan, the buck's stopping place moved from the desk of the president to that of his national security adviser.

NOTES

1. For a perceptive treatment of this matter, see David D. Newsom, "The Executive Branch in Foreign Policy," in *The President, the Congress and Foreign Policy,* ed. Edmund S. Muskie, Kenneth Rush, and Kenneth W. Thompson (Lanham, Md.: University Press of America, 1986), 93-119.
2. Harry S. Truman, *Memoirs,* vol. 2: *Years of Trial and Hope* (Garden City, N.Y.: Doubleday, 1956), 60.
3. Dean Acheson, *Present at the Creation: My Years in the State Department* (New York: W. W. Norton, 1969), 214.
4. Truman, *Memoirs,* vol. 2, 58.
5. Quoted in David Wise and Thomas B. Ross, *The Invisible Government* (New York: Random House, 1964), 167.
6. John Ranelagh, *The Agency: The Rise and Decline of the CIA* (New York: Simon and Schuster, 1986), 341. See also Stephen E. Ambrose, *Eisenhower the President* (New

York: Simon and Schuster, 1984), esp. 226.

7. Charles E. Bohlen, recorded interview May 21, 1964, John F. Kennedy Library Oral History Program, 33.

8. John A. McCone, interviewed by Joe B. Frantz, Lyndon B. Johnson Library, Austin, Texas, August 19, 1970, 18.

9. Richard Helms, interviewed by Paige Mulhollan, April 4, 1969, Lyndon B. Johnson Library, 8.

10. McCone interview, LBJ Library, 23.

11. Helms interview, LBJ Library, 6.

12. Thomas Powers, *The Man Who Kept the Secrets: Richard Helms and the CIA* (New York: Pocket Books, 1981), 256-257.

13. House Committee on Expenditures in the Executive Departments, *National Security Act of 1947*, Hearings, 80th Cong., 1st sess., 1947, 28-29. Published by House Committee on Government Operations and House Permanent Select Committee on Intelligence, 1982.

14. Senate Select Committee to Study Governmental Operations with Respect to Intelligence Activities (Church committee), *Final Report*, S. Rept. 94-755, 94th Cong., 2d sess., 1976, Book IV, 14.

15. The relevant provisions of the National Security Act are found in 50 USC 402 and 403.

16. For much of the historical data in this section, I am indebted to Anne Karalakas, *History of the Central Intelligence Agency*, included in the Church committee's *Final Report*, Book IV. See also Arthur B. Darling, *The Central Intelligence Agency: An Instrument of Government, to 1950* (University Park: Pennsylvania State University Press, 1990).

17. John Prados, *Keepers of the Keys: A History of the National Security Council from Truman to Bush* (New York: William Morrow, 1991), 33.

18. Clark Clifford with Richard Holbrooke, *Counsel to the President: A Memoir* (New York: Random House, 1991), 351.

19. Senate Select Committee on Intelligence, *National Intelligence Reorganization and Reform Act of 1978*, Hearings, 95th Cong., 2d sess., 1978, 30.

20. Martin Anderson, *Revolution* (New York: Harcourt Brace Jovanovich, 1988), 352-369.

21. Quoted in Kent Jenkins, Jr. and Michael D. Shear, "Reagan Issues Letter Denouncing North," *Washington Post*, March 18, 1994.

22. *Final Report of the Independent Counsel for Iran/Contra Matters* (Washington, D.C.: U.S. Court of Appeals for the District of Columbia Circuit, 1993), vol. 1: *Investigations and Prosecutions*, 446.

23. Ibid., 473.

24. Iran-Contra Hearings, Pt. 100-8, 161-162.

CHAPTER 10

Congress

There's a marked lack of curiosity around here.
—Congressional staff member

Congress got into the business of intelligence oversight reluctantly. It was driven to it mainly by a series of spectacular intelligence failures in the 1960s and revelations in the media in the 1970s of intelligence abuses. If the White House had been more diligent and circumspect, the intelligence community might never have had an intrusive Congress to put up with.

In the formative period of congressional oversight (roughly 1975 to 1977), the emphasis in Congress was on preventing mistakes, on keeping things from going wrong. By the late 1980s and early 1990s, Congress was taking a broader view of oversight—making things go better as well as keeping them from going badly.

The intelligence community by and large did not welcome serious congressional oversight. It was not accustomed to outsiders asking sensitive questions. In time its attitude changed. This was partly due to the infusion of younger officers that occurs naturally over fifteen or twenty years. Partly it was due to the realization that Congress can be helpful and even protective.

This chapter traces the evolution of congressional oversight and considers some of the problems of the task. To the extent that is possible when dealing with secrets, it also evaluates how Congress is doing.

EARLY ARRANGEMENTS

In the beginning the intelligence community (except for the counterintelligence functions of the Federal Bureau of Investigation) was under the jurisdiction of the House and Senate Armed Services committees. Those committees had jurisdiction of the National Security Act of 1947, an incidental purpose of which was creation of the Central Intelligence Agency. Most other members of the intelligence community are part of the Department of Defense, which is also under the jurisdiction of the armed services committees. The appropriations committees were (and are) involved because they control the money.

From the creation of the CIA in 1947 until about the middle of the 1950s, there was the barest minimum of congressional oversight. The chairmen and two or three senior members of defense appropriations subcommittees in each house saw to it that the intelligence budget, usually what the director of central intelligence (DCI) wanted, was tucked away out of sight in the much larger defense appropriation bill. The story is told of the time DCI Allen Dulles showed a subcommittee chairman the architect's drawing of the proposed new headquarters building for the CIA in Langley, Virginia, just outside Washington. The chairman commented that the building looked so nice it must cost $25 million.

"Well, no, Mr. Chairman," Dulles said, "I'm afraid it's going to cost $50 million."

"My, my," said the chairman, "that will be a nice building."

End of hearing.

Allen Dulles, his predecessors and immediate successors as DCI, established quiet, confidential relationships with the chairmen and the ranking minority members of the Armed Services Committee and the Defense Appropriations Subcommittee in each house. Contacts, which were infrequent, were initiated by the DCI. According to one CIA official who participated in the process, the budget review was more thorough in the House than in the Senate mainly because of the interest of Rep. George Mahon, D-Texas, chairman of the Appropriations Committee's CIA subcommittee.

Most members of Congress were content with this arrangement; some were probably not even aware of it. But some were uneasy. Among this last group was Mike Mansfield, who was elected to the Senate as a Democrat from Montana in 1952 after serving ten years in the House. Mansfield regularly introduced a resolution to create a joint congressional committee to oversee the CIA along the lines of the Joint Committee on Atomic Energy, which Congress had established to oversee the nation's nuclear program.

The model was a good one. The secrets of the nation's nuclear program in the 1950s were scarcely less sensitive than those of the intelligence community, yet the Joint Committee on Atomic Energy was entitled, by law, to know them all, and it had an exemplary record for not leaking.

The Task Force on Intelligence Activities of the Second Hoover Commission (formally, the Commission on Organization of the Executive Branch of the Government) also recommended a joint congressional committee on intelligence. In its report in 1955, the task force, which was headed by General Mark Clark, presciently warned of "the possibility of the growth of license and abuses of power where disclosures of costs, organization, personnel, and functions are precluded by law." [1]

However, the Joint Atomic Energy Committee's reputation for vigilance as a watchdog was called into question in 1993-1994 by revelations that the old Atomic Energy Commission carried out radioactive medical experiments on unwitting subjects. Apparently, the joint committee itself was also unwitting. There is no reference to the matter in the index to the committee's records, which are now in the National Archives and some of which are still classified. Staff members of the joint committee in the 1950s have no recollection of knowing about the experiments. One suggests the money involved was so little (millions of dollars, or less) that it was overlooked as the committee concentrated on big items (hundreds of millions or billions of dollars). But there was also continuing inattention. As late as 1986, a staff report for the House Energy and Commerce Committee attracted little notice with its disclosures of some of the experiments.[2] There is a moral to be drawn from this by the congressional intelligence committees: it's not how much money is spent; it's what it's spent for.

There are still students of oversight who think a joint committee would be the best device for oversight of intelligence, but by the time Congress got serious about the matter in the 1970s, joint committees were in bad odor on Capitol Hill for unrelated reasons, and most of them were abolished in a congressional reorganization in 1977.

The only time Mansfield was able even to get a vote on his CIA oversight resolution was in 1956. It was rejected, 27-59. The debate was revealing. Sen. Leverett Saltonstall of Massachusetts was the senior Republican on the Armed Services Committee and the second senior Republican on the Appropriations Committee. Opposing the resolution, he said that "at least twice a year" the CIA requested a meeting with the Armed Services Committee and "at least once a year" with the Appropriations Committee. Further, he said, both General Smith and Mr. Dulles, the DCIs in the 1950s,

> stated that they were ready at all times to answer any questions we might wish to ask them. The difficulty in connection with asking questions and obtaining information is that we might obtain information which I personally would rather not have, unless it was essential for me as a Member of Congress to have it. . . .
>
> [I]t is not a question of reluctance on the part of the CIA officials to speak to us. Instead, it is a question of our reluctance, if you will, to seek information and knowledge on subjects which I personally, as a Member of Congress and as a citizen, would rather not have, unless I believed it to be my responsibility to have it because it might involve the lives of American citizens.[3]

In the spring of 1993, thirty-seven years after Saltonstall's statement, a congressional staff member commented on what he called "the marked lack of curiosity" on Capitol Hill.

BROADENING CONGRESSIONAL CONCERN

One result of the 1956 debate on Mansfield's resolution was to prod the Armed Services and Appropriations committees in the Senate to establish subcommittees on the CIA. This was a modest step. The subcommittees were no more active than the chairmen and senior members had been before, but at least they provided a structure.

THE U-2 AND PLAUSIBLE DENIABILITY

In 1960 the Soviets shot down a U.S. reconnaissance aircraft flying over the Soviet Union. The U-2 affair (described in detail in Chapter 4) brought into sharp relief for the first time the contradiction inherent in plausible deniability. Any denial of presidential responsibility for an intelligence operation gone wrong is also necessarily an admission that the president is either (a) duplicitous or (b) not in control of his own government. Either position is politically ruinous in the United States. President Dwight D. Eisenhower dealt with this dilemma by abandoning deniability, which was becoming steadily less plausible in any case. He admitted that he had known of the U-2 flights and had approved of them. Most of his successors have followed this example most of the time.

But the point at which intelligence and diplomacy come together is extremely complicated. The matter is not as simple as it has just been described. The argument can be made that the U-2 affair was almost as embarrassing to Soviet premier Nikita Khrushchev as to President Eisenhower. Khrushchev had known for some time that his country was being overflown by an American spy plane. Eisenhower knew that Khrushchev knew, and Khrushchev knew that Eisenhower knew that he (Khrushchev) knew. They both engaged in a tacit conspiracy of silence. For Khrushchev to have complained about the overflights would have been an admission that he was powerless to stop them. For Eisenhower to have bragged about them would have been needlessly humiliating to Khrushchev.

Suppose Eisenhower had maintained a facade of sweet innocence. Khrushchev would have known he was being disingenuous, and Eisenhower would have known that Khrushchev knew. But Khrushchev might very well have accepted it and gone to the summit, which he badly wanted. This might be good diplomacy (Machiavelli would almost certainly have approved), but in the United States it is not good politics. And it would have been out of character for Eisenhower.

There was a great ruckus in Congress over executive branch contortions with respect to the U-2, but the concept of plausible deniability is not unknown on Capitol Hill. In essence, it is the scapegoat defense described in fancier words. That is why a good many leaks out of Capitol Hill come from the staff, acting under instructions. Then when members are questioned by ethics committees, they can truthfully say they did not leak. One suspects a good many leaks come out of the White House and State and Defense departments under similar circumstances.

The U-2 incident also marked the first breach in the wall that had been erected around the Armed Services and Appropriations committees with respect to intelligence. The community found this arrangement congenial. The standard response of DCIs to other committees was that they would report to Congress under any arrangement that Congress determined, and Congress had determined that it would be to the Armed Services committees. DCIs did come to the Senate Foreign Relations Committee from time to time but only, as a rule, for general surveys.

Now, in the aftermath of the U-2, the Foreign Relations Committee held full-blown intelligence hearings for the first time. The committee's interest was basically political—the relationship between the intelligence gathering mission of the U-2 and the broader foreign policy objectives of the United States. The focus of such oversight of intelligence activities as the Senate Armed Services Committee exercised in those years is unknown. Sen. Richard B. Russell, D-Ga., the principal overseer as chairman of the Armed Services Committee, gave his extensive papers to the University of Georgia; not one paper deals with intelligence. It is probably a good guess that the CIA had not previously faced questions from Congress such as those raised in the U-2 hearings. The administration refused to answer some questions at all (such as what the plane was looking for) and dodged others, but another step had been taken in a long journey.

MORE MOVEMENT IN THE SENATE

Other steps followed at a quickening pace. Less than a year after the U-2 in 1960, the Kennedy administration suffered the disaster of the Bay of Pigs in 1961. (See Chapter 7.) Again the consequences of an intelligence failure were mainly political, not military, and again it was the Foreign Relations Committee, not the Armed Services Committee, that held hearings. One of the conclusions that the Foreign Relations Committee had drawn from the U-2 hearings was that the political implications of the mission had been insufficiently considered. This was even more obvious in the case of the Bay of Pigs. Omission of the political factor suggested the need for closer congressional oversight.

The point was underlined by the fact that the only advice President John F. Kennedy got against the Bay of Pigs operation came from the Senate. This was purely fortuitous and not the result of any established institutional executive-legislative arrangement. It resulted, rather, from the personal relationship between Kennedy and Sen. J. W. Fulbright, D-Ark., then chairman of the Foreign Relations Committee.

That Fulbright was even aware of the plan was itself fortuitous: an official of the executive branch, who was opposed to the idea, had revealed it in broad outline to a member of the committee staff. The leaker's motive was no doubt to enlist the support of a powerful Senate committee or at least its chairman. The chairman's support was forthcoming, but it did not change the policy outcome. This is a classic example of the use of a leak in an effort to influence policy.

Two points are worth particular note. Although Fulbright did not reveal the full extent of his knowledge to Kennedy (he spoke in hypothetical terms), Kennedy showed no sign of surprise or concern that Fulbright knew. Second, after Fulbright had had a full conversation with the president, he let the matter drop. The temptation today, more than thirty years later, would be to make a speech in the Senate and thereby effectively kill the plan.

The Cuban missile crisis in 1962 (see chapters 5 and 8) was probably the closest the United States and the Soviet Union ever came to war. It arose with the introduction of Soviet missiles into Cuba, and it ended with their withdrawal, a success for U.S. diplomacy and intelligence and for the Kennedy administration's crisis management. When it was over, Secretary of State Dean Rusk urged the Senate Foreign Relations Committee to investigate it and promised total access to administration files. The committee, which only eighteen months before had rehashed what went wrong at the Bay of Pigs, was uninterested in exploring what went right during the more serious missile crisis. This is a good demonstration of what is almost a rule of congressional behavior: Congress, like the media, would rather dissect the corpse of a failure than examine the anatomy of a success.

There continued to be bad things for Congress and the media to concern themselves with. In 1963 President Ngo Dinh Diem of South Vietnam was assassinated during a military coup d'état in which the U.S. role was not (and is not) clear. In 1964 U.S. and North Vietnamese ships exchanged fire in the Gulf of Tonkin. Under a misapprehension of what happened (see Chapter 4), Congress gave President Lyndon Johnson broad war powers.

In 1965 President Johnson sent military forces to the Dominican Republic to restore order in the aftermath of an attempted coup d'état that, it was feared, might lead to a communist takeover. An investigation by the Senate Foreign Relations Committee revealed that the administration's public statements had exaggerated the available intelligence about the extent of the disorder and the communist influence. This was a case not so much of the failure of intelligence as of the misuse of intelligence by policy makers, but that, too, is a matter for oversight. In 1967 there were revelations in the media of CIA subsidies of the National Student Association, the Institute of Political Education in Costa Rica, and other organizations (see Chapter 7).

All of these things increased the uneasiness in the Senate about the intelligence community generally. It is important to note that the senators who were uneasy to begin with became more uneasy, but the number of uneasy senators did not significantly increase. In 1966 a resolution to create a Senate Committee on Intelligence Operations got twenty-eight votes; Mansfield's proposal for a joint committee ten years before had gotten twenty-seven. The 1966 resolution originated with Sen. Eugene J. McCarthy, D-Minn., and provided for participation of members of the Foreign Relations Committee, one of whom might be McCarthy himself. This prospect alarmed the DCI, Adm. W. F. Raborn, as well as Senator Russell. Both Raborn and Russell argued to the White House that Foreign Relations sought information on the CIA's sources and methods, the most sensitive parts of the agency's operations.[4] White House opposition played a role in the resolution's defeat.

The following January (1967), Russell gave a little. He invited three members of the Foreign Relations Committee to meet with the Appropriations-Armed Services group, but he insisted on excluding McCarthy. The arrangement did not last long in any event. The members of Foreign Relations found it generally unsatisfactory. They participated by sufferance and not by right; the group met infrequently and was inadequately staffed.

This incident illustrates an aspect of the Senate approach to intelligence that the Senate prefers to keep under the surface. It was aptly described in 1971 by Francis O. Wilcox, a former chief of staff of the Senate Foreign Relations Committee:

> What is basically involved is something it pains the Senate to talk about—personality differences and bureaucratic jealousies. To be blunt about it, and perhaps to overstate it, neither the CIA nor the people who now watch over it fully trust the people who want to watch over it; and the people who want to watch over it do not fully trust either the agency or its present watchers.[5]

This distrust existed not only between different groups within Congress; it existed between Congress and the executive branch. It grew with the divisions engendered by the Vietnam war. By the late 1960s it permeated executive-legislative relations, and it contributed to the monolithic opposition of the executive branch to letting Congress have anything more to do with the intelligence community.

In 1972 in opposing a bill for CIA reports to Congress, the Nixon administration revealed the lengths to which the executive branch was then willing to go to shut Congress out. The bill, the department said, would be "incompatible" with the role of the secretary of state as the president's "principal foreign policy adviser." It would "raise a constitutional question as to separation of powers." And it would "derogate the DCI's capability to protect intelligence sources and methods." [6]

What the CIA says to Congress has nothing to do with the relationship of the secretary of state to the president. The argument was doubly peculiar in this case since the president had already allowed the national security affairs adviser to usurp the role of the secretary of state. A report from the CIA to Congress has no more to do with the separation of powers than does a report from, say, the Agriculture Department. Nor would such a report endanger intelligence sources and methods.

Senator Russell died in January 1971 and was succeeded as chairman of both the Armed Services Committee and the intelligence subcommittee by Sen. John C. Stennis, D-Miss. Under Stennis, intelligence oversight became somewhat more active. Members of the staff who were allowed to know about the subcommittee's work increased from one to two, and the staff even visited some large CIA stations abroad.

CHILE

The movement toward real congressional oversight took a giant leap toward achieving critical mass in Chile in 1973. Chile had enjoyed political stability for many years; it was frequently cited as a paragon of Latin American democracy. In 1964 Eduardo Frei, the leader of the Christian Democratic Party, was elected president with considerable covert help from the CIA. Frei defeated the Socialist Party candidate, Salvador Allende. Under the Chilean constitution, Frei could not succeed himself when his six-year term ended in 1970, and the field that year was fragmented. Allende was again a strong contender for the Socialists. Aging ex-president Jorge Alessandri ran as the leader of a group of businessmen and conservatives. The Christian Democratic candidate was Radomiro Tomic. Compared with what it had done in the past in Chile (in particular, the $3 million the CIA spent to influence the 1964 election), the United States kept its hands off: the CIA had $425,000 for covert anti-Allende propaganda. [7]

Allende finished first in the election in September 1970 but with only 36 percent of the vote. The constitution provided that if no candidate got as much as 50 percent, the matter was to be decided by Congress. Congress had a long tradition of electing the front-runner. It did so in 1970, and Allende assumed office.

Eighteen months later columnist Jack Anderson published internal documents of the International Telephone and Telegraph Company, which had major interests in Chile, indicating that the company had tried to instigate a CIA covert action in 1970 to block Allende's election by Congress. ITT had even gone so far as to offer $1 million to pay for it. Richard Helms, DCI at the time, had turned down the offer, citing a longstanding agency policy against accepting such outside support. (In 1980 Congress passed legislation specifically authorizing the CIA to accept gifts, bequests, and property.)

Anderson's revelations sufficiently piqued the interest of the Senate Foreign Relations Committee that it created a special subcommittee to investigate multinational corporations generally. The committee's interest at that time was directed more toward international business than toward the intelligence community, but its first order of business was inquiry into the activities of ITT in Chile.

Meanwhile, Allende embarked on a program of radical economic reform in Chile going beyond what Frei had instituted, and the Nixon administration embarked on an economic cold war in which the United States cut off public credits, used its influence in international financial institutions to cut off other credits, and strongly discouraged private credits. The Chilean economy went from bad to worse. Political opposition to Allende—some homegrown, some covertly stimulated by the CIA—got noisier. In September 1973 Allende died in a military coup d'état, and Chile entered a period of military government that was notorious for its abuse of human rights.

William Colby, who became the DCI in 1973, gave the Foreign Relations Committee more (but still incomplete) information about the CIA's activities in Chile. These activities were mainly aimed, according to Colby, at supporting opposition political parties, newspapers, and other groups. The object was to preserve a viable opposition in the hope that a moderate candidate could be elected to succeed Allende in 1976.

The following spring (1974) Colby testified on the same subject and in somewhat greater detail before the House Armed Services CIA subcommittee. Rep. Michael Harrington, D-Mass., an outspoken liberal who was not a member of the Armed Services Committee, read the transcript of Colby's testimony under a law that gives any member of the House or Senate access to the records of any committee of the house in which he serves. Harrington was sufficiently upset about CIA involvement in Chile to fire off letters to Senator Fulbright and to Rep. Thomas Morgan, chairman of the House Foreign Affairs Committee, demanding an investigation. Given the history of congressional-CIA relationships, this request was impractical, and neither chairman acted on it. But Harrington's letter, which contained the substance of Colby's secret testimony, leaked to the press. This set off an uproar of mutual suspicions and recriminations. Those who had been privy to the letter wrangled over who leaked it, and those members of Congress who had not been informed complained that they should have been.

The Chile story reveals other complexities of intelligence. In September 1970, in the interim between the Chilean popular election and the election in Congress, there was great concern in Washington about the prospect of Allende becoming president. Most officials in the State Department and the CIA, both in the American embassy in Santiago and in Washington, held the view that, deplorable though this might be, there was little the United States could do to prevent his election. This was not good enough for President Nixon. Privately and orally, he gave DCI Helms direct, explicit orders to do what was necessary to undermine Allende and to do it so secretly that neither the State Department nor the embassy in Chile would know.

This came to be called Track II. As it worked out, the thrust of it was to inspire a coup by the Chilean military to prevent Allende from taking office. It was obviously not successful in September-October 1970. How much the United States had to do with the coup that did overthrow Allende in September 1973 remains fuzzy twenty years later.

After Nixon was reelected in November 1972, he nominated Helms to be ambassador to Iran, and so Helms appeared before the Senate Foreign Relations Committee to be confirmed. Much of the hearing was devoted not to Iran, but to the CIA and to its role in Chile. The following exchange between Sen. Stuart Symington, D-Mo., and Helms took place:

> Senator Symington. Did you try in the Central Intelligence Agency to overthrow the government of Chile?
>
> Mr. Helms. No, sir.
>
> Senator Symington. Did you have any money passed to the opposition of Allende?
>
> Mr. Helms. No, sir.[8]

After Helms's confirmation he was recalled to testify further regarding Watergate and associated scandals. At that later hearing, in May 1973, Sen. Hubert Humphrey, D-Minn., questioned him:

> Senator Humphrey. I have been thinking a great deal about these investigative agencies and how to cut them off from the politics and the political manipulation. . . . I have never been able to find a substitute for character—no mechanism, no machinery, no law. Have you any idea how we can prevent people who think they are extensions of the spirit, the soul, the body, and the heart of the President to quit acting like they are President?
>
> Mr. Helms. Well, Senator Humphrey, obviously I have thought about these things, too. . . . I have to say to you, sir, I don't know how you legislate character and honor and decency.[9]

Helms's testimony was investigated by a grand jury as possible perjury, but there was no indictment. In 1977 the Justice Department brought a criminal information (a device used in lieu of an indictment in the case of lesser offenses) against Helms. It charged that Helms "did refuse and fail to answer material questions." Helms pleaded *nolo contendere* (meaning he did not contest it) and was fined $2,000 and given a two-year suspended prison sentence. At the time of sentencing, U.S. District Judge Barrington D. Parker said to Helms, "You dishonored your oath and you now stand before this court in disgrace and shame." Parker added,

> If public officials embark deliberately on a course to disobey and ignore the laws of our land because of some misguided and ill-considered notion and belief that there are earlier commitments and considerations which they must first observe, the future of this country is in jeopardy.

Afterward Helms's lawyer, Edward Bennett Williams, told the press, "He's going to wear this conviction like a badge of honor." Helms added, "I don't feel disgraced at all. I think if I had done anything else, I would have been disgraced."[10]

THE HUGHES-RYAN AMENDMENT

President Nixon resigned in August 1974, finally undone by the cumulative scandals of Watergate, which by this time included dark tales of a Nixon "enemies list" and of spying on American citizens. Representative Harrington's revelations about Chile, fleshed out by Seymour Hersh of the *New York Times*, hit the press in September.

These two developments moved Sen. Harold E. Hughes, D-Iowa, and Rep. Leo J. Ryan, D-Calif., to use the foreign aid authorization bill as a vehicle for a requirement that covert actions be reported to Congress.

Written in simpler days, Hughes-Ryan referred to CIA operations "other than activities intended solely for obtaining necessary intelligence," and everybody knew it meant covert action. These operations could not be undertaken "unless and until the President found that each such operation was important to the national security of the United States." Each covert operation was to be reported to "the appropriate committees of the Congress." The law named Senate Foreign Relations and House Foreign Affairs; the other committees, by general agreement, were Armed Services and Appropriations in each house. Hughes-Ryan required the reports to be made "in a timely fashion" and to include "a description and scope" of the activity.[11]

The Hughes-Ryan amendment became law at the end of 1974. During the two years remaining of the Ford administration, including the period when George Bush was DCI (1976), reports were made "in a timely fashion" but the "description and scope" which they presented of the activities left much to be desired. The reports were couched in extremely general terms and were delivered orally by the DCI. Senators asked few, if any, questions.

There were two significant aspects of the Hughes-Ryan amendment. It marked the first time that Congress specifically required the intelligence community to report anything. And by requiring a presidential finding with respect to each covert action, it further undermined, if it did not destroy, the doctrine of plausible deniability. The reports Congress received under the amendment led to a legal prohibition in 1975 against covert action in Angola, the first time Congress had done such a thing.

After the House and Senate intelligence committees were established, they were added to the list of those receiving the covert action reports. Critics of the Hughes-Ryan amendment were fond of counting the members of the eight committees and crying with alarm that this expanded the number of people knowledgeable about a given action by about 140. That was the possibility. The reality was far different. After passing a law that said they had to be told, members of Congress became skittish about learning. The Senate Foreign Relations Committee, which only a few years before had made such a fuss about being informed, now delegated the chairman and the ranking minority member to receive the reports. The chief of staff was authorized to be present and to brief other members on request. Few requested.

More Reporting Requirements

Congress was led to reopen the issue of reporting covert actions by the shortcomings of the Reagan administration's reporting on the Iran-Contra affair in 1985-1986, but a major executive-legislative confrontation did not develop until George Bush was president (1989-1993). There were two issues. One was "timely fashion." The other was what should be included in the presidential finding that was sent to Congress.

From its first use in the Hughes-Ryan amendment, "timely fashion" had been universally interpreted to mean either in advance or very soon after the beginning of a covert action. In one finding connected to the Iran-Contra affair, President Reagan specifically directed that it *not* be reported to Congress. Whatever "timely fashion" meant, it certainly meant sometime; but here was a case in which the president at least left open the possibility that it meant never. The Office of Legal Counsel of the Justice Department justified this legerdemain by holding that the president had "virtually unfettered discretion" to decide what "timely fashion" meant.[12] One would think that the discretion would have to be totally, not just virtually, unfettered in order to bridge the gap between sometime and never.

This provoked a controversy where none had existed before: Congress now tried to require that all reports be made in advance. This is indeed the only way to ensure that Congress can have some input in the final decision instead of being informed of a fait accompli, but President Bush resisted it mightily, arguing that some circumstances might be so urgent that time would not permit advance notification. What such circumstances might be was never specified, or even hypothesized, and the debate was carried out on a theoretical level.

Iran-Contra also provoked controversy over what should be included in the report to Congress. When Congress cut off funding for the Contras, one of the responses of the Reagan White House was to seek contributions from third parties—in some cases individuals in the United States; in others, selected foreign governments. Among these were Brunei, Saudi Arabia, Taiwan, and South Korea. The congressional reaction was not to try to stop such activity but only to be informed of it. Again President Bush strongly resisted reporting, and in this case his argument was less theoretical, whatever its merits. A reporting requirement, he argued, might "deter foreign governments from discussing certain topics with the United States at all."[13] What he was trying to avoid was disclosure of third country cooperation in carrying out particular covert actions. Great Britain's MI6 and the CIA had collaborated in removing Mohammed Mossadegh from power in Iran. Sundry foreign organizations and institutions, not a part of an intelligence agency, had collaborated with the CIA on various occasions in acting as cut-outs for channeling money or other assistance to foreign agents involved in covert actions. It was an open question whether a report to Congress would have a chilling effect on this kind of cooperation, but the point could reasonably be argued.

President Bush vetoed Congress's first effort to deal with these problems after Congress had adjourned in 1990. The veto was primarily on the grounds of advance notification and reporting of third party involvement. When Congress returned in January 1991, there began a long and contentious negotiation between the Senate Intelligence Committee and the White House. In the end the White House retreated on almost every point and the Intelligence Authorization Act, Fiscal Year 1991, finally became law (P.L. 102-88) on August 14, 1991. With respect to covert action, there was only one significant difference between the bill that Bush vetoed in 1990 and the bill that he signed in 1991. The 1990 bill provided that a request to a foreign government or a private citizen to conduct a covert action on behalf of the United States would itself constitute a covert action. This was dropped from the bill in 1991, but the requirement to report third party participation remained. The difference was that under the 1990 bill a request to a third party would have to be reported even if the third party said no. Under the 1991 bill the report would have to be made only if the third party complied at least partially with the request.

DISCLOSURES OF DOMESTIC ABUSES

Procedures for implementing the Hughes-Ryan amendment were not even in place when, in December 1974, the *New York Times* published a long story detailing extensive domestic activities of the CIA.[14] Most of these were of the kind prohibited by the National Security Act, and some of them were illegal under other statutes. The White House under Presidents Johnson and Nixon had been obsessed with the notion that opposition to the Vietnam war was inspired from abroad, probably from Moscow, and had ordered massive efforts to find evidence to support this theory. In the course of these efforts, intelligence files were maintained on at least 10,000 Americans. The story also reported other abuses, some dating back to the 1950s and unrelated to Vietnam. They included surreptitious mail openings, break-ins, and wiretapping.

All this and more came from a list that was known in the CIA as the "family jewels." It had been compiled at the behest of DCI James Schlesinger, whose brief and stormy tenure lasted from February to June 1973. Schlesinger was outraged to discover that some of the Watergate burglars, using CIA equipment, had broken into the office of the psychiatrist who had been treating Daniel Ellsberg, charged with disclosing the Pentagon Papers. (See Chapter 8.) The object of the break-in was to find material from which the CIA could prepare a psychiatric profile of Ellsberg for the White House. (This piece of prosecutorial misconduct led the judge in the case to declare a mistrial and clear Ellsberg.)

Schlesinger demanded to know what else the agency was keeping from him and directed that every employee should report every instance of activity that might be outside the agency's legislative charter. Every former employee was invited to do the same. These reports produced a list of 693 pages.

The *New York Times* story stirred the Senate Appropriations and Armed Services subcommittees on the CIA to hold a hearing and even to release publicly the statement made by William E. Colby, by then the DCI succeeding Schlesinger. Colby admitted some improprieties but argued that they were "few and far between" and had been corrected.[15]

Another consequence of the *Times* story was that President Ford appointed his own commission, headed by Vice President Nelson Rockefeller, to investigate the matter. The Rockefeller report in May 1975 was much like Colby's: there had been wrongdoing in the past, but it wasn't happening in the present.

CONGRESS INVESTIGATES

A third consequence of the *Times* story was the creation of the Senate Select Committee to Study Governmental Operations with Respect to Intelligence Activities, which came to be known as the Church committee after its chairman, Frank Church, D-Idaho. A parallel committee in the House was first headed by Rep. Lucien N. Nedzi, D-Mich., and later by Rep. Otis G. Pike, D-N.Y.

The Church committee finished its work in April 1976, only fifteen months after it started. By Senate standards this was a remarkably short time. The committee revealed the Track II program in Chile. It fleshed out many of the family jewels only alluded to by the *Times*. Among its many recommendations, two deserve special mention: that the Senate should have a permanent intelligence oversight committee, and that there should be a legislative charter for all intelligence agencies spelling out what they could and could not do.

The permanent oversight committee was created promptly. Serious efforts were made, especially in 1978, to write a legislative charter, but this proved more difficult than was anticipated. By 1994 it still had not been done, and the effort had been all but abandoned.

The counterpart investigating committee in the House traversed a rockier road. The first chairman was Representative Nedzi, who was also chairman of the CIA subcommittee of Armed Services. Its members included Harrington, who had started the whole affair with his fuss over Chile, and Ronald Dellums, D-Calif., another critic of the CIA. (Dellums rose to the chairmanship of Armed Services in January 1993 when previous chairman Les Aspin became secretary of defense.) The Nedzi committee took three months to hire a staff director, and its internal quarrels led to an extraordinary series of House actions.

In June Nedzi resigned as chairman, but the House voted 64-290 not to accept the resignation. In July the House abolished the committee and immediately created another one with the same name and terms of reference but without Nedzi and Harrington. The new chairman was Representative Pike, but the committee was scarcely more tranquil.

Under Pike the committee was by no means united, but its noisiest quarrels were with the executive branch over its access to classified information and over who had the authority to declassify. To put the matter bluntly, the administration did not trust the committee not to leak. The administration was particularly nervous over the law that gives any member access to any records of a committee. Representative Harrington was no longer a member of the committee, but as a member of the House he could assert his rights to see its records. He had already been reprimanded by the Armed Services Committee for leaks that he acknowledged, but he was unrepentant. Armed Services even voted to deny him access, notwithstanding the law, pending a ruling by the House ethics committee (officially the Committee on Standards of Official Conduct). The latter committee ruled that the Armed Services transcript that Harrington had leaked had not been taken at a legal meeting: there had been no notice, no vote to go into executive session, and no quorum. None of these factors had anything to do with the sensitivity of the information in the transcript or with the appropriateness of disclosing it, but they provided the excuse that the ethics committee was looking for to avoid the issue.

The hullabaloo over Harrington provided a sometimes spectacular side-show, but a more important issue between the Pike committee and the Ford administration was declassification. (See Chapter 6 for a discussion of the rules for classification and declassification.) Most of the time Congress growls and accepts executive branch edicts about what is classified. The Pike committee did not, and in September 1975 it released some documents including material that the administration wanted withheld. President Ford demanded that the committee return the classified documents and warned that it would get no more until it "satisfactorily alters its position."

The committee refused to give up the documents it had and demanded more, firing off subpoenas to Colby and to Secretary of State Henry Kissinger. At one point it voted to cite Kissinger for contempt of Congress for refusing to supply documents relating to covert action. This impasse was resolved when the committee backed down enough to accept an oral briefing in the White House for a small delegation.

The declassification issue had not been laid to rest. The Ford administration wanted certain material deleted from the committee's final report. On January 23, 1976, the committee voted 9-3 to release the report with the material included. On January 29 the House voted 246-124 to prohibit the committee from doing this until the president certified that the report contained no information "which would adversely affect ... intelligence activities."[16] This was followed February 11 by publication in the *Village Voice* in New York of a twenty-four-page supplement containing lengthy excerpts from the report. CBS correspondent Daniel Schorr confirmed that he had given a copy of the report to the *Voice*.

The larger question, of course, was where Schorr had obtained a copy. This brought the ethics committee into the intelligence case for the second time. In an acrimonious investigation the committee predictably failed to determine Schorr's source.

Meanwhile, the Pike committee published its recommendations.[17] The House, the committee said, should have a permanent intelligence committee. There should be closer fiscal controls: the overall budget figure should be public, transfers and reprogramming of intelligence funds should be subject to approval by congressional committees, and the General Accounting Office should have the same authority to investigate and audit intelligence as other agencies. There should be a foreign operations subcommittee in the National Security Council to deal with covert action and hazardous collection. A reorganization of the intelligence community should separate the DCI from CIA and the National Security Agency from the Defense Department, and the Defense Intelligence Agency should be abolished. American citizens associated with religious, educational, or communications organizations should be put off limits to the intelligence community for recruitment.

The furor attendant on the Pike committee left enough bad feeling in the House to delay creation of a permanent intelligence committee for more than a year. This was finally done in July 1977 by a vote of 247-171. Almost thirty years to the day after passage of the National Security Act Congress had in place the mechanism for serious oversight of the intelligence community.[18]

THE INTELLIGENCE COMMITTEES

Four aspects of the intelligence committees make them different from the run-of-the-mill committees of Congress. First, they are "select," not "standing," committees. This means that their members are appointed in the Senate by the majority and minority leaders and in the House by the Speaker and the minority leader. The members of standing committees are chosen by party organizations in each house; seniority is an important factor. The leadership has total control of the appointments to select committees; it can only influence appointments to standing committees. Thus, the leadership has a greater opportunity to shape the character of select committees by determining who is a member and—just as important—who is not.

Second, members of the intelligence committees serve limited terms: eight years in the Senate, six years in the House. Members on a standing committee serve for as long as they want to stay, unless their party suffers such grievous electoral losses that the party ratio on the committee changes and unfortunate junior members are bumped.

Third, the majority and minority leaders in each house are ex officio members of the intelligence committees. This is another way to increase leadership influence on the committees. The ex officio members have no vote on the intelligence committees and do not count in determining a quorum.

Finally, some of the members of the intelligence committees are selected from other committees with particular interests in the intelligence community. On the House Intelligence Committee, there is at least one member from each of the Appropriations, Armed Services, Foreign Affairs, and Judiciary committees. In the Senate there are two members (one from each party) from the same committees. The Judiciary committees are included because of their jurisdiction over the Justice Department, which includes the FBI and its counter-intelligence functions.

There are two important differences between the House and Senate Intelligence committees. The House committee has nineteen members (not counting those ex officio) and no provision is made about allocation of members between parties. That is left up to the Speaker; most of the time the division on the committee reflects the division in the House. The Senate committee has fifteen members (not counting those ex officio), and the rule specifies that, regardless of the party division in the Senate, eight shall be from the majority party and seven from the minority. The chairman of the Senate committee is elected by the majority members of the committee, and the vice chairman is elected by the minority members. In the House committee there is no vice chairman, and the chairman is appointed by the Speaker.

There is also an important difference in committee jurisdiction. The Senate committee has jurisdiction only over the National Foreign Intelligence Program (NFIP). In the Senate the Armed Services Committee retains jurisdiction over Tactical Intelligence and Related Activities (TIARA). In the House the Intelligence Committee has jurisdiction over both NFIP and TIARA. It shares TIARA jurisdiction with the Armed Services Committee. This difference complicates congressional procedures, but it has not seemed to make any substantive difference in the legislative outcome.

Power of Intelligence Committees

In the beginning the power of the intelligence committees came from only two sources. One was reports that the law required the executive branch to make to Congress. Covert action reports under the Hughes-Ryan amendment and its successors have been discussed previously. Mention should also be made of the Case Act (1 U.S.C. 112b). This act, which was passed in 1972, requires that Congress receive the text of all international agreements other than treaties. The sponsors of the Case Act did not have intelligence in mind, but the law affects intelligence oversight because it covers arrangements between U.S. and foreign intelligence agencies.

The other source of the intelligence committees' power was (and is) their legislative jurisdiction over bills authorizing appropriations for intelligence activity. Congress deals with money in two stages. In the first, or authorizing, stage, the committee with primary jurisdiction considers legislation authorizing the appropriation of money for specified agencies for specified purposes. An authorization is usually stated as a ceiling, for example, "there is hereby authorized to be appropriated not to exceed x." The second stage is the actual appropriation bill, which comes from the Appropriations Committee in the House or Senate. The amount may be less but cannot be more than the authorization. It is against the rules of both the House and Senate to appropriate money that has not been authorized, but it is not unusual for this rule to be waived. However, the rule is more stringent in the case of intelligence. Even though funds may be appropriated without having been authorized, they still cannot be spent by the intelligence agencies.

If this provision had been enforced (or enforceable?) after President Bush's veto of the authorization act for fiscal year 1991, it would have left the intelligence community literally without funds. The veto came in the fall of 1990 after Congress had adjourned and after the start of the 1991 fiscal year on October 1. Congress had no opportunity either to try to override the veto or to enact another authorization. However, the intelligence committees agreed informally that they would not insist on the letter of the law, and the White House agreed informally that limits and guidelines on authorizations in the vetoed bill would be followed as though they were the law.[19] This arrangement lasted until a new authorization bill was enacted in August 1991 with less than two months of the fiscal year remaining.

The resolution creating the Senate Intelligence Committee expressed "the sense of the Senate" that department and agency heads should keep the committee "fully and currently informed with respect to intelligence activities," [20] but this has no binding effect. There was no comparable provision with respect to the House committee.

Thus, except for Hughes-Ryan and the Case Act, both of which were subject to some interpretation, the intelligence committees in their early years had no firm legal basis for asserting a right to information held by the executive branch. The committees' control of the intelligence budget gave them a powerful lever. If they insisted strongly enough, they could usually get what they wanted, but a good deal of it had to be negotiated, sometimes painfully, on a case-by-case basis.

In the Intelligence Oversight Act of 1980 (50 U.S.C. 413), Congress gave itself considerably more power. The most significant feature of the law was a requirement that the intelligence committees be kept "fully and currently informed of all intelligence activities . . . including any significant anticipated intelligence activity." A "significant intelligence activity," as the phrase is used here, generally means covert action. In extraordinary circumstances prior notice could be limited to the chairmen and ranking minority members of the two committees, the Speaker and minority leader of the House, and the majority and minority leaders of the Senate, a group that came to be known as the Gang of Eight. Further, the president is to "fully inform the intelligence committees in a timely fashion" of covert actions of which prior notice was not given and is to explain why he did not give prior notice.

Except for this last small loophole, the committees' right to know was thus transformed from a wishful statement of policy to a binding legal requirement. But the right to know in general was still hedged by a wordy preambular phrase:

> To the extent consistent with applicable authorities and duties, including those conferred by the Constitution upon the executive and legislative branches of the Government, and to the extent consistent with due regard for the protection from unauthorized disclosure of classified information and information relating to intelligence sources and methods. . . .

This fuzzy language can mean anything or nothing. Its effect is to give a DCI or a president a basis for argument if he wishes, for whatever reason, to be less than fully cooperative with Congress.

The 1980 law went further than simply requiring the committees to be "fully and currently informed." It directed that they be furnished "any information or material concerning intelligence activities" that either committee requests "in order to carry out its authorized responsibilities."

The law also directed that the committees be informed "in a timely fashion" of "any illegal intelligence activity or significant intelligence failure" along with what the administration has done about it, or plans to do about it.

In 1993 Congress carried this a step farther in the Intelligence Authorization Act for Fiscal Year 1994 (P.L. 103-178, approved December 3, 1993). This law directs the DCI to submit an annual unclassified report on the activities of the intelligence community. The report is to include significant intelligence successes and failures, as well as areas and issues that are expected to require additional attention during the coming year. The report is due when the president's budget is submitted in January, but in 1994 the first report had not been received by August, much to the displeasure of the intelligence committees.

The 1994 authorization act also requires reports, which may be classified, on counterterrorist activities and on intelligence gaps.

OVERSIGHT IN ACTION

The main work of the intelligence committees is the annual intelligence activities authorization act. This is the legislation that contains the intelligence community's budget in a secret annex. The committees have also generated a body of other legislation regulating sundry aspects of intelligence activities. This is beginning to look like a rudimentary intelligence charter enacted in bits and pieces. The committees have held public hearings on proposed legislation and on selected problems of intelligence. They have issued a number of special public reports. And they consider each proposed covert action individually.

AUTHORIZATION ACTS.   The main purpose of the annual act is to authorize the secret appropriations that support the intelligence community. The intelligence committees spend more time on the budget and the authorization act than on anything else they do. The question of whether an overall budget figure should be made public has been regularly considered but not resolved. The Church committee voted 6-5 to pass the buck to the Senate, which has been disinclined to make a decision. (The effect of not deciding, of course, is to keep the budget secret.) The House committee voted specifically in 1979 not to release an overall figure, a curious decision in light of DCI Stansfield Turner's repeated statements that he had no objections to releasing it. (Turner did not release it himself because he felt that would be presumptuous after the House committee's action.) In 1993 the full House rejected, 169-264, a proposal to make the total public.

The Constitution requires that "a regular Statement and Account of the Receipts and Expenditures of all public Money shall be published from time to time" (Art. I, Sec. 9). Notwithstanding, Congress gave President George Washington a secret contingency fund, and the practice has continued and expanded.

Nobody has suggested releasing a breakdown of the intelligence budget. The argument in favor of releasing a total figure is that the public has a right to know at least that much. The argument against releasing even that much is that it would lead to demands to release more. It would be argued that the total could not be sensibly debated while its components were unknown. (This argument is based more on logic than on the way Congress works. Congress regularly debates foreign aid and other large programs with only the haziest notion of their components.) Another argument against release is that trend lines could be discerned over a period of years as the overall program expanded or contracted, and big swings would indicate the start or stop of large covert actions or expensive collection systems. Another argument, not much used in public, is that if the public knew how much is really spent on intelligence, there would be a political outcry to cut it. As a practical matter, the Defense Department budget is shrinking, which makes it harder to conceal an intelligence budget that is not shrinking so much.

Intelligence authorization bills are also used as the vehicle for sundry housekeeping chores, such as enacting changes in the CIA personnel retirement system, and for making a stab at reorganizing the intelligence community. The Intelligence Authorization Act for Fiscal Year 1993 (P.L. 102-496, approved October 24, 1992) contained extensive provisions designed to strengthen the authority of the DCI over the intelligence community as a whole. It created the National Intelligence Council, with members drawn from senior analysts within the community and substantive experts from outside, to produce national intelligence estimates and to be the principal organ of the intelligence community with respect to analysis. The council was made part of the office of the DCI. The act increased the authority of the DCI over the community's budget and over reprogramming of appropriated funds. And it made explicit the DCI's authority to coordinate relationships with foreign intelligence agencies. The secretary of defense was given authority over the National Security Agency, the National Reconnaissance Office, the Defense Intelligence Agency, and a central imagery authority. The heads of all of these agencies were to be appointed by the secretary, either after consultation with, or on the recommendation of, the DCI.

MISCELLANEOUS LEGISLATION.   The intelligence committees have been concerned with building a legal framework for the activity they oversee. Efforts to enact an all-inclusive legislative charter have come to naught, but at least part of a structure has been built ad hoc. In chronological order the three most important parts are the Foreign Intelligence Surveillance Act of 1978, the Classified Information Procedures Act of 1980, and the Intelligence Identities Protection Act of 1982.[21]

The Classified Information Procedures Act was passed in 1980 as a way to deal with the problem of graymail, a defense tactic in criminal prosecutions that stopped short of blackmail though it shared some of the same characteristics. In graymail a defendant seeks from the government classified documents, alleging that they are essential to his or her defense. In some cases the government abandons the prosecution rather than comply and risk compromising the documents. This has occurred, for example, in some fraud cases, especially those involving officers or employees of CIA proprietaries. It occurred in the case of two employees of ITT who were accused of lying to the Senate Foreign Relations Committee about their activities in Chile with respect to the election of Allende.

Under the Classified Information Procedures Act, the court may authorize the government to delete specific items of requested information, or to substitute a summary, or to admit relevant facts without supplying the documents. The government's request for this authority can be made in a written statement, which only the court can see; and the court acts on the request after an ex parte hearing. On the government's request, the court also issues a protective order for any classified information disclosed to a defendant.

If the court denies a government motion to suppress classified information, the attorney general may file an affidavit objecting to disclosure. In this case the court shall: (1) dismiss the indictment; (2) dismiss specified counts; (3) find against the government on any issue to which the excluded information relates; or (4) preclude the testimony of a witness.

The attorney general is to report semiannually to the intelligence committees on cases not prosecuted because of problems related to classified information. There has been about one such case a year, but the attorney general's reports are not made public.

The Classified Information Procedures Act made the graymail defense more difficult, though in the view of some private lawyers, the problem was never as great as the Justice Department made it appear. But the act had the reverse effect with respect to prosecutions brought by independent counsels appointed under the Ethics in Government Act. That act provided for the ap-

pointment of counsels to conduct investigations and prosecutions independently of the Justice Department in cases involving alleged misconduct by high
officials. This procedure stemmed from the Watergate scandals and was devised
by Congress to take prosecutions away from the Justice Department in cases in
which Congress did not trust the department to be sufficiently vigorous and
evenhanded.

The prosecutions brought by the independent counsel in the Iran-Contra
affair were repeatedly impeded by a hostile Justice Department that took advantage of the powers conferred on the attorney general by the Classified Information Procedures Act. In passing that act, Congress had assumed that the
Justice Department would be the prosecutor and had given it weapons to use
against graymail. But in the Iran-Contra cases the Justice Department was to all
intents and purposes a part of the defense and used these same weapons to reinforce graymail. By insisting on keeping certain documents secret, it effectively
quashed the prosecution of Joseph Fernandez, one-time CIA station chief in
Costa Rica, who was charged with lying to investigators.

The Intelligence Identities Protection Act of 1982 was the congressional
response to the activities of a small group of disaffected former intelligence officers. Prominent among them were Philip Agee, author of *Inside the Company:
CIA Diary* (published in Great Britain in 1975), an exposé based on his career in
the CIA in Latin America, and Louis Wolf, co-editor of *The Covert Action Information Bulletin*. This group made a particular point of naming supposed
CIA officers abroad, sometimes with harmful or even fatal results. Richard
Welch, the CIA station chief in Athens, was shot and killed in front of his house
in December 1975 after having been named by the *Athens Daily News* and by a
magazine then published by Agee. Attacks were made on CIA personnel in Jamaica in 1980 and in Nicaragua in 1981 after their names had been published.

The identity of a station chief is really not so secret as the CIA pretends to
wish it were. He or she is the person in the American embassy with a house,
car, and lifestyle exceeding the rank the person is given in the embassy hierar-
chy, and in most countries the station chief is known to the foreign office and
police. But this is not the same thing as plastering his or her name in public
prints. And lesser CIA employees, like lesser bureaucrats of any agency, can
usually count on reasonable anonymity.

The coincidence of timing in the Athens, Jamaica, Nicaragua, and other
cases suggested a cause-and-effect relationship, and the intelligence and judiciary committees in Congress took up the problem of how to prohibit disclosing identities without violating the First Amendment's guarantee of free
speech. The device that was hit upon was to target the prohibition against persons who have, or have had, authorized access to classified information and
then intentionally identify a covert agent. There is a separate prohibition
against engaging in "a pattern of activities intended to identify and expose covert agents and with reason to believe that such activities would impair or impede the foreign intelligence activities of the United States." Penalties range
from $15,000 to $50,000 and from three to ten years.

SPECIAL REPORTS AND HEARINGS.   Some of the intelligence committees' most useful contributions have been in their nonlegislative activities.

Prominent among these have been those related to covert action, the quality of intelligence reporting and analysis, and legislation and treaties pending before other committees of Congress.

The committees are informed of each covert action, almost always in advance. According to both members and staff of the committees, sometimes a proposed action is changed or even abandoned as a result of questions raised in these discussions. The usual course is that the DCI makes some changes to satisfy one or both committees—or to "refine" or "improve" the action, in the phraseology preferred in Congress.

It occasionally happens—perhaps once a year, in one estimate—that a committee chairman and ranking minority member go to the secretary of state or national security adviser or even the president himself with a strong objection. A president does not always see his mistake even when it is pointed out by a member of Congress. In such a circumstance the committee has no power of its own to block the action. If it feels strongly about the matter, it can seek legislation. This has been done twice—once in the case of Angola and once in Nicaragua. Congress eventually reversed itself with respect to Angola, and the Reagan administration ignored the prohibition in Nicaragua. Given the political fallout of Iran-Contra, another administration might well pay more attention if a similar case should arise in the future.

The two intelligence committees have produced many helpful reports about the quality of intelligence reporting and analysis. For example, one report by the Senate committee staff in November 1985 became influential in internal U.S. government debates over policy in the Philippines.[22] The central issue in the debate was whether to continue to support the government of President Ferdinand Marcos, and the central question affecting that issue was Marcos's political survivability. The Intelligence Committee staff expressed "serious doubt" on this point and listed a number of reasons. Their report, together with similar reports from other sources, was used to good effect by senators (including Richard Lugar, R-Ind., then chairman of the Foreign Relations Committee) who were trying to persuade President Reagan that Marcos no longer deserved American support.

In 1978 the Senate engaged in a lengthy, major debate over two highly controversial treaties that would decrease U.S. control and increase Panamanian control of the Panama Canal. The canal would become totally Panamanian in 2000. Under the treaties the United States also would give up its military bases in the Canal Zone, which was to be abolished. Two questions relating to intelligence arose during the debate. One was whether a compromise of intelligence sources during the long negotiations had influenced the outcome. The other was whether the outcome was affected by intelligence activities related to the drug trade in Panama. The Senate Intelligence Committee laid these questions to rest in a report that was presented and discussed in an unusual secret session of the whole Senate.

The Senate Intelligence Committee also made special studies with respect to every arms control treaty, and some arms control proposals, considered by the Senate after 1977. A crucial question with respect to all of these treaties concerned the capability of the United States to monitor Soviet compliance. From time to time Congress debated proposals to limit nuclear testing unilaterally, and the intelligence committees contributed important data, which might not otherwise have been available, about U.S. intelligence performance and capabilities.

In 1986 the House Intelligence Committee held hearings on Angola. At issue was whether U.S. involvement there should be publicly acknowledged and debated. A proposition in favor of public acknowledgment was made a part of the committee's intelligence authorization bill that year; it was aimed not so much at ending American involvement in Angola as at bringing it into the open. The full House did not agree and voted 229 to 186 to strike that section of the authorization bill. Although the committee's hearings and actions did not end the CIA's involvement in Angola, they did accomplish part of their purpose in focusing attention on the question of public policy in covert action.

In another action during consideration of the 1986 authorization act, the House added an amendment prohibiting intelligence cooperation with agencies of the South African government. The intelligence committees sent staff members to South Africa to be sure the prohibition was being observed.

PROBLEMS OF CONGRESSIONAL OVERSIGHT

The intelligence committees have all the problems of oversight that face the standing committees of Congress—problems of bureaucratic obfuscation and rigidity, of policy clashes with the agencies they are overseeing, and of obtaining information. In the case of the intelligence committees, these problems are magnified because of the secrecy in which intelligence business is conducted. In addition, the intelligence committees have special problems arising from the subject matter and the agencies in their jurisdiction.

RELATIONS WITH THE COMMUNITY

The intelligence community generally has come to accept the oversight committees. It was not always this way. The community, perhaps unavoidably, is a particularly closed society, and the appearance of aggressive people from Capitol Hill asking sensitive questions was a traumatic shock. But the community has generally adapted to a new era. (The covert operators have been slowest to change.) Recent DCIs, notably Robert Gates, who served from 1991 to 1993, came to look on Congress as a potential ally and protector in bureaucratic wars within the executive branch. Gates has written of the "policymaker who is politically at the mercy of any CIA briefer who goes to Capitol Hill." [23] Congress can be particularly helpful in shielding the community from political pressure to shape intelligence to support predetermined policy. Many in Congress would no doubt say that the community has not taken advantage of the shield. Congress itself is a potential source of such pressure.

Congress has also been helpful to the community in arguments over the distribution of budget resources, especially in an era of budgetary stringency. Most members of the intelligence community are in the Department of Defense. Although the DCI is supposed to control the overall intelligence community budget, the agencies in Defense are at a disadvantage in fighting for their share of a shrinking pie.

The development of increasingly expensive collection systems, mainly imagery satellites, has been accompanied by the growth of an intelligence industrial complex. This is, and probably will continue to be, small in comparison with the much larger military industrial complex of which it is a part. But it is real. It is a new political influence.

The intelligence committees normally do not insist on knowing the most sensitive matters—the identity of sources. But they say that when they really need to know, they can find out. Thus, when they investigated charges of relationships between the CIA and death squads in the Salvadoran military, a crucial element was the identity of Salvadoran military personnel working for the CIA. Committee investigators were told, and the information was treated on a compartmented basis—that is, a clear need to know was a condition of access. There were no leaks.

MICROMANAGEMENT

All congressional committees make daily decisions, consciously or otherwise, about where to draw the line between policy oversight and micromanagement of detailed operations. This is not any easier for the intelligence committees than for anybody else.

As reconnaissance satellites become more sophisticated and acquire greater capabilities, they become more expensive—very expensive. Whether the National Reconnaissance Office needs one or more new satellites is a legitimate policy question that ought to be decided by Congress. It is akin to questions of whether the navy needs one or more new aircraft carriers or whether the air force needs a new intercontinental bomber. The intelligence committees even have a legitimate interest in the proposed design of a new satellite. Will it work? What is the opinion of nongovernmental experts? But if the committees try to dictate the design themselves, they have crossed the line into micromanagement. According to a former official of the intelligence community, the House committee once even prescribed the radio frequency for a satellite, but this action was overturned.

Micromanagement is not necessarily related to how much money is involved. The intelligence committees consider each covert action project individually, and some of them involve very small amounts of money. Consideration of individual covert actions is not micromanagement; a policy decision must be made whether a covert action, large or small, is to be undertaken at all. It is micromanagement when the committees tinker with the conduct of a covert action.

But in the end, micromanagement tends to be in the eye of the beholder. One member's micromanagement is another member's policy. The executive branch tends to define micromanagement as anything that impinges on its flexibility to do what it wants to, but the executive brings a good deal of micromanagement on itself by not following legislative policy guidelines. Thus, some members of Congress do not take the issue of micromanagement seriously, but it is a serious problem for Congress nonetheless. Congress can get so bogged down in micromanagement (which it does poorly) that it neglects the larger policy issues (which it handles well, most of the time).

CO-OPTATION

The intelligence committees, no less than other committees, are targets for co-optation, the subtle process by which watchdogs are transformed into lap-dogs. Limitations on terms of service for members of the intelligence commit-tees have been criticized as making co-optation easier: members are less experi-enced and therefore more subject to being fooled. But term limitations have a contrary effect as well: repeated new crops of members present new challenges to those who would co-opt them. This gives committee staffs, some of which serve long term, greater responsibility and influence.

There is yet another effect of term limitations. As members move off the intelligence committees, they become part of a widening pool of members of Congress who are knowledgeable about intelligence. This is good in that it raises the level of congressional consideration of intelligence matters. But it means that more people know more secrets, and this violates one of the princi-ples of security.

The degree, if any, to which the intelligence committees have been co-opted seems to have varied over time, with the attitude of the chairman being the principal variable. Sen. David L. Boren, D-Okla., who was chairman of the intelligence committee from 1987 to 1993, was particularly close to DCI Gates. The CIA never had a better friend in Congress than Sen. Barry Goldwater, R-Ariz., chairman of the Senate Intelligence Committee from 1981 to 1985. Gold-water had been a member of the original Church committee. Notwithstanding this experience, he said in 1980 that he would have preferred that there be no congressional oversight of intelligence agencies: "The Russians have a very fine system. . . . No part of their government has any idea of what is going on [in the KGB]. That is the way . . . I wish it were in our country, but it is not." [24]

As committee staff director, Goldwater brought in John Blake, who had worked in the CIA for thirty-two years, rising to be acting deputy director. Blake was succeeded as staff director by Robert R. Simmons, a ten-year veteran of CIA. Recruiting staff from the agencies a committee is supposed to oversee does not necessarily mean co-optation. It may mean that the staff brings a built-in pro-agency bias with it. But it also means that the staff knows the right ques-tions to ask and the right places to look in the bureaucratic maze. It was a for-mer navy officer on the staff of the Senate Foreign Relations Committee who unraveled the Gulf of Tonkin incident.

Despite his pro-CIA disposition, Goldwater was infuriated when he discov-ered that the CIA had been mining Nicaraguan harbors in 1984 without having informed the Senate Intelligence Committee as the law required. Never one to mince words, Goldwater wrote DCI William Casey what is surely the bluntest letter ever to go from a congressional committee chairman to the head of an executive agency:

> Dear Bill: I've been trying to figure out how I can most easily tell you my feel-ings about the discovery of the President having approved mining some of the harbors of Central America.
> It gets down to one, little, simple phrase: I am pissed off! . . .[25]

Senator Goldwater also released the letter to the press, raising a problem for some of the nation's more sedate editors as to whether all of its language was fit to print. Casey apologized, after his fashion, and argued that the committee had been informed. So it had been, but in one sentence of a long statement.

Sen. Daniel Patrick Moynihan, D-N.Y., was so outraged that he resigned from the committee in a huff, only to be placated and return. Later Moynihan charged that the CIA conducted what amounted to a sub rosa disinformation campaign against Goldwater, spreading the word that "well, of course he had been told, but you understand, he is getting old, he can't remember and maybe he wasn't paying attention." [26]

PRESIDENTIAL FINDINGS

Another problem of oversight has to do with what goes into a presidential finding about covert action. Such a finding has been a legal prerequisite for covert action since enactment of the Hughes-Ryan amendment in 1974. The requirement means that the president has to determine (that is, "find") that a particular covert action is "important" to the national security. The problem is in how precise the finding ought to be in specifying the scope and limits of the action.

This is important, because a broad finding can be used to cover activities that were not contemplated in the beginning. A narrow finding would require amendment and return trips to the intelligence committees if activities change. To illustrate the difference, consider a hypothetical example in Country X. Suppose a newspaper published by a political party friendly to the United States is in economic difficulties, and it is proposed that the United States covertly support the paper by buying advertisements or even paying some salaries. A narrow finding would authorize a certain amount of money for support of the particular newspaper. A broad finding would authorize support for the political party in question. Now suppose that a year later the party is involved in an electoral campaign that the United States desires to support. Under a narrow finding, a new finding would be necessary. But under a broad finding, the CIA could engage in the whole range of activities associated with elections—pay party workers, subsidize television and radio broadcasts, and so on. All of these things, of course, would be done through cut-outs so that the American hand would not appear. We hope.

The executive branch tends to write findings in broad language to preserve flexibility for unforeseen contingencies. Congress tends to want findings in narrow language to ensure that if an action grows beyond what was originally contemplated, Congress is brought in at every stage of the expansion.

FOREIGN INTELLIGENCE AGENCIES

Another problem of oversight involves the relations of the intelligence community (principally the CIA) with foreign intelligence agencies. This is one of the more delicate aspects of oversight. It involves some of the things the CIA is most sensitive about, because in many cases neither party to the relationship wants it known that the relationship exists. Agreements with foreign intelligence agencies are supposed to be reported to Congress under the Case Act of

1972, but successive administrations have been most reluctant to do so. In some cases there are no written agreements. This is one of the areas in which the chairmen and vice chairmen of the intelligence committees are likely to be the only members who are informed.

The congressional intelligence committees are reluctant to talk about the extent of their inquiry into this aspect of their jurisdiction. This reluctance might be a way of shielding extraordinarily sensitive data. Or it might be a way of obscuring a lack of oversight.

Sharing intelligence with foreign governments and their intelligence agencies (or withholding it from them) can also be a tool of diplomacy—to cement relations, to express goodwill (or disapproval). The use of intelligence in this way obviously requires great tact and skill. More often the arrangement has been a quid pro quo of intelligence gathering: let us establish a listening base and we'll tell you (part of) what we hear.

Congressional Will

The final, and the biggest, problem of congressional oversight of the intelligence community is the will to do it. The mechanism to do it is in place. Congress has the power to make the mechanism work. Members of the intelligence committees regard themselves as agents of Congress and, indeed, of the American people to ensure that what the intelligence community does in secret is in accord with what the government says in public. The people, perforce, have to trust the committees.

But members of Congress do not have to rely on trust in the committees. Any member of the House can go to the House committee, and any member of the Senate can go to the Senate committee, and read any records the committees have.

Michael Barnes, then a Democratic representative from Maryland, was chairman of the House Foreign Affairs Committee's Latin American Subcommittee during the contentious debates about Nicaragua in the 1980s. He made a point of not asking the Intelligence Committee what it knew about Nicaragua because he felt that would inhibit his freedom in debate.

When the intelligence authorization bills are being debated, any member can look at the secret annexes and at the secret justifications for them. If members see something they do not like, they can demand a secret session, debate the matter, and (if they can get the votes) change it. The number of members who take advantage of this right of access is measured in single digits.

It was this lack of curiosity that made Iran-Contra possible. Members of the intelligence committees at the time say they did ask questions and got lies for answers. This has left them with a helpless feeling. Their mistake was that they did not ask the questions of enough people. Congress could learn from journalists. You have to ask the same question of different people over and over and over. This was more apparent in 1994 than it was in 1985 and 1986, and it is understandable, if not entirely forgivable, that members of Congress would have once accepted lies from responsible officials. It will be neither understandable nor forgivable if they do it again.

NOTES

1. Commission on Organization of the Executive Branch of the Government, *Intelligence Activities*, H. Doc. 201, 84th Cong., 1st sess., 1955, 60.
2. See Keith Schneider, "U.S. Expands Inquiry into Its Human Radiation Tests," *New York Times*, Dec. 31, 1993; and Schneider, "Anguish on Both Sides in Human Experiments," *New York Times*, March 2, 1994; also House Committee on Energy and Power, Subcommittee on Energy Conservation and Power, *American Nuclear Guinea Pigs: Three Decades of Radiation Experiments on U.S. Citizens*, staff report, mimeo, October 1986.
3. *Congressional Record*, 84th Cong., 2d sess., April 9, 1956, 5924.
4. See National Security File, Agency File, Box 9, CIA Vol. II, Memorandum for the President from W. W. Rostow, "Admiral Raborn's View of Compromise on CIA Watchdog Committee," June 1, 1966. See also correspondence from Mike Mansfield, May 25, 1966, and June 1, 1966, Lyndon Baines Johnson Library, Austin, Texas.
5. Francis O. Wilcox, *Congress, the Executive, and Foreign Policy* (New York: Harper & Row, 1971), 86.
6. Letter from David M. Abshire, assistant secretary of state for congressional relations, to J.W. Fulbright, chairman, Committee on Foreign Relations, January 28, 1972. Text is in Senate Foreign Relations Committee, *National Security Act Amendment*, Hearings, 92d Cong., 2d sess., 1972.
7. Nathaniel Davis, *The Last Two Years of Salvador Allende* (Ithaca: Cornell University Press, 1985), 5.
8. Senate Foreign Relations Committee, *Nomination of Richard Helms to Be Ambassador to Iran and CIA International and Domestic Activities*, Hearings, 93d Cong., 1st sess., 1974, 47.
9. Ibid., 102.
10. Anthony Marro, "Helms Is Fined $2,000 and Given Two-Year Suspended Prison Term," *New York Times*, Nov. 5, 1977. For contrasting views of this case, see Richard Harris, "Reflections: Secrets," *The New Yorker*, April 10, 1978; and Thomas Powers, *The Man Who Kept the Secrets: Richard Helms and the CIA* (New York: Pocket Books, 1979), esp. 281-305.
11. The Hughes-Ryan amendment was Sec. 662 of the Foreign Assistance Act of 1961, as amended, 22 U.S.C. 2422. It was itself later amended and then repealed.
12. *Congressional Quarterly Almanac*, 1989, 548. See also Cecil V. Crabb, Jr., and Pat M. Holt, *Invitation to Struggle: Congress, the President, and Foreign Policy*, 4th ed. (Washington, D.C.: CQ Press, 1992), 179-181.
13. Memorandum of Disapproval for the Intelligence Authorization Act, Fiscal Year 1991, November 30, 1990, in *Weekly Compilation of Presidential Documents*, vol. 26, no. 48, December 3, 1990, 1958-1959.
14. Seymour M. Hersh, "Huge CIA Operation Reported in U.S. against Antiwar Forces, Other Dissidents in Nixon Years," *New York Times*, Dec. 22, 1974.
15. The text of Colby's statement is in the *New York Times*, Jan. 16, 1975. See also William Colby and Peter Forbath, *Honorable Men: My Life in the CIA* (New York: Simon and Schuster, 1978), 337-350.
16. H. Res. 982, 94th Cong., 2d sess., agreed to January 29, 1976. The House debate is in *Congressional Record*, 94th Cong., 2d sess., January 29, 1976, 1632-1641.
17. H. Rept. 94-833, 94th Cong., 2d sess. The complete text of the suppressed report has since been published under the title *CIA: The Pike Report* (Nottingham: Spokesman Books, 1977).
18. This section draws heavily on Crabb and Holt, *Invitation to Struggle*, 169-177.
19. See House Intelligence Committee, *Report Pursuant to Clause 1(d) of the Rules of*

the House of Representatives, H. Rept 101-1008, 101st Cong., 2d sess., 1991. (This is the committee's report on its activities during the 101st Congress, 1989-1990.) See also William E. Conner, Intelligence Oversight: The Controversy Behind the FY 1991 Intelligence Authorization Act (McLean, Va.: Association of Former Intelligence Officers, 1993).

20. Sec. 11(a), S. Res. 400, 94th Cong.

21. P.L. 95-511, approved October 25, 1978, 92 Stat. 1783, 50 U.S.C. 1801; P.L. 96-456, approved October 15, 1980, 94 Stat. 2025; and P.L. 97-200, 50 U.S.C. 421-426.

22. Senate Select Committee on Intelligence, The Philippines: A Situation Report, staff report, November 1, 1985, 99th Cong., 1st sess., S. Print 99-96.

23. Robert M. Gates, "The CIA and American Foreign Policy," Foreign Affairs 66 (Winter 1987/1988): 222.

24. Congressional Record, 96th Cong., 2d sess., June 3, 1980, 13104.

25. Expurgated text in New York Times, April 11, 1984, A9; full text in Washington Post, April 11, 1984, A17. For more details of incident, see Bob Woodward, Veil: The Secret Wars of the CIA 1981-1987 (New York: Simon and Schuster, 1987), 319-327.

26. Senate Intelligence Committee, Nomination of Robert M. Gates, S. Hearing 102-799, Vol. I, 102d Cong., 1st sess., 431.

PART IV

The Future

The American intelligence community was a product of the cold war, and the end of the cold war left the community in a state of transition. Some (Sen. Daniel Patrick Moynihan, D-N.Y., prominent among them) called for the abolition of the CIA as obsolete. Others saw new missions that would take the CIA as well as other elements of the community into the next century.

Nowhere were the pressures for change felt more strongly than in the CIA, the flagship agency of the intelligence community. At the same time that it was struggling to adjust to new roles and missions, with fewer people and slimmer budgets, its bureaucratic culture—the lifestyle of the practitioners of espionage—was coming under multiple attacks.

The agency was severely shaken by the Aldrich Ames espionage case, especially as it began to appear that it was the CIA's own habits that left Ames undetected for so long. And then the clandestine services of the Directorate of Operations, long a bastion of white males, was assaulted by complaints and lawsuits charging sexual discrimination.

Chapter 11 suggests some new guidelines for the intelligence community in the post-cold war era. These have to do with constraints on covert action, with shifting resources from the extinct Soviet Union to new targets (terrorism, Islam), and with avoiding the temptation of other new targets (industrial espionage).

A balance sheet finds that as the mechanisms of political control were being strengthened on Capitol Hill, they were breaking down in the White House. This perhaps proved the wisdom of the Founding Fathers in providing for a three-branch government: when one branch becomes aberrant, another can compensate for it. But in fact the compensation was insufficient to prevent Iran-Contra. The mechanism was there, but the vigilance was not.

CHAPTER 11

What Next?

There is no country in which everything can be provided for by the laws, or in which political institutions can prove a substitute for common sense and public morality.

—Alexis de Tocqueville

The question was asked of a former chairman of one of the congressional intelligence committees: "How can an open society assert political control over activities which are necessarily secret?"

The answer came back like a shot: "It can't."

The same question, asked of a former cabinet officer, elicited this answer: "A good question. And one that's never been satisfactorily answered."

Yet neither of these men, nor any of the scores of others interviewed for this book, was willing to abandon the search. For that would be to admit that we cannot make government work.

The intelligence community was very much a creature of the cold war. Intelligence professionals, especially the old boys who moved from the Office of Strategic Services to the CIA, are prone to argue that the community was really a belated reaction to Pearl Harbor and was born of a determination never again to be caught by surprise. But it is hard to imagine that the community would have developed as it did if there had been no cold war—if, for example, there had been only one Germany after 1945; if Poland, Czechoslovakia, and Hungary had held, and abided by, free elections; and if the Soviet Union had walked in good faith through the door that was briefly open for its participation in the Marshall Plan.

Half a century passed between the attack on Pearl Harbor in 1941 and the dissolution of the Soviet Union in 1991. That is almost a quarter of the history of the United States as an independent nation. It is too long to be dismissed as an aberration, but there was very little about this period that could be called normal. It gave shape and character to two generations of Americans and to many institutions of the American government, not least the intelligence community. Many of these changes will not be undone. A great deal can be learned from them.

We developed a fail-safe procedure for launching nuclear warheads, the military weapons of the cold war, but we had no fail-safe procedure for launching secret intelligence operations, the cold war's political weapons. In the end our only reliance is on unremitting vigilance, especially by the media and by Congress. And we must all be skeptics without being cynics.

The atmosphere of the cold war was accurately mirrored in a 1954 report by a committee headed by World War II hero Gen. Jimmy Doolittle:

> It is now clear that we are facing an implacable enemy whose avowed objective is world domination by whatever means and at whatever cost. There are no rules in such a game. Hitherto acceptable rules of human conduct do not apply. If the United States is to survive, longstanding American concepts of "fair play" must be reconsidered. We must develop effective espionage and counterespionage services and must learn to subvert, sabotage and destroy our enemies by more clever, more sophisticated, and more effective methods than those used against us. It may become necessary that the American people become acquainted with, understand and support this fundamentally repugnant philosophy.[1]

It may be considered remarkable that matters have not turned out worse given the fact that the people who should have been overseeing the application of this "fundamentally repugnant philosophy" were not paying attention most of the time. In the early stages of his historic investigation of intelligence activities (and before he had learned enough to know better), Sen. Frank Church, D-Idaho, characterized the CIA as a "rogue elephant." The phrase contained an element of truth, but withal it was an unfair exaggeration. Most of the offenses for which the CIA can justly be held responsible had to do with domestic activities—such things as mail openings, drug experiments on unwitting subjects, and illegal surveillance of American citizens. Even with respect to some of these, it felt driven by beleaguered presidents who were so certain of the rightness of their policies that they thought opponents had to be inspired by communists.

In most of the foreign escapades of the intelligence community that left the United States embarrassed or worse, the CIA was following orders it received from legally constituted authority—the president of the United States. The CIA was not acting on its own when it sent the U-2 on an ill-timed flight, or overthrew sundry governments, or rigged various foreign elections. It had been told what to do by the people it looked to for direction.

All of these things, and more, were thought to be simply steps in implementing a policy on which there was general agreement—namely, the anticommunist, anti-Soviet policy of the cold war. From the earliest days it has been accepted that it is appropriate for a president to conduct certain aspects of foreign policy in secret *provided that what is done in secret is compatible with generally accepted policy and with generally accepted norms of international behavior.*

Most presidents during the cold war—from Harry Truman to George Bush—no doubt thought they were acting in conformity with this principle. But the resources of the CIA gave these presidents means, on a scale not available to their predecessors, to conduct secret foreign policies. This new capability presented the temptation to use secrecy not only to accomplish a foreign policy objective, but also and more importantly to avoid a political debate at home. Thus, the CIA became the instrument—sometimes unwitting, sometimes unwilling, sometimes complicit—of presidential subversion of the American government. It is the CIA that particularly concerns us because the other agencies of the intelligence community deal only with collection and (in the Defense Intelligence Agency) with analysis. The uniformed armed services have some capability of covert action, but that activity is reserved to the CIA by executive order except in time of war. The FBI's counterintelligence activities are, and have been, subject to abuse, but this is more a problem of domestic law enforcement than of foreign policy.

REASSESSMENTS

The end of the cold war left a big part of the intelligence community a bureaucracy searching for a mission. When the Soviet Union disappeared, so did at least half of the community's targets. Some of the targets remain in attenuated form—nuclear missiles, for example. But withal, the collapse of communism set off a frantic search by America's spies for something to do. The community's overseers need to ensure that what is done is done because it needs to be done and not because it makes work for intelligence personnel.

This squeeze on the community was intensified by a governmentwide squeeze on spending generally. The 1993 intelligence authorization act ordered a 17.5 percent reduction in personnel by 1997.[2] More than seven hundred individuals were cut from the CIA's Directorate of Operations, about one thousand from the Directorate of Intelligence.[3] It was reported that the CIA planned to close fifteen stations in Africa.[4]

There remained plenty of viable new priority intelligence targets. Although not a superpower in the sense of the former Soviet Union, China was still communist, was still a nuclear power, and had more than a billion people. North Korea was sending troubling signals of intentions to go nuclear. Chemical and bacteriological weapons of mass destruction are cheaper than nuclear weapons and thus more attractive to some irresponsible governments. Militantly anti-Western Islamic fundamentalists were held responsible for sundry acts of terrorism (including the World Trade Center bombing in New York in 1993).

At a time when the intelligence community generally felt itself to be at a crossroads, the CIA found not only its mission but its lifestyle under attack from several quarters. Most importantly, the agency and the congressional intelligence committees were severely shaken by the arrest of Aldrich Ames and Ames's subsequent plea of guilty to espionage charges (see Chapter 6). The Ames case would reverberate on Capitol Hill and in Langley for a long time. No doubt new procedures would eventually be put into place in the hope of preventing a repetition.

But in a way, the problem Ames posed to counterintelligence was analogous to the problem the shah of Iran posed to intelligence analysts and policy makers during the Carter administration (see Chapter 5). The entire U.S. government had so much invested in the shah, psychologically as well as politically, economically, and militarily, that no one could admit that this particular emperor was not wearing clothes. Similarly, Ames put out all the classic warning symptoms that he was up to no good—he drank too much, he spent too much money, his job performance was poor. But no one in the CIA could screw up the courage to blow the whistle on him.

There were a good many reasons for this timidity, but the basic one was the CIA lifestyle, especially in the Directorate of Operations. Former DCI William E. Colby described it well:

> A bonding does take place among those who share dangers and sacrifice, physical and moral, and we do try to help our fellow officers through personal and other problems without immediately denouncing their failings.[5]

There was another reason the warning signs about Ames were ignored. The old hands at CIA in 1990 remembered the days of James Jesus Angleton, the chief of counterintelligence whom Colby fired in 1974. Angleton terrorized the Directorate of Operations and wrecked several careers with baseless suspicions of collaboration with Soviet agents. The Ames case posed painful questions: Is there a middle ground between camaraderie and suspicion? When does doubt become paranoia?

The eclipse of the KGB may make it easier to find a middle ground, but there is a caveat. Although the danger is reduced that disgruntled spies, needing money, will sell what they know to agents of Moscow, there may be other countries (Libya, Iraq, China?) who would pay for it.

There is a further complication for the CIA. Most of those who share the bonding of which Colby wrote are white men. This is not only incongruous for spies in much of the third world; it is out of tune with late twentieth century America. A former female station chief filed a sex discrimination suit against the CIA under the pseudonym of Jane Doe Thompson. Other female employees were reported to be preparing a class action suit, and there were rumblings on Capitol Hill.[6]

PERIL POINTS

John le Carré, the former British intelligence professional and best-selling author of semifictionalized spy novels, has concluded: "If the Cold War had been fought by the spies, the Soviet Union would have won hands down." [7] That seems too harsh a judgment on Western (including U.S.) intelligence. Britain's MI6, Israel's Mossad, the CIA, National Security Agency, National Reconnaissance Office, and all the rest certainly had their moments. As the saying goes, you win some and you lose some.

Allen Dulles, the director of central intelligence from 1953 to 1961, has explained how the KGB started with an advantage over the CIA because the KGB had already learned many of the tricks of the trade through its experience in an oppressive society. In his view many of the techniques later used to good advantage by the Soviet KGB were developed by Russian revolutionaries under persecution by the czarist police:

> The complicated and devious tricks of concealing and passing messages, of falsifying documents, of using harmless intermediaries between suspect parties so as not to expose one to the other or allow both to be seen together—these were all survival techniques developed after bitter encounters and many losses at the hands of the czar's police. When the Soviets later founded their own intelli-

gence service, these were the tricks they taught their agents to evade the police of other countries.[8]

The CIA, which came out of a free and open society, had a different legacy. Dulles also remarked in the early 1960s that the KGB became the "personal instrument" of the Soviet dictator.[9] A decade later Sen. Stuart Symington complained that the CIA had become the American president's "private army." It was when the CIA began to act like its principal adversary, the KGB, that it began to get into trouble.

Other peril points can be identified, some of them attributable to the intelligence community, some to whoever was president at the time.

How Much Does the President Know?

One of these points comes when the community keeps secrets not only from Congress but also from its boss, the president. On February 18, 1977, less than a month after Jimmy Carter's inauguration, the *Washington Post* reported that the CIA had had an ongoing relationship with King Hussein of Jordan under which the king had been paid millions of dollars.[10] Before printing the story, the *Post* sought White House reaction. Carter received the reporter and editor, and "stunned" them (the editor's word) by saying he had not known of the payments until he received the query from the *Post*.[11]

One of the difficult decisions a DCI has to make is whether the president needs to know about a particular situation (in which case he is told) or whether he doesn't need to be bothered (in which case he is not told). Different presidents have different thresholds of wanting to know and wanting not to be bothered. But when the CIA has an agent as prominent (and as expensive) as King Hussein, a key longtime American ally in the Middle East, there can be no question that the president should have known.

President Carter might well have wondered what else the intelligence community was keeping from him. The media's role of watchdog is usually considered to be to inform the public. In this case it informed the president as well.

The Iran-Contra affair is a more egregious example of the same peril point. There is persuasive evidence that neither President Ronald Reagan nor (especially) Vice President George Bush was totally ignorant. At the least they were certainly inattentive. Nor did either the CIA or the NSC staff do anything to ensure that they were informed.

How Presidents Use Intelligence

Presidents Dwight Eisenhower and Reagan represent the right way and the wrong way of using intelligence. The U-2 incident produced intelligence that convinced Eisenhower that the Soviet Union did not have a lead over the United States in the production and deployment of nuclear missiles (see Chapter 4). He remained silent about this in order to protect the source of the intelligence, but he also resisted demands that the U.S. missile program be accelerated. Democrats' charges of a "missile gap," as it was called in the political rhetoric of the day, later turned out to be false, but in the meantime the charges hurt the administration and contributed to the Republican Party defeat in the close election of 1960.

Thirty years after Eisenhower, the Reagan administration consistently exaggerated intelligence from Central America concerning the extent of communist activity there. The purpose was to build a stronger case for the administration's policy of supporting anticommunist forces in the area.

COVERT ACTION

Policy makers should ask two questions with respect to a covert action. First, is it wise foreign policy? Second, is it something that would be supported by most of the American people if they knew about it?

There is a natural tendency to confuse wise policy with easy policy. It was easier to overthrow Iranian prime minister Mohammed Mossadegh than to live with him. It was easier to overthrow Guatemalan president Jacobo Arbenz Guzmán than to deal with him. It was thought that it would be easier to overthrow Cuban premier Fidel Castro than to live with communist penetration of the Caribbean. But the attempt to overthrow Castro failed, and Cuba has suffered more from communist penetration than has the United States. In all of these cases, and in others, considerations of the cold war clouded the issue. It is perhaps unfair to the policy makers of the time to attempt to second guess them from a post-cold war perspective.

It is argued that a policy maker cannot always judge what the public will or will not support and that therefore it is idle to apply this test to foreign policy moves that are taken in secret and that the public will not know about (or so it is thought). This is a matter of degree. It is doubtful if many Americans cared very much one way or the other about Mossadegh in the summer of 1953; they were a good deal more interested in the final end of the Korean War. Historically, Americans were conditioned to coups d'état in Central America; another one in Guatemala in 1954 did not seem to make much difference, except that the guy who was thrown out was portrayed as a left-leaning commie. But if there had been a Senate Intelligence Committee then, it is by no means certain what its reaction would have been. Sen. Bourke B. Hickenlooper, a solid, conservative Republican from Iowa, was chairman of the Senate Foreign Relations Subcommittee on Latin America in 1954, and he knew about the Eisenhower administration's plans to topple Arbenz. He did not argue much with the administration, but he growled plenty to the committee staff. The basis of his objection was that it is easier to get into things like this than to get out of them. The record of U.S. entanglement in Guatemala over the past forty years makes Hickenlooper appear positively prescient.

A PERSONAL INSTRUMENT

The point at which the question of public support loses all ambiguity is when there is clearly public controversy about an issue, or *a fortiori*, when Congress has expressly forbidden an action and the administration secretly takes it anyway. This was the real mischief of the Iran-Contra scandal.

The rationalization presented by some of the principal wrongdoers in Iran-Contra revealed a frightening failure to grasp the essential principles of how the American government is supposed to work. The failure is even more frightening when such men are so close to the seat of political power.

Said Oliver North, the hard-charging Marine Corps lieutenant colonel on the National Security Council staff: "It is the fault of the Congress for not being able to understand what the problem was." And again: "The Congress is to blame because of the fickle, vacillating, unpredictable, 'on again/off again' policy toward the Nicaraguan Democratic Resistance, the so-called Contras." [12]

And Rear Adm. John P. Poindexter, the national security affairs adviser, explained his approach to answering congressional inquiries: "My objective . . . would have been to withhold information." Again: "My objective all along was to withhold from the Congress exactly what the NSC staff was doing in carrying out the president's policy." Finally: "The point was, and still is, that the President has the constitutional right and, in fact, the constitutional mandate to conduct foreign policy. His policy was to support the Contras." [13]

In other words, Congress did not understand the problem, and Congress vacillated about it; but Congress had no proper role to play with respect to the problem anyway, except to provide appropriations requested by the president. Nobody asked North and Poindexter how withholding information would facilitate congressional understanding. What North meant when he said Congress did not understand the problem was that Congress did not share his—North's—understanding of the problem. North's remarks quoted here and much of the rest of his testimony to the Iran-Contra committee were permeated with an ideological commitment that did not allow for the possibility of reasonable disagreement. Any dissent was due to failure to understand, or worse. Poindexter confused the president's power to conduct foreign policy with the power to make it and thereby arrived at an inflated view of presidential power generally.

The ideological content of Iran-Contra persisted. On Christmas Eve 1992 President George Bush pardoned former secretary of defense Caspar W. Weinberger, who had been indicted for making a false statement to Congress, and five others who had been convicted, or had pleaded guilty, or were awaiting trial on charges growing out of the affair. In a statement accompanying the pardons, Bush said:

> The prosecution of the individuals I am pardoning represents what I believe is a profoundly troubling development in the political and legal climate of our country: the criminalization of policy differences. These differences should be addressed in the political arena, without the Damocles sword of criminality hanging over the heads of some of the combatants. The proper target is the President, not his subordinates; the proper forum is the voting booth, not the courtroom. [14]

Elliott Abrams was assistant secretary of state for Latin America during some of the Iran-Contra years and was one of those receiving a Christmas Eve pardon. He made the same point about the criminalization of policy differences in a book he wrote about the affair—*Undue Process: A Story of How Political Differences Are Turned into Crimes*. [15]

Bush and Abrams had it backwards. It was not the policy differences that were made crimes. It was the policy differences that precipitated the crimes. President Bush was quite right: the proper way to resolve such differences is the political arena. That is precisely how differences over Nicaragua were resolved. Congress debated the matter and cut off the money. The crimes resulted when the Reagan administration refused to accept the results of the political process. That is not only criminal; it is subversive in the most fundamental sense.

Lawrence E. Walsh, the independent counsel appointed to investigate the Iran-Contra case, suggested that without a coverup, which he said Weinberger facilitated, there might have been impeachment proceedings against President Reagan:

> Weinberger's early and deliberate decision to conceal and withhold extensive contemporaneous notes of the Iran-Contra matter radically altered the official investigations and possibly forestalled timely impeachment proceedings against President Reagan and other officials. . . . Weinberger's concealment of notes is part of a disturbing pattern of deception and obstruction that permeated the highest levels of the Reagan and Bush administrations.[16]

Later, in his fourth interim report to Congress, Walsh suggested another motive for the pardons: Bush might have been called to testify as a defense witness and subjected to embarrassing questions.[17]

The actions the Reagan administration took to nullify the results of the political process were secret—for a time. But the administration's activities in Nicaragua that set the process in motion were not secret. Despite the fact that these activities were all carried out under the general rubric of "covert action," they were widely known and openly debated. What a much more complex problem it is when the "covert action" is truly covert and is not known. In these circumstances the political process is stultified.

There was more—and worse—to Iran-Contra. According to North, DCI William Casey saw in the technique of Iran-Contra the possibility of providing a permanent "off-the-shelf" capability for covert action so secret it would be known only to whoever controlled a secret numbered Swiss bank account.[18] We have only North's testimony about Casey's views. Casey died before he could speak for himself.

The intelligence community is supposed to be controlled in the first instance by the president. He necessarily delegates much of this responsibility to the National Security Council and to various interdepartmental committees, not to mention the DCI. But in the end it is the president who is responsible and whom the American people should hold responsible. Beyond the president, there is another mechanism of control, and this is the Congress.

There are many problems of intelligence, but only three raise serious questions of public control of secret activities. These are hazardous collection techniques, hazardous counterintelligence operations, and covert action.

With respect to hazardous collection, the overseers, whether in the White House or on Capitol Hill, need to be especially vigilant against the tendency in the intelligence community to go after a piece of intelligence simply because it is there. Sometimes it is not worth the risk of acquiring it. Sometimes, even if there is no big risk, the intelligence is not worth very much anyway. The overseers need to ask: does the U.S. Government really need to know this, or is it something we are only idly curious about?

The main problem with counterintelligence operations has been the abuse of civil liberties and constitutional procedures in the United States. One can conceive of hazardous counterintelligence operations carried out abroad that might embarrass the United States, or worse, if they went awry. Hypothetical examples include operations against a friendly power or an operation involving one of the more distasteful foreign intelligence organizations. If there have been such operations, they have not backfired.

Greater, and more numerous, dangers lurk in covert action. Here the problem is compounded because presidents cannot be relied on to act always as a restraining influence. In some cases it is the presidents who are the problem. This has especially been the case since presidents discovered that they could use covert action not only to further their purposes abroad but to avoid political controversy at home. All of the burden thus falls on Congress.

Congress did not perform well with respect to Iran-Contra. Those who were on the intelligence committees at the time pleaded that they asked the right questions and were lied to and that this was all they could reasonably be expected to do. They asked the right questions, but they did not ask them of enough people. Their mistake was in assuming that they were getting honest answers and then dropping the matter. If they had kept probing, they most likely would have gotten closer to the truth.

Those who are on the post-Iran-Contra intelligence committees are confident the affair could not be repeated, mainly because—they say—they are in closer contact with intelligence operatives. The rest of us can only hope they are correct.

NEW GUIDELINES?

Efforts to write a comprehensive legislative charter for the intelligence community have been largely abandoned, and properly so. There are too many unforeseeable contingencies. But the experience of almost half a century since passage of the National Security Act of 1947, combined with the end of the cold war, suggests some new approaches.

First, paramilitary covert action has become an oxymoron that should be abandoned as an instrument of policy. One can quarrel over the definition of "success," but certainly in recent years the only such action that would meet most definitions has been the one in Afghanistan. And it was about as public as anything could be.

Second, no covert action of any type should be undertaken unless it advances an objective that has broad support among the public and in Congress.

Third, any proposal for covert action ought to be approached, both in the White House and in Congress, with great restraint. There is a persuasive argument to be made for abandoning covert action entirely as an instrument of policy. The United States no longer has an adversary so threatening as to require it to follow the "repugnant philosophy" described by the Doolittle committee. In any event, if covert action is not abandoned entirely, it should be narrowly defined and limited to the kinds of things for which confidential contingency funds have long been provided to secretaries of state. An example is a largely unreported covert action code-named Operation Yellow Bird that rescued dissidents from China following the Tienanmen Square massacre in 1989. But apparently the initiative in this was taken not by the CIA, but by Chinese who happened to be CIA agents and who then received discreet help from the agency.[19]

We will no doubt continue to have favored candidates in some foreign elections, but there will probably not be many so important to the U.S. national interest as to warrant covert intervention. One can conceive of hypothetical antiterrorist covert actions that would pass muster.[20]

Fourth, it is worthwhile to continue to stockpile intelligence on obscure countries and subjects so it will be there if it is needed five or ten years in the future. In 1987 nobody thought American troops would be in Somalia in 1992; it would have been useful if there had been a larger compendium of basic information on Somalia.

Fifth, a distinction should be made between economic intelligence and industrial espionage. The United States needs economic intelligence worldwide. Most of it is openly available and can be gathered by the Treasury, State, Commerce, and Agriculture departments, all of which have people overseas for this purpose. For some, intelligence targets, reconnaissance satellites, or even old-fashioned spies may be needed. But the United States does not need any kind of industrial espionage—that is, efforts to steal the secrets of individual companies.

The suggestion that it does need industrial espionage is made from time to time by people who want to maintain American competitiveness in the world economy and who argue that other countries are doing it to us. This is a bad argument that starts America back on the road to General Doolittle's "repugnant philosophy." American companies can run their own spies if they want to, but the government ought not to do it for them. And it ought not to defend them if they are caught.

Sixth, the intelligence community should not compete with the Associated Press or Cable News Network. Timeliness is of the essence in tactical military intelligence, but it is less so with other intelligence. The proper role of the intelligence community is to supplement what is reported by news services, not to try to report the same thing first.

Seventh, the intelligence community should not deal in cocktail party gossip. Such gossip can properly be reported but as something for future reference, something that may fit with other bits and scraps to shed light on an individual's behavior or a particular relationship or development. It does no great harm to pass some of the more salacious gossip on to the president (some presidents, as FBI director J. Edgar Hoover well knew, have been particularly titillated by this sort of thing), but the collection of such items should not be a priority. If the intelligence community should not compete with the AP and CNN, even less should it compete with gossip columnists.

Finally, a word needs to be said about the organization of the intelligence community, a perennial source of bureaucratic fudge-making. Intelligence has never really been centralized, as was the original intention, nor is there much prospect that it will be. The technical collection agencies in the Department of

Defense are too dependent on that department's vast infrastructure to make centralization worthwhile, even if it were politically feasible.

The question arises of the relative emphasis on technical and human sources (TECHINT versus HUMINT, in spyspeak). This can be a sterile argument. The specific intelligence being sought will indicate to most sensible people which path to follow. Both had better be kept open.

There is another question over centralization versus diversity in analysis. Too much of either is bad, and it is not hard to recognize how much is too much. A good deal of this argument is fueled, not by the merits, but by bureaucratic loyalties and predilections over what the analytic outcome should be. Of all the members of the intelligence community, the CIA is the only one that does not have an institutional stake in policy outcomes. That is the best reason for not giving cabinet status to the director of central intelligence and for keeping him out of the policy-making machinery.

CONCLUSION

The end of the cold war did not end the problem of responsibly managing a secret intelligence service in an open society. Legitimate intelligence targets remain. Paradoxically, messy international situations proliferate in the post-cold war era with the removal of what was sometimes the Soviet Union's restraining influence. As it becomes more difficult to make policy in these situations without the certainties of the cold war, so it becomes more important to have more knowledge of them. And that means intelligence.

Viewed without the distorting prism of the cold war, the problem of controlling the intelligence community can be seen as part of the generic problem of controlling government. What makes intelligence a unique part of the problem is secrecy. One of the great benefits of the end of the cold war is the opportunity it presents to reexamine secrecy and to end a great deal of it.

"The strength of America," John le Carré has said, "is in her frankness, her mobility of mind, her willingness to declare herself, take risks and change. Not in her secrecy." [21]

NOTES

1. Quoted in Anne Karalakas, *History of the CIA*, in the final report of the Church committee, S. Rept. 94-755, 1976, Book IV, 52-53n. The Doolittle committee was an appendage of the Hoover Commission on Organization of the Government, which endorsed its report.
2. House Permanent Select Committee on Intelligence, *Intelligence Authorization Act for Fiscal Year 1995*, H. Rept. 103-541, 103d Cong., 2d sess., 1994, 22.
3. R. James Woolsey, *National Security and the Future Direction of the Central Intelligence Agency*, address at Center for Strategic and International Studies, Washington, D.C., July 18, 1994. CIA press release, 17, 19.
4. Walter Pincus, "CIA Plans to Close 15 Stations in African Pullback," *Washington Post*, June 23, 1994.
5. William E. Colby, "The CIA: Everybody's Favorite Scapegoat," *Washington Post*,

Aug. 5, 1994.

6. Walter Pincus, "Many Female CIA Officers Allege Bias," *Washington Post*, July 20, 1994, and "Intelligence Panel to Study Discrimination Charges," *Washington Post*, July 25, 1994.

7. John le Carré, "Why I Long for Shy Spies," *Washington Post*, Aug. 8, 1993.

8. Allen Dulles, *The Craft of Intelligence* (New York: Signet Books, 1965), 89.

9. Ibid.

10. Bob Woodward, "CIA Paid Millions to Jordan's King Hussein," *Washington Post*, Feb. 18, 1977.

11. Benjamin C. Bradlee, "The Post and Pelton: How the Press Looks at National Security," *Washington Post*, June 8, 1986.

12. Iran-Contra Hearings, Vol. 100-7, Pt. I, 339, 191.

13. Iran-Contra Hearings, Vol. 100-8, 83, 152, 159.

14. Associated Press, "Text of President Bush's Statement on the Pardon of Weinberger and Others," *New York Times*, Dec. 25, 1992.

15. New York: Free Press, 1993.

16. Reuters, "Independent Counsel's Statement on the Pardons," *New York Times*, Dec. 25, 1992.

17. David Johnston, "Walsh Implies Bush Used Pardons to Avoid Testifying," *New York Times*, Feb. 9, 1993.

18. Iran-Contra Hearings, Vol. 100-7, Pt. I, 124.

19. See Mark Perry, *Eclipse: The Last Days of the CIA* (New York: William Morrow and Co., 1992), 246-250.

20. For a more detailed discussion of covert action criteria, see Loch K. Johnson, "On Drawing a Bright Line for Covert Operations," *American Journal of International Law* (April 1992): 284-309. See also the Report of the Twentieth Century Fund Task Force on Covert Action and Democracy, *The Need to Know* (New York: Twentieth Century Fund Press, 1992).

21. John le Carré, "Tinpots, Saviors, Lawyers, Spies," *New York Times*, May 4, 1993.

Glossary

NOTE: An attempt has been made to include in this glossary the most common acronyms and intelligence terms, both technical jargon and inside-the-community slang. A more extensive compilation is in the House Intelligence Committee Annual Report for 1978 (H. Rept. 95-1975, 95th Cong., 2d sess.). A formidable list of acronyms is in Jeffrey Richelson, *The U.S. Intelligence Community*, Cambridge, Mass.: Ballinger Publishing, 1985.

ACTIVE MEASURES.   Soviet term for influence operations, or covert actions.

AGENT.   An individual who engages in clandestine activity on behalf of an intelligence organization, usually for money, but who is not an officer or employee of that organization.

AGENT OF INFLUENCE.   An agent who is used to influence a foreign government or organization instead of, or in addition to, reporting intelligence.

ASSET.   A paid agent or other source that can be called on.

BAG JOBS/BLACK BAG JOBS.   Surreptitious entries for purposes of burglary or installation of monitoring devices.

BIGOT LIST.   The list of individuals cleared for access to particularly sensitive material.

BLACK.   Free of surveillance; not being followed.

BLOW (v.).   To make known. An operation is blown when it becomes known. See "compromise."

BLOWBACK.   Material clandestinely published abroad, or planted in foreign media, and later unwittingly circulated in the United States.

BRUSH CONTACT.   A brief encounter of an agent with a case officer.

CAS.   Controlled American Source. An agent under the control of a U.S. intelligence agency.

CASE OFFICER.   The intelligence officer who is in charge of an agent. The officer is said to "run" or "handle" the agent.

CHICKEN FEED.   Misleading information channeled to another country's intelligence service.

CIPHER/CODE.   A way to disguise the contents of a written message. In a cipher, letters or numbers are substituted one-for-one according to a key that scrambles the alphabet and that must be known for the message to be deciphered and read. In a code, groups of numbers (usually of four digits) are substituted for words or phrases. Sometimes a code is itself put into a cipher.

CODEWORD.   A designation for a particularly sensitive intelligence source, method, class of intelligence, or intelligence operation. Codewords are used not only to disguise sources and methods but also to limit the number of individuals with access to especially sensitive data.

COMINT.   Communications intelligence, that is, intelligence derived from intercepted communications.

COMPARTMENTATION.   Dividing particularly sensitive intelligence, or operational matters, into separate compartments as a means of improving security through limiting access.

COMPROMISE (V.).   To become known, or to fall into unauthorized hands. See "blow."

CONTROL (N.).   An agent's case officer.

COUNTERESPIONAGE/COUNTERINTELLIGENCE.   Generally, operations undertaken against foreign intelligence services. Counterespionage is directed specifically against the espionage efforts of such services. Counterintelligence includes counterespionage; more broadly, it also includes efforts directed against foreign intelligence services generally such as, for example, efforts to penetrate them.

CRYPTONYM.   The codeword assigned to an intelligence agent to mask his/her true identity. See "pseudonym."

CUT-OUT.   A third party inserted in an intelligence operation or between an intelligence service and an agent in order to make an activity more difficult to trace.

DANGLE (N.).   A false defector "dangled" like bait before an intelligence service in the hope that the service will bite and thereby provide an opportunity for penetration by the "dangle."

DCI.   Director of Central Intelligence.

DDCI.   Deputy Director of Central Intelligence.

DDI. Deputy Director for Intelligence (CIA).

DDO/DDP. Deputy Director for Operations (formerly Plans) (CIA).

DEAD DROP. A place where an agent leaves material for his or her control officer or cut-out to pick up, or where instructions may be left for the agent. It makes it possible to avoid passing material from hand to hand.

DEEP COVER. An occupation or profession unrelated to intelligence used by intelligence officers to explain their presence in a foreign country and mask their true activities. Most intelligence officers abroad operate under the light cover of the State Department or a related agency in an American embassy. Officers under deep cover would identify themselves as employees of an unrelated government agency or of a nongovernmental enterprise.

DEFECTOR IN PLACE. An intelligence officer who defects to a foreign intelligence service but who continues to work for his or her original service.

DIRTY. An operation found to be controlled or exploited by a foreign intelligence service.

DISPATCHED AGENT. An officer sent to penetrate a foreign intelligence service by appearing to defect. See "dangle."

DOUBLE AGENT. An agent who is cooperating with an intelligence service on behalf of and under the control of a foreign intelligence service and who is manipulated by one service to the detriment of the other.

DRYCLEANING. Freeing oneself from hostile surveillance.

ELSUR. Electronic surveillance. It can be taps on telephones or microphones operating independently.

FALSE FLAG. An agent or officer posing as a national of a third country.

FBIS. Foreign Broadcast Information Service.

FEED MATERIAL. Material that a dangle or dispatched agent is authorized to give to a foreign intelligence service in order to establish his bona fides. Feed material is also used by double agents. It must be important enough to excite the other service's interest but not so important that it cannot be compromised for a higher goal. Also termed "giveaway" and "throwaway."

FISUR. Physical surveillance.

FLUTTER. A lie detector test for a prospective agent or defector.

GIVEAWAY. See "feed material."

GRAYMAIL. A tactic by a defendant can use to avoid prosecution by threatening to publicize classified information during trial.

GRU. Soviet Military Intelligence Service.

HONEY TRAP.   A situation contrived by an intelligence service to lead to the sexual compromise of an officer of a foreign government so that he or she can be blackmailed.

HUMINT.   Human intelligence, that is, intelligence derived from a human, as distinguished from a technical, source.

ILLEGAL (N.).   An intelligence officer or agent clandestinely in a foreign country with a false passport. He or she pursues a legitimate occupation while surreptitiously transmitting intelligence reports and/or supervising a group of other illegals. Illegals may spend years establishing themselves or awaiting the development of a given contingency before engaging in espionage.

INR.   Bureau of Intelligence and Research (State Department).

IOB.   Intelligence Oversight Board. Established by President Gerald Ford to receive reports of inspectors general of the intelligence agencies. Disbanded by President Bill Clinton, who transferred its functions to the President's Foreign Intelligence Advisory Board.

KGB.   *Komitet Gosudarstvennoy Bezopasnosti.* Committee for State Security. The major intelligence service of the former Soviet Union. It was divided into two agencies by Russian president Boris Yeltsin: the Foreign Intelligence Service (Russian acronym SVRR), roughly equivalent to the Central Intelligence Agency in the United States and comprising the former first chief directorate of the KGB; and the Federal Counterintelligence Service (Russian acronym MBRF), an internal counterintelligence service roughly equivalent to the United States' Federal Bureau of Investigation.

LEGEND.   The cover story of an intelligence officer working under deep cover or of an illegal. Especially in the latter case, the legend may be a complete, elaborately contrived, and wholly false biography.

MISUR.   Microphone surveillance, that is, electronic listening devices planted in places frequented by the subject.

MOLE.   Someone who has penetrated an intelligence service in behalf of a foreign service.

NFIP.   National Foreign Intelligence Program. U.S. intelligence activities not related to tactical military intelligence.

NID.   National Intelligence Daily. Published by the CIA six days a week and circulated to a limited number of policy-making officials and congressional committees. It is a summary, with individual reports usually no more than two or three paragraphs in length.

NIE.   National Intelligence Estimate.

NSA.   National Security Agency.

OFFICIAL COVER.   The cover used by an intelligence officer when he goes abroad as an ostensible employee of another U.S. government agency.

PDF. President's Daily Brief. The intelligence summary prepared daily for the president by the CIA.

PFIAB. President's Foreign Intelligence Advisory Board.

PITCH. The final approach in recruiting a foreign intelligence agent.

PLAYBACK. Intelligence about how an intelligence service's tactics are affecting the foreign service against which they are directed.

PSEUDONYM. A false name used by an intelligence officer to make it more difficult to trace the officer to a future assignment or to connect him or her to a past one.

ROLL UP. To end a hostile intelligence operation, usually by arresting the agents and/or expelling the officers who have diplomatic immunity. To break a spy ring.

SAFE HOUSE. A house or other premises controlled by an intelligence service so that it is secure against penetration and can be used for clandestine meetings and other activities.

SIGINT. Signals intelligence.

SNIE. Special National Intelligence Estimate.

SPARROW. A female employee or agent who is assigned to sexually compromise a target. See "swallow."

STAY-BEHIND. An agent recruited to remain in a country in the contingency that Americans are expelled. The agent is then expected to send clandestine intelligence reports.

SW. Secret writing.

SWALLOW. A female employee or agent who is assigned to sexually compromise a target. See "sparrow."

SWAN. A male employee or agent who is assigned to sexually compromise a female target.

TARGET. The object of an intelligence operation, usually an organization, facility, or country to be penetrated or an individual to be recruited.

TECHNICAL INTERVIEW. Polygraph (lie detector) tests routinely given to employees of certain intelligence services.

TELINT. Telemetry intelligence, that is, intelligence derived from the telemetry transmitted by missiles and satellites.

TELSUR. Telephone surveillance or wiretaps.

THROWAWAY. Low-level material supplied by a double agent or false defector to establish his bona fides.

TIARA.   Tactical Intelligence and Related Activities. U.S. intelligence programs that are military related, as distinguished from NFIP.

TRADECRAFT.   Tricks of the trade.

UNWITTING.   Unknowledgeable about a particular intelligence source, method, or operation. In some cases an unwitting person may participate in an operation without knowing it.

WALK-IN.   A source, usually a defector, who volunteers, as distinguished from one who is recruited.

WITTING.   Fully knowledgeable about a given intelligence source, method, or operation.

Bibliography

BOOKS

Agee, Philip. *Inside the Company: CIA Diary*. New York: Penguin Books, 1975.

Ameringer, Charles D. *U.S. Foreign Intelligence: The Secret Side of American History*. Lexington, Mass.: Lexington Books, 1990.

Bamford, James. *The Puzzle Palace: A Report on America's Most Secret Agency*. Boston: Houghton Mifflin, 1982.

Berkowitz, Bruce D., and Allan E. Goodman. *Strategic Intelligence for American National Security*. Princeton, N.J.: Princeton University Press, 1989.

Brown, Anthony Cave. *The Last Hero: Wild Bill Donovan*. New York: Times Books, 1982.

Brownell, George A. *The Origin and Development of the National Security Agency*. Laguna Hills, Calif.: Aegean Park Press, 1981.

Brugioni, Dino A. *Eyeball to Eyeball: The Inside Story of the Cuban Missile Crisis*, ed. Robert F. McCort. New York: Random House, 1990.

Cline, Ray S. *The CIA Reality vs. Myth*. Washington, D.C.: Acropolis Books, 1982.

_____. *Secrets, Spies and Scholars: Blueprint of the Essential CIA*. Washington, D.C.: Acropolis Books, 1976.

Cohen, Eliot A., and John Gooch. *Military Misfortunes: The Anatomy of Failure in War*. New York: Free Press, 1990.

Colby, William, and Peter Forbath. *Honorable Men: My Life in the CIA*. New York: Simon and Schuster, 1978.

Conner, William E. *Intelligence Oversight: The Controversy Behind the FY 1991 Intelligence Authorization Act*. McLean, Va.: Association of Former Intelligence Officers, 1993.

Corson, William R. *The Armies of Ignorance: The Rise of the American Intelligence Empire*. New York: Dial Press, 1977.

Darling, Arthur B. *The Central Intelligence Agency: An Instrument of Government to 1950*. University Park, Pa.: Pennsylvania State University Press, 1990.

Davis, Nathaniel. *The Last Two Years of Salvador Allende*. Ithaca, N.Y.: Cornell University Press, 1985.

Donner, Frank J. *The Age of Surveillance: The Aims and Methods of America's Political Intelligence System*. New York: Vintage Books, 1981.

Dorman, William A., and Farhang, Mansour. *The U.S. Press and Iran: Foreign Policy and the Journalism of Deference*. Berkeley: University of California Press, 1987.

Draper, Theodore. *A Very Thin Line: The Iran-Contra Affairs.* New York: Hill and Wang, 1991.

Dulles, Allen. *The Craft of Intelligence.* New York: Harper and Row, 1963.

Dunlop, Richard. *Donovan: America's Master Spy.* New York: Rand McNally, 1982.

Epstein, Edward Jay. *Deception: The Invisible War between the KGB and the CIA.* New York: Simon and Schuster, 1989.

Eveland, Wilbur Crane. *Ropes of Sand: America's Failure in the Middle East.* New York: W.W. Norton, 1980.

Freemantle, Brian. *CIA.* New York: Stein and Day, 1984.

Gentry, Curt. *J. Edgar Hoover: The Man and the Secrets.* New York: W.W. Norton, 1991.

Godson, Roy, ed. *Intelligence Requirements for the 1990s: Collection, Analysis, Counterintelligence and Covert Action.* Lexington, Mass.: Lexington Books, 1989.

Goulden, Joseph C. *Korea: The Untold Story of the War.* New York: Times Books. 1982.

Hinckle, Warren, and William W. Turner. *The Fish Is Red: The Story of the Secret War against Castro.* New York: Harper and Row, 1981.

Immerman, Richard H. *The CIA in Guatemala: The Foreign Policy of Intervention.* Austin: University of Texas Press, 1982.

Johnson, Loch K. *America's Secret Power: The CIA in a Democratic Society.* New York: Oxford University Press, 1989.

———. *A Season of Inquiry: Congress and Intelligence.* Chicago: Dorsey Press, 1988.

Kahn, David. *The Codebreakers: The Story of Secret Writing.* New York: Macmillan, 1967.

Kent, Sherman. *Strategic Intelligence for American World Policy.* Hamden, Conn.: Archon Books, 1965.

Kessler, Ronald. *Inside the CIA: Revealing the Secrets of the World's Most Powerful Spy Agency.* New York: Pocket Books, 1992.

———. *Spy vs. Spy: Stalking Soviet Spies in America.* New York: Scribner's, 1988.

Kimball, Penn. *The File.* New York: Harcourt Brace Jovanovich, 1983.

Kwitny, Jonathan. *Endless Enemies: The Making of an Unfriendly World.* New York: Congdon and Weed, 1984.

Lamphere, Robert J., and Tom Shachtman. *The FBI-KGB War: A Special Agent's Story.* New York: Random House, 1986.

Laqueur, Walter. *A World of Secrets: The Uses and Limits of Intelligence.* New York: Basic Books, 1983.

Layton, Edwin T., with Roger Pineau and John Costello. *"And I Was There": Pearl Harbor and Midway—Breaking the Secrets.* New York: William Morrow and Co., 1985.

Lewin, Ronald. *The American Magic: Codes, Ciphers and the Defeat of Japan.* New York: Farrar Strauss Giroux, 1982.

Mangold, Tom. *Cold Warrior: James Jesus Angleton: The CIA's Master Spy Hunter.* New York: Simon and Schuster, 1991.

Marchetti, Victor, and John D. Marks. *The CIA and the Cult of Intelligence.* New York: Alfred A. Knopf, 1974.

Martin, David C. *Wilderness of Mirrors: The Secret War between the CIA and the KGB.* New York: Harper and Row, 1980.

Miller, Nathan. *Spying for America: The Hidden History of U.S. Intelligence.* New York: Paragon House, 1989.

Morgan, Richard E. *Domestic Intelligence: Monitoring Dissent in America.* Austin: University of Texas Press, 1980.

Newsom, David D. *The Soviet Brigade in Cuba: A Study in Political Diplomacy.* Bloomington: Indiana University Press, 1987.

Perry, Mark. *Eclipse: The Last Days of the CIA.* New York: William Morrow and Co., 1992.

Powers, Francis Gary, with Curt Gentry. *Operation Overflight: The U-2 Spy Pilot Tells His Story for the First Time.* New York: Holt, Rinehart and Winston, 1970.

Powers, Thomas. *The Man Who Kept the Secrets: Richard Helms and the CIA.* New York: Alfred A. Knopf, 1979.

Prados, John. *Keepers of the Keys: A History of the National Security Council from Truman to Bush.* New York: William Morrow and Co., 1991.

Ranelagh, John. *The Agency: The Rise and Decline of the CIA.* New York: Simon and Schuster, 1986.

Richelson, Jeffrey. *America's Secret Eyes in Space.* New York: Harper and Row, 1990.

_____. *The U.S. Intelligence Community.* Cambridge, Mass.: Ballinger, 1985.

Roosevelt, Kermit. *Countercoup: The Struggle for the Control of Iran.* New York: McGraw Hill, 1979.

Schecter, Jerold, and Peter Derabian. *The Spy Who Saved the World.* New York: Macmillan, 1992.

Shulsky, Abram. *Silent Warfare: Understanding Intelligence.* London: Brassey's, 1993.

Smist, Frank J., Jr. *Congress Overseas the United States Intelligence Community, 1947-1989.* Knoxville: University of Tennessee Press, 1990.

Smith, Joseph Burckholder. *Portrait of a Cold Warrior.* New York: Putnam's Sons, 1976.

Stevenson, William. *A Man Called Intrepid: The Secret War.* New York: Ballantine Books, 1977.

Tower Commission. *Report of the President's Special Review Board.* New York: Bantam Books/Times Books, 1987.

Treverton, Gregory F. *Covert Action: The Limits of Intervention in the Postwar World.* New York: Basic Books, 1987.

Turner, Stansfield. *Secrecy and Democracy: The CIA in Transition.* Boston: Houghton Mifflin, 1985.

Twentieth Century Fund Task Force on Covert Action and American Democracy. *The Need to Know.* New York: Twentieth Century Fund Press, 1992.

Wise, David. *Molehunt: The Secret Search for Traitors that Shattered the CIA.* New York: Random House, 1992.

Wise, David, and Thomas B. Ross. *The Espionage Establishment.* New York: Random House, 1967.

_____. *The Invisible Government.* New York: Random House, 1964.

Woodward, Bob. *Veil: The Secret Wars of the CIA 1981-1987.* New York: Simon and Schuster, 1987.

Wyden, Peter. *Bay of Pigs: The Untold Story.* New York: Simon and Schuster, 1979.

ARTICLES

Barnds, William J. "Intelligence and Foreign Policy: Dilemmas of a Democracy." *Foreign Affairs* (January 1969): 281-295.

Gates, Robert M. "The CIA and American Foreign Policy." *Foreign Affairs* (Winter 1987/1988): 215-230.

Johnson, Loch K. "On Drawing a Bright Line for Covert Operations." *American Journal of International Law* (April 1992): 284-309.

_____. "The CIA: Controlling the Quiet Option." *Foreign Policy* (Summer 1980): 143-153.

Turner, Stansfield. "Intelligence for a New World Order." *Foreign Affairs,* (Fall 1991): 150-166.

GOVERNMENT DOCUMENTS

Final Report of the Independent Counsel for Iran/Contra Matters. 3 vols. United States Court of Appeals for the District of Columbia Circuit, 1993.

House Committee on Armed Services. Oversight and Investigations Subcommittee. *Intelligence Successes and Failures in Operations Desert Shield/Storm.* Committee Print No. 5, 103d Cong., 1st sess., 1993.

House Permanent Select Committee on Intelligence. *Congressional Oversight of Covert Activities.* Hearings, 98th Cong., 1st sess., 1983.

House Permanent Select Committee on Intelligence. Subcommittee on Oversight. *The CIA and the Media.* Hearings, 95th Cong., 1st and 2d sess., 1977, 1978.

House Select Committee on Intelligence (Pike committee). *U.S. Intelligence Agencies and Activities.* Hearings, 94th Cong., 1st sess. (1975): Pt. 1, *Intelligence Costs and Fiscal Procedures;* Pt. 2, *The Performance of the Intelligence Community;* Pt. 5, *Risks and Control of Foreign Intelligence; Final Report,* H. Rept. 94-833, 1976.

Senate Select Committee on Intelligence. *Meeting the Espionage Challenge: A Review of United States Counterintelligence and Security Programs.* S. Rept. 99-522, 99th Cong., 2d sess., 1986.

_____. *National Intelligence Act of 1980.* S. 2284, 96th Cong., 2d sess., 1980.

_____. *National Intelligence Reorganization and Reform Act of 1978* S. 2525, 95th Cong., 2d sess., 1978.

_____. *Oversight Legislation.* 100th Cong., 2d sess., 1987.

_____. *Whether Disclosure of Funds Authorized for Intelligence Activities Is in the Public Interest.* Hearings, 95th Cong., 1st sess., 1977.

Senate Select Committee on Secret Military Assistance to Iran and the Nicaraguan Opposition, and House Select Committee to Investigate Covert Arms Transactions with Iran (Iran-Contra committee). *Iran-Contra Investigation.* Joint Hearings, 100th Cong., 1st sess., 1987, Pts. 100-1 to 100-11.

_____. *Report of the Congressional Committees Investigating the Iran-Contra Affair.* H. Report. 100-433, S. Rept. 100-216, 100th Cong., 1st sess., 1987.

Senate Select Committee to Study Governmental Operations with Respect to Intelligence Activities (Church committee). Hearings, 94th Cong., 1st sess. (1975): Vol. 1, *Unauthorized Storage of Toxic Agents;* Vol. 4, *Mail Opening;* Vol. 5, *National Security Agency and Fourth Amendment Rights;* Vol. 7, *Covert Action; Final Report,* S. Rept. 94-755, Books I-VI, 1976.

Index